PANDORA'S KEEPERS

PANDORA'S KEEPERS

NINE MEN
AND
THE ATOMIC BOMB

Brian VanDeMark

LITTLE, BROWN AND COMPANY

Boston   New York   London

First Edition

Library of Congress Cataloging-in-Publication Data
VanDeMark, Brian.
    Pandora's keepers : nine men and the atomic bomb / Brian VanDeMark. — 1st ed.
      p. cm.
    Includes bibliographical references and index.
    ISBN 0-316-73833-6
    1. Nuclear physicists — Biography.   2. Atomic bomb — Moral and ethical aspects.
3. Nuclear weapons — Moral and ethical aspects.   4. Nuclear physics — Moral and
ethical aspects. I. Title.
QC774.A2V36 2003
539.7'092'273 — dc21
[B]   2002043646

10 9 8 7 6 5 4 3 2 1

Q-MART

Designed by Oksana Kushnir

Printed in the United States of America

TO

ROBERT DALLEK AND ROBERT MCNAMARA

———

Mentors and Friends

CONTENTS

This is the story of nine men who helped create the atomic bomb, which forever changed their lives and the world. Their story is a compelling one, filled with elements of great drama, emotion, irony, and tragedy. It is not surprising, therefore, that the story of the bomb's creation has been told often, and well, by others much more knowledgeable about nuclear physics than I.[1] My aim is different. It is to explore the *human* story behind the atomic bomb by probing its creators' thoughts, feelings, and judgments. What motivated them? How did they relate to one another? How did they deal with the political and moral issues posed by nuclear weapons? Put simply: Why did they do it, and what did it mean to them?

People usually think about what the atomic scientists did, instead of who they were, because they do not see them as human beings with personal histories and emotional lives, hearts — sometimes broken — as well as heads. Scientists themselves have contributed to this popular image. Very often they have represented themselves as calmly rational and coldly objective — above human frailty and unaware of man's condition. But scientists are first and foremost people, people who know just how imaginative and human an enterprise science really is.

All of this suggests that the history the atomic scientists made is not as simple as people have usually portrayed it. Numerous myths and caricatures have grown up around the atomic scientists (and the bomb) since 1945. Too often these men (and they were almost all men) have been flat screens on which one-dimensional fictions and fantasies were projected. But the atomic scientists were not all good; they were not all bad. To understand them is to recognize their good intentions and at the same time to confront the doubtful morality of their achievement. Good history does not fear ambiguity, nor does it reduce complex and sometimes contradictory individuals to simple stereotypes.

Physics, like everything that is potentially constructive, can be put to destructive ends. It has two faces, benign and threatening, bringing blessings and curses. Each of the atomic scientists, like each of us, can make imperfect choices that seem reasonable — even responsible — in the context of the times but are impossible to undo once the course is set. They, like us, do things they think are right at the time, and later come to regret them. They, like us, have rich human stories of ambition and disappointment, achievement and failure, cooperation and rivalry, jealousy and revenge. Their story helps illuminate how people deal with circumstances, the legacy of creation, and an imperfect world that sometimes forges good from evil and evil from good. Their story has moral reverberation, that strange and haunting quality generated by a tale that is not always pleasant but that entrances us because it has an effect beyond itself. This effect may be as simple as inspiring us to do something practical about the legacy of their creation, or at least to feel that we should.

Many physicists contributed to the making of the atomic bomb. Clearly, not all of them can be treated, not even in a big book like this one. I therefore used three criteria to select the subjects of this study: 1. those who contributed centrally to the bomb's creation; 2. those who voiced moral and political judgments about the bomb; and 3. those whose views represented a range of opinions and responses. Based on these criteria, I chose to write about the following nine physicists, in alphabetical order:

Hans Bethe
Niels Bohr
Arthur Compton
Enrico Fermi
Ernest Lawrence
Robert Oppenheimer
I. I. Rabi
Leo Szilard
Edward Teller[2]

This book treats these nine physicists as a group rather than as discrete subjects. It seeks to integrate what might otherwise be a string of disparate biographies into something like a history of a scientific generation, and to do so without slighting either the individual physicist or the larger setting. It follows their intertwined lives chronologically, showing how they related to one another and reacted to the history they made together. Part I traces the atomic scientists' effort to build the bomb and, with it, to end World War II. Part II explores how the atomic scientists came to understand the bomb's consequences, both for their own lives and for the world they changed forever through their creation.

Two themes — two morals of the story — emerge along the way. The first is how inexorable was the trap into which the atomic scientists fell, a trap largely of their own making. The atomic scientists were deeply thoughtful men, no fools in any way, yet they were drawn into a frenzy of creation, throwing themselves into the enterprise and laboring beyond all expectations of human capacity to produce a weapon of unprecedented destructiveness. The effort quickly took on a life, and a momentum, of its own, a chain reaction from a chain reaction. When it was done, the bomb they had made horrified and frightened them. The atomic scientists originally sought to build something that would save the world and ended up believing what they created might destroy it. They came to fear the very thing they had built to end fear.

The second theme is the political and moral awakening of the atomic scientists. Twentieth-century physics was a great adventure of imagination and intelligence, and until the discovery of fission it was carried on in an ivory tower, far removed from the world of politics. It was "pure" science — a contest of the human mind with nature; the object was not to change the world but to understand it. Scientists did physics because it was there to be done and because it was wonderfully interesting. They rarely addressed the political implications of their research or applied moral considerations to their work. They were detached and above such things. But their work on the bomb shook the atomic scientists out of their detachment and forced them to confront larger implications. For the first time, they began to ask questions about politics and morality in the same searching way they had always asked them about Nature. And as they asked these questions, they transformed themselves.

Science is a wager on our ability to know the world, but that wager changes the world in ways that escape scientific prediction and understanding. The atomic scientists' struggle to come to terms with what they had done is emblematic of the larger and continuing human struggle created by the opening of the Pandora's box of nuclear weapons. Some of the questions the atomic scientists wrestled with, we are still wrestling with now. Today, as we rush headlong into a future filled with the promise of potentially astonishing scientific and technological advances, we are continually drawn back to the most momentous scientific achievement of the twentieth century — an achievement that raises questions so profound that they seem to transcend time itself.

PANDORA'S KEEPERS

Nine Physicists and the Discovery of Fission

H E FIRST LEARNED the news in late January 1939, just seven months before World War II began. Eugene Wigner, a fellow Hungarian physicist whom he had known since their student days together at the University of Berlin, lay ill in the Princeton University infirmary with jaundice. Although weak, Wigner instantly recognized the short, portly man with curly dark hair, enormous head, flat cheekbones, and gentle, soulful eyes when he walked into the infirmary room. It was Leo Szilard. Szilard had come out of friendship, but business was still permissible, indeed necessary, since Wigner had urgent news: a chemist working at Berlin's Kaiser Wilhelm Institute, Otto Hahn, had split uranium the month before.

Szilard, shocked, wanted details. What Hahn had done, repeating an experiment first conducted by the Italian physicist Enrico Fermi in 1934, was to bombard uranium atoms with neutrons (particles with no charge that could pass through the electrical barrier surrounding the atom). Nuclear physics was still in its infancy, and measurements were done by methods that were often crude and amorphous. Fermi had surmised that the uranium atoms had absorbed the neutrons and, in the process, had been transformed into heavier, man-made "transuranic" elements. German chemist Ida Noddack, following reports of Fermi's experiment in scientific journals, had suggested a chemical analysis of "transuranic" elements to see if they were actually fragments of split atoms. But Fermi had not pursued Noddack's suggestion, because he did not think a slow neutron with very little energy could split the massive uranium nucleus. Had he thought so, he might have discovered fission five years earlier.

Now, several years later, Hahn had followed Noddack's suggestion and did some careful chemistry. Common uranium has 92 protons (positively charged particles) and 146 neutrons, a total of 238 particles in its nucleus. By Fermi's logic, transuranic elements would contain more of both. To Hahn's astonishment, he found barium instead. Barium has a much lighter nucleus than uranium: 56 protons and 82 neutrons — a total of 138 particles. Hahn was puzzled. How could a uranium nucleus be split in half by a slow neutron of very low energy? It was as if a thick steel girder had been cleaved by a rubber band.

Rather than publish his findings immediately, Hahn wrote his former colleague Lise Meitner, a brilliant theoretical physicist who had been forced to leave the Kaiser Wilhelm Institute for Sweden a few months earlier because of her Jewish ancestry. Hahn asked her for assistance in interpreting the unexpected results.

Hahn's letter reached Meitner at the seaside resort of Göteborg, where she had gone with her visiting nephew Otto Frisch, another brilliant theoretical physicist up from Copenhagen to be with his aunt during her first holiday in exile. When she read Hahn's letter to him, Frisch disagreed and almost refused to listen. When his aunt persisted, he suggested they go for a walk, she on foot, he on skis. It must have been a strange sight: the diminutive sixty-year-old Meitner trudging through the snowy woods outside Göteborg alongside her thirty-four-year-old nephew on skis, both struggling to make sense of Hahn's letter. Like all other physicists of the time, they assumed heavy nuclei could not be split in two. Could that assumption be wrong? They now began to question it. Using Danish physicist Niels Bohr's "liquid drop" model of the atomic nucleus as their theoretical guide, Meitner and Frisch reasoned that the stresses on a heavy uranium nucleus triggered by neutron bombardment could make it wobble like a perturbed drop of water and eventually split it into two smaller, lighter nuclei. This might explain Hahn's strange discovery.

Meitner and Frisch then went one fateful step further in their interpretive speculation. Using Albert Einstein's famous formula for the conversion of matter into energy ($E = mc^2$, an enormous number),* they calculated the energy that would be released when splitting apart or "fissioning" the nucleus of a uranium atom. The fig-

---

* The value of c^2 — the square of the speed of light — is 100,000,000,000,000,000,000.

ure was staggering: 200 million electron volts of energy. Two hundred million electron volts is not a large amount of energy — only about enough to nudge a speck of dust — but it is an awesome, almost unimaginable amount of energy from a single, tiny atom. And in just one gram of uranium there is an astounding number of atoms: about 2,500,000,000,000,000,000,000.

As he stood in Wigner's infirmary room, these details struck Leo Szilard like a thunderbolt. What Szilard had dimly imagined for years — yet vaguely dreaded — had been found. Fissioned uranium released a million times more energy than dynamite, which was the most explosive force known at that time. Such energy might be harnessed into a terrible weapon of mass destruction. Such a weapon in the hands of Hitler and the Nazis would give them an instrument with which to enslave the world. This seemed an all-too-plausible danger because Germany had some of the best scientific brains in the world — like Otto Hahn — and the industrial capacity to do the job. Suddenly, a dramatic melancholy fell upon Szilard.

The discovery of fission spread among the other physicists like wind across a field of wheat. Hungarian physicist Edward Teller was looking forward to seeing Szilard at the Third Annual Conference on Theoretical Physics in Washington, D.C., where Teller had sought refuge as a professor at George Washington University after fleeing Nazi persecution four years earlier. The participants at the Washington conference would include Bohr, who was coming from his world-famous institute in Copenhagen, and Fermi, who had been awarded the Nobel Prize the month before for his research on neutrons.

Bohr himself had learned of fission from Otto Frisch just before leaving Copenhagen. "How could we have missed it all this time?" he exclaimed in utter astonishment. When Bohr's ship docked in New York two weeks later, he took the train to Washington and arrived at the home of Russian physicist George Gamow, the conference organizer and a colleague of Teller's, late in the afternoon on the day before the conference began. An hour later Gamow phoned Teller in great agitation. "Bohr says uranium splits," he told Teller. That was all of Gamow's message. It was enough. Teller understood what fission might mean.

Bohr opened the conference the next morning by announcing the discovery. It escaped few, if any, that the atom had been split in Nazi Germany. Teller glanced across the auditorium at Fermi as Bohr spoke. Fermi's wife was a Jew, and he had become uneasy about remaining in Mussolini's Italy, an ally of Hitler's Germany. Leaving everything behind, Fermi had taken his family out of Italy the month before when he left to accept the Nobel Prize. They had used the prize money to travel on to New York, where Fermi was settling in as a professor at Columbia University.

Fermi had learned of fission a few days before the conference began from I. I. Rabi, his colleague on the physics faculty at Columbia who himself had picked up the news at Princeton while his friend Szilard was there. A short time later Rabi saw Fermi standing at his large office window on the top floor of Pupin Hall high above the Columbia campus, looking down the length of Manhattan's grid of skyscrapers crisscrossed by streets teeming with pedestrians and taxis. Fermi cupped his hands as if he were holding nothing larger than a ball. "A little bomb like that," he said simply, "and it would all disappear."[1]

Hans Bethe, who also attended the Washington conference, had fled Nazi Germany the same year as Teller. He pondered the consequences of fission on the long train ride back to Cornell University in upstate New York after the conference. Bethe realized that atomic bombs were now theoretically possible, though he did not believe they were even remotely feasible. The task of making an atomic bomb was simply too big and too difficult from a technical and engineering point of view. There was simply no way, Bethe was convinced, to produce fissionable uranium even in amounts as small as a millionth of a gram; a kilogram of fissionable uranium was far beyond the reach of science, he thought.

Arthur Compton, a Nobel Prize–winning physicist at the University of Chicago who personally knew most of those at the Washington conference, learned of fission while at the McDonald Observatory in the Davis Mountains of West Texas. Could a chain reaction of splitting uranium atoms occur? he wondered. The amount of energy released by such a chain reaction, according to his quick calculations, was enormous. Here was something of great importance, thought Compton, and also of great danger.

Ernest Lawrence, Compton's former graduate student and now a successful and ambitious professor of physics at the University of California, Berkeley, grasped the larger meaning of fission at once. Its military potential — which many physicists such as Bethe considered insurmountable — seemed like a heroic challenge to him. "This uranium business is certainly exciting," he wrote Fermi within weeks.[2]

Lawrence was determined to do what he could to make sure that if an atomic bomb was possible, America would get it first.

Working at the blackboard in his office, Lawrence's charismatic Berkeley colleague Robert Oppenheimer tried at first to prove that fission could not happen. Within a week, however, Oppenheimer the theoretician had decided that it could and that additional neutrons would be released. Within another week there was a crude drawing on his blackboard of a bomb. Oppenheimer wrote to a colleague that a ten-centimeter cube of uranium "might very well blow itself to hell."[3]

Nine physicists. Colleagues and friends. For the European refugees among them, the 1930s had been a decade of indelible scarification. When Nazism first began to spread like a malignant cancer, they had felt secure in their ivory towers, hoping that Hitler was not really a problem or, if he was, that he would go away. They felt no urgency because they believed politics was not a physicist's concern, much less a physicist's responsibility. But the rise of Hitler made politics personal, even for cloistered physicists. The world they knew and the scientific values they cherished were being destroyed, and that deeply painful but inescapable fact became increasingly difficult, and finally utterly impossible, for them to ignore. They wanted to preserve that world and those values. That was the fundamental thing that moved them. But one by one they had realized that if they were to stay in Europe, there would be no future. Deep down, they sensed that the world as they'd known it had only a little more time to run. So they packed what they could and brought their heavy accents and heavy wool suits to a New World that welcomed them.

For the native-born Americans they met in labs and university offices, the 1930s had marked an education in the troubling realities of a world more interconnected and complex than they had thought. American physicists had believed that the United States was insulated and invulnerable, separated as it was by a vast ocean from the misfortunes, follies, and crimes of Europe. This was a sentiment that most of their isolationist countrymen shared in the 1930s. But the experience of their refugee brethren, and their own knowledge of what fission portended, made them imagine, and confront, an ominous future.

"Science can solve every problem" — this was an article of faith among them, physics a pure and lofty calling. They had a detached preference for objective facts over subjective values. Raising moral considerations was not their professional style. Their aim had been to

— 7 —

understand the world, not change it. But with the announcement of Hahn's breakthrough, that would change. What followed would be a tale of unrivaled brilliance and unintended folly. It would also be a tragedy in the deepest and most fundamental sense. For had the atomic scientists not pursued fission, they would have been untrue to their nature and aspirations as physicists; yet having done so, they would be haunted by their quest. It is a sobering paradox not lost on the atomic scientists themselves. "Taken as a story of human achievement, and human blindness," Robert Oppenheimer observed late in his life, it is "among the great epics." And the epic begins with the shadow that the discovery of fission cast over the idyllic world of physics in the 1930s. Hahn had split more than an atom. After his discovery, there would always be a before and an after. Out of little things come big things — but nobody, not even the nine men who would go on to build the bomb, had any idea just what was to come.

PART I

—

A FEARSOME GRAIL

CHAPTER 1

Exodus

ANYONE WHO DID physics before the discovery of fission could remember what that world was like. Pre-fission physics was a beautiful, intimate subject that simmered with purpose. It was attractive, awe-inspiring, and deeply satisfying. Physicists worked in an atmosphere of intellectual and emotional excitement. Things were new, there were surprises, they were turning corners. Physics had no object other than satisfying the human spirit of intellectual adventure. Through every experiment and theory coursed an aesthetic joy and the moral exercise of seeking the truth. More than other scientists, physicists prided themselves that their science did not have any practical use.

Physics was a personal undertaking. A physicist enjoyed autonomy. He chose what work to do. His subject for research was his own, just as much as what a writer selects to write about or a painter to paint. Physicists viewed their work as a calling, as an enlargement of their lives, not just as a career. It meant something to them personally, in the same sense that art or literature did to others. The study of physics was noble, enlightening, and constructive, a model of how life should be lived. And the scientific method was an anchor of predictability and precision in a chaotic and uncertain world. Nature was profound, yet its secrets could be unlocked. The joy of insight, physicist Victor Weisskopf once said, was "a sense of involvement and awe, the elated state of mind that you achieve when you have grasped some essential point. It [was] akin to what you feel on top of a mountain after a hard climb or when you hear a great work of music."[1]

Just as physics existed outside of political and moral concerns, physicists lived on a plane above the nation-state. They eschewed politics; they shunned chauvinism and racism (though not, in many cases, sexism); they preferred cooperation and collaboration. They were cosmopolitan. Language posed no barrier because facts and concepts were communicated by mathematics. Steeped in a common culture of rationalism and humanism, they believed there was one supreme reward for their work: the sense of sharing in the building of knowledge. From this idealism, physicists derived the belief that their true identity was not as a member of a nation or a class but as scientific searchers speaking to other searchers. They believed physics could flourish only in an atmosphere of openness and freedom.

The personal ties among physicists were extraordinarily warm and close. Indeed, they were attracted to the discipline in part because each of them enjoyed being engaged in a collective enterprise. The community was small enough, and intimate enough, that everyone knew everyone else. They all hungrily read the latest scientific journals, but they learned more from talking among themselves, and when not together they communicated constantly by mail and telegram. A physicist could do his work in any country; and when he published the results of his work, they were read all over the world.

It was a time of great opportunity and optimism for all of the sciences, but physicists sensed it was an especially fertile moment and harbored grand expectations of discoveries to come. Nuclear physics, especially, was a beehive of exuberant creativity. The powerful new theory of quantum mechanics, developed by Werner Heisenberg, Pascual Jordan, and Paul Dirac in the 1920s, had given the structure and behavior of the atom a mathematical base. Excitement grew as physicists applied the analytical force of quantum mechanics to a wide variety of physical problems. The theory was such a departure from approaches of the past and shed so much new light that it was as if explorers lost in the desert had been given a map, compass, and water.

Curious, intelligent, and ambitious, physicists journeyed from one research center to another in Europe: Berlin, Cambridge, Copenhagen, Göttingen, Hamburg, Leipzig, Leyden, Munich, Rome, Zurich. A physicist simply decided where he wanted to go and showed up there, unannounced, to witness discoveries and learn insights that excited and inspired him. In 1927 I. I. Rabi spent several weeks at the Cavendish Laboratory at Cambridge observing the work of Ernest Rutherford, then went on to Copenhagen, where Niels Bohr had his

Institute for Theoretical Physics. When Rabi arrived in Copenhagen, he walked to the institute, rang the bell, and said to the secretary who answered the door, "My name is Rabi; I've come here to work."[2] In this informal way, physicists learned new experimental techniques, absorbed new ideas, and made new friends.

This mixing of people and ideas brought European and American physicists into close contact with one another. The peregrinations of one physicist, Hans Bethe, illustrate how the process worked. Funded by a Rockefeller Foundation Fellowship in 1931–1932 — which bestowed a generous stipend during the hard times of the Depression — Bethe traveled first to the Cavendish, then to Rome to study with Fermi. Bethe had been a graduate student at Munich in 1927 when Rabi spent the summer there. While in Europe, Rabi met Robert Oppenheimer and Edward Teller. Rabi and Oppenheimer formed a bond of friendship that grew stronger with the passing years. (Between each of them and Teller, however, existed a subtle friction that would later become the stuff of high drama.)

These transatlantic relationships were cemented through guest lectureships at American universities by distinguished European physicists such as Bohr; pilgrimages that young American physicists made to the great European centers of physics; the prestigious Solvay Conference held in Brussels, where the world's top physicists gathered annually; meetings of the American Physical Society at the National Bureau of Standards in Washington, D.C.; and a summer symposium on theory at the University of Michigan, attended by such rising stars as Bethe and Fermi. Through such personal contacts, a powerful network formed.

As things were, no one had the time to do it all himself. But these close international links stimulated the interplay of ideas, producing one of the most creative atmospheres that had ever existed in physics. Physicists seemed to know when someone was doing interesting work, and almost every idea occurred to several scientists simultaneously. Physics attained a richness and variety of approach — and most important, an expansion of knowledge — that it never would have attained if it had been the work of isolated scientists. It was an immensely exciting time. Few noticed the shadows and thunder in the distance.

When the Nazi attacks on academics came, they initially affected the humanities more than the sciences. The exchange between a professor of physics and a professor of literature at the University of Stuttgart in 1932 captured the mood of academics in Nazism's early days. "Well, Herr Pongs, how are you?" the physicist Paul Ewald asked. "How should I be?" the literature professor answered. "I'm not a physicist. We have to 'relearn' our entire field, looking upon everything '*unter dem Evoelkischen Gesichtspunkt*' [under the racial point of view]." "I really pity you," said Ewald.[3]

Yet if physicists lived under the illusion that politics would never reach into the isolated realm of physics, it did not last for long. Shortly after Hitler came to power, the Nazis issued an edict that the greeting *Guten Tag* (good day) be replaced by *Heil Hitler!* Jewish physicists saw their academic colleagues ridicule the edict at first. Then their colleagues began making a sloppy Hitler salute, and gradually it became more formal. After a while their colleagues started crossing the street to avoid greeting them. Physicists were no longer able to keep politics at bay.

The university community was changing, too. *Studenten Verbindungen* (fraternities) were increasingly nationalistic and anti-Semitic — foreshadowing the growing Nazi movement that would come to power in a few years. Members of these fraternities spent their free time roaming the streets, where they could be heard howling anti-Jewish slogans late into the night. They regularly searched out and beat up Jewish students or those who looked Jewish. Before long, Jewish physicists became one of their favorite targets because physics was so dominated by Jews. Such insults and coercion were part of the Nazis' plan to "free" German education from the Jews' "destructive yoke." The Nazi Party took control of universities and appointed *dozentenschaftsfuerhers* (faculty leaders) who would assemble physics professors and lecture them that there was no such thing as "objective" science, that science was an outcome of "national feeling." A vise was slowly closing.

The vituperation of Nazi academics toward Jewish physicists became increasingly aggressive and outlandish. "German physics?" asked Herr Lenard of Heidelberg University. "'But,' it will be replied, 'science is and remains international.' It is false. In reality, science, like every other human product, is racial and conditioned by blood." Herr Tomaschek of Dresden's Physics Institute went further. "Modern physics," he wrote, "is an instrument of [world] Jewry for the destruction of Nordic science. . . . True physics is the creation of the German spirit. . . . In fact, all European science is the fruit of Aryan, or, better,

German thought." And then there was Herr Mueller of Aachen's Technical College, who in a book titled *Jewry and Science* described a worldwide Jewish plot to pollute science and thereby destroy civilization.[4]

American physicists had an inside view of the tragedy befalling Jewish physicists in Germany. The physics grapevine carried vivid accounts of Nazi persecution, dramatic stories of hasty departures, and desperate inquiries about faculty positions outside of Germany. "We have been three days in Göttingen and the rest in Berlin, and had time to see and appreciate the effects of the present German madness," wrote one American physicist to a colleague back home. "It is simply horrible. In Göttingen, it is quite obvious that if these [Nazis] continue for only two more years (which is unfortunately very probable), they will ruin German science for a generation — at least." Hitler didn't care. He reportedly said: "If the dismissal of Jewish scientists means the annihilation of contemporary German science, then we shall do without science for a few years."[5] (The irony of fate is that Hitler's actions removed the one group of people who would have been able to provide him with the instrument for the world dominance he so eagerly sought.)

One result of all this was the exodus of the cream of European physicists, the prominent and the promising alike. Eleven Nobel laureates in physics left Germany in 1933 alone; one was Albert Einstein. They could not yet imagine the evil of the Holocaust and it was not German anti-Semitism per se that drove most of them away; they had long been used to subtle prejudice in Germany and elsewhere. Instead, it was more the fear, the expectation — almost the certainty — that the Nazis would get into a war and that the physicists caught in Germany would have to work for Hitler. *That* idea was too much.

These years and exile did not destroy the physicists' intellectual and emotional bonds to the best of German culture, which was deeply ingrained in their thinking and feeling, but did profoundly, personally demonstrate to them that unfathomable evil could take hold of a civilized society. They had gone into physics to escape, and now they had to escape to do physics. And it was still not clear whether they had escaped the hangman's noose, or whether the rope had just temporarily loosened.

Leo Szilard lived on the edge of the maelstrom as a researcher in nuclear physics at the Kaiser Wilhelm Institute in the Berlin suburb of Dahlem. A brilliant, sensitive, and intuitive genius who imagined things no one else had imagined before — and could peer into the future as few others could — Szilard was in Dahlem when Hitler took power as chancellor of Germany on January 30, 1933. With the coming to power of the Nazis, Szilard sensed a new chill more potent than Germany's damp and biting winter air. As the situation for Jews in Europe grew darker, the streets of Dahlem seemed to him more and more like a maze, a trap.

Szilard's ideas often appeared bizarre and remote from reality because his thinking was so far ahead of others'. Such foresight was not restricted to physics. His colleagues at the Kaiser Wilhelm Institute thought civilized Germans would not tolerate anything really rough happening under Hitler, but Szilard was not so sure. One night he saw a Nazi torchlight parade end in a square near the institute. A huge pile of books gathered there was put to the torch, and as the flames engulfed them, more books were thrown on the pyre. Among the books tossed into the flames were works of "Jewish physics" by Einstein. As Szilard watched the barbaric spectacle, he remembered that a century earlier the great German Jewish poet Heinrich Heine had written, "Wherever they burn books they will also, in the end, burn human beings."

Szilard possessed a rare combination of concentrated thinking — often about the future — and readiness for immediate action. He reacted to the rise of Nazism by packing his suitcases and keeping them close at hand. He was used to picking up and leaving when things fell apart: he had grown up a Jew in early-twentieth-century Hungary.

Szilard was born in 1898 in the Garden District of Budapest, a neighborhood of wealthy Jewish merchant families who stood just one step below the Magyar nobility in the hierarchy of Austro-Hungarian society. Budapest was one of Europe's most cosmopolitan cities; it had the second-largest Jewish population, after Warsaw. Horse-drawn droshkies carried silk-gowned women and their counts in red uniforms and furred hats to the grand palace of Emperor Franz Josef while coffeehouses teemed with intellectuals espousing socialist revolution. The Hapsburg Empire's official tolerance and rich mixture of nationalities had allowed Jews such as the Szilards to find a home, but beneath the cosmopolitanism lurked a powder keg waiting to explode.

Szilard's mother, Tekla, was a frank and honest woman who taught her son to be candid. "I made up my mind" at an early age, he later wrote, "that if I had to choose between being tactless and being untruthful, I would prefer to be tactless."[6] As an adult, his outstanding characteristic was not to be deterred by conventions of the time. Although Szilard's mother was Jewish, she practiced what she called her "natural religion," which was loosely based on the teachings of Jesus and which she conveyed through vivid parables. As a result, her son developed a strong moral and ethical sensibility, and a deep aversion to violence. He later said that his "predilection for saving the world" was traceable to the stories his mother told him.[7]

Tekla and her husband, Louis, argued often in front of their son, who increasingly exhibited a trait quite likely fostered by their chronic disagreement: a tendency to worry. Playmates kidded Szilard for worrying too much, but he seemed unable to stop thinking about dangers. Intensely inquisitive, and perhaps a bit terrified about endings and abandonment, he was always jumping ahead to the next assignment in school. Most boys his age strove to fit in, but Szilard was — and would forever be — independent and irreverent. His sense of humor also helped him alleviate tension and neutralize opponents, and he cultivated an ironic wit.

Szilard's interest in physics surfaced when he was a teenager. At about the same time, he found himself drawn to politics as well. "Ever since I was 13," Szilard recalled later, "I was interested in physics and in public affairs but I kept these two things in water-tight compartments and it never occurred to me that these two interests of mine would ever meet."[8]

In 1916 Szilard began riding the streetcar from his home, over the ornate Franz Josef Bridge spanning the Danube River, to the Technical University just below Gellért Hill, where he attended classes and discussed with fellow students the Great War raging across Europe. Szilard was drawn into the war the next summer when he was drafted into the Austro-Hungarian army and sent to officers' school, where he acted impertinent and nonchalant. He believed that Austria-Hungary and its ally Germany would eventually lose the war — and said so. He had little patience for what he considered mindless military discipline. His belt buckle was always tugged to one side, his boots always needed a shine.

After the war ended, Szilard returned to the Technical University, where revolutionary turmoil swirled around him. Students, artists, and intellectuals debated issues of the day in sidewalk cafés. Szilard thrived as the gadfly who asked the uncomfortable questions that others avoided. He was sympathetic to the communist regime that had come to power in Hungary at the end of the war under Béla Kun but recoiled at the brutalities that Kun inflicted in the name of the people and feared a conservative backlash. Szilard felt this backlash personally when he was confronted by angry students at the university who shouted, "You can't study here. You're a Jew!" They rushed Szilard, hitting and kicking him. The blood, bruises, and shame left Szilard with a fear of anti-Semitism that he would carry for years to come.

Realizing that, as a Jew, he was in personal danger, Szilard decided to leave Hungary for the University of Berlin. He arrived in Berlin in 1920 and took the university by storm. Berlin's physics faculty included giants such as Einstein, Max Planck, and Max von Laue, and Szilard sensed new developments in the air. In 1932 British physicist James Chadwick discovered the neutron. The neutron had no electric charge, which meant it could pass through the electrical barrier surrounding the atom and penetrate the nucleus. Szilard saw in the neutron's ability to easily penetrate the nucleus the possibility of eventually releasing the vast store of energy contained within the atom.

The same year as Chadwick's discovery, Szilard moved from the University of Berlin to the Kaiser Wilhelm Institute, where he continued his experimental work in nuclear physics. As he probed the mysteries of the atom within the institute, he grew edgy as he observed what was happening outside its walls. Szilard noticed that most Germans stood passively watching the growing Nazi threat. When he asked his German friends, "Why don't you oppose Nazism?" most of them shrugged and muttered, "What good would it do?" Szilard concluded that Hitler would gain power not because Nazism was so appealing to Germans but because so few Germans would resist it.

Unlike most physicists during these years, Szilard had no illusions that things would get better. He saw Nazism for what it was: an evil force that spelled disaster for Germany and all of Europe. Months before Hitler came to power, and years before he engulfed Europe in a bloody war, Szilard's assessment of the problems brewing for Jews in Germany led him to grave predictions. He shared them in a letter to Rabi, whom he had met and befriended in the late 1920s. "As far as the fate of Germany is concerned," Szilard wrote Rabi, "I always was very pessimistic, but I range now with the optimists. (You know, an optimist is a man who jumps out of the window of the 22nd floor and who says smiling when he passes the 10th floor, falling down: 'Well, nothing happened to me up till now.')"[9] Szilard's sarcasm belied his deep pessimism and despair.

On the night of February 27, 1933, Nazi saboteurs set fire to the Reichstag, Germany's parliament. Hitler blamed the arson on a Jewish-Communist plot and bullied Reichstag deputies into granting him dictatorial powers. On April first the Nazis directed a national boycott of Jewish businesses and beat Jews in the streets. On April seventh thousands of Jewish academics lost their positions in German universities. Szilard was particularly incensed by the prohibition against teaching "Jewish science" — any theory, even Einstein's profound theory of relativity, that had been developed by a Jew. He decided the time had come to get out. He grabbed his suitcases and took the night train to Vienna. The following day Nazi border guards stopped the same train and held back everyone whose passport was stamped "Jewish." This close call so frightened Szilard that he kept two suitcases packed and close at hand wherever he lived for the rest of his life.

In Vienna Szilard called on Western embassies and warned them that the Nazi assault on Jews was just beginning. The diplomats listened politely but said, and did, nothing. So Szilard decided to leave the Continent for the greater safety of Britain. He sought a permanent academic position there, but Depression-era Britain had only a limited ability to absorb refugees — there were neither enough positions nor enough money to fund them. Unable to secure a university appointment, Szilard decided to camp out in a modest hotel in London while he contemplated his next step. For the moment, he lived on the income from his patent licenses and money he had saved from tutoring fees.

Szilard was an idea man par excellence. Each day for months he strolled London's busy streets and beautiful parks pondering nuclear physics and his fears for Europe's future. One afternoon, while walking on a sidewalk in Bloomsbury, he had a fateful idea. He later recalled:

> As the light changed to green and I crossed the street, it suddenly occurred to me that if we could find an element which is split by neutrons and which would emit *two* neutrons when it absorbed *one* neutron, such an element, if assembled in sufficiently large mass, could sustain a nuclear chain reaction. I didn't see at the moment just how one would go about finding such an element or what experiments would be needed, but the idea never left me.[10]

Szilard imagined that if a neutron struck a nucleus and split the atom, the breakup might release the binding energy that holds the atom together. Some of that atom's neutrons might in turn be released, which could hit and split other atoms. If more than one neutron was released from each split atom, the process could expand exponentially: one neutron would release two, which would each strike a nucleus to release four, and so on. In millionths of a second, billions of atoms would split.

Suddenly the H. G. Wells novel he had read the year before took on grave new meaning. Published in 1914, just before the outbreak of World War I, *The World Set Free* prophetically described a conflict in which cities were destroyed by atomic bombs. "Of course," Szilard wrote a friend to whom he sent a copy of the novel, "all this is moonshine, but I have reason to believe that the forecast of the writers may prove to be more accurate than the forecast of the scientists."[11]

Szilard stood alone in his belief in a chain reaction. At the time, his mentor and friend Einstein — the world's preeminent theoretical physicist — told reporters that such an effort would be "fruitless."[12] Attempting to unlock the energy of the atom by neutron bombardment, said Einstein, was likely to enjoy about the same chance of success as "shooting birds in the dark in a country where there are only a few birds."[13] A doyen of the scientific establishment, the great experimentalist Lord Ernest Rutherford dismissed the prospect of a chain reaction with devastating British understatement: "The outlook for gaining useful energy from atoms by artificial processes of transformation does not look promising."[14] With comments like these the order of the day, it is easy to appreciate Szilard's difficulty in getting support for exploring the possibility of a nuclear chain reaction.

It was not an idle joke. Recognizing that the days of peace in Europe were numbered and that the future of Western civilization and modern science would depend on the degree of support that could be mustered in the New World, Szilard decided to emigrate to America. About Christmastime 1937 Szilard attended a dinner at Magdalen College in Oxford, where a fellow of the college told Szilard that he was leaving soon on a visit to the United States. "Buy a one-way ticket," Szilard advised him.[15]

Szilard's reasoning was simple. As he told a fellow Jewish refugee planning to leave the Continent, Britain was "a *very* likeable country, but it would certainly be a lot smarter if you went to America. In

America you would be a free human being and very soon would not even be a stranger."[16] In practical terms, he also saw a much better opportunity for nuclear physics research in the United States.

In January 1938 Szilard decided the time had come to depart. He begged his parents in Budapest to join him, but they refused to budge — they were old and did not want to leave the only world they knew. Szilard could do nothing more than bid them a sad farewell. Once in New York, he found himself quickly and happily at home. Nazism was far away. He did not feel like a foreigner. When he had some difficulty adjusting, this nation of immigrants offered understanding and sympathy. He had felt much more like a refugee in Europe.

So, quickly and eagerly Szilard decided to become a U.S. citizen. Emotionally and politically, he felt that he already belonged irretrievably to America. In his thinking and action, he scarcely had any affinity with the mentality of Nazi Germany. Soon he was in touch with other refugee physicists in the United States and was visiting Columbia frequently to see Rabi. With Rabi's help, Szilard resumed his research on the atomic nucleus and began warning anyone who would listen about the looming threat of Nazism.

Although Szilard had conceived the idea of a chain reaction, he lacked the resources — a laboratory, assistants, and financial support — to search for it. That quest fell to another refugee physicist, Enrico Fermi, who had the resources that Szilard lacked — and the brains to match. In contrast to Szilard, who moved from one temporary job to the next, lived in hotel rooms, and proposed experiments to other people, Fermi was a well-established academic who ran a famous physics institute located in a small, quiet park on a hill in central Rome. The park, landscaped with palm trees, bamboo thickets, and a garden that attracted singing sparrows at dusk, made the institute a peaceful and attractive center of study.

A short man with rounded shoulders, narrow nose, thick black hair, and hazel eyes that stood out against a dark complexion, Fermi charmed people by craning his neck forward and flashing a winning smile that exposed a gap between his front teeth. Quiet and unpretentious, he combined disarming personal modesty with an equally disarming self-confidence. He wore a simple leather jacket and always drove his own car. When he encountered a roadblock in front of his institute one day, he leaned out the window and said, "I am His Excellency Enrico Fermi's chauffeur" — which got him waved through. He had such a gift for seeing into the heart of problems and such an easy manner of solving them that other physicists nicknamed him "the Pope."

Fermi was born in 1901 into a middle-class family of civil servants and was educated in Italian public schools. He showed intellectual brilliance from an early age and also a cool, reserved manner. He was more prone to deeds than to talk and carefully guarded his innermost thoughts. Though somewhat cold, he was absolutely impartial. Fermi's most striking trait was his willingness to accept the world and people as they were. "He took people around him at their own value," said a friend. "That's why I was very fond of him."[17] He understood complex theories but preferred making simple points. Likewise, though he did not spend a lot of time analyzing people, he seldom misjudged them. Fermi abhorred confrontation and avoided battles that he was not confident of winning. If faced with superior force, he invariably withdrew from a contest. Consistent with this, he rarely made promises unless he was sure he could deliver on them.

Fermi began his career as a physicist in 1922, the year he received his doctorate from the University of Pisa. That same year, Benito Mussolini marched on Rome at the head of his armed Black Shirts and seized control of the Italian government in the name of Fascism. Preoccupied as he was with physics, the menace of Fascism seemed remote to Fermi. In 1923 he won a fellowship to study in Germany with the renowned Max Born, who had gathered a group of brilliant young physicists around him at Göttingen, including Werner Heisenberg and Wolfgang Pauli. Heisenberg and Pauli did not bring Fermi into their circle of conversation; most of the time the young Italian worked alone in silence. As a result, Fermi, who had succeeded almost effortlessly until then, felt ignored and unappreciated at Göttingen, an unwelcome foreigner in Germany. The experience embittered Fermi, who would remember it for a long time to come.

Fermi returned to Italy and took up a professorship of theoretical physics at the University of Rome. Over the next decade Fermi turned his physics institute into a leading center for the study of the nucleus. Fermi preferred tackling concrete problems. His method was never to waste time and to keep things as simple as possible — a no-nonsense, matter-of-fact, commonsense perspective. In this way, he kept going forward until he reached his goal, like a steamroller that moved slowly but knew no obstacles. He was a master at achieving important results with a minimum of effort. Like Szilard, Fermi saw the significance of the neutron and designed experiments around it. He decided to bombard nuclei of atoms with neutrons and see what happened. Fermi's insight was to slow neutrons down by sending them through paraffin (a particularly dense substance); the slower the neutrons moved, he thought, the more likely they were to stick in the nucleus they were hitting.

Fermi began his neutron experiments in the mid-1930s in typically methodical fashion: by systematically bombarding all the elements in the periodic table. He started with water — testing hydrogen and oxygen at the same time — and finally came to uranium, one of the heaviest elements.

The results were puzzling. Fermi observed that the uranium nucleus captured the bombarding neutron, emitted an unusually large amount of radiation, temporarily became a heavier isotope (with the same chemical characteristics but a different atomic weight), then decayed to an element heavier by one atomic number. The simplest explanation consistent with the known facts — the yardstick typically applied by scientists to interpret experimental results — was that the uranium was mutating up the periodic table. These man-made, very heavy "transuranic" elements should be unstable: their radioactive breakdown could explain the copious radiation being emitted.

During these years Fermi grew increasingly alarmed by Mussolini's policies, first the invasion of Ethiopia, then the intervention alongside Nazi Germany in the Spanish civil war. And there was something else: although anti-Semitism was not yet an issue in Italy, Fermi's beloved wife, Laura, was Jewish. In 1936 Fermi traveled to the United States to lecture at the University of Michigan summer school, where he came into contact with a large number of American and visiting European physicists. Fermi liked what he saw at Ann Arbor: well-equipped labs, eager students, and plenty of praise for his scientific talent. He returned the next two summers as well. Each visit made him like America's people, culture, and institutions more and more. At the same time, he gained perspective on Fascist Italy. America increasingly looked like the future to him, a land of freedom and opportunity far from the troubles of Europe.

Back in Italy, Fermi remained outwardly friendly, but now he kept his own counsel with all but his closest friends. As long as Fermi felt he could work unhindered in physics, he tried to ignore the nature of the Fascist regime and the trend of events. Like many of his country-men, he tried not to see the unfolding truth, because it was too unpleasant to contemplate. But the atmosphere in Italy took a sharp turn for the worse in July 1938. That month Mussolini published the *Manifesto della Razza*, which announced that "Jews do not belong to the Italian race." The manifesto was soon followed by edicts copied from Nazi racial laws. Not long after, the Fascist press began attacking Fermi for "having transformed the physics institute into a synagogue."[18]

Fermi realized that it was time to get his family out of Italy. He wrote to four American universities that had expressed an interest in hiring him. To avoid suspicion, he mailed each letter from a different location in Rome. When all four responded favorably, Fermi chose Columbia University and awaited an opportunity to make his escape. Listening to the radio on the night of November 10, 1938, Fermi and his wife heard that he had won the Nobel Prize during the same broadcast that reported the horrors of Kristallnacht, the murderous anti-Jewish pogrom that had swept Germany the night before, and the institution of a new set of racial laws excluding Italian Jewish children such as their own son and daughter from public schools.

Fermi decided to use the Nobel ceremony in Sweden to spirit his family out of Italy. In early December he, Laura, and their two children left by train for Stockholm. There were tense moments along the way. When they crossed the frontier from Switzerland into Germany, a Nazi border guard slowly and deliberately flipped through their passports. Fermi watched anxiously until the guard moved on to the next compartment. He and his family reached Stockholm safely, where he received the Nobel Prize on December tenth. Two weeks later, on Christmas Eve, the Fermis left for New York. A short time later, Laura Fermi's Jewish father, who had been an admiral in the Italian navy, disappeared into a concentration camp and was never heard from again.

Upon arriving in New York, the Fermis put up at the King's Crown Hotel, on West 116th Street just east of the Columbia University campus, where Szilard had also settled. Szilard had corresponded with Fermi about neutron experiments since 1936, so the two men had much to talk about when they met, by accident, in the hotel lobby one morning. They were the two physicists in the world best able to advance the research that would lead to the atomic bomb. Each man was a refugee from European fascism, and each possessed essential pieces of the atomic puzzle. Fermi was a scientific celebrity because of his recent Nobel Prize. Szilard, by contrast, was an unemployed "guest scholar" with no classes or lab of his own who had kept his pioneering nuclear research secret out of fear that the Nazis would somehow learn about it and use it to make an atomic bomb. "You didn't know what he was up to" was the complaint around Columbia's new Pupin Laboratory. "He was always a bit mysterious."[19] A late sleeper, he often appeared at Columbia only in time for lunch, after which he would drop in on colleagues, posing questions and suggesting experiments. As a result, most Columbia physicists looked upon Szilard as an inconvenient visitor who poked around the department and showed up unannounced in the lab to pester and offer unwanted advice.

One physicist at Columbia knew both men well: Rabi. Rabi bridged the world of transatlantic physics, counting both native-born and refugee physicists as personal friends. He had first met Fermi and Szilard in Germany during the 1920s and had remained in touch with both ever since. He shared with Fermi a passion for physics, but with Szilard he shared even more: similar roots. Although their temperaments were very different — Rabi was affable, politic, and of a sunny disposition, while Szilard was eccentric, impolitic, and moody — they were both Jews who hailed from Central Europe, and thus shared certain shadows.

Isador Isaac Rabi was born in 1898 in a village in what is now Poland but was then the northeasternmost province of the Austro-Hungarian Empire. His parents emigrated to America before he was a year old. "Had we stayed in Europe," he later said, "I probably would have become a tailor."[20] Like millions of other turn-of-the-century immigrants, the Rabis settled in the crowded Lower East Side of New York. It was a tough neighborhood where youngsters grew up fast. A contemporary of Rabi's described the neighborhood's "wisdom of the streets":

We would roam through the city tasting the delights of freedom, discovering possibilities far beyond the reach of our parents. The streets taught us the deceits of commerce, introduced us to the excitement of sex, schooled us in strategies of survival, and gave us our first clear idea of what life in America was really going to be like.

We might continue to love our parents and grind away at school and college, but it was the streets that prepared the future. In the streets we were roughened by actuality, and even those of us who later became intellectuals or professionals kept something of our bruising gutter-worldliness, our hard and abrasive skepticism. You could see it in cab drivers and garment manufacturers, but also in writers and professors who had grown up as children of immigrant Jews.[21]

Synagogues and saloons coexisted on nearly every Lower East Side street, and these contradictory symbols of life in the Jewish ghetto seemed vivid symbols to the young Rabi of the ways of people and the world. The streets made him impish, quick-witted, buoyant, and brash. He always said exactly what he thought, whether or not he believed it would meet with approval. He was cynical, yet compassionate toward others.

Against the worldliness of the streets stood the piety of his parents, David and Sheindel Rabi, devout Jews who raised their son according to strict Orthodox tradition. Hardly a sentence went by in their conversation without a reference to God. Rabi's earliest reading was Yiddish Bible stories. When he was nine years old, his family moved to Brownsville, the Jewish enclave of Brooklyn. One day as he browsed in the local branch of the Carnegie public library near his parents' small grocery store, he stumbled on a book about astronomy. The explanatory power of the Copernican system impressed him deeply. "It was so beautiful, so marvelous," said Rabi years later. "Instead of the idea that there is some special intervention every day for the sun to come up, I came home with this great revelation." Full of delight, Rabi announced to his parents: "It's all very simple, who needs God?"[22]

Rabi began testing other assumptions as well. Orthodox law forbade riding streetcars on the Sabbath. One Saturday he rode a streetcar, expecting God to strike it (or at least him) with lightning, but nothing happened. In synagogue, rabbis held out their tallis-covered hands; the congregation averted its eyes at the risk of blindness. One day Rabi did not, and again nothing happened. As Judaism began to look more and more like superstition to him, his life outside home became increasingly secular as he abandoned the religious practices and rituals of his immigrant parents. But the moral perspective of his Orthodox upbringing — the struggle between good and evil in the world — continued to shape his outlook. "My early upbringing, so struck by God, the maker of the world, this stayed with me," Rabi later said. "There's no question that basically, somewhere way down, I'm an Orthodox Jew."[23]

Rabi's testing of Jewish ritual and his growing exhilaration with science reflected a search for some all-encompassing system to explain both the universe and, more personally, the hard life of his family and friends. As an adolescent, he began to read books about Marxism and to attend neighborhood meetings of the Socialist Club. After a while, though, Rabi began to feel that Marxists were either kidding themselves or trying to kid him. "Part of the Socialist thing was 'equality' — anybody can do this or that," he recalled later. "But after I went to high school and looked at my classmates, I said, 'Those people can't run a government or a world,' and dropped the whole thing."[24]

When Rabi finished high school in 1916, his parents forcefully suggested that he go into Hebrew studies at a yeshiva. Instead, he decided to break away by going "way out west" to Cornell University in upstate New York. Ithaca, with its spectacular waterfalls and nearby Finger Lakes, certainly seemed like romantic country to a New York City boy who had devoured the novels of James Fenimore Cooper. Rabi scraped together enough money to attend college by summering as a sales clerk at Macy's department store and winning two state scholarships. Once at Cornell, he enthusiastically immersed himself in Ivy League culture — but it was not a total immersion: Rabi reaped its rewards, but he also refused to change his personality or diminish his independence.

When Rabi graduated with a degree in chemistry in 1919, he couldn't find a good job because of anti-Semitism and a postwar recession, so he returned to Cornell for graduate study. He soon realized that he should change his focus. His Orthodox upbringing had given him a feeling for the mystery of physics, a taste for generalization, and a belief in the profundity and underlying unity of nature. "When you're doing physics, you're wrestling with a champ," he liked to say. "You're trying to find out how God made the world, just like Jacob wrestling with the angel."[25] Physics brought Rabi nearer to God because the world was his creation. And like God, physics was infinite and certainly not trivial; it had class and drama. Doing good physics was "walking the path of God."[26]

A decade later Rabi was a full professor at Columbia University and an accomplished physicist. He liked the atmosphere of the laboratory, but he was completely uninterested in details — decidedly hands-off.

He studiously avoided nuts-and-bolts issues. "When things were going well and you were getting interesting data," said one of his graduate students, "he was right there on top of the experiment helping with the interpretation. But when there were leaks in the apparatus, he just disappeared."[27] His way of training theoretical physicists was to tell a young man when he arrived that if he was bright enough to be a theoretical physicist, then he was bright enough to find his own problem, solve it, and, when he was finished, come back and tell him all about it.

In 1931 Rabi spent a year at the University of Hamburg, where he watched brown-shirted Nazi hooligans march past the university in an eerie torchlight parade. His Hamburg professors at first dismissed Nazism because the brownshirts were so few in number and so coarse. But his wife, Helen, attending a nearby art school whose students included several Nazis, had a very different and more troubling view. She did not look Jewish, and Nazi students therefore talked openly to her. They told her about the "next war," and there was no doubt whatsoever about their vicious anti-Semitism. Rabi grew more alarmed when Hitler became chancellor in 1933. By then he was back in the United States at Columbia, but he had extensive contacts in Germany, including Szilard, who relayed what was happening there in frightening detail.

When Szilard arrived at Columbia in 1938, he shared with Rabi his idea of a chain reaction and his concern about what it meant for Europe. When Fermi arrived early the following year, the three physicists began a close collaboration. To work on the problems of fission and a chain reaction attended to all of their concerns at once: it was at the center of their scientific interests, the practical consequences might be enormous, and nothing could be more important politically than to guard against the danger that Nazi Germany might get an atomic bomb first. Like Szilard and Fermi, Rabi had become increasingly alarmed by Hitler and feared that the United States might stand by and allow him to take over Europe. Rabi began thinking about what he could do as a physicist to help in the war that he saw coming and that he felt sure would eventually involve America.

Niels Bohr also saw war coming. As a theoretical physicist, Bohr was thrilled and excited by the discovery of fission; but as a Danish Jew, he feared that Nazi Germany might use the discovery to make an atomic bomb. This fear was written on Bohr's face when he arrived in New

York in January 1939 to spend a semester at the Institute for Advanced Study in Princeton, New Jersey. "He stooped like a man carrying a heavy burden," said a friend who saw Bohr standing on the deck of his ship as it pulled alongside the Hudson River pier. "His gaze, troubled and insecure, shifted but stopped on no one."[28]

A tall Scandinavian with a large head and hands, bushy eyebrows, big jowls, and unruly combed-back hair, Bohr had a quiet, unassuming demeanor that masked a lively and profound mind of great creativity, subtlety, and humanity. He looked rather ponderous, but when people drew near him his blue eyes sparkled, exuding the warmth and charm of his personality. His great kindness and reluctance to hurt anyone's feelings, coupled with his insistence on not letting any inexact or wrong statement pass, led to his frequent comment: "I am not saying this in order to criticize, but this is sheer nonsense!"[29]

As a talker, Bohr found it very hard to get to the point. He thought of the implications of everything he said so much that he was unwilling to make any statement without qualifying it. It didn't help that he spoke in a mumbling voice not much above a whisper. An equally laborious writer, he preferred talking to writing. He also could be absentminded. But if he sometimes seemed scatterbrained about what was right before him, Bohr was stunningly acute when it came to what could not be seen. He possessed a powerful mind and formidable theoretical insight into physical processes.

Bohr was as much a philosopher as a physicist. He loved paradoxes. When faced with an apparently insoluble problem, he always said, "Every great and deep difficulty bears in itself its own solution. It forces us to change our thinking in order to find it."[30] Unlike most physicists of his day, who kept science and moral concerns quite separate, Bohr generalized this concept of "complementarity" to fields outside of physics, including politics, believing that rational inquiry, conducted in an open society and led by an informed elite, could harmonize technological progress with humanistic values and smooth out conflicts between nations. He was also deeply aware of the dangers that scientific innovation could pose to society. This concern, which Bohr felt with great intensity, was called *der Kopenhagener Geist* ("the Spirit of Copenhagen") by other physicists. Bohr was widely admired both for his accomplishments as a scientist and for his qualities as a human being; it was on account of both that he enjoyed great prestige among physicists.

Outside the walls of his Copenhagen institute, Bohr fought his anxiety by working tirelessly on behalf of scientists fleeing Nazi persecution: finding out who was in need, raising funds to assist them, circulating lists of names to institutions that might find jobs for them. As the head of the Danish Committee for the Support of Fugitive Intellectuals and Scientists, which he helped organize in 1933, Bohr had become the head dispatcher of an "underground railroad" that delivered many of Europe's most brilliant scientists to Britain and America. Every year, he traveled to both countries to sell "his refugees," including a trip to Princeton in the spring of 1939.

Bohr spent his time at Princeton that last spring before World War II analyzing the theoretical implications of fission. The big question of the moment was whether additional neutrons — what physicists called "secondary neutrons" — were also released by fission. If they were (and there were enough of them), these secondary neutrons could split still other uranium atoms in a multiplying chain reaction — proving true the idea that had come to Leo Szilard while walking on a London street back in September 1933.

Bohr hoped a chain reaction was impossible. He began studying the problem with a young Princeton physicist named John Wheeler in February 1939. He and Wheeler worked in Fine Hall, a Georgian brick pile on Princeton's campus housing the physics and mathematics departments. Bohr's office had bookshelves on one wall, a blackboard on another, and large windows looking out onto a green lawn on another. Bohr began each day standing at the blackboard. Soon he began drawing and writing equations, erasing figures with the sleeve of his coat. He probed and stabbed at the bowl of his pipe as he paced his office for hours, littering the floor with matchsticks. Sometimes he paced the hallway that circled the second floor of Fine Hall, thinking as he walked. Back in the office, Bohr broke one piece of chalk after another in bouts of furious writing at the board. At the end of the day, he would lift the edge of the rug on the hardwood floor and kick broken bits of chalk under it. Otherwise, he would be scolded for messiness by the cleaning lady.

There was a large radio in the common room, and each afternoon at four Bohr would have tea with other faculty members and all of them would listen intently to news of the intensifying crisis in Europe. War seemed inevitable. Bohr took it all in with remarkable equanimity. The Western democracies were making the mistakes now, he remarked, but the Nazis would be making the mistakes in the end.[31]

Amid this tension-filled atmosphere, Bohr and Wheeler pondered the secrets of fission, formulating a hypothesis that fit the known facts. They knew that natural uranium consisted of two isotopes. More than 99 percent of uranium atoms consisted of an isotope of atomic weight 238, and less than 1 percent were of atomic weight 235. They also knew that elements of odd atomic weight tended to be less stable than those of even atomic weight. They reasoned then that only the rare isotope U-235 was fissioning when its nucleus was penetrated by a neutron while secondary neutrons would mostly be absorbed by U-238, which would not fission. The two isotopes were chemically identical and could be separated only by mechanisms that depended on the difference in their weight. Since the weights were so close — differing by only three parts in 238 — it seemed an impossible task to separate the two in any meaningful quantities. Bohr was relieved to conclude that a fission bomb could not be constructed without separation and that the world was safe from destruction after all.

Despite Bohr's conclusion, Szilard labored to keep the possibility of a chain reaction secret. He felt so strongly about the need for secrecy that he decided to withhold his own groundbreaking research from publication. Such self-denial was one way, he thought, of preventing the Nazis from realizing fission's military potential. Another way was to urge other scientists to do the same. This was a major departure from the scientific ethos of the day. Science was open; no scientist hid results; there was no progress without publication. It was quite unaffected by national boundaries.

Szilard learned that neutron experiments were being done by Frédéric Joliot in Paris, so he wrote Joliot, imploring him not to publish his results. "If more than one neutron were liberated, a sort of chain reaction would be possible," he confided to Joliot. "In certain circumstances this might then lead to the construction of bombs which would be extremely dangerous in general and particularly in the hands of certain governments," he broadly hinted. Szilard closed the letter, "In the hope that there will not be sufficient neutrons emitted by uranium, I am . . . ," but then crossed out this closing, simply signed the letter, and mailed it.[32] Joliot refused his request, publishing his results in a European scientific journal later that spring.

Undeterred, Szilard approached Fermi, who was working separately on his own neutron experiments. Although the two had started out together in the Columbia laboratory, it had not worked out — their temperamental differences made collaboration impossible. Szilard preferred brainstorming to manual labor, whereas Fermi expected everyone to roll up his sleeves. Szilard made intuitive leaps from Point A to Point D, whereas Fermi never moved from Point A to Point B until he knew all he could about A — and had reasonable assurances about B. Szilard believed neutron research might well be used for military purposes, whereas Fermi had little confidence that anything militarily useful would result from it. Szilard was disposed to reevaluate things in light of new circumstances; Fermi was by nature a conservative man disinclined to deviate from customary practice.

Fermi considered Szilard a brilliant but very peculiar man who enjoyed startling people. He was certainly startled when Szilard walked into his Pupin Hall office one afternoon and told him that it was his duty to withhold results of his neutron experiments until it was clear whether they were potentially dangerous. This was especially important, Szilard argued, because astute reporters had gotten on the trail after Bohr had announced Hahn's fission results at the Washington conference in early February. With fission, "hope is revived that we may yet be able to harness the energy of the atom," the New York Times reported on February fifth. The February sixth issue of Newsweek also reported on fission. The Times' science correspondent, William Laurence, buttonholed Fermi after a meeting of the American Physical Society at Columbia on February twenty-fourth, and inquired whether uranium could be used to make an atomic bomb. The unusually long silence that followed made Laurence feel that he had asked something important.

"We must not jump to hasty conclusions," Fermi said carefully. "This is all so new. We will have to learn a lot more before we know the answer. It will take many years."

How many? Laurence replied.

"At least twenty-five, possibly fifty years," answered Fermi.

"Supposing Hitler decides that this may be the very weapon he needs to conquer the world," Laurence persisted. "How long then?"

Fermi was guarded, but to Laurence the implications were clear. Fission meant a chain reaction, and a chain reaction meant an atomic bomb.[33]

When Szilard learned from Rabi the next day that Fermi had publicly discussed the possibility of a chain reaction, he was horrified. He rushed to Fermi's office; he wasn't there. Szilard went back to Rabi and asked him to tell Fermi that "these things ought to be kept secret."

Szilard sought out Rabi again the following day:

I said to him: "Did you talk to Fermi?" Rabi said, "Yes, I did." I said, "What did Fermi say?" Rabi said, "Fermi said 'Nuts!'" So I said, "Why did he say 'Nuts!'?" and Rabi said, "Well, I don't know, but he is in and we can ask him." So we went over to Fermi's office, and Rabi said to Fermi, "Look, Fermi, I told you what Szilard thought and you said 'Nuts!' and Szilard wants to know why you said 'Nuts!'" So Fermi said, "Well . . . there is the remote possibility that neutrons may be emitted in the fission of uranium and then of course perhaps a chain reaction can be made." Rabi said, "What do you mean by 'remote possibility'?" and Fermi said, "Well, ten percent." Rabi said, "Ten percent is not a remote possibility if it means that we may die of it. If I have pneumonia and the doctor tells me that there is a remote possibility that I might die, and it's ten percent, I get excited about it."[34]

"We both wanted to be conservative," Szilard noted, "but Fermi thought that the conservative thing was to play down the possibility that this may happen, and I thought the conservative thing was to assume that it would happen and take the necessary precautions."[35]

Szilard grew increasingly frantic that spring the more he thought about fission. For weeks he rushed about the Columbia University labs and faculty offices, bearing witness to the great and dreadful events he foresaw. He was anxious — almost desperate — to prove or disprove a chain reaction. Half in hope and half in fear, he set up an experiment on the night of March third. The setting was the vaultlike laboratory on the seventh floor of Pupin. The experiment was designed to reveal pulses on an oscilloscope that could be expected from the neutrons of split uranium atoms. All Szilard had to do was flip a switch and watch the oscilloscope screen. If pulses appeared on the screen, it would mean that secondary neutrons were emitted in the fission of uranium — and that would confirm a chain reaction.

Szilard flipped the switch, saw the dreaded pulses, and watched them for several minutes with mounting horror. Then he flipped off the switch and walked back in silence to his hotel. "That night," Szilard later recalled, "there was very little doubt in my mind that the world was headed for grief."[36]

CHAPTER 2

The Gathering Storm

T HE SAME NIGHT that Szilard conducted his experiment at Columbia University proving a chain reaction, he phoned Edward Teller with the ominous news. Teller remembered the moment vividly many years later. "I was at the piano, attempting with the collaboration of a friend and his violin to make Mozart sound like Mozart, when the telephone rang. It was Szilard, calling from New York. He spoke to me in Hungarian, and he said only one thing: 'I have found the neutrons,'" and hung up.[1] Teller understood just what Szilard's laconic message meant. And he shared Szilard's sense of dread. "All my worries about nuclear energy — the full realization that it was coming, and coming very soon, and that it would be very dangerous" was clear to Teller. "My sleep that night was uneasy," he recalled.[2]

Teller's sense of foreboding had been building for years. When he arrived at the University of Göttingen in 1930, he saw the goose-stepping, the torchlight parades, the pagan rallies, and found them barbaric rituals unworthy of a cultured people. He saw the critical faculty of Germans being swept away in an emotional frenzy, and every hateful lie that Hitler shouted being accepted as Truth itself. How could this happen? A few Germans were troubled, they admitted to Teller — but what could they do? It was not a question that many Germans asked, or answered. The Nazis' virulent anti-Semitism also bothered Teller. For most German Jews, it came as a terrible shock. They could not grasp how such a thing could happen in an advanced society in the heart of Europe in the twentieth century. Teller, a Hungarian Jew, knew better. What was happening in Germany was an uncomfortable reminder of what he had left behind in his native land.

Teller, like Szilard, had been born in turn-of-the-century Budapest. His father, Max, was a lawyer and associate editor of the major law journal of Hungary who worked from a spacious office apartment on the east embankment of the Danube near the Parliament Building. A quiet and reserved man, Max Teller did all the routine work on the law journal while the chief editor added the flair. His son's own later style, avoiding routine work and constantly offering original ideas, may have been an unconscious reaction against the tedium of his father's life. From his mother, Ilona, Teller inherited a moody temperament and a tendency to worry, though his worries were uniquely his own. As a young boy, he had such a terrible fear of the dark that, until he was seven, his parents always left a light on in his bedroom at night. When the light went out, he worked math problems to help cope with his fear of the dark. The consistency of numbers made him feel safe.

As a schoolboy, Teller annoyed his teachers and classmates with his self-concern and self-assurance even as he awed them with his brilliance. He was opinionated and always eager to show that he knew more than others. Classmates who resented this behavior bullied him as he walked to and from school. His governess later recalled that all he would say was, "I'm working on a plan."[3] After getting a longer strap for his books, Teller, when approached by the gang, whirled his books around him and was never bothered again. It was an early example of defense through a cunning weapon. The bullying engendered in Teller a lifelong sense of being embattled, besieged, alone in a struggle against his enemies. Sensitive but deeply insecure, he took refuge at the family piano, losing himself for hours playing Mozart and Beethoven sonatas with great feeling. Teller also sought escape in the novels of Jules Verne, which carried him into the exciting and imaginative world of science fiction.

The revolutionary turmoil that swept post–World War I Europe hit Budapest when Teller was an impressionable adolescent. He witnessed political violence in the streets from the window of his bedroom. One day walking home from school, he saw a poster of a stern man with an outstretched arm whose large fingertip seemed pointed right at him, warning: "You, hiding in the shadows, you counterrevolutionary, TREMBLE." He did.

When the communists briefly took over Hungary in 1919, Teller's father was labeled a capitalist and the family became social outcasts.

Communist soldiers requisitioned the Teller apartment as "bourgeois excess" and terrorized the family by urinating on houseplants and scrounging for money, which Max had hidden in the lining of his law books. This terrifying ordeal was the eleven-year-old Teller's first taste of communism, and it fed into his preexisting fear of Russia, the great looming presence to the east. "When I misbehaved when I was a small boy," he remembered, "my grandmother told me, 'If you don't behave, the Russians will get you.'"[4] Her threat, and the haunting image it evoked, resonated and would stay with Teller all his life.

Max Teller told his son that the Hungarian Soviet would eventually fail and that anti-Semitism would follow. "Too many of the communist leaders are Jews," he explained, "and all the Jews will be blamed for their excesses."[5] It was a sadly accurate prediction. In the fall of 1919 fascists swept to power in Budapest. Red Terror gave way to White Terror — an especially cruel trap for the Jewish middle class. They never had any use for the Commune, and yet now they became the scapegoats of the fascists. They were publicly vilified and denied access to certain professions, such as law, medicine, and education. For the first time, Teller tasted the bitterness of persecution.

Max Teller pressed two lessons on his son: he would have to leave Hungary, and as a Jew, he would always have to excel just to survive. Edward added two lessons of his own. One was his already deep and abiding anticommunism. The other was a practical view of what a science could do for him. "I loved science," he later said, "but it also offered a possibility for escaping this doomed society."[6] In this, he meant more than just Hungary. Science was a way for Teller to hold his own in a hostile world.

He took these experiences and emotions with him when he left to study in Germany, just weeks before his eighteenth birthday. Teller did work at Karlsruhe, Munich, and Leipzig, where his mentor was Werner Heisenberg. From Leipzig, Teller went to Göttingen, where for the first time he suffered taunts from Nazi students. A Göttingen administrator made plain the danger that he faced. "I would like to help you," the administrator told him, "but you have no future in Germany."[7] The comment shocked Teller, but he took the hint. He emigrated to Britain and took up a temporary lectureship at the University of London, then won a Rockefeller Foundation Fellowship to study with Bohr in Copenhagen. The terms of the award prohibited marriage during the fellowship, but Teller decided to wed his childhood sweetheart, Mici Harkanyi, anyway. (What Edward Teller wanted, he pursued — whatever the rules.) After a year in Copenhagen, he was offered a tenured position at George Washington University in Washington, D.C. Quantum mechanics was still a new discipline, and Teller was one of perhaps a hundred theoretical physicists in the world well educated in the subject.

Teller left for the United States at the beginning of 1935. He traveled aboard a ship from Southampton to New York. The gentle rocking of the ship induced Teller to meditation. He felt suspended between two worlds, not yet in a country where his future was uncertain, yet forced to leave a continent that was no longer home. Never before had Teller so powerfully felt a sense of exile.

Also aboard the ship was Hans Bethe, another refugee physicist forced to leave Germany, headed to Cornell University. Teller and Bethe shared much in common: Jewish roots, the impact on their lives of rising political extremism, the unsuccessful attempt to keep physics above politics, the maelstrom of Nazism. They were unsure what awaited them in America. Anxious about the fate of their families and friends back in Europe, they were in acute need of emotional, professional, and financial support. They found all these things in their adopted country. Like Szilard, both quickly came to love the United States for its embrace of immigrants. "I am speaking English with an accent, but in no other country have I been told that my accent is charming!" Teller reported to longtime friends back in Europe. "I am praised for *mispronouncing* the language!"[8]

The state of American physics was also quite advantageous for newcomers. Experimental nuclear physics was developing rapidly, with experimental results outrunning theory. For a theoretician like Teller, such a situation was made to order. In Europe, Teller — for all his ability — had worked in the shadow of older, more established physicists. In America he was his own man with his own graduate students. These advantages, combined with his awareness of his own intellectual gifts, rapidly gave Teller a brash self-assurance that made him a commanding teacher at George Washington University. His physical presence helped: intense, sad gray eyes stared out from under thick black eyebrows. And he was an impressive speaker, his pauses powerful, his words great blocks of stone laid down one by one. If he sensed he was losing his students' attention, his stentorian voice would go down — not up.

Dramatic and passionate, forceful and egotistical, gregarious and clever, Teller could be irresistibly charming — when it suited his purposes. On such occasions he was a brilliant raconteur with a perfect sense of timing who told good stories and listened attentively to others. Yet coexisting with this warm, charming, vulnerable, and idealistic Teller, there was an alternative Teller, who was melancholy and whose gusto for life was offset by bouts of dark brooding during which he could be bullying, aggressive, devious, intolerant, resentful, vengeful, and self-absorbed. This Teller, when tense, was liable to take a route of no-holds-barred aggression that could include a full-blooded tirade against his opponents, real and imagined. And even when in a good mood, he would always exaggerate the gap between himself and his critics. There was always something angry about the energy and intensity with which he pursued an argument, an unremitting fierce tight focus, like a flame, that put observers in mind of a blowtorch.

People were amazed by Teller's stamina in dispute. Marvelously argumentative, never tired, he possessed a singularity of purpose that brooked no diversion. Given this propensity, it might come as a surprise that Teller kept any friends — but he did. Yet the role of former friends was, in comparison, endless, all of them guilty of making an objection to some aspect of Teller's work, no matter how mild or constructive in spirit. The general rule was: once exiled, exiled forever. Even détente was unthinkable. Onlookers were left openmouthed at the ferocity of the rows and the intensity of the rejections.

Uncomplicated and genuine at one moment, an aggressive salesman driven to impress at the next, slyly political and naive, he was a complex and moody man who remained scarred by political upheaval. Such experience had made Teller an insecure pessimist. Like Szilard or Fermi or Bethe, he loved America, but he was never a happy exile, never able to live from day to day, and the fate of his family — whom he did not know how to protect — in Europe caused him much anxiety and suffering. Conflicts born of such frustrations would embitter Teller for the rest of his life.

The morning after Szilard phoned Teller with the news about neutrons, he took the train from New York to Washington. Teller picked him up at Union Station in the shadow of the Capitol, and they drove to Teller's home on Garfield Street in leafy Northwest Washington. There they talked in Hungarian, long into the night, about fission and a chain reaction. Szilard told Teller it was crucial for fission research to remain secret in order to keep it out of the hands of the Nazis. He understood that science was advanced through the free exchange of ideas and that many refugees like himself had left Germany precisely because the Nazis had censored intellectual inquiry, but Szilard saw war coming and feared that atomic bombs would decide the outcome. Teller agreed.

Szilard felt so strongly about this issue that he decided to lobby Niels Bohr as well. If he could convince Bohr to swing his prestige behind secrecy, then the campaign to hinder German atomic research might succeed. On March 16, 1939, Szilard and Teller went to see Bohr at the Institute for Advanced Study at Princeton. That same evening the radio broadcast ominous news that Hitler had sent German troops into Prague, violating the promise to respect Czech independence he had made to the leaders of Britain and France at the Munich Conference just six months earlier. Awakened at last to Hitler's duplicity, Britain and France now issued guarantees to Poland, next on Hitler's list, and began to rearm furiously. And there was this: Nazi-occupied Czechoslovakia had some of the world's richest uranium deposits.

The news only confirmed the two Hungarians in their advocacy of secrecy, but Bohr disagreed vehemently. "Openness is the basic condition necessary for science," he scolded them. "It should not be tampered with."[9] Physics was an international discipline. The good physicist reported his results so that other physicists could scrutinize them and correct errors. Secrecy would subvert openness and subordinate physics to national competition, substituting petty rivalry for progress.

Bohr also thought Szilard and Teller were being unduly alarmist. Bohr continued to believe that separating U-235 from U-238 and accumulating enough of the U-235 isotope to make a bomb would require a staggering — well-nigh impossible — engineering effort. "You would have to turn the entire country into a factory," Bohr told them.[10] He estimated that an isotope separation factory would have to operate twenty-four hours a day for ten days to produce only a billionth of a gram of U-235. At that rate, it would take 26,445 years to produce one gram. To Bohr, the conclusion was simple and inescapable: U-235 was, thankfully, not a practical source for atomic bombs.

As Bohr's time in Princeton came to an end, colleagues urged him to send for his family and remain in the States — any university position in the country was his for the asking. Bohr certainly saw the handwriting on the wall — that war was imminent — but turned down all invitations to stay because of his loyalty to Denmark. He had to return home, Bohr felt, in order to protect his institute and keep its doors open as a haven for scientists fleeing Nazi persecution. "We are aware that a catastrophe might come any day," he wrote a friend in America after his arrival back in Copenhagen.[11] But still he refused to leave home.

Szilard had concluded that fission was deadly serious business and that physicists could no longer handle it alone. They had to share their knowledge and concerns with the U.S. government — the stakes were simply too big and too grave. In Szilard's mind, the question now was not *whether* to notify Washington, but *how*. He approached the chairman of Columbia's physics department, George Pegram, with his concerns. Pegram had followed Szilard's and Fermi's experiments and agreed that the time had come to notify the government. He mentioned a contact he had in the Navy Department in Washington. Pegram and Szilard asked Fermi to see this contact during an upcoming trip he had planned to Washington.

Fermi had spent his first months in America adjusting to his adopted country. He strove to master the plainsong of American speech and the nuances of American culture — all with a sunny disposition and modest manner. He made a deal with his students: if they corrected his English and taught him Americanisms, he would teach them physics. He and his wife, Laura, bought a house in Leonia, New Jersey, across the Hudson River from Columbia University. Working at night, they dug a hole in the basement, where they buried his remaining Nobel Prize money as a precaution against the chance that it might be taken away from them as enemy aliens in the event of a war.

On March seventeenth Fermi took the train to Washington and called on Admiral Stanford Hooper, technical assistant to the chief of naval operations, at the Navy Department building on the Mall near the White House. "There's a WOP outside," said a lieutenant loud enough for Fermi to hear, rudely foreshadowing the puzzled indifference of the admiral he was about to see. Fermi affected nonchalance, but inside he was fuming. When Fermi was let in to see Hooper, he handed the admiral a letter of introduction from Pegram that described the physicists' discoveries and their implications:

> Experiments in the physics laboratories at Columbia University reveal that conditions may be found under which the chemical element uranium may be able to liberate its large excess of atomic

energy, and that this might mean the possibility that uranium might be used as an explosive that would liberate a million times as much energy per pound as any known explosive. My own feeling is that the probabilities are against this, but my colleagues and I think that the bare possibility should not be disregarded.[12]

Hooper gathered a group of officers and navy civilian scientists. For the next hour Fermi outlined the military potential of fission in his halting English with a thick Italian accent. His audience listened politely as they tried to follow along. Few if any knew what a neutron was, and little came of the meeting. When it was over, Admiral Hooper merely asked to be kept informed. No sooner had Fermi left than a navy scientist who had attended the briefing called another and asked him, "Who is this Fermi? Is he a Fascist or what?"[13] Such was the outcome of the first contact between physicists and the government on the possibility of an atomic bomb.

Fermi rendezvoused with Szilard and Teller in Washington that weekend. The navy's indifference to the dangers and opportunities of fission frustrated and infuriated them. "If we brought a bomb to them all ready made on a silver platter," said Fermi bitterly, "there would still be a 50/50 chance that they would mess it up."[14] They were apprehensive. They had inside knowledge of German science, and much respect for it, even though many of Germany's best physicists had been driven away. There was still enough scientific talent in Germany, they felt, to solve the problem of a fission bomb. German physicists had read the scientific literature about fission and a chain reaction, as they had. Heisenberg had mentioned his interest in uranium on a recent tour of American universities. While some, like Bohr, found the idea of an atomic bomb scarcely credible because of the isotope-separation problem, Szilard, Teller, and Fermi had little doubt that such a bomb could be made. And if such a bomb *could* be made, they reasoned, then one *would* be made. The prospect of such a weapon in Hitler's hands meant nothing short of doom.

Their experience with the Navy Department led them to conclude that ideas presented at a low level of the governmental bureaucracy were likely to go nowhere, but those inserted at the top stood a much better chance of getting results. The president of the United States was more likely to be interested in extraordinary ideas than would unimaginative bureaucrats. Roosevelt had to be warned, but how? What could *they* do? They were well known in physics circles, but nothing more than registered aliens in American society at large. As newcomers to the United States, they lacked the political connections necessary to press their claims effectively in the corridors of power.

Then Szilard thought of his teacher and friend Albert Einstein. A letter from a scientist of Einstein's stature might make the president sit up and take notice. Szilard contacted Einstein and explained the situation. An avowed pacifist, Einstein agonized at the thought of setting in motion a program to build an atomic bomb, so antithetical to his instincts. Einstein struggled with his conscience for some time before finally concluding that bitter necessity required the United States to pursue a bomb — the Nazis must not get it first. Finally, in late July Einstein agreed to sound the alarm on Szilard's behalf. It was unusual for a scientist of Einstein's stature to take such a step. "The one thing most scientists are really afraid of is to make a fool of themselves," Szilard said later, reflecting on Einstein's decision. "Einstein was free from such a fear and this above all is what made his position unique on this occasion."[15]

On August second Szilard set out for Einstein's summer retreat on Long Island with a letter he had drafted for Einstein's signature. Szilard had never learned to drive, so he enlisted Teller, who was teaching physics at Columbia that summer, to take him out there. It was already hot and humid when Teller picked up Szilard outside the King's Crown Hotel early in the morning and drove through Harlem, across the new Triborough Bridge, and past the World's Fair grounds to Long Island. "I entered history as Szilard's chauffeur," Teller later said.[16]

Szilard and Teller knew Einstein's general whereabouts, but not his specific address. Once they reached the north shore of Long Island, they began asking directions to the home of the famous Professor Einstein, but no one could help. Finally they asked a little girl with long braids who said she had never heard of Professor Einstein, but she knew where a nice old man with long white hair lived.

Szilard and Teller reached Einstein's cottage on Peconic Bay in the late afternoon. They found the great man with a massive forehead and an aureole of white hair dressed in an old robe and slippers sitting in the living room, empty except for a few garden chairs and a small table, pondering physics. A picture window looked out on to Long Island Sound, but the shutters were half closed to keep out the heat. Looking like an old-fashioned Swiss watchmaker in a small town who collected butterflies on Sundays, Einstein served his guests iced tea with heavily muscled arms and drank some himself while he reviewed the letter Szilard had drafted for him. His large bulging chocolate eyes followed the text carefully. In it, the physicist who had risked his life during World War I for his outspoken pacifist beliefs said that an atomic bomb might be possible and that the United States should speed up experiments regarding a uranium chain reaction. Szilard and Teller watched silently as Einstein hunched over the dining-room table and signed the letter:

Old Grove Road
Nassau Point
Peconic, Long Island
August 2, 1939

F. D. Roosevelt
President of the United States
White House
Washington, D.C.

Sir:
Some recent work by E. Fermi and L. Szilard, which has been communicated to me in manuscript, leads me to expect that the element uranium may be turned into a new and important source of energy in the immediate future. Certain aspects of the situation which has arisen seem to call for watchfulness and, if necessary, quick action on the part of the Administration. I believe, therefore, that it is my duty to bring to your attention the following facts and recommendations:

In the course of the last four months it has been made probable — through the work of Joliot in France as well as Fermi and Szilard in America — that it may become possible to set up a nuclear chain reaction in a large mass of uranium, by which vast amounts of power and large quantities of new radium-like elements would be generated. Now it appears almost certain that this could be achieved in the immediate future.

This new phenomenon would also lead to the construction of bombs, and it is conceivable — though much less certain — that extremely powerful bombs of a new type may thus be constructed. A single bomb of this type, carried by boat and exploded in a port, might very well destroy the whole port together with some of the surrounding territory. However, such bombs might very well prove to be too heavy for transportation by air.

The United States has only very poor ores of uranium in moderate quantities. There is some good ore in Canada and the former Czechoslovakia, while the most important source of uranium is the Belgian Congo.

In view of this situation you may think it desirable to have some permanent contact maintained between the Administration and the group of physicists working on chain reaction in America. One possible way of achieving this might be for you to entrust with this task a person who has your confidence and who could perhaps serve in an unofficial capacity. His task might comprise the following:

a) to approach Government departments, keep them informed of the further development, and put forward recommendations for Government action, giving particular attention to the problem of securing a supply of uranium ore for the United States;

b) to speed up the experimental work which is at present being carried on within the limits of the budgets of university laboratories, by providing funds if such be required, through his contacts with private persons who are willing to make contributions for this cause, and perhaps also by obtaining the cooperation of industrial laboratories which have the necessary equipment.

I understand that Germany has actually stopped the sale of uranium from the Czechoslovakian mines which she has taken over. That she should have taken such early action might perhaps be understood on the ground that the son of the German Under-Secretary of State, von Weizsäcker, is attached to the Kaiser-Wilhelm-Institute in Berlin where some of the American work on uranium is now being repeated.

Yours very truly,
Albert Einstein[17]

After Szilard returned to New York, he began to think about how to get Einstein's letter to the president. Through a friend, Gustav Stolper, an economist and former member of the German Reichstag who was now a refugee living in New York, Szilard made contact with Alexander Sachs — a Russian émigré, science buff, financier, and well-connected New Dealer with access to the White House. Sachs was an ideal go-between. He understood the concept of fission and the seriousness of what Szilard told him. Sachs agreed to get the letter to Roosevelt.

Events delayed Sachs's meeting with the president. On August twenty-third Hitler and Stalin, ideological enemies but totalitarian twins, signed a cynical "nonaggression" pact that stunned the world and prepared to carve up Poland between them. On September first German tanks crashed into Poland, facing little more than horse cavalry as opposition. The years of threat and bluster and tension were over. World War II had begun. A Polish refugee in America who heard the news on the radio captured the feelings of a whole generation when he said, "I suddenly felt as if a curtain had fallen on my past life, cutting it off from my future. There has been a different color and meaning to everything ever since."[18]

By early October, Szilard had almost given up on Sachs. To Einstein he wrote: "There is a distinct possibility that Sachs will be of no use to us. If this is the case, we must put the matter in someone else's hands. I have decided to accord Sachs ten days' grace."[19] On October eleventh Sachs finally got his appointment with the president, more than two months after Einstein had signed Szilard's letter and six weeks after the war had begun. Reminding FDR that Napoleon had missed the greatest technological marvel of his day when he rejected Robert Fulton's offer to build a fleet of steamships, Sachs tendered Einstein's letter and proceeded to explain the military potential of fission. Einstein had, of course, closed his appeal to the president with a warning that Germany had stopped the sale of uranium from mines in Nazi-controlled Czechoslovakia, one of the world's few sources of the metal, a sure tip-off that Hitler was already at work on an atomic bomb. FDR quickly grasped the point. "Alex," he said, "what you are after is to see that the Nazis don't blow us up." The president called in General Edwin "Pa" Watson, his personal aide, and told him, "This requires action."[20]

At Roosevelt's request, Watson directed the creation of an Advisory Committee on Uranium to explore the feasibility of an American atomic bomb program and report its findings to the president. Lyman Briggs, the director of the National Bureau of Standards, was appointed the committee's chairman. Although Briggs was a physicist, his interests and experience lay outside the field of nuclear physics. Moreover, he was conservative by nature, accustomed to operating — as most bureaucrats do — in a slow, cautious, and methodical manner. For Briggs, fission was an area of scientific research whose possibilities had to be soberly measured against opportunities in other fields.

The Uranium Committee met for the first time on October 21, 1939 — ten long months after the discovery of fission in Germany.

Sachs saw to it that Szilard and Teller were invited to the meeting. Fermi was also invited, but he refused to attend; his experience with Admiral Hooper and the navy made him unenthusiastic about another meeting with government bureaucrats. Fermi did, however, authorize Teller to speak on his behalf.

Szilard opened the meeting by emphasizing the possibility of creating a chain reaction in a uranium-graphite "pile" (or nuclear reactor). He explained to the committee that each time a uranium nucleus split apart, it released tremendous energy. But fission would not occur if one had to keep firing neutrons from an external source at the uranium atoms to break them up. If, on the other hand, the uranium atom released neutrons as it split, then these neutrons could go on and break up other nuclei. The neutrons from these disintegrations would trigger more, producing a chain of fissions. But neutrons had a less than 1 percent chance of fissioning a nucleus of natural uranium — thus no chance for a chain reaction. Neutrons needed to be slowed down. Slow neutrons had a more than 50 percent chance of fissioning a uranium nucleus — thus producing a chain reaction. The best way to slow neutrons was to use a "moderator," which absorbed neutrons. The best moderator was graphite, whose carbon molecules absorbed about 10 percent of neutrons.

All of this sounded terribly exotic to the bureaucrats gathered around the table. The ordnance expert at the meeting, Lieutenant Colonel Keith Adamson, an officer at the army's Aberdeen Proving Ground in northern Maryland, sneered at the idea of an atomic bomb — it was sheer fantasy. The colonel told Szilard and Teller in no uncertain terms that he did not believe "all this junk about complicated inventions." "At Aberdeen," he went on, ridiculing the physicists, "we have a goat tethered to a stick with a ten-foot rope, and we have promised a big prize to anyone who can kill the goat with a death ray. Nobody has claimed the prize yet."[21] Adamson then proceeded to lecture Szilard and Teller about scientific boondoggles in wartime. "He told us that it was naive to believe that we could make a significant contribution to defense by creating a new weapon," recalled Szilard. "He said that if a new weapon is created, it usually takes two wars before one can know whether the weapon is any good or not. Then he explained rather laboriously that in the end it is not weapons which win the wars, but the morale of the troops."[22]

Teller listened to Adamson with mounting frustration and anger. He had studied in Germany for many years and understood their military technology better than most — certainly better than the colonel. Finally he exploded. "If it is morale and not weapons that wins wars," Teller said, his voice rising as his accent thickened, "then why does the Army need such a large arms budget? Perhaps its funding can be cut." "All right, all right," Adamson replied, "you'll get your money."[23] The Uranium Committee authorized all of $6,000 to purchase graphite, though Szilard and Fermi would not actually receive the money for several months. Briggs sent a report of the meeting to President Roosevelt on November first. He heard from the White House on November seventeenth. The president had read the report and wanted to keep it on file. "On file" is where it languished well into 1940.

Szilard and Teller left their meeting with the Uranium Committee frustrated and dejected. They felt trapped in a dilemma: to determine whether a nuclear chain reaction could be the basis for the development of an atomic bomb required a thorough scientific investigation; such an investigation required considerable financial support, but the Uranium Committee would not offer such support without substantial evidence suggesting a high probability of success. Since they could not guarantee that a bomb would be available for wartime use, they could not attract the money for vital chain-reaction experiments. They felt as if they were "swimming in syrup."[24]

Months passed and nothing happened. Szilard's frustration turned to anger. He decided to write a scientific paper about a chain-reacting uranium-graphite pile and threaten to publish it unless the government promised to take some positive action. The ploy worked. Within weeks of making his threat known, Columbia University received a grant of $6,000 for the purchase of graphite. This allowed Szilard and Fermi to begin their experiments. They started by addressing two problems: the absorption rate of graphite and its effectiveness in slowing down neutrons. They set up the graphite in a square column several feet thick. Then they arranged lumps of uranium in a lattice configuration throughout the column, placed a neutron source inside the column, and measured the neutron activity with Geiger counters. The results led Szilard and Fermi to conclude that a very large pile would be needed to create and sustain a chain reaction. What is more, impurities commonly found in uranium and graphite would have to be eliminated because these impurities hungrily absorbed neutrons. All of this meant that a chain-reacting uranium-graphite pile would be very expensive in both materials and labor.

Meanwhile, Szilard traveled again to Princeton to see Einstein. They prepared a second letter for President Roosevelt that emphasized the secret German uranium research underway at the Kaiser Wilhelm Institute, which they had learned about from a Jewish chemist, Peter Debye, who had recently been expelled from the institute. This second Einstein letter also stressed that Berlin had assumed direct responsibility for fission research and was stepping up its efforts to achieve a breakthrough.[25] In March 1940 Sachs sent the letter to FDR, who ordered the White House to consult the Uranium Committee. Briggs and Adamson cautiously said that nothing more should be done, pending the outcome of Fermi's and Szilard's work on neutron absorption in graphite. Bureaucratic caution prevailed once again.

Meanwhile, security officials busily developed a mind-set of distrust toward Szilard, Teller, Fermi, and other refugee physicists "of queer types and backgrounds."[26] Agents categorized them as "aliens," or in the case of Fermi, who came from Italy — an Axis country — as an "enemy alien." A confidential report prepared by Army Intelligence in the summer of 1940 offered the following assessment of Fermi and Szilard:

(1) ENRICO FERMI. Department of Physics, Columbia University, New York City, is one of the most prominent scientists in the world in the field of physics. He is especially noted for breaking down the atom. He has been in the United States for about eighteen months. He is an Italian by birth and came here from Rome. He is supposed to have left Italy because of the fact that his wife is Jewish. He has been a Nobel Prize winner. His associates like him personally and greatly admire his intellectual ability. He is undoubtedly a Fascist. It is suggested that, before employing him on matters of a secret nature, a much more careful investigation be made. Employment of this person on secret work is not recommended.

(2) MR. SZELARD. It is believed that this man's name is SZILLARD. He is not on the staff of Columbia University, nor is he connected with the Department of Physics in any official capacity. He is a Jewish refugee from Hungary. It is understood that his family were wealthy merchants in Hungary and were able to come to the United States with most of their money. He is an inventor, and is stated to be very pro-German, and to have

remarked on many occasions that he thinks the Germans will win the war. It is suggested that, before employing him on matters of a secret nature, a much more careful investigation be made. Employment of this person on secret work is not recommended.[27]

Allegedly based on "highly reliable" sources, the report was riddled with errors. To security investigators, Szilard and Fermi were simply foreigners with strong accents, suspicious backgrounds, and a string of fanciful ideas. Briggs informed Szilard and Fermi that the Uranium Committee had decided to limit further financial support of their research. The committee was afraid that if it supported a substantial research effort that failed, Szilard's and Fermi's foreign backgrounds would prove an embarrassment in case of a congressional investigation. The explanation Briggs gave them was that the possibility of a costly failure loomed too large. It seemed the American government would never seriously embrace the possibility of building an atomic bomb.

CHAPTER 3

The Manhattan Project

I F WASHINGTON FAILED to perceive the importance of an atomic bomb early in the war, London did not. British scientists were furiously studying the feasibility of a bomb, their motivation simple and urgent: to beat Hitler to the punch. This was crucial, for by mid-June 1940 France had fallen to the Nazis. Britain now stood alone, and many people feared that Germany would soon cross the English Channel. The notion that Hitler was ahead in the atomic race had become so deep-rooted that it was treated as a certainty. "We were told day in and day out that it was our duty to catch up with the Germans," recalled a British physicist.[1] In 1940 it was still difficult for Americans to think about the war, while it was the only concern for the British.

The principles of fission and a chain reaction were clear enough to British scientists by 1940. Far less clear to them was the feasibility and expense of separating U-235 and constructing a weapon in time to be useful. Three questions overshadowed all others: How could a sufficient amount of fissionable material be collected? How much material would constitute the critical mass necessary to sustain a chain reaction? And how could the material be assembled rapidly enough so that it exploded, rather than simply fizzled like a pile of gunpowder?

The advanced state of British efforts and the desperate need to work quickly combined to effectively override whatever bureaucratic obstacles might normally have interfered with fission research. The imperative of survival concentrated British scientific minds dramatically.

Two of them, refugees Rudolf Peierls and Otto Frisch — the latter for the second time playing a decisive role — got together in early March 1940 to discuss the implications of fission. Peierls remembered: "I had a conversation with Frisch in the course of which he asked, 'Well, Bohr and Wheeler have made it quite clear that the fission is due to 235. What would happen if one had a pure uranium 235 in a sufficient quantity? How much would you need? And if you got it, what would happen?'"[2]

Frisch and Peierls came up with startling answers to these questions. Early estimates of the "critical mass," the amount of U-235 needed to start a chain reaction, had run to several tons — far too much for a deliverable weapon. But Frisch and Peierls produced an estimate that only one kilogram (just over two pounds) of U-235 could create a critical mass that would explode with a force equivalent to that of several thousand tons of dynamite. Eighty generations of neutrons would multiply in millionths of a second, yielding temperatures as hot as the interior of the sun and as deadly in radiation, before the swelling explosion separated the atoms of U-235 enough to stop the chain reaction.

"Our first reaction was to realize that this was no longer an academic exercise, but a highly practical problem, in spite of the almost science-fiction nature of large-scale isotope separation," Peierls recalled later. "Then it struck us that, as the idea had come to us so easily, it was likely to have occurred to the Germans, and the thought of such a weapon in Nazi hands was frightening."[3] Something had to be done immediately. They decided to draw the attention of the authorities to this possibility and its implications. In a three-page memorandum, they described their calculations and a practical mechanism for a bomb: making a U-235 sphere in two parts "which are brought together when the explosion is wanted." As soon as the hemispheres touched, the whole assembly "would explode within a second or less." The yield would be immense. Lethal radiation would be emitted on a large scale, against which "effective protection is hardly possible."[4]

"I have often been asked," Frisch wrote years afterward, "why I didn't abandon the project there and then, saying nothing to anybody. Why start on a project that, if it was successful, would end with the production of a weapon of unparalleled violence, a weapon of mass destruction such as the world had never seen? The answer was very simple. We were at war, and the idea was reasonably obvious; very probably some German scientists had had the same idea and were working on it."[5]

The Frisch-Peierls memorandum consisted of not more than a thousand words, but it was all there. They not only asked the right questions, they also answered them. They made isotope separation sound easier than it turned out to be, and their estimate of the amount of U-235 needed was too small, but these errors only encouraged official attention to and acceptance of their analysis. An atomic bomb had seemed like science fiction to government officials. Now it seemed *feasible*.

Otto Frisch was an Austrian, and Rudolf Peierls was a German. They should have been making their pioneering calculations at the Kaiser Wilhelm Institute in Berlin. But instead they made them at the University of Birmingham, in England. The reason for their relocation was simple: they were Jews.

British authorities referred their paper to a scientific committee code-named MAUD. Over the next fifteen months — through the successive shocks of the invasion of Norway, the fall of France, the Battle of Britain, the London Blitz, the fall of Yugoslavia and Greece, and the attack on the Soviet Union — the MAUD Committee carefully reviewed the two refugee physicists' conclusions. By the middle of 1941 their conclusions had persuaded London to undertake an atomic bomb program. The MAUD Committee recommended "that this work be continued on the highest priority and on the increasing scale necessary to obtain the weapon in the shortest possible time."[6]

The British government preferred to keep the whole project (and thus its control) in the United Kingdom, but it would require an immense industrial effort. It was one thing to talk of separating U-235 isotopes on this scale, but a formidable job to do it. The country was at war and was struggling to survive, which meant that its scientific talent and resources had to be devoted to projects with immediate practical military value — like radar. Britain's ally, America, on the other hand, was still not in the war and possessed vast industrial resources. The British government decided to go ahead as fast as possible with research, and then — if the work was promising — to persuade the United States to build a production plant for the bomb. London understood what this would mean down the road: Washington, by contributing the majority of technical and industrial effort, would effectively control the bomb. But London had little choice; such an effort in Britain was impossible because of the strain on

British resources and the danger to British project sites from German bombing. Hence, it was decided to lobby the Americans.

As part of its lobbying effort, the British government dispatched an Australian physicist working at the University of Birmingham with Frisch and Peierls named Mark Oliphant across the Atlantic in the late summer of 1941 to proselytize for an atomic bomb. His mission was to stir American physicists to action. "If Congress knew the true history of the atomic energy project," Leo Szilard said modestly after the war, "I have no doubt but that it would create a special medal to be given to meddling foreigners for distinguished services, and Dr. Oliphant would be the first to receive one."[7] Oliphant was a blunt, forceful, and persuasive man who was chosen by the British government to seek out one American physicist in particular, a striver of immense self-confidence and practical genius named Ernest Lawrence.

A tall, broad-shouldered man with slicked-back strawberry blond hair atop a boyish face colored by pale blue eyes set behind rimless glasses, Lawrence was a talented gadgeteer and charming yet shrewd promoter from the prairie heartland of America. There was something enormously vital in his movements, in the energetic way he walked and talked. He moved so quickly that he always seemed to be on the run. He was not a brilliant physicist, but he loved to build great big powerful machines, and his enormous drive got them built.

Born in South Dakota in 1901, Lawrence inherited his drive from his father, Carl, a small-town Babbitt who built a big house, became a leading citizen, and constantly kept his eye out for the main chance. His son showed a similar knack from the time he was in college at the University of South Dakota. He was so enthusiastic and persuasive in his request to the dean of students for funds to buy radio equipment that the dean gave him the money on the spot and urged him to take up the study of physics. He told Lawrence about another country boy named Ernest from New Zealand (Rutherford), who had won the Nobel Prize for his insights into atomic structure. What adventure could equal that of searching for nature's secrets? he said, firing the young man's imagination. Who knew what might be discovered next?

After college Lawrence attended graduate school at the University of Chicago, where he came into contact with Arthur Compton, and later moved to Yale. He developed beautiful technique as an experimenter, with not only remarkable physical intuition but also the confidence to believe in his instincts. While at Yale, he invented the "cyclotron," an atom smasher that provided an entirely new way of studying the nucleus. His first cyclotron was a bellows-shaped glass instrument just four inches wide and covered with red sealing wax against vacuum leaks. It worked by accelerating electrically charged particles in a magnetic field and then aiming them at a target. The subatomic pieces that broke off on impact provided clues to the internal structure of the atom. The cyclotron quickly earned Lawrence what he wanted most: publicly acknowledged success. He became the boy wonder of American science.

The University of California, Berkeley, which sought to build up its physics department, wooed Lawrence from Yale by offering him tenure, graduate students, and opportunity for rapid advancement — uncommon perquisites for a fresh-faced academic at an Ivy League university. Lawrence moved to Berkeley in 1928, settling into an office on the second floor of LeConte Hall, the physics building. He set up shop in an old wooden building next to LeConte Hall that he saved from demolition, renamed the Radiation Laboratory, and made his personal fiefdom.

The instruments in the "Rad Lab" were first-class, but almost nothing else was. The centerpiece was a twenty-seven-inch cyclotron — twenty-seven inches for the size of the poles of its eighty-ton electromagnet. The electromagnet was massive, twelve feet high and twelve feet long in its semicircular arch. Inside the arch, set on its side, was a metal spool shaped like a giant barbell. From the narrow neck of the spool spread out a web of wires and cables. Here the particles were accelerated and the targets set. The building was so full of static electricity that one could light up an electric bulb by touching it to any metal surface.

Before Lawrence, there had been a tradition — almost a pride — that a physicist conducted research only with tools he made himself. The cyclotron demanded a large team; Lawrence even introduced shift work to keep it constantly running. This was all part of Lawrence's plan. Teamwork had the benefit of being enormously stimulating intellectually. Lawrence's approach was to assemble teams concerned not only with solving particular problems but with crossing disciplines to apply discoveries. By bringing together physicists, chemists, biologists, physicians, and engineers, he increased his odds of producing the practical applications that would bring him the fame and funding he wanted.

The Rad Lab was an exciting place for an experimental physicist. Lawrence had a tremendous enthusiasm for the work, an enthusiasm that was very infectious. Everyone wore a wraparound apron with a sash tied in front — it was a kind of badge that showed you were "in." Everyone knew it was one of the most outstanding physics laboratories in the world. They felt a sense of adventure and participation in an important activity with important people — especially Ernest Lawrence, whom they affectionately called "the Maestro." Occasionally Lawrence would don an apron himself and work alongside everyone else. When he did, things went a little faster, his focus on the acquisition of physical data, not on what the data meant.

Operating independently of the physics department, Lawrence was a scientific entrepreneur who had shrewd business sense and was skilled at raising money for his laboratory. Measured against the standards of later years, the money he raised was small, but it was an astronomical sum for science during the Depression, especially for what was then considered an esoteric field. Introducing the big-machine approach to science, he became a sovereign in his own realm.

He also put Berkeley on the map. Lawrence knew he had arrived when he was invited to the prestigious Solvay Conference on Physics, held in Brussels in October 1933, the only American so honored. Other invitees included such giants of physics as Einstein, Bohr, and Fermi. By the mid-1930s Lawrence was the youngest full professor at Berkeley, with an army of graduate students. Berkeley's chancellor, Robert Sproul, exaggerated only a little when he quipped, "I don't know whether I'm running a university with a cyclotron attached to it or a cyclotron with a university attached to it."

The boyish, clean-cut Lawrence was an exceptional salesman and handler of people. He instinctively knew how to make a good impression — particularly on those he sought to flatter — and was scrupulously polite, even to those he did not particularly like. As he worked a room like a master politician, foundation officers and industrialists found him hard to resist. His presence and salesmanship grew out of an inexhaustible energy and optimism that impressed everyone who met him.

Underneath the charming smiles and friendly backslaps, however, lurked an intense, driven man who clenched his jaw and had little time for "nonsense." When his temper flared, a vein in his left temple bulged out — it became a warning sign to everyone. Assertive and at times overbearing, he identified personally and passionately with the Rad Lab. It was *his* laboratory — he had created it from scratch — and he ran it with an iron fist. "This was Lawrence's domain," said Philip Abelson, one of his graduate students. "He was number one. He was running the show."[8] Lawrence was omnipresent, demanding, and dominating. He hung a huge microphone from the lab's ceiling so that he could talk to the staff from his office — and listen to them. Some staffers found him overbearing and pompous — "a man with an inflated ego."[9] During midmorning coffee breaks, Lawrence used a fine china cup and silver spoon, while everyone else made do with thick porcelain mugs. At the end of the break, the cup and spoon went into a locked drawer conspicuously marked RESERVED FOR THE DIRECTOR.[10] His cyclotrons cost loads of money to construct and operate, yet the staff who ran them had to make do with small salaries and no benefits such as medical insurance.

Lawrence was quintessentially American — he believed anyone could do anything if he just put his mind to it. "Keep your nose to the grindstone, there's nothing more interesting than physics," he often said.[11] He chose his staff carefully, preferring uncomplicated people willing to work long hours. Laziness was not tolerated. "He wouldn't hesitate to bawl you out or tell you [that you] were doing things wrong," recalled Edwin McMillan, whose years in the Rad Lab eventually won him a Nobel Prize. "The greatest sin was not working hard enough. That was a worse sin than doing something badly."[12] He dropped in to the Rad Lab at odd hours of the night — often dressed in black tie after a dinner party at Sproul's house — just to see how things were going. He also kept a radio by his bedside at home tuned to the cyclotron frequency to know that it was running. If it was not, he would get on the phone and bark, "What the hell's the matter? Having coffee, or were you out for a beer?"[13]

As the administrative and fund-raising burden increased, Lawrence grew distant from the day-to-day work of the Rad Lab. He was often away in New York, where his main financial supporters were located. These trips occupied more time than necessary, since he insisted on going by train — he would have nothing to do with airplanes. In spare moments he hosted friends at favorite restaurants like DiBiasi's in Albany and played tennis to win. His family and friends worried that he wouldn't be able to keep up the frenzied pace and that one day his health would suffer. But Lawrence was not the worrying type.

By the late 1930s Lawrence had made himself and his Rad Lab world-famous. MIT's president wrote him: "I believe [the Rad Lab] to be the most interesting and important scientific work now going on anywhere in the world."[14] In Russia, cyclotrons were called "Lawrences." When a model cyclotron was set up at the Golden Gate International Exposition on Treasure Island in San Francisco Bay in 1939, Lawrence spoke about it on a national radio hookup with a showmanship worthy of P. T. Barnum. That same year he won the coveted Nobel Prize in physics.

Lawrence was sarcastic and impatient with Berkeley colleagues who explored schemes for alleviating the lot of humanity. Political issues did not excite or engage him. His view of international affairs was even more naive and simplistic. Like the vast majority of Americans during the isolationist 1930s, he thought Europe's "shenanigans" should be ignored because they were not America's business. In October 1938 he wrote to Wilfred Mann, a British physicist who had done research at the Rad Lab, commenting on — among other things — the recent Munich Conference, where Britain and France had sacrificed Czechoslovakia to Nazi Germany on the altar of appeasement:

Dear Wilfred:
You have been having a very anxious time recently, but let us hope the war clouds have passed and that we have ahead of us at least a decade of peace. I don't think it absurd to believe it is possible that we have seen a turning point in history, that henceforth international disputes of great powers will be settled by peaceful negotiations and not by war.

Cordially,
Ernest[15]

"I still think war is going to be avoided," he wrote his parents on August 29, 1939, adding confidently: "All this discussion certainly must mean that Hitler is backing down."[16] Three days later Nazi Germany invaded Poland and started World War II.

Oliphant and his British sponsors knew that if they could convince Lawrence of the feasibility of a bomb, Lawrence would grab hold of the idea and push it relentlessly in American scientific circles, while leaving the political ramifications to others. They thought Lawrence would get it done without asking too many questions. And although Lawrence was quite clearly a political naïf, they had chosen just the right man.

The relationship between Britain and America was growing closer when Oliphant traveled to Berkeley in late September 1941. Though still a nonbelligerent, the United States was far from neutral. Its sympathies lay with the hard-pressed British, who had survived a Nazi aerial blitz the previous summer. In the fall of 1940 the Roosevelt administration had transferred fifty destroyers to Britain in return for U.S. rights to build bases in British possessions in the Caribbean and the western Atlantic, and Congress had passed the first peacetime military draft in American history. In the spring of 1941 direct Lend-Lease aid to Britain began. The United States was edging toward war on the side of Britain.

On Sunday, September 21, 1941, Lawrence picked up Oliphant at the San Francisco train station in his car and drove up into the green hills above the Berkeley campus, where the magnet for his giant new 184-inch cyclotron was being erected on the summit of Charter Hill. It was a beautiful autumn day and far below, beyond the gardens and lawns of Berkeley, the bridges of San Francisco Bay shone in the sun. Lawrence's driving petrified Oliphant. Pressing the accelerator to the floor and keeping his face turned toward his passenger, Lawrence threw the car forward in jerks and spasms, swaying from one side of the twisting dirt road to the other, cutting corners at full speed, paying no heed to other cars as they passed.

Nervously gripping the door handle, Oliphant told Lawrence about Frisch and Peierls's calculation that a bomb could be made with just a few kilograms of U-235, and about the methods under study in Britain for separating the isotope from natural uranium. Lawrence was deeply impressed by the serious view of British scientists not only that atomic bombs were quite possible but that Nazi Germany might be working on the problem. He suggested the possibility of extracting U-235 through electromagnetic separation using his new 184-inch cyclotron. He began to describe to Oliphant a fantastic vision of gigantic laboratories and industrial complexes, armies of specially trained scientists and arsenals of newly invented tools and instruments, his voice rising with excitement. It was a contagious exuberance that overwhelmed doubt and drowned all sense of reality in a flood of buoyant optimism. When Lawrence was talking, it was impossible not to fall under the almost hypnotic spell of his enthusiasm — he even convinced himself. Here was something big enough, Oliphant thought, for Lawrence's talents and ambition. That other physicists might find such a vision fantastic would only spur him to prove them wrong.

Lawrence immediately put his Rad Lab staff to work. A chemist at the Rad Lab, Glenn Seaborg, had recently hit upon the discovery that neutrons absorbed by U-238 transformed uranium into a heavier element — plutonium — that also was fissionable by slow neutrons. This was an accidental but important discovery, just like fission had been. Not only could plutonium be made in a chain-reacting pile, but it was a different chemical element, not just another isotope of uranium, and could therefore be separated from U-238 through a comparatively easier and less expensive process than U-235. Lawrence reasoned that plutonium might supplement U-235 as a source for atomic bombs.

In the fall of 1941 — a time when the war was going very badly for Hitler's enemies — Lawrence instructed Rad Lab scientists to convert the cyclotrons for use in the electromagnetic separation of U-235. It was an extremely slow, complicated, and expensive way to produce fissionable material for a bomb. By February 1942 the Rad Lab had produced three samples of U-235 weighing all of seventy-five micrograms each. A microgram was a speck barely big enough for the eye to see, and each sample contained only 30 percent "enriched" U-235. Lawrence had a long way to go — how was he going to separate *kilograms* of pure fissionable U-235? Lawrence had committed himself to the goal, however, and was absolutely determined to see it through. "That was just the beginning," he said with great assurance.[17] He told his contacts in Washington that the project should be expanded to bring in more scientists and to build the infrastructure necessary to accomplish the task.

Driven by a determination that Hitler not get the bomb first, Lawrence drove himself and his staff relentlessly. He demanded complete dedication to the task at hand. He worked long hours and expected others to do the same. When delays occurred or things went wrong, he bawled people out unmercifully, though he never asked others to do anything he would not do himself and he showed appreciation for results. He led by example and maintained his leadership through the intensity with which he followed the isotope-separation work. He believed that if you wanted something to come true, you made it come true by pushing like hell. Somehow a way could be found, and he had faith that he would get there. With such effort, he thought, nothing was impossible.

Lawrence met the Rad Lab staff every morning at eight. People took pains to be already in their seats. The Maestro made a grand and lordly appearance, stomping in, slowly striding the length of the room, pounding the floor with his feet. Beaming at the assembled staff, he took his seat in a big red leather armchair facing sideways between a blackboard and the audience. The thing to do, he would then announce, was *to get the job done* — he expected everyone to share his sense of urgency. Later in the day he would walk unannounced through the lab and query people about their work. He did not say much. Often it was simply, "What are you doing? Why are you doing that?" If they answered hesitantly or pessimistically, Lawrence frowned. If they went into detail, he looked impatient. Above all, he hated idleness; there was an important job to be done and no time to waste in doing it. "The esprit has perked up considerably with everybody conscious of the necessity to work like the devil," wrote one Rad Lab staffer after a surprise visit by the director.[18]

The fast pace, constant work, and self-imposed stress took its toll on Lawrence. His full head of blond hair began to recede. His thin, muscular face grew puffier and pastier. Once remarkably energetic, he now was slowed by frequent and severe colds and a chronic backache. On those rare occasions when he went home early for an evening with his family, he usually tired after a few minutes of hugging and tossing around his children. Neighborhood kids, used to congregating noisily at the sprawling Lawrence home in the afternoon, frayed his taut nerves and were abruptly ordered out. He found it much more difficult to relax than to wrestle with the atomic project.

Lawrence felt in his bones that an atomic bomb could be made. He was confident that America possessed the ability and resources to do it. He insisted that prudence required stepping up research, if only because of what the Nazis might be doing. Szilard and Teller had said much the same before, but as refugees they were not trusted by close-minded government bureaucrats. They also lacked Lawrence's dogged optimism.

But although Lawrence's hard sell worked with many people, it did not with Vannevar Bush. A fit man of fifty-two who looked uncannily like a beardless Uncle Sam, Bush was a shrewd Yankee who was also an astute administrator. He had a distinguished career behind him: an inventor with numerous engineering patents to his credit, vice president of MIT and dean of its school of engineering until 1938, then head of the Carnegie Institution of Washington, a key research organization. Now he was the scientific adviser to President Roosevelt, and in that capacity, head of the Office of Scientific Research and Development (OSRD), which had been established by executive order (under the name National Defense Research Committee)* on June 27, 1940, the day after the Nazis occupied Paris.

---

* The NDRC became the OSRD in June 1941.

The mission of the OSRD, which had absorbed the Uranium Committee, was to mobilize the nation's scientific resources and apply them to national defense. This included support of research that would result in weapons applicable to the present war. To Bush, the defense of the free world in the fall of 1941 was in such a perilous state that only research efforts likely to yield quick results were worthy of serious consideration. He therefore thought physicists such as Lawrence should concentrate their efforts on projects that promised results within a matter of months, or at most a year or two — like radar and sonar. In Bush's opinion, America could not afford to devote its limited scientific resources to an extravagant program of uncertain success.

More significant than Lawrence's prodding was the MAUD Committee Report, which a British scientific liaison officer passed along to Bush on a visit to Washington in early October 1941. The report's optimism about techniques for isotope separation and the prospects for development of an atomic bomb diminished his skepticism at the same time that it increased his fear of Germany's success in exploiting fission. Bush took the MAUD Report to the White House on October ninth. He summarized its conclusions for the president: that the explosive core of a fission bomb might weigh twenty-five pounds; that it might explode with a force equivalent to nearly two thousand tons of TNT; that a vast industrial plant would be necessary to separate the fissionable U-235; and that British scientists estimated the first bombs might be ready in two years. He emphasized that he based his statements "primarily on calculation with some laboratory investigation, but not on a proved case," and therefore could not guarantee success.[19]

Roosevelt's mood had changed considerably since Einstein's letter two years earlier. The war felt much nearer and more nearly inevitable for the United States in 1941 than it had in 1939. If the British were pursuing such a promising line of research, it seemed quite possible that the Germans were, too. No president could assume anything less. Thus, FDR endorsed an American atomic project and directed that consideration of policy — what might be done with a bomb, if it was made — be restricted to a Top Policy Group consisting of Vice President Henry Wallace, Secretary of War Henry Stimson, Army Chief of Staff George Marshall, Bush, and Bush's OSRD deputy, James Conant, a noted chemist and president of Harvard University. Roosevelt emphasized the importance of keeping knowledge of the project within the smallest possible circle, a theme he would stress again and again throughout the war. Within the next few months the organization, the tempo, and the attitude of the American government toward research on an atomic bomb would alter dramatically.

The United States was not yet committed to building an atomic bomb, but it was now committed to exploring whether one could be built. With Roosevelt's permission, Bush ordered a feasibility study and a timetable. What were the prospects of making an atomic bomb? Could it be finished in time to help win the war? Should Washington fund an all-out effort when research funds were limited and other projects of more immediate promise and effectiveness — such as radar and the proximity fuse — existed? To answer these questions, Bush chose a senior American physicist with a Nobel Prize, excellent contacts, and long experience on the national scientific scene named Arthur Compton.

Broad-shouldered and athletic with a thick mustache, deep-set gray eyes, and a strong chin, Compton was a professor of physics at the University of Chicago. Principled and firm yet pragmatic, Compton fit neatly and easily into the project: he was popular in scientific circles, he had an agreeable disposition, and he had powerful connections. Scion of a famous American scientific family — his brother Karl was president of MIT — Compton was not policy-oriented like Bush but was trusted by high officials in Washington whose background and upbringing was similar to his own: a midwestern childhood in a midwestern family with midwestern Protestant beliefs. Compton moved easily in the world of the American Establishment.

As a boy, Compton had listened spellbound as his father described the discovery of a new chemical element that glowed with brilliant luminosity: radium. What especially intrigued him was that radium was warm to the touch. Where did such heat — radioactivity — come from? Could this heat be exploited for energy? Such questions stirred his imagination. When Compton was twelve, he sat on the front porch one night. The winter air was crisp and clear as he watched pinpricks of starlight. He felt a sense of wonder and sat up "all night, astonished, among the stars."[20] Soon he was spending every night in the backyard, searching the face of the moon with binoculars until he memorized its cratered features. He bought a telescope with his savings and used it to view the moons of Jupiter. By putting a piece of welder's glass in front of the telescope, he even watched the sun. He began to feel a "strong emotional stirring," as he later put it, about science.[21]

Compton became a physicist and demonstrated his brilliance early in his career when he won a Nobel Prize in 1927 for his study of X rays, following that up with pioneering work on cosmic rays in the 1930s. Compton's bold experiments in the new field of cosmic rays were carried out at high altitudes in the Himalaya, the Andes, and the Artic, and at the Equator. Travel to far-flung corners of the globe taught the midwesterner that other people of other cultures and colors were just as human as he. And it introduced him to such European physicists as Szilard, Fermi, and Bohr, whom he came to know well.

Compton visited Fermi at Columbia in October 1941 to gather firsthand information on neutron fission. He also heard from Lawrence, who warned him that an atomic bomb "might well determine the outcome of the war."[22] Compton told Lawrence to make his case directly to Conant: the Harvard president and Lawrence both planned to be in Chicago soon to attend celebrations honoring the fiftieth anniversary of the founding of the University of Chicago. The following week the three met at Compton's rambling home on Woodlawn Avenue a few blocks north of the campus. It was a crisp autumn evening. With steaming cups of coffee, the three scientists gathered around the fireplace in the wood-paneled study. Lawrence reviewed British calculations that a bomb could be made with just a few kilograms of fissionable material. He also mentioned his lab's discovery of plutonium, emphasizing that it fissioned like U-235 but could be chemically separated from U-238 much more easily. He insisted that an atomic bomb could be made. No other physicist would stake his reputation on such an unproved assumption. But Lawrence's confidence was supreme; his enthusiasm swept away whatever doubts lingered — in Compton's mind, at least.

Conant was still reluctant. A seasoned administrator and savvy player well schooled in the cautious bureaucratic ways of Washington, Conant believed physicists should work on problems *certain* to be helpful because the country could not afford to waste limited resources on projects of questionable military value. Looking at Lawrence, he said, "Ernest, you say you are convinced of the importance of these fission bombs. Are you ready to devote the next several years of your life to getting them made?" "If you tell me this is my job," Lawrence said without missing a beat, "I'll do it." Conant asked Compton to examine the evidence and get a report to Bush as soon as possible. "If this matter is as critically important as you men indicate," Conant said, "we mustn't lose a day."[23]

Compton presented his report to Bush on November sixth. It was brief and to the point. He took the problem apart, examined it thoroughly, and reached firm conclusions on all the subjects within his scientific competence. He endorsed the brilliant insight of the Frisch-Peierls paper with the authority and depth of an American Nobel Prize winner — credentials that were indispensable to the task of persuading official Washington. He reported that *"a fission bomb of superlatively destructive power will result from bringing quickly together a sufficient mass of element U-235"* and that *"the separation of the isotopes of uranium can be done in the necessary amount."* Compton also addressed the crucial issues of time and cost. Three to five years would be needed, he estimated, and several hundred million dollars. His bottom line was this: atomic bombs could be made.[24]

Bush was impressed. He concluded that the possibility of a wartime bomb was strong enough that every effort must be made to find out if it could be built. Bush knew how to get this done. He kept his memoranda short and cogent. He took no public credit for getting things accomplished. He understood the bureaucracy and the military. And he knew how to persuade President Roosevelt.

Compton was not above some personal lobbying of his own. After submitting the report to Bush, he arranged a game of tennis with his personal friend, Vice President Wallace. As they chatted on the court, Compton told Wallace that Bush would soon be showing the president a report. "Please give it your most careful attention," he said. "It is possible that how we act on this matter may make all the difference between winning and losing the war."[25]

Bush carried Compton's report to the White House on November twenty-seventh. The weather that day was cold and the news was bleak. Hitler's armies, which had invaded Russia in June, had reached the outskirts of Moscow and a crisis was brewing between America and Japan in the Far East. Bush proposed to Roosevelt an all-out effort to build a bomb. He told FDR that although Britain was ahead of the United States in bomb research, it lacked the resources to build one and looked to America to do so, if it was possible. The United States was the only country with uncommitted and protected resources sufficient to make an atomic bomb during the war.

Roosevelt followed intently. He had listened to Sachs and his account of the refugee physicists' fears, and had politely thanked Einstein. But what he had now was not a vague idea but a clear proposal for action that came with the combined authority of British science and an American scientist whom he trusted. This combination had the commanding prestige that was necessary to give credibility to something as implausible as a one-kilogram device with an explosive force of some two thousand tons. And so, on December 6, 1941 — just one day before Japan attacked Pearl Harbor and plunged the United States into the war — FDR put the vast resources of the government behind an all-out effort to build an atomic bomb.[26] The authority for deciding how the bomb would be used went to the Top Policy Group he had named earlier. The assumption that the bomb would be built quickly for use during the war was implicit in the decision to develop it.

Now the entire governmental machine began to get to work on the effort, code-named the Manhattan Project, after the headquarters of the Army Corps of Engineers' district tasked to manage it. Bush appointed Conant to oversee the scientific project from Washington and gave Compton responsibility for academic research throughout the country. Bush also made clear the government's intent to maintain authority over the project and to transfer it to the army's control when large-scale production of fissionable materials became necessary. His reasons were simple: Bush knew the money was running out from sources at his disposal and much more was going to be needed. By bringing in the army, he could hide the project's expenditures within the Corps of Engineers' massive budget under line items labeled "Procurement of New Materials" and "Expediting Production." Roosevelt did not want to have to defend the Manhattan Project to the Congress. This would result in unacceptable delay and would undermine the absolute secrecy in which he felt the project had to be cloaked.

Many of the physicists who would soon be brought into the Manhattan Project were refugees, recent immigrants to the United States. This was partly because they included some of the world's best physicists, but there was another reason as well: many native-born American physicists had been swept up earlier in military research on radar and the proximity fuse, which appeared to have a more immediate military application to Allied success in the war. As a result, refugees were the main remaining source of available scientific brainpower to work on the project. The very restrictions and limitations imposed upon refugee scientists — which had delayed the government's embrace of the project — facilitated their leading roles in the bomb's development once the government decided to support it. This irony would have a significant, if unstated, impact down the road, when disputes arose about the long-term political consequences of what the scientists and the government were doing.

In the end, the refugee physicists and their native-born colleagues did not protest their loss of control over the project in December 1941. Most of them, in fact, welcomed it because they thought it would insulate them from political pressure and criticism. Their acceptance of this condition was the tacit price of their admission into the project. It was also a measure of their loyalty by those at the top. "I think [Ernest Lawrence] now understands this," Bush said, "and I am sure Arthur Compton does, and I think our difficulties in this regard are over."[27] The government was giving physicists, whom Bush and others in top councils considered "somewhat naive and lacking in discretion,"[28] the responsibility for making an atomic bomb, not for helping to decide how it would be used.

Oak Ridge was a quiet rural area of oak- and pine-covered ridges around the meandering Clinch River eighteen miles from Knoxville, Tennessee. It was a beautiful countryside, with rolling hills covered with dogwood and full of partridge and deer. To the east were the Great Smoky Mountains, to the west the peaks of the Cumberland Mountains. It answered all the requirements for a sprawling plant to separate U-235 isotopes: an isolated area in the midst of the vast power grid of the Tennessee Valley Authority, an abundant water supply, relatively few people to relocate, good access by road and train, and a mild climate that permitted outdoor work the year round. Here on a 59,000-acre site, 32,000 construction workers built and 47,000 operating personnel maintained a gigantic forty-two-acre separation plant flanked by facilities covering some fifty additional acres and containing more than six thousand miles of pipe that was the largest factory complex on earth when it was finished.

U-235 was separated at Oak Ridge by three different methods — no one knew which would prove most effective. The first method was electromagnetic separation, using giant cyclotrons designed by Ernest Lawrence. Uranium atoms were stripped of electrons in a vacuum.

Then they were electrically charged and thus made more susceptible to outside magnetism. The heavier U-238 was more sluggish, so the lighter U-235 could gradually and painstakingly be separated out. The enormous separation chambers contained vacuum pumps, more powerful than any ever built, that pushed through millions of gallons of oil a day; the magnet coil windings required 27,750,000 pounds of silver (the metal, worth $400 million at 1940s prices, was borrowed from the Treasury Department).

The second method was gaseous diffusion, developed by Columbia University physicists Harold Urey and John Dunning. When ordinary uranium was mixed with fluorine, the resulting compound — uranium hexafluoride — was a gas. When the uranium hexafluoride gas was forced through the microscopic membrane holes of a filter (or "barrier," as it was also called), the lighter U-235 passed through faster and the gas on the far side was marginally enriched with the desired isotope. When the process was repeated, the proportion of U-235 increased a little more. Bomb-grade uranium — containing 90 percent U-235 — required thousands of passes through the filters.

The third method of U-235 separation was thermal diffusion, pioneered by a former student of Lawrence's working at the Naval Research Laboratory named Philip Abelson. The apparatus was simple. Long, vertical, concentric pipes were enclosed in cylinders that resembled a gigantic church organ. Each cylinder was composed of a thin nickel pipe within a copper pipe. These two pipes, in turn, were encased in a third one made of galvanized iron. When uranium hexafluoride gas was passed between the hot nickel pipe and the cool copper pipe, the lighter U-235 concentrated near the hot nickel wall and moved upward, while the heavier U-238 moved downward along the cool copper wall. The enriched uranium was then skimmed off at the top. Thermal diffusion could increase the percentage of U-235 in natural uranium by only a small amount, but the enrichment was sufficient to supplement the gaseous diffusion method as another source of material for the electromagnetic racetracks, whose efficiency soared tremendously when fed with even slightly enriched uranium.

The names of the processing plants at Oak Ridge sounded like the combination to a safe: X-10, Y-12, S-50, K-25. All plants except X-10, a plutonium research lab, performed the same function: extracting precious U-235 from U-238. At S-50, thermal diffusion was employed; at Y-12, electromagnetic separation was applied; at K-25, the process was gaseous diffusion. K-25 was the largest building ever constructed up to that time. It was a sight to behold. Spread over 2 million square feet, the U-shaped structure was half a mile long and four hundred feet wide on each side. It was so vast that foremen rode bikes from one part of the building to another. Twelve thousand people, working in three shifts, kept K-25 running day and night, seven days a week. When it was operating, a continuous hum — a high-pitched sound resembling the buzzing of a bee swarm — came from the plant, mixing weirdly with the noises from the nearby woods. The electricity for these mammoth facilities came from the nearby TVA and an on-site powerhouse that was the largest power installation ever built. By war's end, Oak Ridge would be consuming the equivalent of the total power output on the American side of Niagara Falls — or one-seventh of all electricity generated in the United States.

Lawrence toured the sprawling complex as it was being built, and thrilled at the spectacle. "What you're doing here is very important," he told construction workers assembled to hear him give a pep talk. Oak Ridge was a realization of his vision of big physics, and it made him feel proud — like King Henry V addressing his troops before the Battle of Agincourt. "A hundred years from now, people may not remember that there was a war on now," he told them, emotion rising in his voice, "but they will remember what you were doing."[29] Privately, Lawrence was awed by what lay ahead. "When you see the magnitude of that operation there," he wrote after returning to Berkeley, "it sobers you up and makes you realize that whether we want to or not, we've got to make things go. We must do it!"[30]

The magnets of the cyclotrons that Lawrence had built at Oak Ridge were 250 feet long, and each contained thousands of tons of steel. They were a hundred times larger than the magnet of the 184-inch Berkeley cyclotron — previously the largest in the world. Their magnetic field was so strong that a wrench would be wrested from a workman's hand, or if he held onto it, he would be pulled against the magnet. But the U-235 separated by these giant cyclotrons offered itself up in only minuscule quantities. Yields were so low from the tons of uranium ore being processed that workers carefully plucked mere specks from their white overalls with tweezers. There were times when they got down on their hands and knees to look for tiny bits of the precious fissionable material.

In south-central Washington State, the small town of Hanford sat in the midst of a vast area of sagebrush and sand, twenty miles north of Richland, bounded on three sides by a huge bend in the Columbia

River. This unusual combination — large amounts of water flowing through sparsely inhabited desert — made the site ideal for another prong of the Manhattan Project. The Columbia River would provide the enormous amount of water needed to cool three gigantic piles to be built there for the production of plutonium, an alternative (and more easily obtained) source of fissionable material for the bomb. The remote location — the population density was just 2.2 persons per square mile — would mitigate the effects of any accidental radioactive release and be easy to guard. Eventually the Hanford facility would grow to more than 428,000 acres — 500 square miles, half the size of the state of Rhode Island.

To recruit a massive labor force of construction workers for the Hanford site at a time when every war industry in America was begging for manpower was an extraordinary task. The White House cabled regional employment offices, giving preference by direction of the president himself to the Hanford Engineering Works, as it was called, and authorizing them, if necessary, to draft workers from the aircraft industry. In some towns of the Northwest, clergymen were asked to promote Hanford from the pulpit. Veterans of many big public works projects — men who had helped construct huge dams and power plants — had never seen so many people working in the same place at the same time. Living in barracks and trailer camps, they created a massive, sprawling physical plant. The statistics were staggering: 540 buildings, more than 600 miles of roads, 158 miles of railroad track, vast quantities of water, concrete, lumber, steel, and pipe. Eventually, 132,000 workers (working 126 million man-hours) were hired — almost as many as had worked on the Panama Canal. Hanford soon became the fourth-largest city in the state of Washington. The total cost to build and run Hanford during the war would reach $358 million, or nearly $5 billion in 2003 dollars.

Hanford's three all-important piles — each one processed two hundred tons of uranium, cooking it for two hundred days — produced the plutonium, but equally important were the chemical-separation plants that treated the uranium slugs irradiated in the piles. These slugs were so radioactive when they came out that they glowed. Three chemical-separation plants were built in isolated and heavily guarded desert areas south of nearby Gable Mountain. For safety reasons — the plutonium in the irradiated slugs was also highly radioactive — the plants were placed ten miles from the nearest pile and well apart from one another. No one wanted to discover an atomic blast by accident.

The separation plants were sinister-looking, windowless structures with walls eight feet thick — in effect, huge concrete coffins eight hundred feet long and eighty feet wide. Each contained an underground row of forty cells where the irradiated slugs were processed. The operating gallery that ran above the cell rows was a silent, deadly radioactive tunnel with glaring electric lamps, where no human being could survive. Because of plutonium's deadly toxicity, metallurgists had to be specially trained to handle it. They wore rubber gloves, worked behind protective shielding, and manipulated the plutonium with long tongs. Not only was the air filtered and ventilated, but a microscopist was hired to analyze its dust. In these gargantuan coffin-like structures, workers operating remote-control machinery around the clock tortuously squeezed out plutonium in a concentration of about 250 parts per million, a half-pound radioactive pellet from every ton of irradiated uranium.

To build a bomb from materials that didn't yet exist in measurable quantities, involving the commitment of an extraordinary range of human and material resources, in the midst of a global war — it was an improbable undertaking. Yet out of nothing would be created a vast industrial enterprise. Bohr's prediction had not been far off the mark: before the war was over, the Manhattan Project would consume more than $2 billion, employ 500,000 people directly and indirectly, and mobilize vast material resources. The project exemplified human ingenuity and determination, a prodigious adventure into which industrial power was launched, secretly and boldly, at a colossal cost and with unprecedented effort. There was something quintessentially American about the Manhattan Project: a gigantic experiment on the scale of an entire continent. No other country in a world at war had the necessary resources and industrial power to attempt such a thing.

An all-out race to build an atomic bomb was now under way after a delay of more than two years. Scientists entered the race — against German scientists believed to have a two-year head start — convinced that the outcome of the war depended on their ability to recover lost time. For them, the bomb's rapid development was the single most important necessity of the war. It was a matter of survival.

CHAPTER 4

The Met Lab

UNDAY, DECEMBER 7, 1941, found Arthur Compton on the morning train from Washington to New York. At the Wilmington, Delaware, station a passenger boarded his compartment and shouted nervously that the Japanese had attacked the U.S. Pacific Fleet at Pearl Harbor, bringing America into the war at last. The news sent Compton into a reverie as the train left Wilmington and raced north across the lush pastureland of rural New Jersey. Compton could see the neo-Gothic towers of Princeton University off in the distance. There was the Graduate College, where he had lived, and the Palmer Physical Laboratory, where he had conducted experiments as a graduate student two decades before. How different those buildings now seemed to Compton. They were still outwardly peaceful ivory towers, but Compton knew that within their walls were active and creative minds working on an immensely destructive weapon that might decide the outcome of the war that America had just entered. He felt conflicted about his own work on an immensely destructive weapon because of a pacifist upbringing by his Mennonite mother. And yet he felt he had no other choice, especially now.

When Compton reached New York that afternoon, he took a taxi from Penn Station up to Columbia University, where he met with Rabi, Szilard, and Fermi to discuss producing plutonium in a chain-reacting pile. This was crucial because producing plutonium by bombarding uranium in a cyclotron — what had been done at the Rad Lab — was not a practical method: at Berkeley, a kilogram of uranium bombarded for a week produced less than a millionth of a gram of plutonium. At that rate, a yearlong bombardment might produce fifty micrograms (smaller than a single grain of sand); it would take 20,000 years to make a kilogram — much better than Bohr's early estimate of 26,445 years to produce one gram, but still nowhere close to what was needed. No one knew exactly how much plutonium would be necessary for a bomb, but estimates ran to several kilograms. Szilard and Fermi expressed confidence that a chain-reacting uranium-graphite pile would be a feasible method of producing large amounts of plutonium.

Until the War Department took control of the Manhattan Project in the fall of 1942, Compton was the de facto leader. Project research was then under way at universities scattered across the country. Compton thought it all should be centralized in one location to avoid duplication, ease communication, and save precious time. He called a meeting in Chicago in late January 1942 to decide where. Compton had the flu, and ran the meeting from a sickbed in one of the spare bedrooms on the third floor of his house. Szilard and Lawrence were both there. "Each was arguing the merits of his own location," Compton later wrote, "and every case was good. I presented the case for Chicago."

First, Compton stressed that he already had the support of the University of Chicago. "We will turn the university inside out if necessary to help win this war," its vice-president had told him.[1] Second, more scientists were available in the Midwest than on the coasts, where universities had already been drained for other war work. Finally, Chicago was conveniently and centrally located for travel to other sites.

"You'll never get a chain reaction going here," scoffed Lawrence. "The whole tempo of the University of Chicago is too slow." He argued in favor of moving everyone to Berkeley. Compton had known Lawrence since Lawrence was a graduate student at Chicago and Compton was chairman of its physics department and a dean; he had no intention of now becoming Lawrence's subordinate. "We'll have the chain reaction going here by the end of the year," Compton bristled. Needing to make a decision, he announced that Chicago would be the site. The decision made sense. Compton was in a powerful position there, and the university's administration had pledged truly unqualified support, which would be important — entire buildings would have to be emptied to provide space for the researchers. Chicago's location in the middle of the country also made it a compromise relocation site for scientists on both coasts.

Lawrence told Compton that plutonium would be highly radioactive and thus dangerous, but the chemical-separation work could be done. He promised to commit the Rad Lab's best chemists to the job, perfecting the process in the lab and then applying it on an industrial scale at Hanford. Armed with this information, Compton laid out an ambitious timetable for Washington: "By July 1, 1942, to determine whether a chain reaction was possible. By January 1943, to achieve the first chain reaction. By January 1944, to extract [plutonium] from uranium. By January 1945, to have a bomb."[2]

Szilard stated that his first loyalty was to the project and not to a particular location. However, he disliked the idea of transferring to the Midwest because he would be cut off from colleagues on the East Coast. Better, he thought, to concentrate the work on the eastern seaboard — or move everyone to Berkeley. Furthermore, Szilard argued that Compton had to be especially solicitous of Fermi, who might need coaxing from Szilard to "overcome his strong preference for Columbia." "It would be obviously wrong," he said, "to decide in favor of a place as long as Fermi had a strong objection."[3]

But although Szilard preferred to stay in New York, he understood the importance of centralizing research work and admired Compton's talents as an organizer and a leader. "Most people consider him as the only hope to bring order into the present mess," Szilard had observed the month before. (If anything, he felt Compton was not aggressive enough. "Compton seems to be too modest to realize that he could carry this matter by the sheer weight of his personality," Szilard wrote.)[4] So Szilard would go to Chicago.

Having persuaded Szilard to move, Compton phoned Fermi and asked him to relocate to Chicago as well. Fermi was reluctant. He resented that he did not have full security clearance for war work because he was still a "registered enemy alien," but now he was being asked to take a leading role in the country's most secret military project. He told Compton that he liked Columbia and enjoyed his home in New Jersey. Yet his adopted country was now at war and Fermi wanted to prove his patriotism. He agreed to go.[5]

All-out work at the University of Chicago's Metallurgical Laboratory began in February 1942. The primary purpose of the Met Lab was to achieve a chain reaction in order to test the feasibility of producing plutonium in an atomic pile. There was also the question of how to separate the plutonium once it was produced. Physicists and chemists exploring the properties of this strange element worked in Eckart and Ryerson Halls, three-story gray stone neo-Gothic buildings that stood side by side on the northeast corner of the University of Chicago quadrangle. Their cramped labs and offices were partly lighted by leaded-glass windows that shook against the bitter-cold winds of a midwestern winter.

The war was going very badly for the United States and its allies in early 1942. Nazi Germany controlled most of Europe and was threatening to take over Russia and North Africa. The bulk of the American Pacific Fleet lay at the bottom of Pearl Harbor. Japan was continuing its onslaught in the Pacific. The Philippine capital of Manila had fallen, and American troops were retreating to the island of Corregidor. Japanese troops had made it as far as New Guinea and Alaska's Aleutian Islands. Not until the Battle of Midway, four months away, would the tide of the war in the Pacific at last begin to turn; the tide of war in Europe would not turn until the Battle of Stalingrad almost a year away.

The refugee physicists watched in horror as their homelands fell to the Axis like dominoes, and feared that America might be next. They felt a sense of impending doom. They were not alone. The atmosphere at the Met Lab was nervous and embattled. "We felt behind the Germans," said a scientist who was there — in danger of losing the race for the bomb.[6] Met Lab staff knew that Hahn, the discoverer of fission, had a two-year head start and that German engineering was the most respected in the world, especially when it came to arms; panzer tanks rolling across Europe in the blitzkrieg seemed unstoppable. The feeling of desperation was especially keen among the refugees, most of whom had studied in Germany, knew Germany as the prewar center of nuclear physics, and were inclined to give the Germans much credit for what they could do.

Compton tried to calm the refugees' anxiety, but he was less successful than Fermi, who was one of them yet still managed to joke that the Nazis could not fight a war and build an atomic bomb at the same time. Despite this bravado, Fermi privately began to think about what country he and his family should escape to next if America fell to the Nazis. Another leading refugee scientist balked at being fingerprinted by security officials at the Met Lab. "If the Germans win, they'll use these prints to track us down and kill us all!" he nervously protested.[7]

Few things focus the mind like the bark of a bloodhound. There was the constant fear that with one small error — one lost day — the scientists might awaken one morning to read the news that Nazi Germany had unleashed a powerful new bomb. "The feeling was that we were a small group of people with a terribly important mission," recalled a physicist at Chicago. "If we failed, the United States and its allies might come into terrible harm. We were afraid."[8] They worked long hours without complaint, putting in a full day and then returning to the Met Lab in the evening after dinner, six days a week. Every day, every moment, counted.

Heavy security heightened the stress. "I am determined to have secrecy observed to the utmost," Compton told lab personnel. "We are at war."[9] Anyone mentioning the word *uranium* or *plutonium* received a stare and a warning. Each newcomer to the Met Lab was shown a film that darkly depicted the ominous consequences of negligence and carelessness. A list was passed around at each meeting where new information was revealed, and every scientist signed his name, with the date, showing that he had attended. (One refugee scientist hesitated to sign, fearing that the lists would fall into the hands of the Nazis if America lost the war.) Posters shouting DON'T BE A BLABOTEUR were plastered everywhere.

On the outside, Chicago looked like any university. But if anyone entered Eckart or Ryerson Hall, he was quickly confronted by armed guards who asked what business he had being there. There were security passes, papers marked TOP SECRET, and an unlimited budget. Spending during the first six months of 1942 reached $590,000 for materials and $618,000 for salaries — enormous sums for physicists accustomed before the war to conducting research on a few thousand dollars per year. "Within a year," said one Met Lab physicist, "I was ordering a million dollars' worth of material at a time without a qualm."[10] In March 1942 there were only 45 people at the Met Lab, including secretaries. By June there were 1,250. At its peak six months later, the Met Lab employed 2,000 people.

Arthur Compton was an effective leader of the Met Lab, steady and imperturbable. He could be irritable, but he had great resources of temperament and knew that this was too serious a time to let irritability flash. His door was always open. He tracked problems carefully. He trusted refugees at a time when many in Washington did not. He understood personalities and egos: how to accommodate them, how to assuage them when they clashed, how to mold them into an effective team. He also realized that scientists needed freedom to exercise their imagination. He understood their strengths and weaknesses and treated them with sensitivity. He combined skill in research with finesse in administration.

Compton needed all these qualities because overseeing a bunch of bright scientists was no easy task. They were all independent, and more than a few were prima donnas. That certainly was true of Szilard. Opinionated, immodest, pushy, and demanding, Szilard was a difficult man even for his friends and rubbed many people — especially bureaucrats and soldiers — the wrong way. "He was odd," said a colleague who liked him. "There was no doubt about it: eccentric."[11] "He's a queer fish," thought another, "very pleased with his own ability as a physicist." Szilard even threatened at one point to resign from the project and "file patent applications" if his salary wasn't raised.[12] So adept was he at offering his opinions and telling others what to do that colleagues took to calling him "the General."

A gadfly and an iconoclast, Szilard moved through the Met Lab like a whirlwind, firing off hectoring memos to Compton and kibitzing other scientists. His passion for politics began to rival his interest in physics in June 1942, when he learned of a visit by two army colonels to Compton's office. Szilard had assumed that one atomic bomb would be enough to sober humanity into forsaking war. "You've got to sit down and get reoriented," the colonels had instead told Compton's assistant. "The thing we're talking about is not a few bombs; what we are talking about is *production capacity* to continue delivering bombs at a given rate. That, you will discover, is a very different problem."[13] Their comment shocked Szilard and his Met Lab colleagues, who began to fear where the military was taking the project.

The military, for its part, viewed scientists as nonconformists with strange accents, no discipline, and a lot of arrogance. Generals and admirals were horrified at the absence of a chain of command below Compton and at the freewheeling structure of the Met Lab, and were skeptical about the likelihood of physicists producing anything useful.

Army Brigadier General Leslie Groves, whom the War Department appointed czar of the Manhattan Project on September 17, 1942, certainly felt this way. Groves was a career officer and son of an army chaplain who was a strict disciplinarian. He had grown up a service brat shaped by the military culture and the traditional American values of God and country. He had attended the U.S. Military Academy at West Point, where he graduated fourth in his class in

1918 — too late to take part in the fighting in World War I — then joined the Corps of Engineers. As a construction engineer, he had never commanded troops in combat, but he was very patriotic and very ambitious.

Alert and confident, Groves assumed a commanding manner. But his authority and pugnacity were belied by his appearance. He had an oversize waistline that gave a midriff bulge to his starched khakis. He was addicted to ice cream, and there was always a box of chocolates in his office safe. All this, along with a small mustache and too-tight collar, made Groves look rather like an Oliver Hardy in uniform. But his steel-blue eyes were penetrating, and his facial expression was decisive. He knew his business and he knew how to get things done.

Groves saw the world only in black and white, with no shades of gray. Extremely judgmental about people, he sized others up quickly and immediately decided whether they were acceptable or not — there were few second chances. With Groves, you had better do your job, do it well, and do it on time. If you did not, he screamed and threatened and his neck veins popped out in anger. He had no patience for procrastination, no tolerance for sloppiness, no time or talent for small talk. An army subordinate remembered Groves as

> the biggest sonovabitch I've ever met in my life, but also one of the most capable individuals. He had an ego second to none, he had tireless energy — he was a big man, a heavy man but he never seemed to tire. He had absolute confidence in his decisions and he was absolutely ruthless in how he approached a problem to get it done. But that was the beauty of working for him — you never had to worry about the decisions being made or what it meant. I hated his guts and so did everybody else but we had our form of understanding.[14]

Most of Groves's subordinates feared him; only a few liked him. He preferred it that way.

The bitterest day of Groves's life was when he was ordered to assume direction of the Manhattan Project, which Roosevelt and Stimson transferred to the Army Corps of Engineers' control when it became clear that its scale would be far beyond the managerial and logistical capacities of Bush and Conant. "What little I knew of the project," Groves later wrote, "had not particularly impressed me."[15] He had spent the first year of the war overseeing construction of the

Pentagon and expected to be assigned a field command as a reward. Now he would spend the rest of the war overseeing a bunch of "long-hairs" on a potential boondoggle — "a crazy Buck Rogers project," he called it — with a budget that amounted to less than what he had spent on the Pentagon in a week. But even though he was not pleased, he knew what it meant to be a good soldier, and Groves considered himself a very good soldier. He would make the most of it. He would throw himself into the project with enormous energy and no letup. He expected friction with scientists who lacked discipline and did not know how to take orders. But now *he* was in the driver's seat — he was the boss. And in time, Groves became as obsessed with winning the war with the atomic bomb as scientists were with winning the race for it.

Groves's brusque demeanor explained much of the tension that would develop between him and the Manhattan Project scientists. Vannevar Bush wrote a memo after meeting him that said in part: "Having seen Groves briefly, I doubt whether he has sufficient tact for such a job. I fear we are in the soup."[16] Other scientists were appalled at the general's apparent lack of intellectual curiosity. Groves told Ernest Lawrence during one of his trips to Berkeley, "I'm not the least bit interested in the scientific knowledge of the world, except insofar as it gets the job done."[17] The story spread among scientists like wildfire.

From the beginning, Groves distrusted the scientists, particularly the accented foreigners and their tendency to break into incomprehensible languages when they talked to one another in his presence. What were they saying? He viewed scientists as curious, undisciplined people, ready to wander from their tasks unless confined by enforceable rules. They neither understood nor respected the military ethos of obedience and conformity. It was a clash of cultures. Trouble was bound to come, and it did.

In September 1942 Szilard circulated a memo around the Met Lab:

> Compton delegates to each of us some particular task and we can lead a very pleasant life while we do our duty. We live in a pleasant part of a pleasant city, in the pleasant company of each other, and have in Dr. Compton the most pleasant "boss" we could wish to have. There is every reason why we should be happy and since there is a war on, we are even willing to work overtime.

Alternatively, we may take the stand that those who have originated the work on this terrible weapon and those who have materi-
ally contributed to its development have, before God and the
World, the duty to see to it that it should be ready to be used at the
proper time and in the proper way.

I believe that each of us has now to decide where he feels that his
responsibility lies.

Szilard insisted that scientists pay more attention to the consequences
of their work:

It is within our power to construct atomic bombs. What the existence of these bombs will mean we all know. It will bring disaster
upon the world even if we anticipate them [i.e., the Germans] and
win the war, but lose the peace that will follow. . . . One has to visu-
alize a world in which a lone airplane could appear over a big city
like Chicago, drop his bomb, and thereby destroy the city in a single
flash. Not one house may be left standing, and the radioactive sub-
stances scattered by the bomb may make the area uninhabitable for
some time to come.

It will be for those whom the constitution has entrusted with
determining the policy of this country to take determined action near
the end of the war in order to safeguard us from such a "peace." . . .

Perhaps it would be well if we devoted more thought to the ultimate political necessities which will arise out of our present work.
You may feel, however, that it is of more immediate concern to us
that the work which is pursued at Chicago is not progressing as rapidly as it should.[18]

Thanks to comments like this, Szilard's colleagues at the Met Lab
looked upon him as the conscience of the project. He was the one who
got them thinking about the moral and political implications of what
they were doing. Groves, on the other hand, looked upon Szilard as a
troublemaker and a menace. "What a pain in the neck Szilard was,"
Groves complained to an interviewer after the war.[19] "Sure, we should
never have had an atom bomb if Szilard had not shown such determination during the first years of the war. But as soon as we got going, so
far as I was concerned he might just as well have walked the plank!"[20]
Groves even tried to send Szilard to an internment camp. The general
drafted a letter for Secretary of War Stimson that said: "It is considered

essential to the prosecution of the war that Mr. Szilard, who is an enemy alien, be interned for the duration of the war."[21] Stimson refused to sign it.

Although Stimson denied Groves's request, the general found other ways to harass Szilard. He required that "enemy aliens" account for their whereabouts at all times and further compelled Szilard to obtain army authorization every time he wanted to leave Chicago. The restrictions became new rules to be broken, and Groves reacted by ordering security agents to shadow Szilard. The agents' reports on his movements read less like a John le Carré novel than a Marx Brothers' script:

> Surveillance reports indicate that Subject is of Jewish extraction, has a fondness for delicacies and frequently makes purchases in delicatessen stores, usually eats his breakfast in drug stores and other meals in restaurants, walks a great deal when he cannot secure a taxi, usually is shaved in a barber shop, speaks occasionally in a foreign tongue, and associates mostly with people of Jewish extraction. He is inclined to be rather absent minded and eccentric, and will start out a door, turn around and come back, go out on the street without his coat or hat and frequently looks up and down the street as if he were watching for someone or did not know for sure where he wanted to go.[22]

Szilard usually knew exactly where he wanted to go but was often so annoyed by his tails that he deliberately tried to trick them. Other times he took pity on the agents and invited them along for a taxi ride or a cup of coffee. "Why can't you be a good American?" a security agent once asked him, half exasperated, half begging. "Like who?" "Well, like me." "*Ugh*. No," said a smiling Szilard.[23]

When the surveillance turned up nothing, Groves ordered Szilard's phone tapped and his mail opened. He had the power to dismiss Szilard from the project and at one point took a step in that direction by threatening to make him take "an indefinite leave of absence without pay." Groves told a security officer that "the investigation of Szilard should continue despite the barrenness of the results. One letter or phone call once in three months would be sufficient for the passing of vital information and until we know for certain that he is 100% reliable we cannot entirely disregard this person."[24]

But Szilard was irrepressible. That — and his talents as a physicist — made him a favorite of Compton, despite their very different backgrounds and temperaments, and when Groves pressured Compton to fire Szilard, Compton protected him, even writing to officials in Washington in praise of his efforts:

> Szilard was the first in this country, perhaps anywhere, to advocate trying to secure a chain fission reaction using unseparated [uranium]. He has perhaps given more concentrated thought on the development of this project than has any other individual. As an experienced physicist and engineer and a man of unusual originality, his thoughts have been of great value in determining the direction of our work. He has likewise been from the beginning actively concerned with the more far-reaching problems of organization and civil and military uses of the process. Even though not all of his ideas are practical, I consider him one of the most valuable members of our organization.

Compton also cited Szilard's early efforts to keep scientific secrets from Germany, his research on the chain reaction, and his vocal advocacy of a bomb program. Compton concluded his assessment by characterizing Szilard as "an independent individualist, vitally and I believe unselfishly concerned with the effective progress of our program."[25]

Szilard was not alone: another maverick had joined the Manhattan Project by 1942. Nearly every physicist involved in the project knew of him because he was the kind of man one talked about, the sort of character that makes a novelist's fingers itch. Mood-swept and arrogant, yet insecure. A brilliant and charismatic man, a genuine heavyweight of personality, he was a gifted theoretical physicist at Berkeley named Robert Oppenheimer. Famed for his genius, Oppenheimer was the object of admiration and jealousy by colleagues.

The grandson of German Jewish immigrants, Oppenheimer was born in New York City in 1904. He grew up in a spacious apartment at Eighty-eighth Street and Riverside Drive overlooking the Hudson. The family dining room was decorated with a van Gogh painting, and they spent summers at a rambling cottage on Long Island Sound. Oppenheimer stood apart from other youths in more ways than just his family's wealth. He collected minerals, read poetry, and studied languages as well as a great deal of science. Although tremendously gifted intellectually, Oppenheimer was weighted down by his mother's demanding expectations and his Jewishness — both of which he carried as a personal burden. "He reminded me very much of a boyhood friend about whom someone said that he couldn't make up his mind whether to be president of the B'nai B'rith or the Knights of Columbus," said I. I. Rabi, who came to know Oppenheimer well. "Perhaps he really wanted to be both, simultaneously."

Oppenheimer's outlook was shaped by his education at the elite Ethical Culture School facing Central Park on the Upper West Side of Manhattan. The progressive school imparted a pragmatic, liberal philosophy to its students that stressed ethical values over moral laws, which it saw as changing over time to meet the needs of society. The result was a high-minded relativism leavened by selflessness — doing "the noble thing," as it was known at the school. Oppenheimer learned well; he was valedictorian of his class.

To toughen him up and round him out, Oppenheimer's parents had one of his teachers, Herbert Smith, take him out West during the summer before he entered Harvard College. For several weeks during June and July 1922, Oppenheimer and his teacher roamed the southern Rockies together on horseback. The trip opened a whole new world to Oppenheimer. For starters, he learned to appreciate the breathtaking beauty of the West. He also learned that he could stand on his own feet, that he could do what he thought ought to be done, that he did not need to lean on anyone for approval. It was the discovery of an internal grit and stamina that gave him much needed self-confidence.

The high point of the summer was a pack trip in the mountains and volcanic mesas of northern New Mexico. On one of these mesas, Oppenheimer and Smith came upon a cluster of rustic cabins shaded in cottonwood trees: the elite Los Alamos Ranch School for Boys. Oppenheimer loved the extraordinary light and breathtaking vistas of the high desert, the fragrant juniper cedars and piñon pines, the wildflowers colored a palette of muted browns, reds, and yellows. It made an indelible impression on him. He would return two decades later for a very different reason.

Oppenheimer entered Harvard that fall with an astonishing appetite for work. Typical was this note he wrote: "I am now going regularly to 10 courses, & doing my research, & I have started to learn

Chinese."[26] He spent hours alone in his dorm room overlooking the Charles River, surrounded by oils, etchings, and a samovar, subsisting on chocolate-covered raisins. He found studying easy but socializing difficult. "He was often very unhappy," a roommate recalled. "He was lonely and felt he didn't fit in well with the human environment. There was something that he lacked, perhaps some more personal and deep emotional contact with people."[27] Exhibiting symptoms of a manic-depressive, he alternated between periods of furious study and severe depression that led to periodic sessions with a psychiatrist, which continued for several years after Harvard.[28] He struck his friends with the pathos of a sensitive and thoughtful young man, lacking in self-knowledge, constantly struggling with a major repression or conflict that he could neither dislodge nor resolve.

Oppenheimer started out at Harvard in chemistry but was soon drawn to the physics underlying it. The study of nature's harmony and order touched a deep chord in Oppenheimer, appealing to the philosopher and poet in him. After graduating summa cum laude in just three years, he applied for postgraduate work under Ernest Rutherford at Cambridge. His Harvard mentor, the future Nobel laureate Percy Bridgman, wrote a letter about him to Rutherford that was perceptive and prophetic. Oppenheimer had a "perfectly prodigious power of assimilation," Bridgman wrote, and "his problems have in many cases shown a high degree of originality in treatment and much mathematical power." He conceded that "it is a bit of a gamble as to whether Oppenheimer will ever make any real contributions of an important character, but if he does make good at all, I believe that he will be a very unusual success."[29]

Rutherford was unimpressed with Oppenheimer's credentials and rejected his application. Oppenheimer next wrote to J. J. Thomson, another renowned experimentalist at the Cavendish. Thomson accepted Oppenheimer as a research student and put him to work in a corner of the laboratory. "I am having a pretty bad time," he wrote to a high school friend in November 1925. "The lab work is a terrible bore, and I am so bad at it that it is impossible to feel that I am learning anything." When Max Born visited the Cavendish in the summer of 1926 and suggested that Oppenheimer pursue graduate studies at the University of Göttingen, a center for theoretical physics, Oppenheimer readily accepted the plan. It was at Göttingen that Oppenheimer first became aware of the problems perplexing European physicists. At that time, Born, Heisenberg, and Pascual Jordan were all in Göttingen, formulating the theory of quantum mechanics. Oppenheimer profited a great deal from his association with such prominent European physicists.

In 1929 he returned home to take up a prestigious joint appointment at the University of California, Berkeley, and the California Institute of Technology in Pasadena. Before Oppenheimer, American theoretical physics did not inspire high blood pressure in the seminar rooms of Europe. There were a few adept experimentalists, such as Lawrence, Compton, and Rabi, but most universities had no theoretical physicists as such. At the University of Hamburg in the late 1920s, the *Physical Review*, the research journal of the American Physical Society, was considered to be of such scientific insignificance that copies of the monthly magazine were permitted to pile up for a year before being unwrapped for use in the library.

Young Professor Oppenheimer cut a very dramatic figure. He was six feet tall, slightly stooped, with a mobile, expressive face and a body as thin as the wisps from the cigarettes he constantly smoked. His gestures and temperament were much closer to the coffeehouses of Europe than to anything American. He led an almost prototypical ivory tower existence. "I was almost wholly divorced from the contemporary scene in this country," he later said. "I never read a newspaper or a current magazine like *Time* or *Harper's*. I had no radio, no telephone. The first time I ever voted was in the Presidential election of 1936."[30] He learned of the Wall Street crash from Ernest Lawrence six months after it happened. "Tell me," Oppenheimer once said to a student, "what has politics to do with truth, goodness and beauty?"[31] To his brother, Frank, he wrote, "I need physics more than friends."[32]

An inherited income allowed Oppenheimer to live far better than most during the Depression. His first residence was an apartment on Shasta Road built into the wall of a steep canyon in the hills above campus. The furniture was simple, and a few lovely Navajo rugs covered the floors. "I have a little house up on the hill," he wrote Frank, "with a view of the cities [of Oakland and San Francisco] and of the most beautiful harbor in the world. There is a sleeping porch; and I sleep under the stars."[33] His second residence was an elegant house on the crest of Eagle Hill Road that he bought with a check the afternoon he toured it. "I do not have much time for diversions, but I ride about once a week," he wrote in another letter to Frank. "There are good horses, and lovely country among the hills overlooking San Francisco

Bay. From time to time I take out the Chrysler, and scare one of my friends out of all sanity by wheeling corners at seventy."[34]

At Berkeley, Oppenheimer wore gray suits, blue shirts, and blue ties. He was finely cultivated, ever poised and graceful. As a host, he had impeccable manners, made potent martinis (icing them first), cooked gourmet meals, and told droll stories. Spouses of colleagues received red roses; dates received gardenias — both found him irresistible. It was his intellect, however, that impressed people most. He had a mind that could penetrate to the heart of things, that could grasp the essential nature of a physical phenomenon, a book, even a person. Many of those who encountered Oppenheimer considered him the fastest thinker they had ever met — a true genius. In scientific conversation he always assumed that others knew as much as he did. This seldom being the case, and few persons being willing to admit their ignorance, his partner often felt at a distinct disadvantage.

Yet there was a flaw in his genius. He was brutally intolerant of anyone he considered slow or foolish. Those who struck him as intolerably stupid were denounced to their faces. It was called the "blue-glare treatment" in Berkeley circles: when aroused, Oppenheimer's eyes seemed to turn a vivid blue, his voice dropped way down, and his caustic tongue erupted. "He could be devastating if he chose," said one who witnessed the blue-glare treatment, "and sometimes he chose to be so at the wrong time."[35] His cutting tongue wounded people where they were most sensitive. "Robert could make people feel they were fools," a fellow physicist recalled.[36] Oppenheimer acknowledged his behavior in a letter to his brother, Frank, but added that "it is not easy — at least it is not easy for me — to be quite free of the desire to browbeat somebody or something."[37] He called the behavior "beastliness." Those at the receiving end of his cutting tongue put it differently: "He was very snooty," said one.[38] Many victims of Oppenheimer's tongue-lashings nursed a lingering resentment that would be repaid in later years.

Oppenheimer grew into a teaching legend at Berkeley, but he was hardly one at first. He didn't speak loud enough, he didn't face his class, and he scrawled equations at random all over the blackboard while lacing his delivery with obscure references to classics of literature and philosophy. Although desperately eager to reach his pupils, he was too impatient. He lectured to the most advanced students in the class, leaving all the others lost. Frequently he would make big jumps in the presentation of some theory and then turn toward the class, a cigarette dangling from his lips, and say offhandedly, "I hope I'm not being too pedestrian."[39] He applied his sharp tongue freely to students who were doing their best to keep up. Many took his course one year and then again the next in order to understand what it was all about. They would work in pairs, one taking notes and the other one listening.

Gradually Oppenheimer realized this was not a good system. He began trying to connect with and hold all of his audience. He dropped his pace of delivery and took pains to make the links between ideas clearer. He learned to slow down when students could not keep up. He became more relaxed in the classroom. His language evolved into an oddly eloquent mixture of erudite phrases and pithy slang, and he learned to exploit an extraordinary talent for elucidating complex technical matters. The brilliance of his ideas, the flow of his voice, and the feeling in his beautifully chosen words now began to hold students spellbound. His performance was a stimulating combination of sophistication and elegance mixed with a pinch of intellectual arrogance. Even non–physics majors found him one of the most charismatic professors on campus. Students cut other classes to sit in on his lectures, which were usually filled beyond capacity.

If Oppenheimer was a good lecturer, he was a great mentor, caring openly and deeply about his graduate students. He inspired them with his passion for the excitement and discovery of physics. He praised them, patiently answered their questions in his office until midnight, even asked them to collaborate with him on scholarly articles. His charm, eloquence, and humor captivated them, and the scope of his knowledge and the quickness of his mind awed them. He had new and exciting concepts to communicate; it was as if physics seemed to be unfolding from day to day in his seminar room.

Oppenheimer's appeal extended beyond the classroom. He was cultivated, well read, and wealthy enough to indulge his tastes. He liked to have a coterie of students around him. His chats with them often spilled out into hallways, campus quadrangles, and local restaurants, where he ordered students living on tiny stipends expensive meals and picked up the bill. He played classical music albums for them — Bach's Overture in B Minor was his favorite — took them to concerts, and read original Greek and Sanskrit literature to them. His style and his vision of life ignited them. In his presence they became more intelligent, more poetic, more prepared to discuss the nuances of any subject. They felt themselves stretched beyond their expectations and experiences. He was irresistible.

Oppenheimer's charisma was so great and the veneration of his students so deep that they imitated his gestures and mannerisms. They mumbled, "Ja, ja," in affirmative response to questions. They held their heads a little to one side. They splayed their feet when they walked. They coughed slightly between sentences. They held their hands in front of their lips when they spoke. They clicked open a lighter whenever anyone took out a cigarette. They referred to him not as Professor Oppenheimer, but simply and reverently as "Oppie" (sometimes spelled *Opje* by the very *in*). "I was very much under his influence," recalled Robert Christy, one of Oppenheimer's graduate students, more than sixty years later. "I would effectively do anything that he wanted me to do."[40]

During summers Oppenheimer would retreat to his northern New Mexico ranch, which he impishly named *Perro Caliente* ("hot dog" in Spanish). It was a beautiful, tranquil place nestled in the high alpine meadows of the Pecos Valley near Cowles. A rough-hewn log cabin on six acres, it had few conveniences and no electricity. The atmosphere was bohemian: everyone would sit in front of the fireplace, eating Indonesian food, playing tiddledywinks, and talking. Oppenheimer prepared wild strawberries with Cointreau for dessert. Guests rode horses by day — sometimes as far as Taos — and slept on Navajo rugs on the porch at night.[41]

One visitor to Perro Caliente in 1936 was an attractive, complex young woman who captivated Oppenheimer. Her name was Jean Tatlock. Tall and slender with green eyes and dark hair, always immaculately and severely dressed, she was pursuing a doctorate in psychiatry at Stanford Medical School. She was bright, passionate, and compassionate, an idealist and a rebel who was subject to fits of deep depression. Her spontaneity and forcefulness impressed Oppenheimer. Her beauty and intelligence entranced and infatuated him.

The daughter of a right-wing English professor at Berkeley, Tatlock had become increasingly involved in left-wing activities and was a member of the Communist Party by the time she met Oppenheimer. Oppenheimer had lived up to then for himself alone, or at any rate in his own fashion. She awakened him to the suffering in the world around him, stimulated his social conscience, and introduced him to leftist intellectuals at a time when it seemed to many people that communism offered the only alternative to the failure of capitalism in Depression-ravaged America and to the fascism that was spreading in Europe.

Oppenheimer had been remarkably ignorant of politics up to this point in his life. Whenever colleagues mentioned the rise of Nazism, he brushed them off. He wanted to discuss physics. Now he embraced politics with a neophyte's passion. Once Oppenheimer got interested in something, he would jump in with both feet. He championed the progressive causes of the day, from the plight of migrant farmworkers to struggling labor unions to unemployment among university gradu-ates. Said Oppenheimer, "I saw what the Depression was doing to my students. Often they could get no jobs, or jobs which were wholly inadequate. And through them, I began to understand how deeply political and economic events could affect men's lives."[42] He read the *People's Daily*, made the acquaintance of a number of California com-munists, and belonged to nearly every communist-front organization on the West Coast. The Loyalist cause in Spain was for him, as for many others on the Left during the decade, of particular concern. The capitalist nations, such as Britain and France, had done nothing about Nazi intervention in the Spanish civil war. Instead, it was the Soviet Union that was fighting fascism.

Although some people saw the American Communist Party as a cynical means to extend Soviet influence, this was an uncommon view in the 1930s. Many Americans believed the gloom and resignation caused by the Depression contrasted sharply with the hopefulness and purposefulness of workers in the Soviet Union. Thousands of Ameri-cans visited Russia in the 1930s and returned home with favorable accounts. Ignoring or discounting the human toll of collectivization and the terror famine, they regarded the rational planning of a com-mand economy as superior to the vagaries and hardships of a market economy on the ropes. Even the news of Stalin's bloody purges, which was slowly emerging from Russia, did little to shake their belief that communism was a movement with great potential for constructive social change. To them, even brutal communists were simply "pro-gressives in a hurry."

The politically unsophisticated Oppenheimer sympathized with many of these views. Communism was attractive to the humanitarian in him because it presented itself as a utopian vision of society in which injustice and oppression would cease to exist. It was attractive to the scientist in him because it presented itself as a "logical" and "objective" philosophy of politics and history. In these senses, he was certainly a fellow traveler; he may have been even more.* But at a time when overt expressions of patriotism were unfashionable among intellectuals in general, and particularly among those on the Left, he never hid his love for America. Oppenheimer was naive in his understanding of communism, and he would pay dearly one day for his naïveté. His political flirtation would come back to haunt him.

Other factors compelled Oppenheimer's transformation from cloistered academic to social activist. His mother had died after a long battle with leukemia in late 1931; his father died suddenly of a heart attack in 1937. His attachment to his parents — especially his mother — had been exceptionally strong. For the first time in his life, he knew the pain of personal loss, the two deaths marking the unworldly physicist's most intimate discovery of suffering in the world. And as the 1930s went on, human suffering was increasingly hard for a Jew to ignore. He later explained it this way: "I had a smoldering fury about the treatment of Jews in Germany. I had relatives there, and was later to help in extricating them and bringing them to this country." His aunt Hedwig and her son escaped from Nazi Germany and settled nearby in Oakland. They arrived only a few days after his father's death, and he and his brother, Frank, assumed responsibility for getting them on their feet.

Though Oppenheimer's conscience had been awakened, his activism had a quality of immature gullibility to it. He relied on Tatlock and her circle of radical friends as political mentors. One of them was a handsome, charming, and cultivated thirty-five-year-old professor of French literature at Berkeley named Haakon Chevalier, whom Oppenheimer first met in 1937. They became close friends, founding a campus branch of a teacher's union and sponsoring benefits for leftist causes. Chevalier was fascinated by Oppenheimer's intellect and restlessness. When Oppenheimer sat, he shifted constantly — flicking his fingers stained with nicotine from chain-smoking, crossing and uncrossing his legs. There was a driven — almost Byronic — quality to his life that reflected an inner turmoil.

---

* Evidence has recently come to light suggesting that Oppenheimer was an "unlisted" member of a Communist Party cell at Berkeley into the early 1940s. No concrete evidence has emerged, however, that he ever committed espionage against the United States on behalf of the Soviet Union. See Jerrold and Leona Schecter, *Sacred Secrets: How Soviet Intelligence Operations Changed American History* (Brassey's, 2002), pp. 316–17; and Herken, *Brotherhood of the Bomb*, pp. 31–32, 54–57, 111, 251, 289, 340–41.

Oppenheimer's inner turmoil made what had now become a full-fledged affair with Tatlock a stormy one. Despite their intimacy, their relationship swung back and forth. They were on again, then off again. "We were at least twice close enough to marriage to consider ourselves engaged," said Oppenheimer later.[43] Each time, it was Jean who shied away from commitment. Much of the problem stemmed from her severe bouts of depression. Their love affair continued tempestuously for three years, but it never seemed to provide Jean with what she was seeking. In early 1939 their relationship ended.

In August of that year Oppenheimer met Kathryn Puening Dallet Harrison at a party given by mutual friends in Pasadena, where Oppenheimer spent part of each year teaching at Caltech. Petite and dark, with a broad, high forehead, brown eyes, prominent cheekbones, and a wide, expressive mouth, "Kitty" Harrison resembled Jean Tatlock in many ways. She was politically engaged. She was bright, strong-willed, and controversial. The wife of a young British doctor in residence at a Pasadena hospital (a marriage that was not working out), Kitty had been married twice before — the first time to a European musician (the marriage had been annulled), the second time to an American ccommunist union organizer who had been killed fighting for the Loyalists in Spain. When she met Oppenheimer, the effect on both of them was electric. Their secret affair did not last long. On November 1, 1940, Kitty obtained a quick Nevada divorce and married Oppenheimer the same day. They returned to Berkeley to make a home for themselves and their expected child, a boy named Peter, who was born on May 15, 1941.

"When I met her," Oppenheimer later said of Kitty, "I found in her a deep loyalty to her [deceased second] husband, a complete disengagement from any political activity, and a certain disappointment and contempt that the Communist Party was not in fact what she had once thought it was."[44] Oppenheimer had also begun to reexamine his own political views. Because of his earlier insulation from politics, he had suffered a late awakening to the totalitarian realities beneath the socialist facade of the Soviet Union in the Stalin era. In 1938 two physicists who had just returned from an extended stay in Russia, Victor Weisskopf and George Placzek, paid him a long visit at Perro Caliente. What they told Oppenheimer of purge trials, tyranny, and the lack of personal and scientific freedom shocked him. He later described their reports as "so solid, so unfanatical, so true, that they made a great impression" on me.[45] The fall of France in June 1940 further jolted him. He was deeply troubled by the turn of events in the war — France had just fallen and Britain was in imminent danger. "What are we going to do about Europe?" he asked another physicist that summer.[46] Hitler seemed unstoppable, and Oppenheimer suddenly realized not only that something had to be done but that communism wasn't going to do it. A friend recalled this moment as "the first occasion when Oppenheimer talked about political matters not from the standpoint of the Left, but from the standpoint of the West."[47]

And then it was clear. Although he was the intellectual equal of the greatest physicists of his generation, Oppenheimer knew he was never going to make a grand success out of pure physics. He was a proud man and scientifically ambitious, but he was never able to immerse himself completely in a particular problem with the intensity of a Bohr or Fermi. His wide range of interests worked to his disadvantage and he lacked the creative confidence shared by those who made major discoveries. He had no great scientific achievement to his name, he had won no Nobel Prize; yet he now saw a way to achieve lasting distinction: by using his scientific knowledge in the fight against Nazi Germany. He began plotting a story with himself as the hero.

It was Lawrence who brought Oppenheimer into the Manhattan Project. The two first met when Oppenheimer arrived at Berkeley in August 1929, and quickly began a friendship that shaped the rest of their lives. It was an unlikely relationship. Lawrence — highly intuitive and extroverted, by turns taciturn and brash — was a doer who built big and never doubted himself. Oppenheimer — highly cerebral and introspective, by turns arrogant and charming — was a dreamer who used a piece of chalk as his basic working tool and suffered severe depressions. Lawrence was practical and pragmatic; Oppenheimer was bookish and intellectual. Lawrence liked sports and movies; Oppenheimer liked poetry and music. Lawrence dressed in three-piece suits and behaved like a captain of industry; Oppenheimer dressed in a bohemian manner and was proud of his reputation for mixing drinks.

"Between us was always the distance of different temperaments," Oppenheimer later said, "but even so, we were very close."[48] They dined together at Jack's, an upscale restaurant in San Francisco; rode horses together in the Berkeley and Piedmont hills; and took long drives together to Yosemite and Death Valley. They grew so close that Lawrence named his second son Robert. When Oppenheimer rushed East in the summer of 1931 to the bedside of his gravely ill mother, he wrote to Lawrence:

Dear Ernest,

It has not been easy to write to you before this; but I want you to have some little word from me. I know your understanding and your sympathy; and very deeply I appreciate it.

I found my mother terribly low, almost beyond hope. . . . She is in very great pain and piteously terribly weak. . . . I have been able to talk with her a little; she is tired and sad, but without desperation; she is unbelievably sweet.

For my father alone I should have been glad to come. I think that it has been something of a comfort. He is brave and strong and gentle beyond all telling. . . . You know that I shall come back as soon as I possibly can, and that, if I stay away so long, it is only because what I can do here seems incommensurate with the Berkeley duties.

I hope things are going well, that you are by now done wholly with the administrative horrors, and are having time for work and tennis and an occasional ride. I feel pretty awful to be away so long; you will do what you can for the fatherless theoretical children, won't you?

Affectionately,
Robert[49]

It helped, of course, that they were not rivals. Instead, they perfectly complemented each other. Lawrence's cyclotrons yielded precious physical data that Oppenheimer then used to construct exciting new theories. Their collaboration minimized the gulf separating them culturally and temperamentally. It also allowed Lawrence to dominate American experimental physics much as Oppenheimer dominated American theoretical physics.

Where they differed was in politics. Oppenheimer's political engagement mystified Lawrence, who thought his friend was wasting his time and talent. "You're too good a physicist to get mixed up in politics and causes," Lawrence told him. One day Oppenheimer came into the Rad Lab and wrote on the blackboard: "Cocktail Party Benefit for Spanish Loyalists, everyone at the Lab invited." When Lawrence saw Oppenheimer's message, he stood silently for a minute clenching his jaw, then furiously erased it. Their political differences would sunder their close friendship after the war.

Oppenheimer, like Lawrence, had followed the discovery of fission in December 1938 with great interest. But he had not learned about the secret bomb project until September 1941 — and only then because Mark Oliphant talked indiscreetly to Lawrence in Oppenheimer's presence. Assuming Oppenheimer already knew about the bomb project, Oliphant suggested using him in a more active way. Lawrence agreed. There was opposition in some quarters in Washington to Oppenheimer's participation because of his leftist politics, but Lawrence personally vouched for his reliability and considered the project too important to forgo his talents. "I have a great deal of confidence in Oppenheimer," Lawrence wrote Compton, "and, when I see you, I will tell you why I am anxious to have the benefit of his judgment in our deliberations."[50] On October 21, 1941, Lawrence took Oppenheimer to a meeting that Compton had called at General Electric's research laboratory in Schenectady, New York, to discuss problems of assembly and critical mass (the smallest amount of fissionable material that will support a self-sustaining chain reaction). The final report of the meeting, containing Oppenheimer's estimate of how much U-235 would be needed, became the blueprint for the bomb.

Oppenheimer became intensely interested in the project, even as he continued to teach. He was stirred not only by the technical challenge but also by a sense of mission: he loathed Nazism and wanted to do what he could to help defeat it. After Pearl Harbor, Oppenheimer was invited to meetings in Chicago, where Compton was organizing the Met Lab. Compton felt that a group of physicists should start studying bomb design and construction in addition to the work on a plutonium-producing pile. Oppenheimer was eager for such work, but he told a colleague that his leftist past probably meant that he would not receive the necessary security clearance.[51] A temporary clearance came through, however — owing to Compton's intervention in Washington — and Oppenheimer moved to Chicago at the beginning of 1942. It was the start of what he would later describe as "an adventurous time."[52]

Compton initially put Oppenheimer to work under Gregory Breit, a University of Wisconsin theoretical physicist. Breit was a good scientist but a poor administrator with a weak personality and an inordinate obsession with secrecy. He interpreted his duties as "Coordinator of Rapid Rupture" by locking all documents he was given in a big safe and making sure that nobody else had the combination or copies. Compton eased out Breit in May 1942 and named Oppenheimer his successor. It was the job for which Oppenheimer had been born. "Under Oppenheimer," Compton later wrote, "something really got done, and done at astonishing speed."[53]

The biggest obstacle to progress in Oppenheimer's mind was the lack of coordination among physicists working on bomb design. To fix this problem, Oppenheimer summoned the nation's top theoretical physicists to Berkeley in July 1942 for a brainstorming conference. Heading the list of those he invited was Hans Bethe. Bethe was a theoretical physicist who talked slowly and deliberately but possessed immense intellectual strength and self-confidence. He reminded one of seeing an elephant run: what was astonishing was the rate of progress of an apparently lumbering giant. He was famous for the quantity of food he ate, and in a way, that was similar to his appetite for physical problems. For Bethe, problems existed to be solved — not worried about. And by knowing what to do and where to go, he usually got there with remarkable speed and success.

Born in Strasbourg in 1906 when the Alsacian city was part of the German empire, Bethe was the son of a Prussian professor of physiology and a Jewish mother who converted to Lutheranism before she married. Their only son, Hans, was brought up a Lutheran, but religion did not interest him much. Hans was more interested in numbers. His godfather often asked him questions about arithmetic. Once, when Hans was five years old, his godfather asked, "What is point five divided by two?" A few days later Hans figured it out and ran across the street through thick traffic to tell him the answer.[54]

Before long, Bethe was astonishing his teachers with his ability to do long calculations in his head and to make big tables of the powers of numbers. He loved algebra and calculus. Deciding to pursue a career in analytical mathematics, he enrolled at the University of Frankfurt in 1924. There, a sympathetic professor counseled him to leave for a university that specialized in theoretical physics. Bethe did so, and went to study with Arnold Sommerfeld at the University of Munich. Sommerfeld was a great physics teacher — perhaps the greatest of the twentieth century — whose students included Heisenberg and Wolfgang Pauli, both future Nobel Prize winners.

Bethe was present one afternoon in the spring of 1931 when Sommerfeld entered his seminar room and immediately noticed his students' shocked silence. Curious as to what was wrong, Sommerfeld glanced toward the blackboard and saw scrawled in bold, angry letters the words *Verdammte Juden* — "Damned Jews!"[55] Such an expression of hatred in a German university — particularly toward someone of Sommerfeld's stature — shocked Bethe.

Shortly after finishing his doctorate, Bethe took a job as lecturer in theoretical physics at the University of Tübingen. Tübingen was a conservative Bavarian town near Stuttgart that seethed with the resentments that would soon bring Hitler to power. It was a hotbed of the Nazi Party, and most of Bethe's faculty colleagues were ultranationalists who fantasized about restoring the German empire and railed against the unfair treatment it had received since World War I. Many of his students wore brown shirts and swastika armbands. The night Hitler became chancellor, Nazis marched with torchlights through the city.

Bethe did not feel threatened by what was happening — at first. A month after the Nazis came to power, he told friends that Hitler could never do all the things he proclaimed he would do in *Mein Kampf*. It was inconceivable. Bethe's uneasiness grew, however, when he began hearing rumors about how prisoners were being treated at nearby Dachau concentration camp. Bethe openly discussed these rumors with visiting American postdoctoral students. One day the departmental handyman — a wise old man — approached him and whispered, "Child, don't do that. Don't talk so loud, because there are Nazis here. You don't want to go to Dachau."[56]

In the spring of 1933 the Nazis promulgated their Orwellian Law for the Restoration of the Professional Civil Service, which decreed that "civil servants of non-Aryan descent must retire." Bethe did not think that the law applied to him — even though his mother was Jewish — because he identified with his Protestant father and had been brought up a Lutheran. He felt safe until one day a student called and said he had seen a story in the local newspaper listing Bethe among those to be dismissed. A short time later Bethe received a curt, officious note informing him that he was fired.[57]

He left Nazi Germany, knowing that his life would never be the same. He took temporary posts at the Universities of Manchester and Bristol in Britain, where he met Arthur Compton at a physics conference in London. Bethe never thought of emigrating to the United

States, but when Cornell University sought to strengthen its physics department by appointing him an assistant professor — a post that held the possibility of tenure — he immediately accepted. After his ship docked in New York in January 1935, he spent a day walking the streets of Manhattan, marveling at the skyscrapers and the sidewalk bustle, listening to conversations and trying to pick up the thread of American life. The energy of America amid the Depression lifted his spirits. The next morning he took the train to Ithaca and gazed with astonishment at the open fields and dense forests west of the Hudson River — it seemed such a big and empty country, full of promise.

The physics department at Cornell University and the community of Ithaca, New York, welcomed Bethe with open arms. They were eager to get to know him and to learn about nuclear physics. He encountered no native anti-Semitism and very little professional jealousy. He was treated as an equal — a new American, not a foreigner. "I felt at home almost immediately," he said later with much affection and appreciation. "I was one of the group, which I had not felt even in Germany."[58]

Bethe found that he enjoyed far greater scope and opportunity as a physicist in America than he would have in Germany, even without the Nazis. In Germany it was customary for a professor to lecture his class from an Olympian distance; in America students asked questions whenever they wished, about whatever they wished. Bethe was unprepared for such informality and lack of hierarchy at first, but he quickly grew to like and thrive on it. His straightforward demeanor and strong voice were well suited to the American classroom. His decency and sense of humor made him popular in the faculty lounge and the lecture hall alike.

Of course, there were some drawbacks. One in particular was the phenomenon of faculty meetings, a ritual of participatory democracy that did not take place in highly authoritarian and centralized German universities. The first faculty meeting he attended at Cornell in the fall of 1935 was held in a conference room that was overheated and was devoted almost entirely to the question of whether there should be a vending machine in the basement of the physics department building. It went on for hours.

Bethe came to love his adopted country as much as he hated what the Nazis had done to his native land. When he returned briefly to Germany in the summer of 1936 to visit his parents, he bittersweetly realized that it was no longer home. Bethe expressed his mixed feelings in a letter to his mentor Sommerfeld after the war. "For those of us who were expelled from our positions in Germany," he wrote bitterly, "it is not possible to forget." More important than Bethe's negative memories of Germany, however, were his positive feelings about America:

> It seems to me (already for many years) that I am much more at home in America than I ever was in Germany. As if I was born in Germany only by mistake, and only came to my true homeland at age 28. The Americans (nearly all of them) are friendly, not stiff or reserved, nor brusque (*gar ablehnend*), as most Germans. It is natural here to approach all other people in a friendly way. Professors and students relate in a collegiate way without any artificially erected barrier. Scientific research is mostly cooperative, and one does not see competitive jealousy between researchers anywhere. Politically most professors and students are liberal and reflect about the world outside — that was a revelation to me, because in Germany it was customary to be reactionary (long before the Nazis) and to parrot the slogans of the German National (*Deutschnationaler*) Party. In brief, I find it far more congenial to live with Americans than with my German *Volksgenossen*.
>
> On top of that, America has treated me very well. I came here under circumstances which did not permit me to be very choosy. In a very short time I had a full professorship, probably more quickly than I would have gotten it in Germany if Hitler had not come. Although a fairly recent immigrant, I was allowed to participate in work and to have a prominent position. . . . Understand what I love in America and that I owe America much gratitude (disregarding the fact that I like it here). Understand what shadows lie between myself and Germany. And most of all understand . . . I am very grateful to you.[59]

Bethe eased his adjustment to America by befriending fellow refugee Edward Teller. When Bethe began courting Rose Ewald, the daughter of a German physicist who had been one of Teller's teachers, Teller and his wife, Mici, assumed the role of chaperones. In the summer of 1937 the four of them made a driving trip across the country. Their first destination was Rocky Mountain National Park in Colorado. From there, they drove to the Tetons in Wyoming, then on to Mount Rainier in Washington and Crater Lake in Oregon before ending their journey at a physics conference in California. "It was a happy time for the Tellers and for me," recalled Bethe.[60] Although they did not know it at the time, their warm friendship would later bend and break under the pressure of war and politics.

Bethe's first meeting with Robert Oppenheimer had not gone so well. Oppenheimer had cuttingly dismissed a paper that Bethe presented at a conference in Germany in 1929. They remained in touch, however, and Bethe began to perceive depths of intellect and culture in Oppenheimer that he had not noticed at first. At a physics meeting in Seattle in the summer of 1940, Oppenheimer gave what Bethe considered a "beautifully eloquent speech" about the danger that Nazism posed to Western civilization. Afterward, Bethe and Oppenheimer talked passionately about the threat posed by Hitler.

After the fall of France, Bethe decided to help the West's defense efforts by studying the penetration of armor plate by artillery shells. His paper on the subject was so valuable that the army promptly classified it and gave him a security clearance. He was then asked to help with radar, the most important science project of the war up to that time. In May 1942 he moved from Cornell to MIT, where work on radar was being conducted in the greatest secrecy. Bethe was at MIT when Oppenheimer asked him to come to Berkeley and work on the bomb. He initially turned Oppenheimer down, thinking the project was an "improbable boondoggle."[61] If a physicist wanted to help win the war, he thought, he should stick to something practical like radar. But after much arm-twisting by Oppenheimer, he accepted the invitation to Berkeley. In the end, strong feelings about the Nazis and scientific curiosity persuaded him. "The fission bomb had to be done," he later said, "because the Germans were presumably doing it."[62]

On the way to Berkeley, Bethe stopped for two days in Chicago, where Teller briefed him in detail on the work of the Met Lab. Bethe learned for the first time of Fermi's work on the pile, of plans for plutonium production, and of U-235 isotope separation. Though Lawrence's uranium-separation strategy struck him as an unbelievably expensive method using brute force, Bethe was greatly impressed by the talent and creativity with which Fermi was working on a chain reaction. Teller continued the trip west with him, and they joined Oppenheimer and a few other physicists in Berkeley in early July.

The purpose of the Berkeley conference was to determine whether an atomic bomb could actually be made. There were many questions to be answered: How many neutrons were released with each fission of a uranium nucleus? How did neutrons from one fission produce a secondary fission when they hit another uranium nucleus? Were there other fissionable materials besides uranium, with higher yield? How was fissionable material assembled fast enough to produce an explosion? What happened during the explosion? How could the explosive power be maximized? It was a demanding list.

The conferees met throughout July 1942 in Oppenheimer's office on the third floor of LeConte Hall. Oppenheimer's office had French doors opening onto a balcony with a magnificent view looking down the eucalyptus-covered Berkeley hills, across San Francisco Bay to the Golden Gate. The conferees met under what, for those days, were considered strict security arrangements. The windows were covered in wire mesh, including the exit to the balcony, and the door was fitted with a special lock with a single key that was given to Oppenheimer. Most of Berkeley's students were away on vacation or military service that first summer of the war, and the physicists had practically the whole campus to themselves.

Each scientist played his role. Oppenheimer posed penetrating questions. Teller threw off ideas like sparks. Bethe subjected them all to exhaustive scrutiny. They sifted through report after report, filling the blackboards in Oppenheimer's office and LeConte Hall classrooms with calculations and diagrams. They had been thinking about the key problems, they knew the general picture, but they had not yet pulled together all the pieces of the puzzle. Now they did. "We are up to our ears in every kind of work," Oppenheimer reported to another physicist during the conference.[63]

Among many things they discussed was a far-fetched idea that Teller had hatched with Fermi the year before: could the explosion of an atomic bomb heat the nuclei of heavy hydrogen (deuterium) enough to begin thermonuclear fusion? Such a bomb would be infinitely more destructive than even a fission bomb. Out of curiosity, Oppenheimer vigorously pursued the idea of a "superbomb" based on thermonuclear fusion. He and the other conferees made extensive calculations, which were disappointing — such a weapon apparently could not be made. Yet the concept of a "superbomb" would remain a nagging challenge to Teller's restless mind, one that he took secretly to heart and would nurse for years to come.

The Berkeley conference was the first and only time Oppenheimer and Teller discussed physics with the shared purpose that they enjoyed with other colleagues throughout their lives. "We had a few days of quite violent discussion by which we even learned something," Teller reported to Fermi at the end of their deliberations.[64] Teller attributed the progress they had made to Oppenheimer. It was a pleasant surprise for Teller, who had first glimpsed Oppenheimer four years earlier at a physics colloquium in Berkeley. After the colloquium Oppenheimer had taken Teller to dinner at a Mexican restaurant in San Francisco. Teller had found the dishes spicy and Oppenheimer overwhelming, even intimidating.

Now, during the summer conference, Oppenheimer and his wife, Kitty, invited Teller and his wife, Mici, to dinner at their home on Eagle Hill. The other guests at dinner that night were Haakon Chevalier and his wife, Barbara. Teller brought along a record of his favorite Mozart piano concerto as a hospitality gift, which he felt Oppenheimer found uninteresting. His feeling was subtly reinforced by *mikosh*, a cultural inferiority complex that Teller, a Hungarian Jew, felt toward Oppenheimer, a descendant of German Jews. Teller had imagined or actually experienced this superior feeling of Germans toward Hungarians as a graduate student at Leipzig and Göttingen and was sensitive — perhaps hypersensitive — to it. Oppenheimer may have been born in New York, but to Teller he represented the Germany that had always been out of reach, even to the son of a respected and socially responsible Hungarian lawyer. That they were both Jews made little difference, since in Oppenheimer Teller saw a Jewish elite far above his orbit, an elite whose riches and status commanded respect and opened doors. Oppenheimer, unlike Teller, did not hail from the trembling class.

Feeding the electricity between Oppenheimer and Teller were their differing personalities and temperaments. Teller was gregarious and extroverted, Oppenheimer was shy and introverted. However, both were arrogant, ambitious, charismatic, and intense. Both wanted to be "top dog" and resented those whom they thought were rivals. Running through their relationship from the beginning was an unstated but unmistakable — and inescapable — tension. Their fates were intertwined, although each barely sensed it at the time.

At the end of the Berkeley conference, Oppenheimer, Teller, and Bethe concluded that an atomic bomb *could* be made, but it would require an immense scientific and engineering effort. They now realized the sheer scale and complexity of what was involved, and how much of themselves would be required to make the bomb a reality.

The design and construction of the bomb would be a major task, but until enough plutonium could be produced, bomb design was of secondary importance. The task of constructing a chain-reacting pile that would yield plutonium fell to Fermi, with help from Szilard. One of the biggest problems was the impurity of uranium and graphite supplies. Szilard immediately set about convincing the main U.S. graphite producer, Union Carbon and Carbide, to produce very large quantities of incredibly pure graphite. He also had Compton call Westinghouse and ask, "How soon can Westinghouse supply three tons of pure uranium?" Compton heard a gagging sound at the other end of the line, but the firm's response was positive. Using uranium ore spirited out of the Belgian Congo at the time of the fall of France and sent to a warehouse in New York, Westinghouse stepped up purification from eight ounces a day to over five hundred pounds, and by November 1942 had delivered the three tons.

Fermi worked countless hours with younger scientists planning the pile and calculating the uranium and graphite needed. He was not above doing tedious work himself. "Fermi was doing it with all the rest of us," said a young physicist who helped construct the pile. "When he was on shift, he was on shift — the same as the rest of us."[65] It made him a beloved figure. He found release from the strain and long hours of work by swimming on hot summer afternoons in the choppy waters of Lake Michigan off the huge breakwater rocks from the Fifty-fifth Street Promontory to the Sixty-eighth Street Pier. He did a funny dog paddle but had amazing stamina.

The site of the pile's construction was a large squash court beneath the west stands of Stagg Field, whose masonry facade and crenellated towers facing Ellis Avenue between East Fifty-sixth and Fifty-seventh Streets a block north of Eckart Hall concealed a warren of indoor courts and locker rooms. Scarcely anyone had come this way since the university abandoned participation in intercollegiate football several years before. But here, on November 7, 1942, assembly of the world's first nuclear reactor — called Chicago Pile One (CP-1) — began. There was nothing ceremonial about it. A couple of physicists finished sweeping the floor of a square-shaped gray rubber balloon that would enclose the pile. The huge balloon was hung from the ceiling, with one side left open; then, in the center of the floor, a layer of graphite bricks was placed in a circle and braced by a wooden frame. Somebody jokingly shouted, "Well, Enrico, why don't you lay the cornerstone?"[66] Fermi grabbed a graphite brick and placed it with a grin.

The concept was to build a lattice of graphite bricks, interspersing plugs of uranium oxide until it was big enough to maintain a critical reaction. There were no plans or blueprints, just layer after layer of dark, slippery graphite bricks four inches wide and deep and sixteen inches long and uranium plugs weighing six pounds each and spaced eight inches apart. A layer of solid graphite blocks alternated with a layer of graphite blocks filled with uranium plugs. The pile had an odd shape. The base was square like a windowless brick house, but the top was tapered in the form of a roughly flattened sphere. Before the work was finished, 45,000 graphite bricks with uranium plugs were stacked into a sphere twenty-five feet wide at its midpoint and twenty feet high enclosed within the square rubber balloon.

Fermi directed assembly of the pile from his office in Eckart Hall and then from the balcony of the squash court as the work progressed. Young physicists laying graphite bricks carefully lined up slots for control-rod channels of neutron-absorbing cadmium that passed at various points through the pile. As it grew, layer by dusty layer, they assembled wooden scaffolding to stand on and ran loads of bricks up to the working surface on a portable elevator. "It was hard work, and it was dirty," said one who helped build the pile. "You'd look like you came out of a Kentucky coal mine at the end of a shift."[67] Fine black powder covered faces, lab coats, shirts, trousers, walls, flooring — everything. A dark haze dispersed light in the floodlit air. The only white to be seen was the gleam of teeth. "The people were all black with red eyes peering out," recalled an eyewitness. "It was like a scene from hell. It was a different world."[68]

As the pile neared completion, Compton had to decide whether to bring the pile to critical mass (initiating a self-sustaining chain reaction) right in the middle of a crowded city. "We did not see how a true nuclear explosion, such as that of an atomic bomb, could possibly occur," Compton later wrote with more calm and certainty than he probably felt at the time. "But the amount of potentially radioactive material present in the pile would be enormous and anything that would cause excessive radiation in such a location would be intolerable."[69] He asked Fermi about the probability of controlling a chain reaction; Fermi said it could be controlled.

Compton gave Fermi permission to go ahead, but he chose not to inform University of Chicago president Robert Maynard Hutchins. "The only answer he could have given would have been — no. And this answer would have been wrong. So I assumed the responsibility myself."[70] If the number of neutrons generated became too large, the pile would heat up and melt down. No one, including Fermi, could be sure that a meltdown would not occur and take all Chicago, or even Illinois, with it, so two young physicists volunteered to form a "suicide squad." The two would stand on scaffolding overlooking the pile with buckets of liquid cadmium in their grip. If all other controls failed and the pile started to melt down, they would hurl the cadmium on it.

As the pile grew larger, the neutron strength became stronger, so it became easier to predict when it could be made to go critical. When the fifty-seventh layer of bricks was completed on the night of December first, the work was halted. All the control rods but one were removed and the neutron count was taken. It was clear from the count that once the remaining rod was removed, the pile would go critical. Since it was late, the control rods were put back in and locked up for the night. The pile contained 771,000 pounds of graphite and 12,400 pounds of uranium, assembled at the cost of $1.5 million. Fermi was confident that the next day's experiment would be a success: he would start — and control — a chain reaction. And if he could not? asked one of his colleagues. "I will walk away — leisurely," he breezily answered.[71]

Szilard also doubted that the pile would run out of control, but he brooded nonetheless and seemed withdrawn. That night he walked to Culver Hall, where a psychologist whom he knew often worked late. "Come to dinner with me," Szilard said, and the psychologist, who enjoyed Szilard's speculative conversations, accepted. As they walked through the bitter-cold night to a nearby restaurant, Szilard admitted that he had already eaten but would have a second dinner "just in case." "Just in case what?" asked the psychologist. "In case an important experiment doesn't succeed," said Szilard with a typical air of mystery.[72]

December 2, 1942, dawned brutally cold. The temperature was ten degrees and a strong, raw wind rattled the Windy City. Ellis Avenue was strangely empty. Inside under the west stands of Stagg Field it was as cold as it was outside. Fermi put on his gray lab coat, which normally matched the color of his hazel eyes but now was black with graphite, entered the squash court, and went up to the balcony. Compton took his place next to Fermi. The balcony was now filled with control equipment glowing and radiating some grateful heat. It was unusually quiet in the vast, drafty room. Only the silhouettes of half a dozen physicists could be seen around the pile, which squatted black and menacing, watched by a roomful of hopeful and nervous eyes.

At 9:45 A.M. Fermi ordered all but one of the control rods withdrawn from the pile. The last control rod would be withdrawn by measured increments. Everyone stopped talking; only Fermi's voice could be heard in the silence. He instructed a young physicist to move it out halfway. The pile was still below critical mass. Fermi's fingers moved quickly over his small slide rule as his eyes checked the monitoring equipment. As usual, he looked completely self-confident. He had thoroughly prepared every detail of the experiment and was going to make a good show of it. He wanted to demonstrate how completely he understood the process. He wanted to prove that his predictions were accurate. Not only was he going to a witness a new phenomenon, he was going to be its master. "Fermi was playing this like an orchestra leader," said a young physicist who was there.[73]

He ordered the final control rod moved out another six inches. The tension in the room mounted as the Geiger counters registering neutrons from the pile began to click faster and faster, until their sound became a rattle. The physicists watched, fascinated, as the curve climbed steadily upward. Then the automatic control rod (which had been set for too low a neutron count) slammed back into the pile with a clang. "I'm hungry," deadpanned Fermi. "Let's go to lunch."[74] The other rods were inserted and the pile quieted down. He was drawing out the suspense like an accomplished showman.

At 2 P.M. everyone gathered again in the squash court. This time a crowd stood on the balcony. Szilard and Compton watched Fermi standing above what looked like an ominous black beehive. One by one, on Fermi's orders, the control rods were withdrawn, the counters clicking faster. The pile was alive with neutrons now. But it was not quite a chain reaction. Fermi ordered the control rod out another foot. He was enjoying himself tremendously. The pile was nearly critical. "This is going to do it!" Fermi announced. "Now it will become self-sustaining!"[75] An eyewitness recalled:

At first you could hear the sound of the neutron counter, clickety-clack, clickety-clack. Then the clicks came more and more rapidly, and after a while they began to merge into a roar; the counter couldn't follow anymore. That was the moment to switch to the chart recorder. But when the switch was made, everyone watched in the sudden silence the mounting deflection of the recorder's pen. It was an awesome silence. Everyone realized the significance of that switch; we were in the high intensity regime and the counters were unable to cope with the situation anymore. Again and again, the scale of the recorder had to be changed to accommodate the neutron intensity which was increasing more and more rapidly. Suddenly Fermi raised his hand. "The pile has gone critical," he announced. No one present had any doubt about it.[76]

If anything unpredictable was going to happen, now was the moment. The "suicide squad" waited nervously, ready to pour their liquid cadmium onto the pile. "Fermi was cool as a cucumber," an eyewitness wrote in his diary that night, "much more so than his associates who were excited or a bit scared."[77] Fermi waited a long minute, then another, then another. When it seemed that the anxiety in the squash court had become too much to bear, he ordered the control rods back in. There was applause, but no one cheered. The excitement in that cold and shadowy room was felt and shared by everyone. Someone produced a bottle of Chianti in a straw basket and gave it to Fermi. He and the others sipped the Chianti from paper cups quietly in the midst of that dingy, gray-black room without a word or a toast. While many dreamed of releasing the power of the atom as a peaceful source of energy, everyone present knew that destruction was the ultimate aim of the experiment. No one gave expression to his thoughts and feelings, but each one knew the others too well not to sense what was in their minds. There was greater drama in the silence than if words had been spoken.

Compton left the squash court; walked down Ellis Avenue, through Hull Court, to his Eckart Hall office; and called Conant in Washington. "Jim," he said, using coded language on an insecure telephone line, "you'll be interested to know that the Italian navigator has just landed in the New World." Conant's voice betrayed his excitement. "Were the natives friendly?" he asked. "Everyone landed safe and happy," replied Compton.[78]

The experiment brought to fruition years of theory and planning. Man had controlled the release of energy from the atomic nucleus for the first time, demonstrating dramatically that the chain reaction worked. An atomic bomb was no longer merely a theoretical possibility. Later that month President Roosevelt approved the expenditure of $400 million for uranium-separation plants and a plutonium-producing pile. At long last, Washington had decided to go all-out to build an atomic bomb.

Those present beneath the west stands of Stagg Field that cold December day had witnessed a moment of history. Many had cherished the hope that something ultimately would make a chain reaction impossible — if impossible for them, it would be impossible also for the Germans. Now what they dreaded was on the way to reality. "We began to say things to one another," an eyewitness said, "but there were no words that could express adequately just what we felt."[79] Another eyewitness remembered:

> For some time we had known that we were about to unlock a giant; still, we could not escape an eerie feeling when we knew we had actually done it. We felt as, I presume, everyone feels who has done something that he knows will have very far-reaching consequences which he cannot foresee. . . . Even though our hearts were by no means light when we sipped the wine around Fermi's pile, our fears were undefined, like the vague apprehensions of a man who has done something bigger than he ever expected to.[80]

There was no sign of emotion on Fermi's face. His expression was so calm, it was hard to believe. The experiment had worked — it was as simple as that in his mind. Fermi told everyone to go home and get some sleep. Tomorrow they would get on with the next step. He was the cool man of action.

Nearby, Szilard loitered silently, brooding about the past and the future. For more than two years he had collaborated with Fermi on the pile, and now he had witnessed their vision come true. To Szilard, who had feared this moment for years — and had secretly hoped that it would never come — Fermi's calm reaction was unnerving. Szilard now knew that an atomic bomb could be built. As everyone filed from the squash court into the cold evening, he and Fermi found themselves standing alone. "I shook hands with Fermi," Szilard remembered, "and I said I thought this day would go down as a black day in the history of mankind."[81]

That night a young physicist named John Manley came home from the Met Lab visibly shaken. His wife, Kay, was already in bed. She sensed that something was preoccupying her husband. "John came in very quietly," she remembered many years later. "I knew that he was concerned about something. Something was affecting his thinking very strongly. He looked at me and said, 'The world will never be the same.' That was part of his thinking from then on."[82]

CHAPTER 5

Los Alamos

THE ROAD NORTH from Santa Fe undulated gently for several miles along a string of hills and then opened out onto a valley floor more than seven thousand feet above sea level. On the west side of this valley road the land stretched out for miles to the gray, silver, and timber shades of the Jemez Mountains. In between, stunted brown tree-shrubs dotted the high desert land in countless tufts. At sunrise and sunset the wide valley was a spectrum of rich colors — the tans, mauves, and ever changing lavenders of the desert — but sunrises and sunsets were just moments in the long days here where time and the land alike seemed almost infinite. On the east side of this valley road, the Sangre de Cristo Mountains stood blood-red in the distance, including majestic snowcapped North Truchas Peak, at 13,102 feet one of the highest in all of New Mexico. The air possessed that lucid clarity of the desert. In the wide-open country of the American Southwest, the eye could roll out to the distance and the soul could expand into the great spaces.

At just this point a smaller road crossed the valley floor to the west. It spanned the Rio Grande, only a muddy stream here, and then started a slow climb toward the peaks of the Jemez Mountains, some darkened with trees, some lightened by scree. Large lava beds were visible, and black escarpments. Then salmon-colored cliffs towered skyward. The empty foreground filled suddenly with swellings of mesas, and abruptly trees — slim piñon pines and stubby juniper cedars — appeared over the canyons and the mesas. The air cooled and smells sharpened. The road rose, curved, cut back, then continued up, the mesas gradually taking shape. As the road crested the edge of one mesa, five suddenly appeared, splayed out from the gigantic volcanic mountain mass of the Jemez Caldera like the fingers of a hand sifting the sands of time. In the mesas' walls were a honeycomb of hollowed caves whose ceilings had been blackened by the smoke of long-ago fires. Etched into them were drawings of animals, birds, masked beings, dancing men, symbols of rain and sun.

The Pajarito Plateau opened like a huge fan from an arc of blue mountains. It was grooved by canyons that radiated out like the crudely drawn spokes of a wheel. The canyon walls rose through many-colored layers of hardened volcanic ash, rose and buff, like petrified waves. Some of the ridges between the canyons were narrow. Others were wide and flat, dotted with the mounds of pre-Columbian Indian villages and fields where Hispanic families cultivated beans in summer, returning in winter to their adobe homes along the Rio Grande. Atop one of the ridges of the Pajarito Plateau, where trees grew and the air smelled of pine needles, was the Los Alamos Ranch School for Boys. The school was named after the canyon that bordered the mesa to the south and was dotted with cottonwood trees (*los alamos* in Spanish) along the sandy trickle of its stream. All was quiet in this awesomely beautiful place. It was as far from the war-torn world as one could possibly be in September 1942.

That month General Groves, who had just taken charge of the Manhattan Project, decided to create a new laboratory where the widely scattered work on bomb theory and design could be brought together and the fissionable material produced at Oak Ridge and Hanford could be assembled. There was also the issue of security: if scientists were brought together in one place, it would be a lot easier to control their talking and movements. As leader of this new lab, Groves wanted someone with an intellect broad and quick enough to grasp a whole range of scientific problems, the imagination to suggest novel solutions to those problems, and the charisma to keep everyone working together as a team. He wanted someone who would get the "longhairs" to deliver their "gadget" on time.

Groves needed someone with enough authority and prestige to attract the best people available, ride herd on them, and coordinate their work. None of the Nobel laureates in physics could be spared to administrate. Lawrence was an outstanding experimental physicist and had gained good administrative experience running the Rad Lab at

Berkeley, but he was committed to the electromagnetic separation of U-235 at Oak Ridge and could not be spared. Compton was another obvious choice, but he was already doing more than his share running the Met Lab at Chicago. And it would be unthinkable in Groves's mind to assign the most secret military program to a foreign-born "enemy alien" such as Fermi, who was badly needed in Chicago, anyway.

In the absence of a more important figure, Groves chose Oppenheimer. They first met when Groves visited Berkeley on an inspection trip in early October 1942. Strangely enough, they hit it off well together right from the start. Oppenheimer was straightforward, did not act like a typical scientist, and seemed to be realistic about the importance of security, a matter of grave concern to the general. Oppenheimer, a persuasive talker and a consummate actor, convinced Groves that he was his man.

It was a most unorthodox choice. I. I. Rabi voiced the reaction of many physicists when he called it "a most improbable appointment. I was astonished."[1] Oppenheimer had never administered anything more complicated than a graduate seminar. He had no experience in organizing a large laboratory and had shown no predisposition for teamwork before. He was a theoretician, whereas the lab would be concerned primarily with experiments and engineering. He had no Nobel Prize to distinguish him — would other scientists follow his leadership? Then there was Oppenheimer's left-wing past, which "included much that was not to our liking by any means," as Groves later wrote.[2] Oppenheimer's former fiancée, his wife, his brother, and his sister-in-law had all been members of the Communist Party — perhaps he himself had been, too. Neither Bush nor Conant was enthusiastic. Compton and Lawrence also had reservations about his capacity as an administrator. "Do you know a better man?" Groves asked them.[3]

Yet while the conservative Groves found Oppenheimer politically naive, he found nothing in his security file to doubt Oppenheimer's loyalty to the United States, even though War Department investigators had characterized him as "strongly communistic" and had reported his connection "with radical organizations for years on and off the campus of the University of California."[4] Groves was so confident of his judgment that he personally ordered Oppenheimer's clearance, overruling the objection of Army Intelligence officers on the grounds that Oppenheimer was "absolutely essential to the Project."[5] His order caused consternation and resentment among project security officers, but Groves wanted Oppenheimer — who else *was* there? — and forced through his choice. (The security people never forgave him or Oppenheimer for that act and continued to harass the director at every opportunity.) Groves barely knew Oppenheimer, yet he sensed that this man of great charm and persuasiveness could somehow bring together very difficult personalities and get them to work as a team. Groves's intuition told him that Oppenheimer was a man equipped not only with scientific insight but with strong character and a capacity for decision. That was what Groves wanted, that was what he needed. There was no time to lose. The atomic bomb was only an idea on paper, and he had to make it a reality.

It was a brilliant choice.

The general and the physicist quickly developed a good working relationship. They always addressed each other formally as "General Groves" and "Dr. Oppenheimer" — an indication of the constant if subdued contest between them, each admiring yet suspicious of the other's abilities. Groves treated Oppenheimer with more respect and deference than he did any other project scientist — almost delicately, like a fine musical instrument that needed to be played just right. Oppenheimer, who could be cuttingly sarcastic with colleagues, never was with Groves. He patiently answered every question the general asked. He had not expected to like Groves — the military culture, after all, was definitely not his cup of tea — yet he found himself grudgingly admiring the general. "Groves is a bastard," he would say privately, "but he's a straightforward one."[6] They were an odd and improbable couple locked in a strange union that superseded quarrels and irritation — married, first and last, to the success of the project. They got along because each saw the other as the way to fulfill his ambition to achieve personal glory. "That combination made the thing work," Rabi astutely observed.[7]

Groves and Oppenheimer's first task together was to choose a site for the bomb lab. Oppenheimer remembered the mesa of Los Alamos, where he had spent a happy summer riding horseback and camping. The characteristics that had made the location a place of glory to him — its remoteness and isolation, but also its spare, intense beauty — was especially important to the aesthete in Oppenheimer, who knew the quality of the scientists whom he hoped to attract there and believed they would respond to surroundings that stretched and enriched the spirit.

Oppenheimer proposed this "little gray home in the west"[8] to Groves, and together they drove up to the Ranch School in an unmarked car on November 16, 1942. They arrived there late in the afternoon. A light snow was falling. Despite the cold November wind, the boys were out on the playing fields in corduroy shorts. The founder of the school, Ashley Pond, was an enthusiastic advocate of the vigorous outdoor life and did not even believe in heated sleeping quarters. Oppenheimer and Groves remained outside the gates, taking in the fresh mountain air as they pored over maps and looked out over the surrounding countryside. Log houses and school buildings were scattered amid pastures and cropland. It was a lovely place, this clearing in the pine trees 8,500 feet above sea level. The flat green mesa, separated from the rest of the plateau by the vertical walls of two deep canyons, offered perfect isolation. After taking it all in, General Groves said simply, "This is the place."[9]

The only obstacle to his decision was A. J. Connell, the headmaster of the Los Alamos Ranch School, where forty-three wealthy boys had been sent, mostly from the East, to be educated and toughened up. When an army officer told the headmaster that the school had come to the end of its days and would be taken over, Connell replied, "You must be mistaken. The property is not for sale." The boys were permitted to finish the school year, but that was it. By the time they left, in the early spring of 1943, MPs were already guarding the mesa. Connell retired to Santa Fe a broken man, where he died two years later. That is how the secret lab known as Site Y or the Hill came to be.

On March 16, 1943, Oppenheimer left California by train for New Mexico. He arrived in Santa Fe a few days later and took up residence at 109 East Palace Avenue in Santa Fe under the alias Mr. Bradley until Kitty and Peter joined him and together they moved up to the Hill in May. Oppenheimer's plan was to build an atomic bomb there with just thirty other physicists. It would be a small community. They would live in the schoolmasters' houses and eat at the main lodge. What labs were needed would be squeezed in between the canyon rim and the little pond that graced the front of the lodge. As the realities of the immense challenge set in, however, Oppenheimer would be forced to recruit more physicists, as well as mathematicians, chemists, metallurgists, ordnance experts, machinists — all sorts of personnel. By war's end, Los Alamos would secretly employ more than four thousand civilian and two thousand military personnel.

Oppenheimer's original estimate had been low because of inexperience and his lack of ability to understand the dimensions involved. He had foreseen a theoretical physics laboratory whose main function would be to determine the critical mass, ensure against predetonation in assembly, and perform the necessary subcritical experiments to test the theory. Oppenheimer had given little thought to the engineering aspects of a weapon, which would prove to be awesome.

The laboratory started out with nothing except the library books that the Ranch School boys had read and the equipment they had used to go horseback riding. The only link with the outside world was a hand-cranked Forest Service phone line. Water was scarce and electricity was intermittent. At the center of Los Alamos was Ashley Pond, named after the school's founder. To its east stood Fuller Lodge, the main dining hall. Across an open field was the Big House, which served as a dormitory for arriving scientists. Between the main road and the mesa's southern rim were the laboratories, dubbed the Tech Area, one- and two-story white clapboard and green sheetrock buildings scattered among tall ponderosa pines. The streets created were unpaved and unnamed.

The scientists who would work in the Tech Area had many questions to answer: How many neutrons were released each time a uranium nucleus fissioned? How were they absorbed or scattered? How did the neutrons from one fission produce a second fission when they hit another uranium nucleus? How was a critical amount of fissionable material assembled fast enough to create a powerful explosion? What would happen during the explosion? The questions sounded very academic, but this was no college campus: a fenced guarded by MPs surrounded the Tech Area, and special white badges were required for admission.

Oppenheimer knew the physicists he needed would not readily pass up work at established war projects such as radar at MIT, the proximity fuse at Johns Hopkins, or sonar at San Diego to come to this unknown site in the desert. They would come only if America's top physicists were coming, too. So Oppenheimer recruited the stars first, and the others followed fast. Some he terrified by stressing the prospect of a Nazi atomic bomb. Others he attracted by his descriptions of the immense beauty of New Mexico. But to all he imparted the feeling of how exciting it would be to participate in the pioneering work. "He spoke with a kind of mystical earnestness that captured our imagination," recalled one recruit.[10] By describing the projected work as crucial to the war effort and exerting a kind of "intellectual sex appeal,"[11] as another recruit put it, Oppenheimer managed to get almost everyone he wanted. "Oppenheimer was the best recruiter and salesman I've ever seen," said one who eagerly bought his sales pitch. "He expressed his enthusiasm for the project, and aroused ours."[12] The list of current and future stars was astonishing: Robert Bacher, Robert Christy, Richard Feynman, Donald Hornig, Edwin McMillan, Philip Morrison, Norman Ramsey, Emilio Segrè, Victor Weisskopf, and Robert Wilson, to name just a few.

If Oppenheimer needed additional ammunition in his recruiting effort, he had it in the form of a personal letter from President Roosevelt. Addressed to Oppenheimer but meant for everyone on the Hill, the letter conveyed FDR's appreciation of the project's urgency and the country's thanks for the scientists' labors:

Secret   *June 29, 1943*

My dear Dr. Oppenheimer:

I have recently reviewed with Dr. Bush the highly important and secret program of research, development and manufacture with which you are familiar. I was very glad to hear of the excellent work which is being done in a number of places in this country under the immediate supervision of General L. R. Groves and the general direction of the Committee of which Dr. Bush is Chairman. The successful solution of the problem is of the utmost importance to the national safety, and I am confident that the work will be completed in as short a time as possible as the result of the wholehearted cooperation of all concerned.

I am writing to you as the leader of one group which is to play a vital role in the months ahead. I know that you and your colleagues are working on a hazardous matter under unusual circumstances. The fact that the outcome of your labors is of such great importance to the nation requires that this program be even more drastically guarded than other highly secret war developments. I have therefore given directions that every precaution be taken to insure the security of your project and feel sure that those in charge will see that these orders are carried out. You are fully aware of the reasons why your own endeavors and those of your associates must be circumscribed by very special restrictions. Nevertheless, I wish you would express to the scientists assembled with you my deep appreciation of their willingness to undertake the tasks which lie before them in spite of the dangers and the personal sacrifices. I am sure we can rely on their continued wholehearted and unselfish labors. Whatever the enemy may be planning, American science will be equal to the challenge. With this thought in mind, I send this note of confidence and appreciation.

Though there are other important groups at work, I am writing only to you as the leader of the one which is operating under very special conditions, and to General Groves. While this letter is secret, the contents of it may be disclosed to your associates under a pledge of secrecy.

Very sincerely yours,
Franklin D. Roosevelt[13]

Oppenheimer answered Roosevelt's letter with these words:

July 9, 1943

Dear Mr. President:
Thank you for your generous letter of June 29th. You would be glad to know how greatly your good words of reassurance were appreciated by us. There will be many times in the months ahead when we shall remember them.

It is perhaps appropriate that I should in turn transmit to you the assurance that we as a group and as individual Americans are profoundly aware of our responsibility, for the security of our project as well as for its rapid and effective completion. It is a great source of encouragement to us that we have in this your support and understanding.

Very sincerely yours,
J. R. Oppenheimer[14]

The few who were not moved by Roosevelt's letter were moved by the advantages that scientists enjoyed at Los Alamos. They got everything they wanted; cost was unimportant. They were given top priority for scarce wartime materials. They interacted daily with the finest minds in the world. "I was twenty-three years old when I went up to the Hill and met people I never expected to meet," recalled a veteran of Los Alamos. "I hadn't even known that Niels Bohr was still alive, never mind that I might actually be sitting across the table from him. I was totally overwhelmed by all these people I had read about in textbooks."[15] Yes, there would be isolation. But the professional intimacy would make up for it.

Oppenheimer hoped scientists would be inspired to excellence by the beauty of Los Alamos. For many, this happened during their first meal at Fuller Lodge. In the morning, through a picture window, the rugged chain of the Sangre de Cristos ran like a dark silhouette along the horizon. Then the sun rose over the ridgeline and the room suddenly filled with brilliant light. In the evening the ridgeline darkened from violet blue to crimson at sunset. The mountains, the bright clear air, the deep blue sky, the warm sunshine and cool wind, the wildflowers exploding with color in summer, the walks beneath shimmering aspen trees that turned brilliant yellow in autumn — all these things exhilarated and sustained scientists in their efforts. This was the world they hoped to save and understand, and it was breathtaking. They had only to open their hearts a little and the mesa breathed itself into them, sending them climbing in an elation to a height that no fear could reach.

The mesa was off-limits to outsiders, and armed guards patrolled the perimeter on horseback. Los Alamos did not appear on any map; its very name was classified. People were fingerprinted and photographed and lectured about the need for secrecy. They were forbidden to tell anyone the location of the project. They could travel only within a limited radius, and telephone calls were monitored. It was illegal to mail a letter except in authorized drops, and all mail was censored. Driver's licenses and tax returns were made out to numbers rather than to names. Birth certificates for children born there listed simply "Box 1663, Sandoval County Rural." The secrecy extended to occupations. Even words such as *physicist* and *chemist* were taboo; they were called "fizzlers" and "stinkers" instead. Everyone lived and worked behind a heavily guarded fence topped with three rows of barbed wire. The fence was a tangible barrier and a constant reminder of Los Alamos's separation from the rest of the world and of the war that was somewhere out there.

Oppenheimer accepted the heavy security as a wartime necessity, but he adamantly refused to accept secrecy in one area: scientific discussion. Here, the normal security procedure of compartmentalization — limiting discussion to a "need to know" basis — was not followed, despite protests from Army Intelligence. Oppenheimer held weekly symposia on the pressing technical problems of the moment, inviting solutions not only from the groups working on the problems but from the important cross-fertilization of agile minds from other disciplines with novel approaches and solutions. Just as in fission itself, one small suggestion could set off a chain reaction of ideas at a rapid rate. This fostered a cooperative spirit that maintained high morale. It was also a major reason why the bomb was built in such a short time.

Although the army guarded and administered Los Alamos, the heart of the Tech Area was run by Oppenheimer for the University of California under a government contract. Scientists came to Los Alamos as civilians, sharing with the military one mission: to build an atomic bomb as fast as possible and, with it, end the war. The similarities between them began and ended there. The gulf between their two cultures was immense, the tension almost inevitable. While scientists resented army regimentation and restrictions, the military found it irritating to have to pander to eccentrics who did not behave according to regulations. Soon after things got under way, Groves came to Los Alamos and told his staff behind closed doors: "Your job won't be easy. At great expense we have gathered here the largest collection of crackpots ever seen."[16] On another occasion he told Arthur Compton, "Your scientists don't have any discipline. You don't know how to take orders and give orders."[17] Groves could not appreciate the creative dimension of scientific work.

But ultimately Groves did not care what the scientists thought or said about him behind his back as long as project security was maintained and its mission was accomplished. He knew exactly what he wanted: to keep the project a secret, to build an atomic bomb as fast as possible, to win the war with it, to tell the British as little as necessary, and to tell the Russians nothing. He was not above misleading the scientists if he thought it was for the good of the project. He would, for example, deliberately give Los Alamos excessively optimistic reports about what was being accomplished at Oak Ridge; likewise, he would give Oak Ridge excessively optimistic reports about how things were going at Los Alamos. In this way, he could make both groups work harder, since each group would think it was the bottleneck and therefore get things done faster. On the other hand, Groves was willing to stick his neck out for the scientists. They asked for tremendous amounts of expensive and difficult-to-obtain equipment, and if they made a convincing case to him, he was willing to go a very long way to get it. If the Manhattan Project failed, the man who would be the target, and victim, of subsequent congressional investigations into why $2 billion had been squandered on a useless project would be Groves, not them — and he knew it.

The scientists at Los Alamos were young — their average age was only twenty-seven — and almost no one was older than forty.[18]

Oppenheimer, the lab's director, was all of thirty-nine. They were inexperienced and starting from scratch, but they were full of spirit. They worked most every night, but they still found time — and energy — to explore cave dwellings in nearby canyons, ski, ride horses, mountain climb, and dance. Occasionally they visited Santa Fe on Saturday nights, but the city was terribly crowded and the few bars were swarming with security agents from Army Intelligence, immediately recognizable by their snap-brimmed felt hats and poorly fitting civilian clothes.

"Life is not at all hard on this 'magic mesa,'" reported one young physicist. "The group is large enough so that people can choose friends to their liking, and living conditions are entirely comfortable. Soon after arriving, I purchased a spirited part-Morgan horse that is the love of my life. I have taken several pack trips and have just returned from deer hunting."[19] Singles sponsored dorm parties fueled by punch spiked with grain alcohol. Sometimes the liquor flowed too fast and the noise lasted too long. One dormitory received this warning from army authorities:

> It has come to the attention of this headquarters that parties held in your dormitory are getting slightly out of hand and that on the morning after, your dayroom is littered with broken beer bottles and similar debris, fire hose is found unrolled down the corridor, and other evidences of abuse of Government buildings and property appear.
>
> This situation must be corrected at once, as abuse of Government property cannot be tolerated; and any further reports coming to this headquarters will make it necessary to revoke the privilege of having parties in your dormitory.[20]

Parties at Los Alamos were so intense because they were one of the few ways to relieve the pressure. "I've never drunk so much as there," recalled one wartime resident, "because you had to let off steam, you had to let off this feeling eating your soul: 'Oh God, are we doing right?'"[21] The future Nobel laureate Richard Feynman, then in his early twenties, relieved the stress by playing bongo drums, challenging censors with coded letters, and picking combination locks of safes containing classified documents. Scientists at Los Alamos could not unburden their souls by bringing their doubts and complaints to outsiders; they had to remain either within themselves or within the community.

Coexisting with this tension, however, was the pride of being part of a historic enterprise. "I have never seen such esprit de corps in a scientific group," wrote a physicist at the time.[22] Here was a chance to show the world how powerful, important, and useful physics could be: Western civilization was threatened by a fanatic barbarism, and it looked as though only science could save it. "There was this amazing feeling that what you did was very important, that you damn well better do it right, and that everybody else around you was in the same fix," said one who was there.[23] Oppenheimer voiced this feeling of excitement and purpose later when he wrote:

> Almost everyone realized that this was a great undertaking. Almost everyone knew that if it were completed successfully and rapidly enough, it might determine the outcome of the war. Almost everyone knew that it was an unparalleled opportunity to bring to bear the basic knowledge and art of science for the benefit of his country. Almost everyone knew that this job, if it were achieved, would be a part of history. This sense of excitement, of devotion and of patriotism in the end prevailed.[24]

It was hard to remain unaffected while working amid a remarkable array of scientific talent striving to harness a great force of nature in a race with an evil regime. The interest of technical developments, the interplay of brilliant personalities, the belief that the weapon they were making would decide the outcome of the war — all these things drew scientists deeply and completely in what appeared to be a good, and urgent, cause. That perception, in turn, dampened a lot of personal frictions. It would be hard to exaggerate the intensity of life at Los Alamos during the war. The whole thing lasted a little more than two years, but these were years that shaped for life the people who were there. It was their great moment. But the moment was always clouded by the awareness of the project's purpose, and its possible consequences.

Everyone at Los Alamos felt Robert Oppenheimer's presence. "When he walked into a room — boy, you knew he was there without even looking up," recalled one scientist.[25] A slender figure in a close-fitting suit with a beaklike nose and close-cropped hair — he had cut it when he left Berkeley — he habitually wore a wide-brimmed hat that exaggerated the thinness of his face. His nervous energy and piercing blue eyes seemed to take in everything at a glance. Early each morning, he left his home at 1967 Peach Street on "Bathtub Row" and walked to his Tech Area office on the far side of Ashley Pond. From the moment he reached his office, Oppenheimer threw himself into an endless round of progress reports, phone calls, and meetings. He paced constantly, smoking and coughing. When he spoke, he spoke slowly, thinking out what he wanted to say and phrasing it eloquently. The voice was educated and genteel, but when it told you to do something, you did it. He never seemed in doubt. His mind was as sharp as a knife and his powers of concentration and understanding were phenomenal. "He was so quick that he gave you an inferiority complex," said a friend.[26]

Such leadership was not instantaneous. At first Oppenheimer strained to bring the new laboratory into existence. "Every time I think about our problem a new headache appears," he confided to a colleague just a few weeks into his new job; "we shall certainly have our hands full."[27] Groves was accustomed to pushing subordinates, but Oppenheimer threw himself into his new role with such heedless intensity that even Groves was afraid he might break. He applied his familiar talents — his quick and broad intellect, his personal charisma, his thoughtfulness for others — to the problems of a large and multi-faceted project. And just as he had done years earlier, when making the disastrous start to his university teaching career, Oppenheimer learned fast. But the most important factor was the change that seemed to have taken place in Oppenheimer's personality. He showed a new determination and clarity, as if iron had entered his soul. Soon he was overseeing activities on the Hill with a self-evident competence and outward composure that almost everyone came to depend on.

Creating a new laboratory was stimulating work for Oppenheimer at first. Then an inevitable reaction set in; Oppenheimer realized the enormity of the task and became discouraged. His wife, Kitty, struggled to settle into life on the Hill and began to drink heavily. Time with his son, Peter, and daughter, Toni, born in December 1944, was limited to fleeting moments. He was kept under constant surveillance, his home and office bugged by security officials who remained suspicious of him and who picked over the details of his past. Brusquely dismissing others' complaints about the opening of their mail, he told Teller, "What are they griping about? I am not allowed to talk to my own brother."[28] In the summer of 1943 he confided to his close friend, theoretical physicist Robert Bacher, that he was going to give it up. He

felt overburdened by the many problems of the project and his difficulties with the security people. He felt overwhelmed — he could not
go through with it. "There isn't anybody else who can do it," Bacher
told him.[29]

There wasn't, and Oppenheimer knew it. Decades before, he had
come to Los Alamos and found strength. Now, once again, he dug
deep and confronted and overcame his personal demons. Some sort of
Rubicon had been crossed, and suddenly Oppenheimer was all focus.
Whenever a difficult problem arose, he helped to solve it. Whenever
an experiment reached a critical stage, he was there to watch it. He
kept the various threads of the project in his mind, identified the critical issues, and made smart judgments. He was attuned to every sight
and sound and nuance. His supreme talent lay in judging the ideas
of others, in knowing which to back and which not to back. When
tensions developed between personalities, as they inevitably did, he
defused them with a light hand. He put people at ease through his
informality and his interest in personal as well as technical matters.
Oppenheimer was "one of them" — the fellow scientist who used per-
suasion rather than the boss who gave orders.

Occasionally, a side of Oppenheimer appeared — triggered by the
pressure and the tension he lived with constantly — that close
acquaintances remembered from Berkeley. This Oppenheimer would
alternate between encouraging someone with thoughtful, generous
words and wounding him with cutting remarks and intellectual super-
ciliousness. On one occasion, he lashed out at a scientist so suddenly
that others in the room were stunned and embarrassed. "He was thoroughly entitled to [his intellectual arrogance] because he really was a
lot smarter than most of the people there," said a witness to his verbal
lashings, "but some people were irritated by the fact that he made
them feel that he knew it."[30]

Oppenheimer's arrogance betrayed his underlying lack of confidence. It was not something most people sensed on the surface. He
exuded authority, seemed effortlessly good at everything, and was
very charismatic. "He could charm the socks off of people, even if he
really didn't like them that well," one of his secretaries recalled.[31] Yet
it was all a fragile, frantic, uncertain act. Because he was plagued by
inner doubts, Oppenheimer was skilled at sensing — and targeting —
the insecurities of others. And yet he perceived and manipulated not
just people's deepest fears but also their desires, and this made him an

effective leader. "I don't think anybody ever believed he had it in him," said his successor at Los Alamos, director Norris Bradbury, "but he surely did."[32]

Teller was eager to move to Los Alamos. The action was shifting there, and he wanted to be a part of it. He had, after all, helped Oppenheimer organize Los Alamos, select and recruit its staff, and plan its work. Meanwhile, Teller sought to lift the lid on his security clearance caused by the fact that his parents and other relatives were living in Nazi-occupied Hungary. After finally receiving clearance for secret work, Teller, his wife, Mici, and their newborn son, Paul, arrived on the Hill.* That Teller had been invited to Los Alamos was a tribute to his reputation and talents as a theoretical physicist. That he was kept on at Los Alamos would be a tribute to the patience and forbearance of others.

Teller brought with him to Los Alamos a personal possession vital to his peace of mind: a Steinway baby concert grand piano that Mici had bought for him at a Chicago hotel auction. The piano — affectionately called "the monster" — filled the living room of the Tellers' small apartment. It became the primary form of relaxation for Teller — and torment for his neighbors. Teller would stay up late at night — until 3:00 in the morning — playing sonatas on the piano. Once he asked the wife of another physicist who was an accomplished singer to accompany him. She agreed, flattered by Teller's invitation. But flattery quickly turned to disappointment. "I couldn't sing with him," she recalled, "because he drowned me out completely."[33]

Watching him stir a huge mound of sugar into his coffee mug, Los Alamos scientists wondered how a man like Teller could be so genuinely friendly and at the same time so ruthlessly self-absorbed. "Lovable and selfish," concluded a perceptive observer.[34] He could often be seen walking absentmindedly with his heavy, uneven gait (the result of a tramway accident in Munich in the 1920s that had left him with an artificial left foot), his bushy eyebrows moving up and down as he pursued some new idea. As he had always been, he was a gifted and imaginative physicist, with a mind capable of tackling immensely complicated problems, but he was also a temperamental and argumentative man

---

* Teller's security clearance was expedited at the specific request of Oppenheimer, whose own clearance would be withdrawn a decade later as a result of hearings at which Teller testified as a key witness against him. See chapter ten, pp. 277–281.

who aroused frustration and sometimes anger in others. He pursued his ideas with a vain insistence that made him seem a prima donna to his colleagues and found it very difficult to work with people who did not agree with him. Although he could be kind, humorous, and likable, he was also egotistical and unhappy playing second fiddle to anyone. He "was not a team player," said Hans Bethe. "That's right I wasn't," Teller conceded years later. He was devoted to physics, but also ambitious and hungry for recognition.[35] Someone was free to sing, but he would bang his piano louder.

"Teller was brilliant but flighty," said a physicist who worked with him at both the Met Lab and Los Alamos. "He would jump from one idea to another. He did not systematically go through things."[36] Oppenheimer alluded to this quality of Teller's when he told Groves that "there are a few people here whose interests are exclusively 'scientific' in the sense that they will abandon any problem that appears to be soluble."[37] Teller particularly resented doing the tedious computational work involved in making an atomic bomb. He was bored by details, especially if he thought they could be worked out by lesser minds than his own. Instead, he preferred the puzzle of a thermonuclear bomb, and he insisted on working only on it. This exasperated and alienated those who viewed the atomic bomb as the number one wartime priority.

For this reason, Oppenheimer, with I. I. Rabi's encouragement, decided to give the job of Theoretical Division leader to Bethe rather than Teller.[38] Oppenheimer thought Bethe was more likely to get this crucial job done, and that mattered more than Teller's feelings. Though not as creative or imaginative as Teller, Bethe was far more adroit and effective at dealing with others. Oppenheimer also thought Bethe's logic and thoroughness would better serve the project at a stage when detailed calculations had to be carried out and a good deal of administrative work was inevitable. "We had to sit down in our offices and actually work something out," said Bethe, "and this was against [Teller's] style."[39]

Teller bitterly resented Oppenheimer's decision. "When [Oppenheimer] told Bethe and me that he had named Hans to head the division, I was a little hurt," Teller wrote years later with considerable understatement.[40] A proud man with a strong belief in his own ability, Teller felt he ought to have been doing Bethe's job — and would have done it much better. He had been part of the Manhattan Project longer than Bethe, and he considered himself intellectually superior. He considered Bethe a "brick-maker" physicist — thorough, meticulous, but unimaginative — while he considered himself a "bricklayer" — a synthesizer who understood the underlying structure of physics. "I was not happy about having him as my boss," Teller later admitted. "[Bethe] and I did not work well together. He wanted me to work on calculations, while I wanted to continue not only on the hydrogen bomb, but on other novel subjects." Teller brooded about being Bethe's subordinate. The arrangement, Teller later wrote, "marked the beginning of the end of our friendship."[41]

Seeing that Teller was unhappy, Oppenheimer moved him out of Bethe's division and gave him his own group, despite the manpower shortage. Oppenheimer also continued to meet with Teller weekly for an hour of freewheeling discussion — a remarkable concession, given the enormous demands on his time. And though he liked Teller personally, he came to find him inordinately vain and sensitive to slight. One evening, when Oppenheimer gave a party for a visiting British physicist, he inadvertently failed to invite the deputy of the British mission. Oppenheimer sought out the deputy the next day and apologized, adding: "There is an element of relief in this situation: it might have happened with Edward Teller."[42] He also began belittling Teller in private. "In wartime he is an obstructionist," Oppenheimer told one of his confidantes, "and in peacetime he will be a promoter."[43] Teller, for his part, focused much of his resentment toward Bethe on Oppenheimer, whom he began to view with coolness and even hostility.

When Bethe had first arrived in New Mexico, the arid landscape — like the work that lay ahead — frightened and intimidated him. Bethe kept imagining himself walking through the high desert without a drop of water. He coped with his anxiety by throwing himself into his work. The pressure he felt was tremendous. "I had the feeling of pushing a big load," he confessed decades later, adding: "It was probably the most concentrated work I have done in my life."[44]

Bethe was equal to the task. Calm, cool, and thoughtful, he was a patient and effective leader who worked well with others. A tall and heavyset man, Bethe moved and spoke somewhat slowly, but behind his slow speech and movements lay a mind of formidable speed and power that earned him the affectionate nickname "the Battleship." Solid, dependable, and well liked, Bethe was mature and wise in his dealings with people. "You never had any feeling that Hans was going to get upset and fly off the handle," said a friend. "He didn't hesitate to state his particular position on anything, but it was done in a calm and rational manner."[45] His methodical and detail-oriented approach allowed him to face problems squarely, analyze them quietly, and plow straight through them.

Bethe was effective in his work in part because he was highly motivated politically. He understood through bitter personal experience just how evil and threatening were the Nazis. To him and other refugee physicists, they *had* to be defeated. "I went to beat Hitler," he said of his decision to work at Los Alamos. He had no qualms about using the bomb against his native land. "We hoped very much to use it against Germany," Bethe recalled, "and I entirely concurred with that, even though my father and his second wife were still there."[46] A strong sense of teamwork, and the knowledge that their work was vital to the war effort, gave Bethe and his colleagues in the Theoretical Division a strong sense of mission. It kept them going ten hours a day, six days a week.

I. I. Rabi urged other physicists to move to Los Alamos, but Rabi himself never did, only visiting from time to time as a troubleshooter and a consultant — one of the few exceptions to Groves's rigid policy of compartmentalization, which permitted each scientist to know only as much as necessary to do his job, thus restricting the exchange of information within and between project laboratories. Rabi always arrived on the Hill dressed immaculately in a suit topped with a homburg and swinging a large umbrella. "It hasn't rained for months." Oppenheimer and Bethe would smile to him in greeting. Then it would invariably begin to rain, Rabi would open his umbrella, and the other two would get soaking wet as they walked together to the Tech Area. Oppenheimer and Bethe took to calling Rabi the "Rainmaker from Hoboken."

The Rainmaker from Hoboken was savvy, perceptive, and wise. "He was interested in everybody and could talk to anybody — I was very fond of him," said a Los Alamos resident.[47] Careful and deliberate, he preferred to make his points with humor. "One listened to Rabi with great care," said Rose Bethe, voicing a common opinion among those who knew him well, "because, even though he told you things as jokes, they were always serious."[48] Rabi had a special instinct for dealing with people in extraordinary situations. He found it hard to tolerate fools, and he could be quite rough. But if there was something to be done, as Rabi said, "What choice do you have?"[49]

From the beginning of Los Alamos to its end, Rabi appeared on the Hill when needed. His most important function at Los Alamos was his self-described role as Oppenheimer's "fatherly adviser."[50] Oppenheimer was comfortable with Rabi and confided his troubles to him. Rabi listened patiently and offered useful advice. A youth spent in the streets had taught Rabi to be a shrewd judge of people and how to operate effectively in the world of power. He had administrative experience at the MIT radar lab; he had worked with the military; he understood organizations and how to move them — he had tough-minded wisdom. Oppenheimer did not want to formally structure Los Alamos at first. Rabi told him, "You have to have an organization. The laboratory has to be organized in divisions and the divisions into groups. Otherwise, nothing will ever come of it."[51] Should the laboratory be put under military control? Rabi adamantly opposed the induction of scientists into the army. Oppenheimer listened.

Rabi counseled Oppenheimer discreetly, but he never hesitated to stand up to Oppenheimer's intellectual bullying, which paradoxically had a calming effect on the Los Alamos director. Rabi also never hesitated to speak frankly and bluntly with Groves. When he learned about the housing that Groves planned for the Hill, he told the general, "You are treating these scientists as if they were privates in the Army. You should realize that there are fewer fellows of the American Physical Society than brigadiers [Groves's rank] in the US Army."[52] The housing arrangements were improved.

Offered the laboratory's deputy directorship by Oppenheimer, Rabi turned it down, resisting the pressure of personal friendship and Oppenheimer's considerable charm. Rabi did so because, as he explained to Oppenheimer, he did not want to make the atomic bomb "the culmination of three centuries of physics."[53]

All of them felt the pressure of the work. They knew the project involved tens of thousands of people at sites across the country. They knew it was enormously expensive. And "if we ever forgot any of this," Hans Bethe remembered, "General Groves would tell us."[54] Many had family and relatives in concentration camps. A Polish physicist did not know whether his wife and children, left behind in Poland, were dead or alive. A British physicist had lost his wife to a German bombing raid. The war came close even on the Hill when Teller listened to a radio broadcast on fighting in Hungary, and said somberly, "My family is there." Anxiety and fear haunted them day and night.

One physicist received a postcard from his brother in the fall of 1944, written from the front lines in Italy. Its complete message was "Hurry up!" The brother was killed in action that October.[55]

A fear of success also existed among them, for they were building a weapon so horrible that its use, which seemed the logical culmination of their efforts, could not easily be distinguished from barbarism. It was necessary for them to fear that the Nazis were working toward the same end, for only this could ease their concerns about the destructiveness of the bomb they were making — that and the hope that such a weapon might end war because nations couldn't afford its cost in human lives. They often lay awake at night wondering, "Is this right?" Still, it never occurred to anyone to stop. In their minds, they were doing their duty — in some cases, for no other reason than it was their duty; in other cases, because they were unable to conceive of any other course or were, perhaps, afraid to think of any other course. It was not a matter of choice but necessity. This was the morality imposed by brute circumstance, by habit, by the unspoken social demand that most did not have the strength to refuse, or, often, to imagine refusing.

The reactions to such tensions varied. Some thought, "We've worked on this thing and let's use it — that's what it's for — and see if we can't get the war stopped."[56] Some secretly hoped the technical difficulties would prove insurmountable. If it *was* impossible to develop an atomic bomb, there wouldn't be any danger of the Nazis getting one either. Some of them hoped the war would end before the bomb could be finished. Some harbored moral qualms about the bomb, but many more were preoccupied by work or were lulled into unreflective self-importance by the weapon's power. Gradually, as they became more deeply involved in the work, their misgivings began to fade — or were buried — and the tension of achievement took over and became the driving force, a kind of Faustian fascination about whether the bomb would really work. They had to achieve what they had set out to do. All of them sensed they were involved in something momentous, but they did not see clearly exactly what it was.

Each coped with these complicated feelings in his own way. Oppenheimer tried to relax at night behind the walls of his stone-and-timber cottage set behind a stand of poplars and spruces at the end of Bathtub Row. The furniture was Spanish rustic and rattan, an easy chair with a laurel pattern, serapes on the sofa, and black pueblo pottery on the fireplace mantel. A Picasso lithograph and pictures of the Hindu god Krishna hung on the walls. Oppenheimer drank a martini while Kitty sat nearby, her legs curled beneath her on a sofa, an ash-tray in her lap. But the project was never far away; soldiers patrolled outside the house around the clock. His Native American house-keeper sensed the anxiety. "Dr. Oppenheimer was quiet. . . . He was worried. You could tell it by his face; it was down. Even his wife was worried. I sensed a lot of tension."[57]

Occasionally, Oppenheimer would drive down to a teahouse at Otowi Bridge over the Rio Grande that was run by Edith Warner, a quiet and reserved woman who lived as a neighbor to the Indians of nearby San Ildefonso Pueblo. He drew strength from the warmth that Warner radiated. Juniper wood burned in her adobe fireplace. Often there was the smell of bread that had just been taken from the oven and covered with a cloth on the table under the kitchen window. Black pottery plates stood upright on open shelves along one wall, with cups and saucers in terra-cotta colors from Mexico. Orange candles and red-and-black-striped Chimayo squares brightened the wall; a Navajo rug covered part of the rough floor.

There Oppenheimer drank tea and ate cake in a small room that looked through large windows toward the Sangre de Cristos. Warner, who observed these mountains daily, described what Oppen-heimer saw:

> Sometimes the light makes each range stand out, casting sharp shadows on the ones behind. Occasionally when the air is very clear, there is a strange and breath-taking shining light on the green aspen leaves. At evening the twilight may run quickly from the valley, shrouding almost at once the highest peaks. Or mauve and rose move slowly upward, turning to blood-red on the snow above. One morning they may be purple cardboard mountains sharpcut against the sky. On another they will have withdrawn into themselves. Sometimes I have watched ghost mountains with substance only in their dark outline. It seems then as if the mountains had gone down into their very roots, leaving an empty frame.[58]

Caught up as he now was in the whirlpool of war, the furious plans to construct a deadly weapon, the impossible and often agonizing decisions that had to be weighed and implemented every day, often every moment, Oppenheimer had a particular need for tranquility and quiet reflection that these hours at Edith Warner's teahouse filled. As one whose daily thoughts were involved with techniques of destruction, he found healing here for his divided spirit.

Teller, when burdens seemed greatest, would sit down at his concert grand piano and play the soothing sounds of Bach and Mozart. He gave occasional recitals in the Fuller Lodge dining hall. The room, with a running balcony and a massive stone fireplace at either end, had walls of honeyed pine and looked more like the dining room of a national park lodge than the army-camp messes where most of Los Alamos ate. The center of attention, Teller would beam with satisfaction. His technique was loose but his playing showed a lot of determination and feeling and musicality. Teller also delighted in simple pleasures. His favorite author was Lewis Carroll, and he read Carroll's stories and poems to his son, Paul, long before the child could understand them. He could be as playful as his little boy when he narrated fairy tales on community radio station KRS — a deep voice with a Middle European accent telling bedtime stories. When he reached a funny passage, he let out a very loud, high-pitched giggle.

Bethe relieved the pressure by hiking nearly every Sunday in the nearby mountains, frequently climbing Lake Peak (12,500 feet) across the Rio Grande Valley in the Sangre de Cristos. At the top, through a fringe of cedars, spread an alpine meadow extravagantly carpeted with purple mariposa lilies. These hikes gave Bethe a chance to unburden himself by giving his body exercise and his mind a chance to wander. Others went on weekend camping and fishing trips, rock-gathering expeditions, pueblo visits, and other activities that relieved the tensions of the project and the weight of the moral justifications of bomb making. Some would ride the bus to Santa Fe and sit in the plaza in the center of town, drowsing in a sunny siesta, then dine at the La Fonda, an adobe hotel with exposed beams and wooden balconies. Others walked the quiet streets of old Santa Fe, peering over adobe walls that seemed to soak up the abundant sunshine into the romantic and exotic gardens within. Some found that they could never leave their work behind. They were missing something.

On December 30, 1943, an older man arrived on the Hill as a consultant to the British delegation. His security guards referred to him as "Mr. Nicholas Baker" but physicists instantly recognized "Mr. Baker" as Niels Bohr. Bohr's long odyssey from Copenhagen to Los Alamos had begun in April 1940, when Germany invaded and occupied

Denmark. Half Jewish, Bohr was put under surveillance and his phones were tapped. Secretly communicating with the Danish resistance, he urged his country's leaders to fight Jewish deportations from Denmark, even as German troops patrolled the street in front of his institute.

In late September 1941, as German troops neared Moscow and looked poised to knock Russia out of the war, Bohr received a visit from Heisenberg. The two had once been very close — mentor and beloved protégé. Now Heisenberg was back as the leading scientist of a nation that seemed on the verge of conquering all of Europe. Bohr greeted his former student with careful politeness and invited him into his office at the institute. They busily avoided each other's eyes as they began their conversation. Shy and arrogant, Heisenberg expressed his confidence that Germany would win the war but told Bohr that if the war lasted long enough it would be decided by atomic bombs, said that he was involved in such research for Nazi Germany, and had no doubt that it could be done. After the war, Heisenberg would claim that he was subtly hinting at moral qualms about building an atomic weapon in wartime and suggesting that physicists on both sides of the conflict should refuse to do so. But Bohr, fearful and shaken, did not see it that way. He later recalled that Heisenberg "gave no hint about efforts on the part of German scientists to prevent such a development."[59] Visibly startled by what Heisenberg had said but trying to contain his deep fright, Bohr said nothing and suddenly cut short the conversation. Afterward, he told his family that Heisenberg had tried to pump him for information about fission and, by implication, the Allied atomic project. Hans Bethe was probably closest to the truth when he later remarked that "one talked with one set of assumptions and the other with a totally different set of assumptions."[60] The meeting, however, unquestionably intensified Bohr's suspicion, and fear, that the Nazis were racing toward an atomic bomb.

Two years later, in September 1943, Bohr learned from the Swedish ambassador in Copenhagen that deportation of Danish Jews would begin soon. The ambassador hinted that Bohr, whose mother was Jewish, would be arrested himself. Confirmation came the next morning from an informer at Gestapo headquarters in Copenhagen who had seen orders for Bohr's arrest and deportation. Late that afternoon, Bohr and his wife, Margrethe, walked to a seaside garden and hid in a gardener's shed. They waited anxiously for nightfall. Then, at a pre-arranged time, they left the shed and crossed to the beach. From the beach a motorboat took them out to a fishing boat. Dodging German minefields, they crossed the choppy sound between Denmark and Sweden by moonlight.

When Bohr landed in Sweden, a Swedish officer was told to bring him to Stockholm and to attract no attention on the way. (The officer was too proud of having the famous Dane in his charge, so despite orders he stopped in many places for a drink, each time saying, "Do you know whom I am escorting to Stockholm . . . ?"[61]) When Bohr reached Stockholm the next day, he was put up in the home of a Danish diplomat and never went out alone. Britain moved its diplomatic pouch in and out of Sweden in a fast, unarmed bomber that flew at a high altitude to avoid German antiaircraft batteries along the coast of Norway. The plane's bomb bay was fitted for a single passenger. Temporarily leaving his wife behind, Bohr boarded the plane for the flight to England on October sixth. Once in London, he learned from British scientists that fission research had progressed a great deal since his stay in Princeton four years earlier. An atomic bomb was being made at Los Alamos, the British were preparing to send a team there, and they wanted Bohr to join it.

Bohr agreed to join the British team at Los Alamos. When he reached the United States in December, his first stop was the sprawling U-235 separation plant at Oak Ridge. Seeing what he saw, and being one of the most farsighted of men, he had no doubt now that the atomic bomb would be built, and would be a presence in the world forever. Groves joined him afterward at the Met Lab, and together they boarded a train for Los Alamos. Bohr did most of the talking as their train hurtled south across the Plains and then west over the Rockies, Groves straining to listen as the clicking of the wheels on the tracks and the clanking of the railroad cars almost drowned out Bohr's mumbling voice. When they finally reached Los Alamos, Oppenheimer was there to greet them. He noticed that Groves looked tired and irritated. He asked the general what the trouble was. "I've been listening to Bohr," he grumbled.[62]

Oppenheimer arranged a reception for Bohr at his home with other physicists. When Bohr spotted Teller, he said, "Didn't I tell you that you could not make a nuclear explosive without turning the whole country into a huge factory? Now you have gone and done it."[63] Bohr then related an account of his personal adventures, including his conversation two years earlier with Heisenberg. He said that Heisenberg and other talented German physicists were diligently working on a bomb. The thought of how far the Nazis might have come in the years since the discovery of fission was enough to make everyone at the reception shudder. Bohr also related what he knew about Nazi-occupied Europe to those who had left loved ones behind. The atmosphere was very somber.

The first question Bohr put to physicists at Los Alamos was: "Is it really big enough?" — was the atomic bomb they were building big enough to make future wars too destructive to be sane? Bohr made a clear distinction between the bomb's wartime use, which he considered an all but inevitable military decision, and its political and diplomatic implications, which bore on the longer-range issues of world peace and security and relations among nations. "What role it [the bomb] may play in the present war," Bohr wrote, was a question "quite apart" from the overriding concern: the need to avoid an atomic arms race.[64]

Bohr's thinking was shaped by two assumptions: first, the bomb's destructiveness would be unprecedented and indiscriminate; and second, such a weapon could not be monopolized — sooner or later it would be developed by other nations — thus posing the frightful prospect of a nuclear arms race. Bohr had no doubt that scientists in the Soviet Union would also grasp the significance of the bomb and convey their understanding to Stalin just as scientists in the United States had conveyed their understanding to Roosevelt. He also believed that if statesmen could be made to see the military and political implications of atomic weapons, they would respond positively to international control. There were no historical precedents to guide them, he knew, but the threat of a nuclear-armed world was also unprecedented. If national security was not achieved by nations through international control of atomic energy, he concluded, they would inevitably indulge in an arms race that would plant the seeds of their own destruction. These ideas would become Bohr's central preoccupation from 1943 until the end of the war.

Bohr spent many hours that winter discussing his ideas with Oppenheimer, who was deeply impressed. Bohr had articulated thoughts and sentiments that lay unformed and unexpressed in Oppenheimer's own mind and conscience. Indeed, Oppenheimer was so taken by the depth and insight of Bohr's thinking that he began to regard him as a kind of sage. One afternoon, as Oppenheimer and his assistant David Hawkins were escorting Bohr from the Tech Area back to his room at Fuller Lodge, they skirted Ashley Pond and Bohr tested the ice along the bank. "My God," Oppenheimer whispered to Hawkins, "suppose he should slip? Suppose he should fall through? What would we all do then?"[65]

Oppenheimer noticed that Bohr never seemed relaxed. He always had a sad expression on his face and looked as though he carried all of the cares of the world on his broad shoulders. In a very real sense he did, and he knew it. Bohr forced his colleagues to come to terms with what they were doing. He inspired them to begin their soul-searching — and to think about the future. Numerous Los Alamos physicists poured out their worry and guilt to him in private discussions that went on far into the night. He understood; he spoke the same language; he shared the responsibility. He did not need to remind them of the evils of Nazism or the horror of an atomic bomb in Hitler's hands, but he did not shy away from the ethical and moral problems raised by building a weapon of mass destruction and the terrifying potential of a nuclear arms race.

Bohr spoke the bravest words in the most hesitant and gentle voice. He always seemed to look straight at his listener and his face was difficult to forget, with its eyes full of intelligence and sadness. He addressed matters squarely and frankly. Always the paradoxist, he continued to argue that every problem bore the seeds of its own solution. And here he believed that the atomic bomb could not only end this war but even end war as a means of settling disputes between nations. His thinking brought hope to others who wanted to believe that such a devastating weapon would make leaders see that future wars would be suicidal.

Bohr used hikes with other physicists in the mountains and canyons around Los Alamos to spread his message. As he had done during the train ride with Groves, he placed huge demands on his listener. He spoke very low and softly, often with a pipe clenched in his teeth. People closed in around Bohr to hear, but as they pressed near his voice fell further, until finally the listeners formed a straining, hushed knot around him. "He speaks, everyone listens," was the saying on the Hill. "And you had to listen," remembered a physicist who was there, "because he spoke in such a low voice that you couldn't hear if you didn't."[66] "This is the keston," Bohr would say. "What does 'keston' mean?" a frustrated listener would say. "Keston means question," someone would finally realize.[67]

Convinced that international control could be achieved only if the Soviet Union was told about the Manhattan Project before the bomb was a certainty and before the war was over — thus creating a postwar political climate of cooperation rather than confrontation — Bohr set out to convince President Roosevelt and British Prime Minister Winston Churchill to approach Stalin on this all-important subject. Bohr did not think technical details of the bomb should be revealed to the Russians; he simply thought that informing them of the bomb's existence might open the way for some sort of international arms control agreement. He understood that such an initiative did not guarantee the Soviet Union's postwar cooperation; but he also believed that its cooperation was unlikely, if not impossible, unless such an initiative was made. The timing, moreover, was crucial: the initiative had to be made before developments proceeded so far as to make an approach to the Russians appear more coercive than friendly.

Bohr contacted Roosevelt through Supreme Court Justice Felix Frankfurter, a friend and adviser of FDR whom Bohr had befriended at the University of Oxford before the war. Frankfurter invited Bohr to lunch at the Supreme Court when Bohr returned to Washington in February 1944. There, in the privacy of Frankfurter's chambers, Bohr presented his ideas. Frankfurter relayed them to the president in an Oval Office meeting at the end of the month. Roosevelt confronted a dilemma: on the one hand, to exclude Stalin from any official information about the bomb — even though FDR had been informed by Army Intelligence that the Soviet Union was already getting information about vital secrets through espionage — was bound to affect Soviet perceptions and thus the prospects for postwar cooperation; on the other hand, to continue to withhold such information might yield diplomatic leverage and military advantages vis-à-vis Russia after the war against Nazi Germany was over.

Whatever his thinking, Roosevelt left Frankfurter with the impression that he was "plainly impressed" by Frankfurter's account of the matter. When Frankfurter had suggested that the solution to the problem of the atomic bomb might be more important than the plans for a United Nations, FDR had ostensibly agreed. Moreover, he had authorized Frankfurter to tell Bohr that he might inform "our friends in London that the President was most eager to explore the proper safeguards in relation to [the bomb]." Frankfurter also told Bohr that Roosevelt was "worried to death" about the bomb and was very eager for all the help he could get in dealing with this problem.[68]

In April, Bohr traveled to Britain specifically to see Churchill. While waiting for an audience with the prime minister, he was sent a letter by a Russian physicist. After alerting British security officers, Bohr went to the Soviet embassy in London to pick up the letter, where a Soviet diplomat asked him what information he had about secret war work by American and British scientists. Bohr finessed the question by quickly changing the subject, but to Bohr the inquiry meant that the Soviets knew of the Manhattan Project and were probably working on a bomb of their own. This reinforced Bohr's conviction that the only solution was international control.

Bohr finally won an appointment at 10 Downing Street on May 16, 1944. The meeting misfired from the start. Churchill was preoccupied, with D day only three weeks away. Bohr began by mumbling in his typically discursive way. Churchill grew impatient — why didn't he come to the point? Here was a scientist presuming to advise *him* about international affairs and naive enough to urge informing the Russians about the most secret Anglo-American project of the war. The prime minister curtly told him: "I cannot see what you are talking about. After all, this new bomb is just going to be bigger than our present bombs. It involves no difference in the principles of war. And as for any postwar problems, there are none that cannot be amicably settled between me and my friend, President Roosevelt." Churchill preferred an Anglo-American monopoly of the bomb to postwar international control as a way to check Soviet adventurism and to preserve Britain's influence in the world. Before he would tell Stalin anything about the bomb, he wanted some assurance of cooperation. To Bohr, that was putting the cart before the horse. As the meeting ended, Bohr, sensing failure, asked if he could send the prime minister a letter developing the points he wanted to make. "It will be an honor for me to receive a letter from you," answered Churchill, but then added tartly, "But not about politics."[69] "We did not speak the same language," Bohr said ruefully afterward.[70]

Churchill's assumptions about the bomb and his expectations about the future were, of course, governed by his understanding of the past. He did not anticipate that the bomb would revolutionize international relations and he did not believe anything could be gained by surrendering the atomic monopoly he thought America and Britain would enjoy after the war.

Bohr returned to the United States less than a week after D day, buoyed by the thought that the war was entering its final phase but discouraged by his failure to persuade Churchill. He reported to Frankfurter on his dismal meeting with the prime minister and Frankfurter carried the news to Roosevelt, who expressed a willingness to see the Danish physicist again. The meeting was arranged for August twenty-sixth. FDR received Bohr in the Oval Office late that afternoon for an hour and a half of private talk. He welcomed Bohr with a big smile. Bohr sat down beside the president's desk. In front of him windows framed a view of the Washington Monument and the Jefferson Memorial. Roosevelt was warm, cordial, and amiably sympathetic, as usual.

The two men spoke in a frank and encouraging manner. Bohr told his son, Aage, after the meeting that Roosevelt agreed an approach to the Soviet Union had to be tried along the lines that Bohr suggested. The president said he was optimistic that such an approach would yield a "good result." In his opinion, Stalin was enough of a realist to understand the bomb's revolutionary importance and consequences. FDR also expressed confidence to Bohr that Churchill would come around to his view of things. The two leaders had disagreed before, he said, but they always resolved their differences in the end. Roosevelt suggested another meeting might be useful after he had spoken with Churchill about the matter at the second Quebec Conference scheduled for the following month.[71]

Bohr was hopeful as Roosevelt met Churchill in Quebec on September eleventh and the two leaders then traveled to the president's estate along the Hudson River in upstate New York a week later to continue their talks more privately. High on their agenda was the Manhattan Project. Seated amid the brilliant foliage of a Hyde Park autumn, FDR and Churchill signed a secret agreement that codified their position on the bomb. The heart of their joint agreement said this:

> The suggestion that the world should be informed regarding [the Manhattan Project] with a view to an international agreement regarding its control and use, is not accepted. The matter should continue to be regarded as of the utmost secrecy . . . Enquiries should be made regarding the activities of Professor Bohr and steps taken to ensure that he is responsible for no leakage of information, particularly to the Russians.[72]

Roosevelt and Churchill had resolved to maintain the Anglo-American atomic monopoly — despite Bohr's warning that it was a chimera — as a counter against Stalin's postwar ambitions. The two leaders, unable to grasp the technical fact that fission was common knowledge among scientists throughout the world and that Japan, Germany, and Russia — like Britain — had not pursued a bomb because they lacked the resources in the middle of a war, could not conceive of forgoing an advantage they thought would assure the peace on terms they felt deep in their hearts were best for mankind. Their agreement may also have reflected their fear that Stalin's mistrust would only be aroused if he were informed of the project's existence and then did not receive detailed information about it. Whatever the reasons, Bohr was never invited to meet with either leader again. There would be no attempt at international control *before* the bomb became a reality. And at the very moment FDR and Churchill signed their secret agreement, a member of the British team at Los Alamos, Klaus Fuchs, was busy betraying many of the details of the bomb to Soviet agents. The hoped-for monopoly would not last long.

CHAPTER 6

The Decision to Use the Bomb

BETWEEN HIS MEETING with Churchill in September 1944 and his death in April 1945, Roosevelt underwent no change in his attitude toward the bomb. But in the laboratories of the Manhattan Project, particularly the Met Lab, scientists became increasingly concerned during late 1944 and early 1945 about the implications of their work. To their earlier anxiety about military control was now added the dawning fear that they might succeed in making a weapon of mass destruction. This was especially true of Leo Szilard. The big question in his mind shifted from "Can an atomic bomb be made?" to "What will happen once it is?"

This question increasingly consumed Szilard's thinking as his workload decreased. With a chain-reacting pile achieved and plutonium production underway at Hanford, the Met Lab had essentially completed its task. The focus of effort had shifted to Los Alamos. This gave Szilard more time to reflect, and the more he reflected the less enamored he became of the bomb. Sitting in his room — the space practically bare except for an old traveling bag which served as a closet — at the Quadrangle Club of the University of Chicago or strolling the green expanse of the Midway south of the university on evenings and weekends, he turned his far-reaching mind to a host of questions: Should Russia be told about the bomb? If Germany was defeated before the bomb was ready — as seemed increasingly likely — should it be used against Japan? Could international control be achieved, and if so, what form should it take?

Szilard first addressed these questions in January 1944, when he sent Vannevar Bush a memorandum emphasizing for the first time not the urgency of beating Nazi Germany to the bomb but what it would mean to the world once the bomb was made. "If peace is organized before it has penetrated the public's mind that the potentialities of atomic bombs are a reality," he wrote, "it will be impossible to have a peace that is based on reality." And yet he acknowledged a stark dilemma: "It will hardly be possible to get political action along that line unless high efficiency atomic bombs have actually been used in this war and the fact of their destructive power has deeply penetrated the mind of the public."[1]

Other Met Lab scientists also began contemplating the bomb's implications. The most sophisticated and far-reaching study was conducted by a group that included Fermi. The report, formally titled "Prospectus on Nucleonics," and known as the Jeffries Report after its chairman, physicist Zay Jeffries, called for a general statement to the American public revealing the existence of the Manhattan Project, the destructive potential of the bomb, and the fact that it would inevitably affect relations between nations in the future. The report owed its inspiration to Compton, who had asked Met Lab scientists for their ideas the year before. From then on, with Compton's encouragement, the group devoted serious thought to postwar problems.[2]

The Jeffries Report, submitted to Compton in November 1944, reflected a broad spectrum of scientific opinion. The quality and quantity of viewpoints — the report was sixty-five typewritten pages in length — showed that the implications of the new weapon had been discussed in considerable detail. Its assessment was presented in the form of a warning, coupled with a set of recommendations. A world armed with atomic bombs was analogous to two people armed with machine guns locked in a room, the report said. Since the person who shoots first kills his rival, it is likely that one of them will do so to remove the fear of being attacked. The prospect of this kind of preventive warfare would become a grim reality — as America's road to war against the specter of a nuclear-armed Iraq under Saddam Hussein half a century later attests — unless mutual understanding were achieved and the production of atomic bombs were either prevented entirely or limited to a carefully controlled pool for checking any potential disturbance of the peace. The report also noted that "it would be surprising if the Russians are not also diligently engaged in such work." A peace based on uncontrolled and perhaps clandestine development of nuclear weapons was little more than an armistice and was bound to end, sooner or later, in catastrophe. A central authority for the control of atomic energy was necessary if the world was to avoid disaster. Compton submitted the Jeffries Report to Groves, who chose not to pass it along to policy makers.[3]

Bohr decided to make one last approach to policy makers himself. In early April 1945, he prepared a detailed memorandum on the bomb's postwar implications for Roosevelt. The memo included many farsighted proposals later adopted by the U.S. government for the international control of atomic energy: technical inspection, an international inspection agency, and a distinction between "safe" and "dangerous" activities in the realm of nuclear research. Bohr was arguing that the only hope for humanity in the long run depended upon an unprecedented act of statesmanship in the short run.[4] Bohr asked British Ambassador Lord Halifax and Felix Frankfurter to get it to the president. Halifax and Frankfurter discussed Bohr's request on a stroll through Rock Creek Park on the afternoon of April twelfth. It was a beautiful spring day in Washington, the sun bright and warm and the leaves and grass emerald green. Suddenly church bells began to toll until the air filled with their sound. Halifax and Frankfurter saw people hurrying to speak to others. Roosevelt had died of a cerebral hemorrhage in Warm Springs, Georgia. With that, Szilard's initiative was halted.

Several weeks before, Szilard had also prepared a memorandum for FDR. Remarkably perceptive, the memo addressed a number of central problems: the escalation of nuclear weapons technology from atomic to thermonuclear bombs, the vulnerability of an urbanized nation like the United States to nuclear attack, and challenges involving control of raw materials and on-site inspections. Szilard predicted that America faced a stark choice: strike an agreement with the Russians or compete with them in an atomic arms race after the war. The great danger of such a race was "the possibility of the outbreak of *a preventive war*. Such a war might be the outcome of the fear that the other country might strike first, and no amount of good will on the part of both nations might be sufficient to prevent the outbreak of a war if such an explosive situation were allowed to develop." Only international control could avert this danger. The U.S. government was about to arrive at decisions, he warned, that would control the course of events after the war. Those decisions ought to be based on careful estimates of future possibilities, not simply "on the present evidence relating to atomic bombs."[5]

Szilard had discussed his memo with Lawrence. They met at the Chicago rail station, Lawrence reading and commenting on the memo as he waited to change trains.[6] Lawrence encouraged Szilard to forward the memo to the president through First Lady Eleanor Roosevelt, who agreed to see him. With a White House appointment thus set, Szilard went to Compton's office armed with his memorandum. He was nervous as Compton slowly read the memo, expecting to be scolded for again going outside official channels. To Szilard's astonishment, Compton cheered him on, saying, "I hope that you will get the President to read this." "Elated by finding no resistance where I expected resistance," Szilard recalled, "I went back to my office. I hadn't been in my office for five minutes when there was a knock on the door and Compton's assistant came in, telling me that he had just heard over the radio that President Roosevelt had died."[7]

FDR's death shocked Szilard and the entire nation. Vice President Harry S Truman now assumed the burdens of commander in chief in a war that — especially against Japan — was growing fierce and pitiless. Between February and March 1945, three Marine divisions had slugged their way across Iwo Jima, a western Pacific island of volcanic ash, rock, and stinking sulfur fumes. The island's 21,000 Japanese defenders meant to make its conquest so costly that Americans would recoil from invading their homeland. The battle for Iwo Jima became a nightmare of relentless attacks and swarms of flies feeding on dead flesh. One Marine despaired, "They send you to a place and you get shot to hell and maybe they pull you back. But then they send you right up again and then you get murdered. God, you stay there until you get killed or until you can't stand it any more."[8] Five weeks of fighting on Iwo Jima cost the Marine Corps nearly 7,000 dead and 22,000 wounded out of 60,000 committed — the highest casualty rate in Marine Corps history. Its three divisions had to be rebuilt with teenage replacements. The Japanese on Iwo Jima perished almost to a man, having inflicted more casualties in killed and wounded than they suffered for the first time in the war.

Things would be even worse during the Battle of Okinawa between April and June, when Americans encountered the most savage Japanese resistance of the war. Kamikaze suicide bombers slammed into navy ships offshore, turning destroyers into flaming junk heaps manned by bloody remnants of their crews. The kamikaze attacks were alien and terrifying; they confirmed for Americans the extent of Japanese doggedness and desperation even as the United States ground down Japan's war machine. The navy suffered 10,000 casualties, half of them killed. Fighting on the island was a slaughter. Before it was over, more than 100,000 Japanese soldiers and another 100,000 native Okinawans had perished. The U.S. army lost 40,000 men, a fourth of them killed in action. Thousands of Americans and Japanese were being killed on the beaches and in the jungles of the Pacific every week.

In the skies over Japan, giant American B-29 bombers were running massive raids against cities, wiping them off the map, one after another, like the wrath of God. The results were devastating and appalling. Twenty-two million Japanese — 30 percent of the country's entire population — were rendered homeless by fire raids that razed 178 square miles of densely populated urban areas. The fire raids inflicted 2,200,000 civilian casualties, including approximately 900,000 killed. The number of Japan's civilians killed exceeded its combat casualties of approximately 780,000.

Nothing illustrated the escalating violence of the Pacific War — and the declining restraint of its combatants — more vividly than the B-29 fire raid against Tokyo in March 1945. At the start of the war, Roosevelt had entreated all combatants to refrain from bombing civilians and recalled with pride that "the United States consistently has taken the lead in urging that this inhuman practice be prohibited."[9] Now America launched a thousand-plane bombing raid deliberately designed to burn Japan's capital city — and its civilian inhabitants who lived there, crowded in wood-and-paper houses — to ashes.

Shortly after midnight on March tenth, residents of Tokyo peered out of their air-raid shelters and saw an eerie sight above the city. Reflecting spectral colors from flak bursts and searchlights, hundreds of B-29s descended slowly, their bomb bays filled with six-pound incendiary bomblets that spewed burning gelatinized gasoline that stuck to its targets and was inextinguishable. The bomblets were intended to set the city afire and they did, splashing a flaming dew across wooden roofs and spreading fire everywhere. Wind whipped hundreds of small fires into great walls of flame, a thermal hurricane that leapt streets, firebreaks, and canals at dizzying speed. It acted like a giant bellows, superheating the air to eighteen hundred degrees Fahrenheit. B-29s in later attack waves spotted the growing cauldron while still far out at sea. As they flew over the boiling city, they bounced violently as thermal updrafts from the vast and intense conflagration below knocked them about like paper airplanes. At six thousand feet the heat was so intense that crews had to don oxygen masks to breathe. Even at this altitude, American airmen could smell the soot and the burning flesh and vomited. A bombardier who flew above Tokyo that night remembered it as "the most terrifying thing I've ever known."[10]

Fire was not the only danger to Japanese civilians below. Superheated vapors rushing ahead of the flames killed or knocked victims unconscious even before the fires reached them. Death came in many agonizing ways: oxygen deficiency, carbon-monoxide poisoning, radiant heat, direct flames, and the trampling feet of stampeding crowds. Canals and ponds through the city offered no relief; luckless bathers were boiled alive or drowned as frantic crowds pushed them down in the superheated water. When the raid was over, sixteen square miles had been burned out, one million people were homeless, and upward of 100,000 had perished. Only a few sounds could be heard across the smoking moonscape of vast desolation the next morning: the coughing and gasping of victims with scarred lungs, the occasional call of the name of a loved one.

In an eerie — almost unbelievable — irony, on the same night as the massive B-29 fire raid on Tokyo, a high-altitude Japanese balloon dangling two small incendiary bombs, after drifting across the Pacific Ocean on the jet stream, flukishly fell on the Hanford nuclear reservation in remote south central Washington state. Ropes dangling from the balloon became entangled in the electrical line feeding power to the building housing a nuclear pile. The pile had to be shut down at once, though the power was restored a few hours later. It was this plant that was producing the plutonium that would devastate Nagasaki.

The Manhattan Project, like the war itself, was nearing its climax in the spring of 1945. The project had proceeded with Roosevelt's steadfast support, and although the responsibility was now Truman's, the new president was constrained by the choices of his prestigious predecessor. FDR had refused to broach the subject of international control with Stalin and had indicated his intention to use the bomb to help win the war. Such policies molded the outlook of his successor, who was uninformed, unprepared, and unsure of himself. Truman had met with FDR only *twice* between his inauguration as vice president on January twentieth and Roosevelt's death on April twelfth — both times on trivial matters. He was unaware of the agreement FDR and Churchill had reached at Hyde Park. Nor did Truman's experience as chairman of the Senate Committee to Investigate the National Defense Program prepare him to deal with the Manhattan Project, because the secret had been withheld from him. In a subtle but important respect, the new president was at the mercy of decisions already made and events rapidly unfolding.

To compensate for his inexperience, his ignorance, and his anxiety to do well the job suddenly thrust upon him, Truman relied heavily on his inherited advisers, particularly Secretary of War Henry Stimson and James F. Byrnes, a close confidante of Truman who had been his mentor in the Senate, a Supreme Court justice, and war mobilization director under Roosevelt. The race for the atomic bomb was consuming an increasing amount of Stimson's time by April 1945, even as the war in the Pacific grew fierce and the weight of his seventy-seven years left him in need of rest every afternoon; and as he became more deeply involved with atomic matters, he began to ponder and reflect.

Stimson inclined toward the bomb's wartime use and to hold the secret of the bomb as a reward to induce Stalin's cooperation. Although he knew the Soviets were spying on the project, he did not believe they had acquired any crucial information; and while he was troubled about the possible effect of continuing to keep them officially uninformed about the enterprise, he believed that it was essential, as he wrote in his diary at the end of 1944, "not to take them into our confidence until we were sure to get a real quid pro quo from our frankness." Stimson had no illusions about the possibility of keeping such a secret permanently, but he did not think "it was yet time to share it with Russia."[11] Stimson did not intend to threaten the Soviet Union with the new weapon, but he expected that once its power was demonstrated, the Soviets would be more cooperative about postwar issues.

At the end of Truman's first Cabinet meeting, hastily convened after he was sworn in on April twelfth, Stimson remained behind. He would explain the details later, he said, but before departing he wanted to inform the new president of "a new explosive of almost unbelievable destructive power."[12] Two weeks later, on April twenty-fifth, Stimson and Groves briefed Truman on the details of the Manhattan Project. They told him scientists would soon complete "the most terrible weapon ever known in human history," one of which "could destroy a whole city." They were confident the weapon would bring the bloody war to a rapid conclusion, thereby justifying the years of effort, the vast expenditures, and the judgment of officials responsible for the project. A serious and thoughtful man, Stimson also reflected on the bomb's larger meaning in an accompanying memo. The world, "in its present state of moral advancement compared with its technical development[,] would be eventually at the mercy of such a weapon," he warned the new president, adding: "Modern civilization might be completely destroyed." Stimson asserted that "a certain moral responsibility" flowed from U.S. leadership in this field that the nation could not shirk "without very serious responsibility for any disaster to civilization which it would further."[13]

To cope with this difficult challenge, Stimson suggested the establishment of a committee to consider the proper use of the bomb once it was finished and the postwar problems inherent in its development. Truman agreed, and the Interim Committee, as the advisory group came to be known, was created on May 1, 1945.* Stimson sought to keep the Interim Committee small enough to conduct meaningful discussions but varied enough in its membership to represent diverse viewpoints. More than a year after Bohr had urged policy makers to begin looking ahead, machinery was finally established to consider the most momentous and dangerous development of the war. Stimson's charge to the committee asked for advice about *how*, but not *whether*, the bomb should be used against Japan. That the bomb would be used once it was ready seems to have been a foregone conclusion.

A Scientific Advisory Panel to the Interim Committee was also created, composed of Compton, Lawrence, Oppenheimer, and Fermi, the first three chosen because they were directors of the Chicago, Berkeley, and Los Alamos laboratories; Fermi, because of his unrivaled knowledge of nuclear physics. The Scientific Advisory Panel reflected policy makers' desire for expert advice, but it was also an attempt to preempt discontent among scientists if decisions were made about how to use the bomb without consulting those who had made it.

Somewhat like Szilard, Oppenheimer, after much soul-searching,

---

*The Interim Committee had seven members: Stimson, as chairman (with his special assistant George Harrison as deputy); Ralph Bard, an undersecretary, representing the Navy Department; Will Clayton an assistant secretary, from the State Department; experienced scientific administrators Vannevar Bush, James Conant, and Karl Compton; and James Byrnes, as Truman's personal representative.

had concluded that the bomb he and others at Los Alamos were making *had* to be used because that was the only way to awaken the world to the necessity of abolishing war altogether. No demonstration — even if it was possible under wartime conditions, which he doubted — could take the place of actual combat use, with its horrible and sobering results. Moreover, Oppenheimer thought it would be very difficult if not impossible to get political action on international control *unless* the bomb's immensely destructive power deeply penetrated the popular mind. "My own view," he asserted later, "is that the development of atomic weapons can make the problem more hopeful because it intensifies the urgency of our hopes — in frank words, because we are scared."[14] He hoped that a military demonstration of the bomb would compel a general recognition that pre–atomic age calculations had to give way to new realities.

Oppenheimer privately worried to Szilard, however, that Washington officials had inadequately pondered these sobering new realities. Oppenheimer's worry intensified Szilard's own fears. Referring to the prospects of a "superbomb" infinitely more powerful even than an atomic bomb, he asked Oppenheimer "what men like Stimson and Wallace would think if they were fully advised of the turn which the technical development can be expected to take within a few years."

Using the bomb did not necessarily mean using it on a civilian target. Szilard knew, however, that he faced an uphill battle persuading Oppenheimer to oppose dropping the bomb on a Japanese city. "I expect that you who have been so strenuously working at [Los Alamos] on getting these devices ready will naturally lean towards wanting that they should be used," he told him.[15] In this, Szilard was perceptive. Work on the atomic bomb had begun in the spring of 1939 out of fear that the Nazis were building one of their own, but the surrender of Germany in the spring of 1945 brought the resignation of only *two* scientists at Los Alamos. If others thought of leaving — or debating use of the bomb — a meeting that Oppenheimer called a few days after Germany's surrender stopped them in their tracks. Oppenheimer told them they should finish their task and leave the politics to policy makers in Washington. "He was very uncompromising and very sharp," remembered one who attended the meeting. "He indicated that he would not tolerate that kind of discussion and he implicitly invited those who felt that way to get out."[16] No one else left.

The project had long ago assumed a momentum and a life of its own. It had become a monumental scientific and engineering endeavor, involving prodigious effort and expense and labor. It was now a hurtling train moving forward — like the Pacific War itself — with awesome, almost unstoppable force. Most scientists were too involved in their work and too committed to achieving their goal to stop and reflect. "Most people just didn't think too much about what would happen," recalled a physicist on the Hill that spring — "No, that was somebody else's problem."[17] What had begun as a fearful race with Nazi Germany had become an end in itself. "I don't think there was any time where we worked harder at the speed-up than in the period after the German surrender and the actual combat use of the bomb," Oppenheimer recalled after the war.[18]

Ethical and moral concerns had been eclipsed by their emotional and psychological investment and the intensity they brought to problem solving. The physics existed; it simply waited to be revealed. They believed the bomb was going to be built by someone, and they wanted it to be them. The intensity of collaborative work with extraordinarily gifted people also had enormous appeal. That camaraderie, shared in the exploration of an arcane and forbidden realm, provided a rare sense of intimacy, a sense of transcendence that combined strong creative satisfaction with feelings of individual power — how many people could resist that? And like most Americans in 1945, they found it hard to empathize with the fate of a people whose soldiers had committed atrocities against Americans and who were so physically and culturally different. There was not a single Asian American among the Manhattan Project staff, and it was easy for the scientists to think of the Japanese as "the other." There was some private debate about the morality of dropping the bomb on a city, but most felt it was no worse than the fire raids then devastating Japan and that it was justified if it ended the war. In addition, most scientists believed — or wanted to believe — that once this horrible weapon was used, there could never be another war. This made the idea of using the bomb to kill large numbers of civilians emotionally easier for those who were building it.

Szilard was determined to do all he could to prevent this. On May twenty-eighth, he and two fellow scientists that he persuaded to come along traveled to South Carolina to see James Byrnes, who was now secretary of state designate. Szilard was directed there by the president's appointments secretary after an unsuccessful attempt to speak personally with Truman. Szilard and his two companions traveled by train to Spartanburg, a small town nestled in the piney foothills of western South Carolina, and walked from the red brick railroad station to Byrnes's house nearby.

The meeting between Szilard and Byrnes echoed the one between Bohr and Churchill the year before. It was a tense, unsatisfactory exchange between different men with different assumptions and perspectives. A purse-lipped man with a wiry frame, beaklike nose, and sharp eyes that peered at others with steely geniality, Byrnes was a savvy politician thoroughly schooled in the practicalities of power. He had grown up in the 1880s, when the southern up-country still had an ethos of a frontier society — when gouging, biting, and knifing were the way fights were settled. Byrnes was brought up to believe that when you fought, you fought with everything you had. He had little patience, or sympathy, for the moral arguments of a physicist with a foreign accent, though he concealed his lack of interest beneath the mask of amiability that politicians always have on call.

Once seated in Byrnes's living room, Szilard handed the secretary of state designate a copy of the memo he had prepared for Roosevelt shortly before the president's death. Even before Byrnes could finish reading the memo, Szilard began lecturing him about the danger of using the bomb against Japan as a way to impress Russia. Byrnes replied that demonstrating the bomb would make Russia more manageable in Europe. "You come from Hungary," he said — "you would not want Russia to stay in Hungary indefinitely." But Szilard did not share Byrnes's assumption that the bomb would make Russia more manageable and he countered that the "interests of peace might best be served and an arms race avoided by not using the bomb against Japan, keeping it secret, and letting the Russians think that our work on it had not succeeded." Byrnes was appalled and incredulous. The nation had spent more than $2 billion on the bomb's development, he said — Congress would demand to see results. As he had told FDR shortly before the president's death, the administration might well avoid embarrassment during the war if the bomb remained in doubt, but afterward, "If the project proves a failure, it will then be subjected to relentless investigation and criticism."[19]

Szilard left Spartanburg acutely frustrated. How could he communicate with politicians insensitive to the bomb's revolutionary power and implications? "I thought to myself," he later wrote, "how much better off the world might be had I been born in America and become influential in American politics, and had Byrnes been born in Hun-

Leo Szilard (1898–1964), Hungarian-born American physicist who helped initiate the Manhattan Project in 1939 yet vigorously opposed dropping the atomic bomb on Japan's cities in the summer of 1945. After the war, he became an ardent promoter of international control of nuclear weapons. (Bulletin of the Atomic Scientists, *courtesy AIP Emilio Segrè Visual Archives*)

Enrico Fermi (1901–1954), Italian-born American physicist who conducted early neutron experiments and directed the first controlled nuclear chain reaction in December 1942. He reluctantly supported use of the atomic bomb against Japan and development of the superbomb after the war. (*AIP Emilio Segrè Visual Archives, Segrè Collection*)

I. I. Rabi (1898–1988),
American physicist who consulted
at Los Alamos during the war, where
he acted as an adviser and consultant to
his close friend, Robert Oppenheimer.
He served in many government advisory
posts after the war and vigorously
defended Oppenheimer against
charges of being a security risk.
(© *AP/Wide World Photos*)

Niels Bohr (1885–1962),
Danish theoretical physicist whose
concern about the terrifying prospects
for humanity posed by atomic weapons
led him to lobby British prime minister
Winston Churchill and American
president Franklin Roosevelt during
the war in favor of international control.
He was unsuccessful. (*National Archives
and Records Administration, courtesy AIP
Emilio Segrè Visual Archives*)

Edward Teller (1908–), Hungarian-born American physicist who helped convince the U.S. government to build an atomic bomb and later pushed for development of the superbomb. A staunch anticommunist, he sought American nuclear superiority over the Soviet Union during the Cold War. (© *CORBIS*)

Ernest Lawrence (1901–1958), American experimental physicist who invented the first high-energy particle accelerator, the cyclotron, and founded the Berkeley and Livermore National Laboratories. An early advocate of government support for atomic research in 1941, he opposed development of the superbomb immediately after the war but later changed his mind. (*Ernest Orlando Lawrence Berkeley National Laboratory, courtesy AIP Emilio Segrè Visual Archives*)

Arthur Compton (1892–1962), American physicist who chaired the governmental advisory committee in 1941 that assessed fission's military potential. He later directed the Metallurgical Laboratory at the University of Chicago, where scientists researched plutonium and the nuclear chain reaction. He abandoned weapons work after the war. (*AIP Emilio Segrè Visual Archives, W. F. Meggers Gallery of Nobel Laureates*)

Robert Oppenheimer (1904–1967), American theoretical physicist who led development of the atomic bomb as director of the Los Alamos National Laboratory from 1943–1945. After the war, he sought to resolve the political and moral problems arising from nuclear weapons but fell victim to an anticommunist witch-hunt. (*AIP Emilio Segrè Visual Archives*)

Hans Bethe (1906–   ), German-born American physicist who led the Theoretical Division at Los Alamos during the war and reluctantly participated in development of the superbomb after the war. He later became a leading critic of the nuclear arms race and the policy of nuclear superiority championed by Edward Teller. (© *CORBIS*)

Niels Bohr (second from left) stood at the center of a close-knit network of European and American physicists in the 1920s and 1930s. Here he meets with younger colleagues, including Edward Teller (second from right) and Otto Frisch (far right). (*AIP Emilio Segrè Visual Archives, Wheeler Collection*)

Robert Oppenheimer (wearing hat) and I. I. Rabi (holding sheet), two American postgraduates in Zurich, summer 1930, with Wolfgang Pauli (far right). In Europe, Oppenheimer and Rabi learned the latest physics, witnessed the rise of Nazism, and watched war clouds gather over the Continent. (*AIP Emilio Segrè Visual Archives*)

Robert Oppenheimer and Ernest Lawrence summering at Oppenheimer's New Mexico ranch, 1931. They were very different, but they complemented each other professionally and liked each other personally — until political differences after the war sundered their friendship. (*Molly B. Lawrence, courtesy AIP Emilio Segrè Visual Archives*)

Robert Oppenheimer, Enrico Fermi, and Ernest Lawrence at the Rad Lab, Berkeley, in the summer of 1937. Fermi was visiting America from Italy, which he would leave the following year to escape Fascist persecution of his Jewish wife and children. (*Ernest Orlando Lawrence Berkeley National Laboratory, courtesy AIP Emilio Segrè Visual Archives*, Physics Today *Collection*)

Participants at the Washington Conference on Theoretical Physics, January 1937. The annual conference attracted talented physicists from both sides of the Atlantic. Those attending in 1937 included Hans Bethe (front row, fourth from left), I. I. Rabi (above Bethe's left shoulder), Niels Bohr (front row, second from right, wearing scarf), and Edward Teller (partially obscured, standing directly behind Bethe, two rows up). (*AIP Emilio Segrè Visual Archives, Gamow and* Physics Today *Collections*)

Leslie Groves (1896–1970),
U.S. army general who directed
the Manhattan Project during the war.
He oversaw all aspects of the project:
scientific, production, security, and
planning for use of the bomb. Under
his direction, project plants were built
at Oak Ridge, Tennessee; Hanford,
Washington; and Los Alamos, New
Mexico. (© *CORBIS*)

A weekend hiking excursion in the Jemez Mountains near Los Alamos, winter
1944–1945. Such outings offered one of the few opportunities for scientists such as
Enrico Fermi and Hans Bethe (first and second on left) to relieve the stress of working
on the bomb. (*AIP Emilio Segrè Visual Archives, Segrè Collection*)

Niels Bohr on the ski hill above Los Alamos, January 1945. Bohr used such occasions to listen to other physicists' anxieties about the bomb and to share his own views about the bomb's revolutionary implications. (*AIP Emilio Segrè Visual Archives, Segrè Collection*)

Robert Oppenheimer and Leslie Groves at the Trinity Site near Alamogordo, New Mexico, two months after the July 16, 1945, test. Intense heat generated by the world's first atomic explosion vaporized the hundred-foot steel tower holding the bomb, gouged an enormous crater in the ground, and fused the surrounding sand into jadelike crystals. (© *Bettmann/CORBIS*)

Hiroshima, Japan, after the atomic bomb attack on August 6, 1945. The explosion caused widespread destruction, vividly illustrated by this photograph taken shortly after the attack. Civilians outnumbered soldiers in Hiroshima more than six to one. Over 75,000 inhabitants of the city perished that day, and tens of thousands more afterward due to burns, radiation, and other sicknesses. (© *Bettmann/CORBIS*)

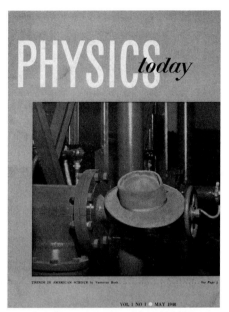

Robert Oppenheimer's signature porkpie hat on the cover of the May 1948 issue of *Physics Today* eloquently conveyed his fame after the war. Until his downfall in 1954, Oppenheimer remained America's most celebrated and influential physicist. (*Ernest Orlando Lawrence Berkeley National Laboratory, courtesy AIP Emilio Segrè Visual Archives,* Physics Today *Collection*)

Ernest Lawrence and Robert Oppenheimer together at Berkeley, 1946. Growing political differences between them after the war — over the superbomb in particular — eroded their storied friendship, which had been weakened when Oppenheimer left Berkeley for Princeton in 1947 and ended as a result of Oppenheimer's security hearing in 1954. (© *AP/Wide World Photos*)

Edward Teller and Enrico Fermi together at the University of Chicago, 1951. By this time, the superbomb had become Teller's fixation. But he failed to convince his good friend Fermi to support a crash program to develop the thermonuclear weapon. (*AIP Emilio Segrè Visual Archives*)

As his lobbying for the superbomb and his testimony against Oppenheimer estranged him from many other physicists in the 1950s, Edward Teller increasingly sought the friendship and support of political conservatives and military officers (such as General Joseph Garvin, pictured here). (*National Archives and Records Administration, courtesy AIP Emilio Segrè Visual Archives*)

Enrico Fermi boating off the island of Elba, 1954. This photograph, taken during Fermi's last visit to his homeland a few months before his death, shows the ravages that undiagnosed stomach cancer had begun to take on the previously vigorous Fermi. Physicists mourned his premature death later that year. (*Amaldi Archives, Dipartimento di Fisica, Università "La Sapienza," Rome, courtesy AIP Emilio Segrè Visual Archives*)

Ernest Lawrence sitting on a hill above the Berkeley campus and the dome of the sprawling Rad Lab, surveying the extraordinary empire he had built, 1958. The ulcerative colitis that had plagued this energetic and driven man finally killed him later that year. (*AIP Emilio Segrè Visual Archives,* Physics Today *Collection*)

Niels Bohr receiving the prestigious Atoms for Peace Award from President Eisenhower, with Arthur Compton (second from left) and Lewis Strauss (far left) looking on, 1957. Strauss had orchestrated the vendetta that brought down Bohr's good friend Robert Oppenheimer three years earlier. Bohr and Compton both died in 1962. (*Niels Bohr Archive, courtesy AIP Emilio Segrè Visual Archives*)

Leo Szilard with former first lady Eleanor Roosevelt, a few years before his death from a heart attack in 1964. Until the end, Szilard remained what he had always been: a dreamer, a gadfly, and the moral conscience of his generation of physicists. (Bulletin of the Atomic Scientists, *courtesy AIP Emilio Segrè Visual Archives*)

A chastened and reflective Robert Oppenheimer after the revocation of his security clearance, late 1950s. His story was a personal tragedy — and the tragedy of his generation of physicists, who opened Pandora's box and ushered nuclear weapons into the world. (*AIP Emilio Segrè Visual Archives*, Physics Today *Collection*)

I. I. Rabi at the fortieth anniversary commemoration of the founding of the Los Alamos National Laboratory, 1983. At the commemoration, Rabi spoke with conscious and courageous irony of "how well we meant." He died in 1988. (*Photograph by Sam Treiman, courtesy AIP Emilio Segrè Visual Archives*, Physics Today *Collection*)

Edward Teller in his eighties, in a photograph taken in his office at the Hoover Institution in Stanford, California, where he continued in interviews to voice the argument for nuclear weapons well into his nineties. (© *Roger Ressmeyer/CORBIS*)

An insecure pessimist, Edward Teller found refuge from his anxieties at the piano, where he played sonatas by Mozart and Beethoven. (*Photo by Fred Rothwarf, courtesy AIP Emilio Segrè Visual Archives*)

Hans Bethe in his nineties, the grand old man of American physics in the early twenty-first century and sharp critic of the nuclear arms race. Bethe and Teller became two lions contesting the legacy of their momentous creation. (*AIP Emilio Segrè Visual Archives, Segrè Collection*)

gary and studied physics. In all probability there would have been no atomic bomb, and no danger of an arms race between America and Russia." Szilard was convinced that Byrnes, and by implication President Truman, were inclined toward a shortsighted policy that would make a postwar atomic arms race inevitable.[20]

On the way back to Chicago, Szilard stopped in Washington to see Oppenheimer, who was in the capital for an upcoming meeting of the Interim Committee. Szilard told Oppenheimer about his unsuccessful meeting with Byrnes and stressed how important it was to persuade policy makers to inform the Russians about the bomb before it was used against Japan. "Don't you think if we tell the Russians what we intend to do and then use the bomb in Japan, the Russians will understand it?" Oppenheimer asked. "They'll understand it only too well," Szilard answered.[21]

Three days after the Spartanburg meeting, on May 31, 1945, the Interim Committee and its Scientific Advisory Panel met in Stimson's Pentagon office to work out a recommendation for President Truman on the use of the atomic bomb. Nazi Germany had surrendered only three weeks earlier. Fighting for Okinawa had entered its bloodiest phase. Japan's militarists seemed unwavering in their determination to fight to the finish. It would be another seven weeks before the first atomic bomb would be tested.

In preparation for the meeting, Arthur Compton drafted a memorandum for the other participants. In it, he stressed that the use of the atomic bomb on Japan was "more a political than a military question because it introduces the question of mass slaughter, really for the first time in history. Essentially, the question of the use to be made of the new weapon carries much more serious implications than the introduction of poison gas." He called the question of the bomb's use "first in point of urgency." "This whole question," Compton wrote skeptically, "may well have received the broad study it demands. I merely mention it as one of the urgent problems that have bothered our men because of its many ramifications and humanitarian implications."[22]

Those gathered in Stimson's office that morning shared two unstated assumptions: that the atomic bomb would have a decisive impact on Japan's leaders; and that the American public, if they knew of its existence, would demand that it be used to save the lives of American servicemen. The expenditure of billions of dollars; mounting U.S. casualties in the face of tenacious Japanese resistance; the bomb's

expected salutary effect on postwar relations with the Soviet Union —
all these factors bolstered a predisposition toward use. "Throughout
the morning's discussion," Compton later wrote, "it seemed to be a
foregone conclusion that the bomb would be used. It was regarding
only the details of strategy and tactics that differing views were
expressed."[23]

Although Stimson sought to create an atmosphere in which everyone felt free to discuss any problem related to atomic energy, he opened
the meeting by reminding Compton, Lawrence, Oppenheimer, and
Fermi that he and Army Chief of Staff Marshall were the ones responsible for making recommendations on military matters to the president. Stimson was anxious, however, to impress upon them "that we
were looking at this like statesmen and not like merely soldiers anxious
to win the war at any cost."[24] To corroborate his point, Stimson read
from handwritten notes he had prepared for the meeting:

Its *size* and *character*
We don't think it *mere* new *weapon*
Revolutionary Discovery of Relation of man to universe
Great History Landmark like
Gravitation
Copernican Theory
But,
Bids fair [to be] *infinitely greater,* in *respect* to its *Effect*
— on the ordinary affairs of man's life.
May *destroy* or *perfect* International *Civilization*
May [be] *Frankenstein or* means for World Peace[25]

Compton then gave a terrifying seminar on the future of nuclear
weapons. He explained that the atomic bombs nearing completion
were only the first step along the road of nuclear weapons technology.
In the not too distant future, Compton soberly observed, loomed the
awesome prospect of a "superbomb" perhaps a thousand times more
destructive. Oppenheimer then explained how unimaginably destructive a superbomb would be: an atomic bomb was expected to have an
explosive force of 2,000 to 20,000 tons of TNT; a superbomb might
produce an explosive force of 10,000,000 to 100,000,000 tons of
TNT. If an atomic bomb could effectively destroy a city, those present
could only wonder in fright at what an explosive force of this magnitude would destroy.

The implication to Lawrence was inescapable: the United States would be in mortal danger if and when another country acquired such a bomb. Lawrence urged staying ahead of the rest of the world by expanding the weapons lab at Los Alamos and stockpiling atomic bombs. Compton agreed. Oppenheimer did not, fearing an arms race as soon as the Soviet Union took up the challenge.

The committee then took up the issue of international control. Byrnes asked how long it would take for the Soviet Union to catch up.[26] Groves estimated at least twenty years. The scientists disagreed, estimating Russia could build a bomb in four to six years.* Oppenheimer put the point vividly. "Our monopoly is like a cake of ice melting in the sun," he said.[27] Drawing on his talks with Bohr at Los Alamos, Oppenheimer urged that Washington contact Moscow promptly about joining in a system of international control without giving them details of the progress achieved. Marshall agreed, saying it might be desirable to invite Russian scientists to witness the first atomic bomb test scheduled for July in New Mexico. Byrnes strenuously objected. He said Stalin would ask to be brought into the project — and that was unacceptable. Byrnes believed the bomb's diplomatic utility would be diminished if Stalin was informed of the weapon prior to its use. He favored seeking international control while maintaining U.S. atomic superiority. Such a strong statement by a man of Byrnes's influence and prestige was not to be dismissed lightly. No one challenged him — nor expressed the contradiction between these objectives.

Everyone except Marshall then adjourned to a dining room across the hall for lunch. The conferees sat around four tables. Discussion centered on whether or not to use the bomb against Japan — the *only* time this crucial and fundamental question would ever be formally addressed. Given the bomb's momentous implications, and in light of all the subsequent controversy about its use, it is striking how virtually no one in the inner circle of decision making seriously contemplated not dropping it. To a degree that later generations would find remarkable, the advent of the nuclear age was heralded by little formal deliberation. Events were in the saddle, and they rode men hard.

The talk was brief, lasting ten minutes. Lawrence repeated a suggestion he had made that morning for a nonmilitary demonstration. A political naïf, he thought the weapon would not actually be used. "The bomb will never be dropped on people," he had assured the

---

* The USSR successfully tested its first atomic bomb in late August 1949. See chapter 9, p. 221.

chairman of Berkeley's physics department. "As soon as we get it, we'll use it only to dictate terms of peace."[28] Compton asked whether it was possible to give the Japanese an opportunity to witness the weapon's tremendous power before it was dropped on them. Stimson invited comments. The reaction was negative: the weapon might be a dud; a failure would strengthen Japan's morale; if the Japanese received a prior warning, they might take steps to block it; fanatical militarists would be unimpressed by a demonstration; the Japanese might move American prisoners of war into the test area.

Oppenheimer then reported an estimate prepared at Los Alamos of the number of deaths that would be caused if an atomic bomb were exploded over a city. (The estimate — twenty thousand — was based on the erroneous assumption that a city's inhabitants would seek shelter before the bomb went off.) A participant soberly noted that this number would be no greater than the number killed in the Tokyo fire raid — far less, in fact. The outcome, Compton later wrote, was that "no one could suggest a way in which [a demonstration] could be made so convincing that it would be likely to stop the war."[29]

Returning to Stimson's office after lunch, the participants took up the bomb's probable impact on Japan's will to fight. Someone again observed that its destructive effect might not differ much from the B-29 fire raids incinerating Japan's cities. Oppenheimer predicted that the visual effect of the bomb would be "tremendous" and for the first time mentioned radiation, but he did not mention the possibility of lingering illness.

Stimson expressed the conclusion, on which there was general agreement, that the Japanese should not be given any warning. He said the bomb should not be dropped on a civilian area, but an attempt should be made to make a profound psychological impression on as many Japanese as possible. The preferred target would be a war plant closely surrounded by workers' homes. None of those present, however, noted the contradiction in their logic: a bomb powerful enough to destroy an entire city would surely kill thousands — probably tens of thousands — of civilians if dropped anywhere near workers' homes. Compton, Lawrence, Oppenheimer, and Fermi perhaps understood this contradiction best because they knew best how destructive the bomb would be, but at no time did they point it out. Perhaps it was because the four of them felt such views would find little sympathy at such a meeting. Perhaps it was because they themselves were too invested in the project. Or perhaps it was because they did not want to admit to themselves what the human costs of their creation's use would be.* But the dilemma that policy makers and scientists preferred not to face was all too real. And it remained on Compton's mind. "What shall I tell Szilard?" he asked Oppenheimer as the session broke up. Oppenheimer gave no answer.[30] Stimson informed Truman of the committee's recommendation on June sixth. The decision to use the bomb was inherent in the decision made years before to build it. The momentum of that process was rapidly building toward an all but inevitable climax.

Compton returned to Chicago knowing that he faced a growing gulf between the views of the Interim Committee and the Met Lab scientists under his direction. He reported to his restless constituents on the afternoon of June second, immediately after his arrival from Washington. Constrained by the secrecy rule that the Interim Committee had imposed on its science advisers, Compton did not disclose that a recommendation had been made to drop the bomb on Japan without warning. Instead, he told his audience that the Science Advisory Panel would meet again in mid-June in Los Alamos.

Szilard sat in the audience glumly listening to Compton. His respect for policy makers had hit a new low after his meeting with Byrnes in Spartanburg. Szilard also lacked confidence in the Scientific Advisory Panel. He believed that Oppenheimer would not oppose dropping the bomb after laboring so long and hard to make it; that Fermi would state his views privately but would not speak up; and that Compton would not risk incurring the displeasure of the Washington Establishment. And he faced the renewed wrath of Groves, who had learned about his unauthorized trip to Spartanburg.

Groves demanded an explanation from Szilard's Met Lab boss — a military officer who had taken Szilard's approach of going through outside channels might well find himself court-martialed or assigned to some remote Aleutian Island. The usually even-tempered Compton exploded in an answering letter to Groves. "I believe the reason for their action is that with regard to the Project their responsibility to the nation is prior to and broader than their responsibility to the Army, and

---

* Policy makers also indulged in self-deception. Stimson told Truman on May sixteenth: "I am anxious to hold our Air Force, so far as possible, to the 'precision' bombing which it has done so well in Europe. I believe the same rule of sparing the civilian population should be applied, as far as possible, to the use of any new weapons." (Henry L. Stimson Diary, Sterling Library, Yale University.) Truman, for his part, insisted to the end of his life that the bombings of Hiroshima and Nagasaki were directed against "military" targets.

they felt that a situation had developed in which they could not perform their duty to the nation working through me or through the Army." Compton made it clear to Groves that he shared their uneasy feelings:

> The scientists who were responsible for initiating and developing this project have felt that its control has been taken from them, that they are uninformed with regard to plans for its use and its development, and that they have had little assurance that serious consideration of its broader implications is being given by those in a position to guide national policy. The scientists will be held responsible, both by the public and by their own consciences, for having faced the world with the existence of the new powers. The fact that the control has been taken out of their hands makes it necessary for them to plead the need for careful consideration and wise action to someone with authority to act. There is no other way in which they can meet their responsibility to society.

After pointing out that time and again their efforts to get their concerns to those with authority to act had been bottled up in channels, Compton asked, "To whom then were the scientists to go in order to obtain an effective consideration of their views on the use and further development of the Project?" He pointedly added that the Jeffries Report, which he had passed to Groves, had not reached policy makers. The gentle Compton even permitted himself an attack on outgoing Secretary of State Edward Stettinius for failing to explain the atomic dilemma to the founding conference of the United Nations in San Francisco on April twenty-fifth. "His appreciation was so limited as possibly to serve as a hazard to the country's welfare," Compton charged. He placed the blame for this squarely on Groves, who had briefed Stettinius about the bomb before the UN conference.[31]

To meet both Groves's demand that scientists adhere to the chain of command and the Met Lab scientists' concern that policy makers consider their opinions about the use of the bomb, Compton organized a committee to study and report on the bomb's implications. Compton promised to deliver their findings personally in Washington. Chaired by Nobel laureate and Nazi refugee James Franck, the committee produced a perceptive study. Franck was a highly principled physicist who had openly criticized the Nazis — a rare and courageous gesture — before being driven out of Germany. In 1934 he went to Copenhagen to join his friend Bohr; later, he moved on to

America — first to Johns Hopkins University and then to the University of Chicago, which became his home. Other physicists considered Franck a saint and a martyr. Mournful looking, retiring, and unpretentious, Franck fretted about the consequences of weapons work and had taken charge of the Met Lab's chemistry section in 1942 only after securing a promise from Compton that he would be heard at a high level when the time came to decide how the bomb would be used.

The Franck Report took as its fundamental premise the fact that "the manner in which this new weapon is introduced to the world will determine in large part the future course of events." It warned that the bomb opened the way to "total mutual destruction" of all nations. It predicted the almost limitless destructive power of nuclear weapons and the elusive security that any attempt at monopoly would bring. And it stressed the widening gap between technological progress and traditional conceptions of war:

> Nuclear bombs cannot possibly remain a "secret weapon" at the exclusive disposal of this country for more than a few years. The scientific facts on which their construction is based are well known to scientists of other countries. Unless an effective international control of nuclear explosives is instituted, a race for nuclear armaments is certain to ensue following the first revelation of our possession of nuclear weapons to the world. . . .
>
> We believe that these considerations make the use of nuclear bombs for an early unannounced attack against Japan inadvisable. If the United States were to be the first to release this new means of indiscriminate destruction upon mankind, she would sacrifice public support throughout the world, precipitate the race for armaments, and prejudice the possibility of reaching an international agreement on the future control of such weapons.

The Franck Report argued against using the bomb, even "if one takes the pessimistic point of view and discounts the possibility of an effective international control over nuclear weapons at the present time." In this case, the report concluded, "the advisability of an early use of nuclear bombs against Japan becomes even more doubtful — quite independently of any humanitarian considerations. If an international agreement is not concluded immediately after the first demonstration, this will mean a flying start toward an unlimited armaments race." The report rested its argument against dropping the bomb on Japan on the ground that announcing its existence to the world in this way would make international control virtually impossible. The report urged instead a demonstration of the bomb over an uninhabited area before a group of international observers. "A demonstration of the new weapon might best be made before the eyes of representatives of all the United Nations on the desert or a barren island. This may sound fantastic, but in nuclear weapons we have something entirely new in order of magnitude of destructive power, and if we want to capitalize fully on the advantage their possession gives us, we must use new and imaginative methods." The scientists hoped to shock the world into international cooperation.[32]

Compton kept his word by accompanying Franck to Washington to discuss a preliminary draft of the report with Vice President Wallace at a breakfast meeting arranged by Compton on April twenty-first.[33] They also tried to see Secretary of War Stimson at the Pentagon on June twelfth, but the secretary did not make himself available. Compton left the Franck Report for Stimson with a covering note that faulted it for failing to consider what Compton thought was the most important issue at hand. "While it calls attention to difficulties that might result from the use of the bomb," wrote Compton, it "does not mention the probable net saving of many lives,* nor that if the bomb were not used in the present war the world would have no adequate warning as to what was to be expected if war should break out again."[34]

Unlike Franck, who hoped to avert an atomic attack, Compton hoped such an attack would be the last terrible act of World War II and serve notice that there must be no World War III. This grandson of pacifist Mennonites knew all too well the destruction and human agony the bomb would cause; he had been living with this realization for four years. "But I wanted the war to end," Compton later wrote. "I wanted life to become normal again. I saw a chance for an enduring peace that would be demanded by the very destructiveness of these weapons. I hoped that by use of the bombs many fine young men I knew might be released at once from the demands of war and thus be given a chance to live and not to die."[35] Compton was especially haunted by the semester he had spent at the University of Cambridge in the fall of 1919. Among his students that fall were many who had been crippled and blinded during the Great War. He often saw

---

* In fact, the Franck Report stated: "The saving of American lives achieved by the sudden use of atomic bombs against Japan may be outweighed by the ensuing loss of confidence and by a wave of horror and repulsion sweeping over the rest of the world."

crutches leaning against chairs in the lecture halls. It was a sadly poignant sight — they were so young. What had sunk most deeply into Compton's soul was not the sight of legless young men but the awareness that so many others who should have been there lay buried in the mud of Flanders' fields.

Compton took the Franck Report along with him to a meeting of the Scientific Advisory Panel in Los Alamos on June sixteenth. The panel was meeting in Oppenheimer's office that day when Stimson's assistant George Harrison phoned and said they, not the Interim Committee, should consider the Franck Report and examine the possibility of devising a nonmilitary demonstration that would be sufficiently convincing to effect Japan's surrender. Harrison's call charging the panel to reconsider use of the bomb against Japan in the light of the Franck Report created a tense and soul-searching atmosphere. Compton later described the harsh dilemma that he and his three colleagues felt at that moment:

> We were keenly aware of our responsibility as the scientific advisers to the Interim Committee. Among our colleagues were the scientists who supported Franck in suggesting a nonmilitary demonstration only. We thought of the fighting men who were set for an invasion which would be so very costly in both American and Japanese lives. We were determined to find, if we could, some effective way of demonstrating the power of an atomic bomb without loss of life that would impress Japan's warlords. If only this could be done!
>
> The difficulties of making a purely technical demonstration that would carry its impact effectively into Japan's controlling councils were indeed great. We had to count on every possible effort to distort even obvious facts. Experience with the determination of Japan's fighting men made it evident that the war would not be stopped unless these men themselves were convinced of its futility.[36]

The possible failure of a demonstration bomb also worried them, as did the specter of a bloody invasion of Japan if the bomb failed to end the war. But, of course, they had more than just the war in mind. In their opinion, the weapon's postwar influence depended on a widespread recognition of new realities — the new weapon required a new attitude toward war. If Japan did not accept this view, the war might continue; if the Soviet Union ignored it, the peace would be lost. They concluded that combat use of the bomb would make a deep impression on both countries, convincing those who needed to be convinced to end the war, and persuading those who needed to be persuaded that postwar cooperation was imperative. Compelled initially by fear of German progress, and now terrified by the consequences of their own success, these men of sensibility, culture, and peace were driven to recommend policies that they would have found abhorrent in other circumstances.

There was not unanimous agreement, however. Lawrence again pressed for a demonstration, or at least an explicit warning, before the bomb was dropped on Japan. Fermi also resisted. This was highly unusual. Fermi disliked expressing political opinions. Now, he boldly argued not for a demonstration, but for no drop at all. Nations will always fight wars, he said, therefore scientists could not responsibly place atomic bombs in national arsenals. It took Compton and Oppenheimer until 5:00 the following morning to "talk him down," Oppenheimer later noted.[37] In the end, Fermi gave in, Compton and Oppenheimer's logic prevailing: it was better to have the bomb used *once* so that people everywhere learned just how awful it was.*

Oppenheimer reported to Washington the panel's conclusion that it could "propose no technical demonstration likely to bring an end to the war" and that there was "no acceptable alternative to direct military use." "Our hearts were heavy as we turned in this report to the Interim Committee," Compton later wrote. "We were glad and proud to have had a part in making the power of the atom available for the use of man. What a tragedy it was that this power should become available first in time of war and that it must first be used for human destruction."[38]

Oppenheimer would later regret publicly the lack of farsightedness and political courage that the Scientific Advisory Panel demonstrated at this crucial weekend meeting in June. His feeling of failure may have been compounded by the realization that if he, Compton, Lawrence, and Fermi had endorsed the recommendation of the Franck Report that weekend, their endorsement might have forced a high-level reconsideration of use-without-warning. But then no one in Washington, either, spent a fraction of the time and thought reviewing the arguments of the Franck Report that its drafters put into

* Fermi came to resent Compton's (if not Oppenheimer's) pressure that night. When a colleague complained to Fermi a few years later, "Why does [Compton] talk so much these days about God and philosophy and brotherhood?" Fermi replied acidly, "Current need. What did the country need most during the war? The Bomb. What does it need now? Religion." (Quoted in Davis, *Lawrence and Oppenheimer*, p. 249.)

formulating them. The remarkably prescient report made little impression on policy makers who saw their first responsibility as ending the war victoriously.

Compton, Lawrence, Oppenheimer, and Fermi also had made ending the war, rather than the bomb's impact after the war, their controlling consideration. This was not surprising. To have acted otherwise, at the time and under the circumstances, would have required political vision and courage that the atomic scientists, at this juncture, did not possess. This was clear when, having made their recommendation to Stimson, they added: "With regard to these general aspects of the use of atomic energy, it is clear that we, as scientific men, have no proprietary rights. It is true that we are among the few citizens who have had occasion to give thoughtful consideration to these problems during the past few years. We have, however, no claim to special competence in solving political, social, and military problems which are presented by the advent of atomic power."[39] To some extent, they were just being polite. But to another, their recusal was evidence that despite increasing awareness, they subscribed to the axiom — common in their day — that scientists should not offer political judgments. Their attitude would change dramatically in subsequent years.

Bohr, however, felt no reluctance about speaking out. After the May thirty-first Interim Committee meeting, Oppenheimer went over to the British Embassy, where Bohr was staying. "I met Bohr and tried to comfort him," Oppenheimer remembered later, "but he was too wise and too worldly to be comforted. . . . He [was] quite uncertain about what, if anything, would happen."[40] Tellingly, Oppenheimer added this about Bohr (and himself) years later: "He was for statesmen; he used the word over and over again. He was not for committees and the Interim Committee was a committee."[41]

Bohr felt that time was running out. Before leaving the United States to return to his liberated Denmark, Bohr asked Frankfurter to arrange one last meeting for him with Stimson. On June eighteenth, Stimson's assistant Harvey Bundy sent the following in a message to his boss: "Do you want to try and work in a meeting with Professor Bohr, the Dane, before you get away this week?" Stimson scrawled no in the margin of the message.[42] Bohr gave up and a few days later sailed for Europe.

Szilard sensed that things were moving fast now, and that he must act quickly if he hoped to avert what he considered a tragedy. Appalled at the firebombing of civilians, he felt frightened by the gathering force of events. In early July he decided to draft a petition to President Truman arguing against use of the atomic bomb on moral grounds.[43]

The sense of urgency and responsibility that Szilard felt came through forcefully in his covering letter to colleagues:

Enclosed is the text of a petition which will be submitted to the President of the United States. As you will see, this petition is based on purely moral considerations.

However small the chance might be that our petition may influence the course of events, I personally feel that it would be a matter of importance if a large number of scientists who have worked in this field went clearly and unmistakably on record as to their opposition on moral grounds to the use of these bombs in the present phase of the war.

Many of us are inclined to say that individual Germans share the guilt for the acts which Germany committed during this war because they did not raise their voices in protest against those acts. Their defense that their protest would have been of no avail hardly seems acceptable even though these Germans could have had protests without running risks to life and liberty. We are in a position to raise our voices without incurring any such risks even though we might incur the displeasure of some of those who are at present in charge of controlling the work on "atomic power."

The fact that the people of the United States are unaware of the choice which faces us increases our responsibility in this matter since those who have worked on "atomic power" represent a sample of the population and they alone are in a position to form an opinion and declare their stand. . . .[44]

In the petition Szilard argued that the United States bore special moral responsibility for being the first nation to develop the bomb:

The development of atomic power will provide the nations with new means of destruction. The atomic bombs at our disposal represent only the first step in this direction, and there is almost no limit to the destructive power which will become available in the course of their future development. Thus a nation which sets the precedent of using these newly liberated forces of nature for purposes of destruction may have to bear the responsibility of opening the door to an era of devastation on an unimaginable scale.

If after this war a situation is allowed to develop in the world which permits rival powers to be in uncontrolled possession of these new means of destruction, the cities of the United States as well as the cities of other nations will be in continuous danger of sudden annihilation. All the resources of the United States, moral and material, may have to be mobilized to prevent the advent of such a world situation. Its prevention is at present the solemn responsibility of the United States — singled out by virtue of her lead in the field of atomic power.

The added material strength which this lead gives to the United States brings with it the obligation of restraint and if we were to violate this obligation our moral position would be weakened in the eyes of the world and in our own eyes. It would then be more difficult for us to live up to our responsibility of bringing the unloosened forces of destruction under control.

Szilard opposed the atomic bombing of Japan on the moral ground that it would open "the door to an era of devastation on an unimaginable scale."[45]

Sixty-seven Met Lab scientists signed Szilard's petition. The scientists who did not told Szilard that more lives would be saved by using the atomic bomb than by continuing the bloody war without it. Thousands of American — to say nothing of Japanese — soldiers were being killed each week, and they felt they would be guilty of permitting this slaughter to continue if they did not urge use of the bomb to end the war. Still others felt that patriotism demanded the bomb's use. "Are we to go on shedding American blood when we have available the means to speedy victory?" one note angrily demanded. "No! If we can save even a handful of American lives, then let us use this weapon — now! These sentiments, we feel, represent more truly those of the majority of Americans and particularly those who have sons in the foxholes and warships of the Pacific."[46]

Szilard also sent a copy of his petition to friends at Los Alamos. "I hardly need to emphasize that such a petition does not represent the most effective action that can be taken in order to influence the course of events," he wrote to Oppenheimer and other scientists on the Hill. "But I have no doubt in my own mind that from a point of view of the standing of the scientists in the eyes of the general public one or two years from now it is a good thing that a minority of scientists should have gone on record in favor of giving greater weight to moral arguments."[47]

Szilard urged Teller to both sign the petition and gather signatures for it. Before deciding what to do, Teller went to see Oppenheimer, who answered him in a polite and convincing way by questioning Szilard's political judgment. "What does he know about Japanese psychology?" Oppenheimer told Teller. "How can he judge the way to end the war? The people in Washington are very wise, they know all the facts. Szilard knows nothing. Don't do anything."[48] Teller complied, and wrote Szilard a letter to that effect:

Dear Szilard:

Since our discussion I have spent some time thinking about your objections to an immediate military use of the weapon we may produce. I decided to do nothing. I should like to tell you my reasons.

First of all let me say that I have no hope of clearing my conscience. The things we are working on are so terrible that no amount of protesting or fiddling with politics will save our souls.

This much is true: I have not worked on the project for a very selfish reason and I have gotten much more trouble than pleasure out of it. I worked because the problems interested me and I should have felt it a great restraint not to go ahead. I can not claim that I simply worked to do my duty. A sense of duty could keep me out of such work. It could not get me into the present kind of activity against my inclinations. If you should succeed in convincing me that your moral objections are valid, I should quit working. I hardly think that I should start protesting.

But I am not really convinced of your objections. I do not feel that there is any chance to outlaw any one weapon. If we have a slim chance of survival, it lies in the possibility to get rid of wars. The more decisive a weapon is the more surely it will be used in any real conflict and no agreements will help.

Our only hope is in getting the facts of our results before the people. This might help to convince everybody that the next war would be fatal. For this purpose actual combat-use might even be the best thing.

And this brings me to the main point. The accident that we worked out this dreadful thing should not give us the responsibility of having a voice in how it is to be used. This responsibility must in the end be shifted to the people as a whole and that can be done only by making the facts known. This is the only cause for which I feel entitled in doing something: the necessity of lifting the secrecy at least as far as the broad issues of our work are concerned. My understanding is that this will be done as soon as the military situation permits it.

All this may seem to you quite wrong. I should be glad if you showed this letter to Eugene [Wigner] and to [James] Franck who seem to agree with you rather than with me. I should like to have the advice of all of you whether you think it is a crime to continue to work. But I feel that I should do the wrong thing if I tried to say how to tie the little toe of the ghost to the bottle from which we just helped it escape.

With best regards.

Yours,
E. Teller[49]

Teller did not mention Oppenheimer's opposition to the petition in his letter to Szilard because he knew that Oppenheimer would see the letter before it was sent.[50] In later years, Teller looked back on his refusal to sign Szilard's petition — and the bombing of Hiroshima and Nagasaki — as mistakes. In 1962 he wrote:

I am convinced that the tragic surprise bombing was not necessary. We could have exploded the bomb at a very high altitude over Tokyo in the evening. Triggered at such a high altitude, the bomb would have created a sudden, frightening daylight over the city. But it would have killed no one. After the bomb had been demonstrated — after we were sure it was not a dud — we could have told the Japanese what it was and what would happen if another atomic bomb were detonated at low altitude.

After the Tokyo demonstration, we could have delivered an ultimatum for Japanese surrender. The ultimatum, I believe, would have been met, and the atomic bomb could have been used more humanely but just as effectively to bring a quick end to the war. But to my knowledge, such an unannounced, high altitude demonstration over Tokyo at night was never proposed.[51]

And in 1987 he wrote:

I eventually felt strongly that action without prior warning or demonstration was a mistake. I also came to the conclusion that, although the opinions of scientists on political matters should not be given special weight, neither should scientists stay out of public debates just because they are scientists. In fact, when political decisions involve scientific and technical matters, they have an obligation to speak out.

I failed my first test at Los Alamos, but subsequently I have stood by that conviction.[52]

"Could we have avoided the tragedy of Hiroshima?" he wondered. "Could we have started the atomic age with clean hands?"[53] The questions would haunt him to the end of his life.[54]

I. I. Rabi did not share Teller's opinion. When Rabi arrived on the Hill in mid-July, he told Oppenheimer that the war was almost over, that the Japanese were as good as defeated, but that it was wishful thinking to expect Truman not to use the bomb. Rabi, who had an office in Washington and understood the mood of the capital, could sense the determination — even the zeal — there to end the war quickly and decisively. Rabi's view was equally jaundiced about cowing Japan with a demonstration. He saw no way to shake them with such a gambit. Who would evaluate such a demonstration — the emperor? "This is absurd," he told Oppenheimer. It would be empty "fireworks." Only the destruction of a city would be "incontrovertible."[55]

Oppenheimer was under intense pressure from Groves to prevent political debate over the bomb on the Hill. Oppenheimer's job, the general repeatedly told him, was to finish the "gadget" — nothing else. Early on, Oppenheimer had fought compartmentalization by telling Groves that scientists would work more effectively if they were permitted unfettered discussion among themselves. Groves had acceded to Oppenheimer's request, but he had extracted a promise in return: Oppenheimer would limit discussions strictly to scientific matters. Groves used the bargain he struck with Oppenheimer in the spring of 1943 to restrict debate about use of the bomb in the summer of 1945.

Although Oppenheimer stopped Szilard's petition, no one at Los Alamos was more concerned than he was about the role atomic bombs would play after the war. But Oppenheimer did not think that scientists could do much about postwar problems while the war was still going on. Better informed than any other scientist on the Hill about the state of play in Washington, Oppenheimer perhaps also realized that scientists, at the end of the day, had no real voice in the decision to use the bomb. He also probably knew that those who did have a voice had no need for the opinions of those at Los Alamos or the Met Lab.

An incident earlier in the year suggested Oppenheimer was right. As Allied forces raced toward the heart of Germany, U.S. Army Intelligence discovered that the Nazis had no atomic bombs. Soon after this was learned, the sensational news swept like wildfire through the Manhattan Project laboratories, where it was eagerly discussed. "Isn't it wonderful that the Germans have no atom bomb?" a physicist said to an army liaison officer at one of the labs. "Now we won't have to use ours." The officer, schooled in the ways of the military and of Washington, looked at him for a long moment, rolled his eyes, shook his head, and said, "Of course you understand that if we have such a weapon we are going to use it." His reply shocked the naive physicist.[56]

Truman never saw Szilard's petition. Szilard gave it to Compton on July nineteenth, and asked him to keep the signers' names secret from Groves. Compton did so, sealing it in a manila envelope addressed "To The President of the United States." Also included in the envelope was a poll of 150 Met Lab scientists who had been asked to choose among five possible courses of action. By far the largest number, 46 percent, voted to "give a military demonstration in Japan, to be followed by a renewed opportunity to surrender before full use of the weapon is employed." The phrase "military demonstration in Japan" was later interpreted by officials in Washington to mean an attack without warning, but many of the polled scientists subsequently contended that they meant just the opposite: the phrase "before full use of the weapon is employed" meant that they first wanted a demonstration that would not kill a large number of civilians.[57]

After checking with Groves, Compton sent the package to Groves's deputy, Colonel Kenneth Nichols, on July twenty-fourth, noting that "since the matter presented in the petition is of immediate concern, the petitioners desire the transmission occur as promptly as possible."[58] When Nichols received the package on July twenty-fifth, he sent it by special military courier to Groves in Washington, urging "that these papers be forwarded to the President of the United States with proper comments."[59] Groves delayed sending the package to Secretary Stimson's office until August first — after Truman had left Washington for the Potsdam Conference and a telex from Tinian Island in the western Pacific had assured him that the atomic bomb was ready for combat use against Japan.

In the end, the decision was one for policy makers, not scientists, to make. From the time the project got underway in October 1941, policy makers saw the bomb as a legitimate part of the overall war effort. They asked whether it would be ready in time, not whether it should be used if it was. Their chief purpose was to win the war at the least possible cost in American lives. They also considered the effect of the bomb's use on Japan, which they hoped would be shocked into surrender, and to a lesser degree on the Soviet Union, which they hoped might be made more cooperative after the war. These anticipated effects dampened any inclination to question the bomb's use, to consider an advance warning, or to ponder its broader moral and political consequences. Truman and his advisers concluded that using the bomb against Japan would achieve their primary aim of bringing the war to a speedy end and would further, rather than impair, the prospects of postwar peace. From their point of view, the greater the shock effect in Tokyo, the more quickly the war would end; and the greater the shock effect in Moscow, the more willing Stalin would be to deal in a friendly way with the United States. That was their assumption.

It was time to test it.

July 1945 was unusually hot and dry in Los Alamos. Instead of the usual summer rains, electrical storms rolled like loose cannonballs down from the Jemez Mountains, the blue sky forboding and crackling with branches of white lightning. Plutonium was arriving from Hanford and U-235 was arriving from Oak Ridge. The thump from explosives tests on nearby mesas could be heard more frequently each day. Nerves visibly tensed. Oppenheimer smoked constantly and grew painfully thin and gaunt, his porkpie hat looking bigger and bigger as his face grew thinner and thinner.

The approaching climax, coming after two years of constant strain and pressure, produced drawn faces on the scientists, who seemed to one spouse to be "driven by demons."[60] Failure was unthinkable, and yet some couldn't suppress the thought as the enterprise entered its final phase.

They had come a long way since the laboratory opened in April 1943 and Ernest Lawrence scoffed that "thirty scientists could design this bomb in three months if we had the fissionable material."[61] Then, they had known almost nothing about bomb design. How much fissionable material was needed to make the explosion? What was the best way to get the biggest explosion? What should be the material's shape? How should it be detonated? Could the force of the explosion be predicted?

Time had passed, problems had been solved, and work had progressed with increasing speed. Things were moving fast now. Two types of bombs neared completion. To obtain a powerful explosion, sufficient fissionable material had to be brought together quickly, then kept together long enough to release a lot of energy. The most obvious and direct assembly method was a uranium bomb, using a simple and tested "gun" design in which a cannon fired a subcritical slug of U-235 into a subcritical core of U-235, bringing them to a critical mass that generated a tremendous radioactive explosion. Because U-235 was in extremely short supply and because Oppenheimer and his colleagues felt highly confident that the straightforward design of the gun would work, the decision was made not to test it.

Not so for the second type: a plutonium bomb. The gun-assembly method could not be used with plutonium, since this new element exploded too *easily*. Plutonium emitted alpha rays and would be a source of background neutrons. Calculations strongly suggested that these background neutrons would be strong enough to predetonate a gun-type weapon; that is, even at the highest possible muzzle velocities, the chain reaction would start before the two pieces of the core had come close enough together to become a critical mass. In that case the reaction would fizzle and the weapon would release only a minute fraction of its explosive energy. It would be a dud.

An alternative to the gun method, called implosion, was proposed by Caltech physicist Seth Neddermeyer and developed by Harvard chemist George Kistiakowsky. Instead of shooting two subcritical masses of plutonium together, implosion involved taking a subcritical mass and compressing it to criticality in millionths of a second. If a sphere could be uniformly squeezed tight enough over its entire surface, the plutonium molecules would be compressed to a higher density at which the subcritical mass would become critical. The great speed of compression would also eliminate the danger of predetonation.

Plutonium was considerably easier to produce than U-235, but there was also considerably more uncertainty whether the implosion design would work. Oppenheimer and most of his division leaders, including Bethe, were skeptical at first. The technical problems of implosion were tremendous. If one point of the plutonium sphere were detonated more than one-millionth of a second later than another point, implosion would not work. More than six hundred Los Alamos scientists ended up working on the problem and devising feasible solutions, but without a test, there was no way to tell if the implosion bomb would work.

Nagging doubts persisted as Oppenheimer and his colleagues went about their last weeks of preparations, and a gloomy parody repeated up and down the halls of the Tech Area: "From this crude lab that spawned a dud / Their necks to Truman's axe uncurled / Lo, the embattled savants stood / And fired the flop heard 'round the world."[62] Each scientist on the Hill gave a different estimate of the chance of success, but all agreed that the answer was uncertain. They were reaching into the unknown.

Oppenheimer argued that delays in development, as well as the tight schedule in production of fissionable material, made it necessary to postpone the test date. But Groves was unrelenting. He insisted that the bomb be tested before July seventeenth (when the final wartime conference between Truman, Churchill, and Stalin was scheduled to begin at Potsdam). On July second, Groves phoned Oppenheimer to discuss the test schedule. Oppenheimer requested a delay; the implosion device, he said, would not be ready before July seventeenth. Groves insisted that the target date of July sixteenth be kept, and explained why. Oppenheimer, who had few reserves left, said it went against his own feeling, but if the general wanted it that way, he would do it.[63] As they had been for the past two years, Oppenheimer and the other scientists at Los Alamos would be pushed to the limit.

At the beginning of July, large numbers of scientists began making mysterious trips off the mesa to a destination in southern New Mexico. Nearby canyons echoed with explosions as test work on implosion reached a climax. Then the explosions suddenly stopped. Excitement was at fever pitch. It seemed to everyone that something big was about to happen.

On July fifth, just six days after enough plutonium had arrived from Hanford, Oppenheimer wired Lawrence: "Anytime after the 15th would be a good time for our fishing trip. Because we are not certain of the weather we may be delayed several days. As we do not have enough sleeping bags to go around, we ask you please not to bring any one with you."[64]

The test site, codenamed Trinity — it had been named by Oppenheimer while he was reading seventeenth-century English poet John Donne: "Batter my heart, three-person'd God." — lay in a vast, empty, and forbidding sweep of desolate land fifty miles northwest of

Alamogordo, New Mexico. It was bounded on the west by the Rio Grande River and on the east by the Sierra Oscura Mountains, which rose low and broken on the distant desert horizon. Dotted with mesquite, yucca, and cactus and inhabited by a menagerie of desert insects and reptiles, the site was originally part of the royal road north from Mexico City to the farthermost regions of Spain's New World empire. The area had been known ominously from Spanish times as Jornada del Muerto — the dry and dangerous Dead Man's Trail, the Journey of Death.

Apaches roamed here originally, but during the nineteenth century it became ranch land where cattle and sheep grazed as best they could. The state of New Mexico owned most of the land, but leased it to a handful of homesteaders at minimal cost. After Pearl Harbor the Jornada became the northwest sector of the Alamogordo Air Base. The Army Air Corps leased a ranch in the middle of the Jornada, and ten miles north of the ranch house marked out Ground Zero. At points 10,000 yards north, west, and south from Ground Zero, contractors built observation bunkers with concrete slab roofs supported by sturdy oak beams. South-10,000 would serve as the control bunker for the test. Another five miles beyond South-10,000 was a base camp of tents and barracks. Behind the camp, desert brush ran all the way to the Oscura Mountains. Here — on the endless stark desert, empty almost all the way to Mexico — was the Trinity site in all its strangeness, an oasis willed into existence overnight.

The convoy carrying the precious plutonium core from Los Alamos arrived at Alamogordo in the early evening of July twelfth. The core, transported in a shock-mounted case, was carried into a room at the ranch house, which was guarded throughout the night by heavily armed MPs. The next morning — a Friday the thirteenth — a team of physicists gathered in white labcoats at the ranch house to begin the assembly. On a table in the room, the assemblers spread brown wrapping paper and laid out two hemispheres of plutonium warm to the touch and plated in nickel to make them safe to handle, a shiny beryllium/polonium initiator and, to confine these elements, several pieces of plum-colored natural uranium. With Oppenheimer walking in and out like an expectant father, adding to the already considerable tension in the room, the assemblers carefully nestled the small cylinder with the initiator between the plutonium hemispheres, then the nickel ball in the hollowed tamper of uranium.

Late that afternoon, the eighty-pound bomb core, readied at last, was placed in a sedan and carefully driven to Ground Zero. The following day, a team of physicists working under Oppenheimer's close and constant attention gingerly completed the final assembly. The team, many of them shirtless, worked inside a muslin tent to protect them from the scorching rays, a soft light guiding their work. Everyone in the tent seemed outwardly calm, but each felt the tension in the air. The plutonium core, suspended by a chain from a hoist, was slowly lowered into the center of a sphere of high explosives, like the pit in a peach. The team finished its work under lights in the late evening.

At 8:00 the next morning, the tent was removed, and the plutonium bomb started its slow ascent to the top of the steel tower. Several mattresses were stacked under the bomb in the hope of softening the impact of an accidental drop. Powered by a motor, the hoist rose slowly, only a foot a minute. Workers climbed just ahead of the bomb, guiding its passage from platform to platform until they finally placed it in a sheet-steel cage on top of the tower. Dozens of fragile detonators, arranged symmetrically on the outside surface to be triggered simultaneously by an electric circuit, were then delicately attached. Late that night, the work was finished. Finally everything was ready.

The steel tower at Ground Zero looked like an oil rig without the pipes, a spindly structure of steel beams and tie braces. Concrete footings supported its four legs, spaced thirty-five feet apart. Braced with crossed struts, the tower rose one hundred feet to a wooden platform that was roofed and sheltered on three sides with sheets of corrugated iron. The bomb atop the tower was five feet around and weighed five tons, but the plutonium core was not much bigger than a grapefruit. Cables connected the bomb's sixty-four detonator ports to electrical boxes. Out of the boxes' switchboard backs an equal number of cables hung down to the firing unit, a padlocked aluminum case. Below on the desert floor, hundreds of six-foot wooden poles strung with five hundred miles of wire fanned out from Zero to measuring instruments anchored miles away. Zero Hour was fixed for Monday morning, July sixteenth.

The early morning of July 16, 1945, was dark — not a star could be seen. A tropical air mass thick with humidity hung over the Jornada, and winds gusted to thirty miles an hour. A low, unbroken belly of clouds stretched from one end of the valley to the other. Lightning was striking everywhere. In every arc of the horizon a bolt was hitting. One report of thunder overlapped and muffled another. As lightning flashed, everyone, tense and nervous, glanced apprehensively toward Zero. A bomb of similar size, but filled with ordinary explosives, had been hauled up the tower a few days before to test the measuring instruments. That bomb had been struck by lightning and exploded with a thunderous bang. If a bolt were to strike now, who knew what might happen? The desert was damp, and the waiting scientists shivered.

Oppenheimer, even more nervous and tense than usual, paced back and forth in the doorway of South-10,000, peering at the weather outside. It was miserable. A colossal storm had raged all night long. The bunker was damp and wet. Oppenheimer had passed the night stirring restlessly on his bunk, racked with coughing from chain-smoking. "He was very tense," recalled a young scientist who was in the bunker that night. "I tried to be funny, to lighten the situation. He seriously debated firing me on the spot."[65]

Oppenheimer spent the final, harrowing hours before the test with Groves. The physicist seemed to totter on the verge of a nervous collapse. Groves made an effort to keep him away from the mounting tension in the dugout. Each time that Oppenheimer seemed on the point of breaking down, Groves would take him out and walk with him in the rain, reassuring him that everything would be all right. Oppenheimer wanted the test to succeed. Yet just two nights before, in a mood of foreboding, he had recited to a friend a stanza from the sacred Hindu epic poem the Bhagavad Gita: "In battle, in forest, at the precipice in the mountains / On the dark great sea, in the midst of javelins and arrows / In sleep, in confusion, in the depths of shame / The good deeds a man has done before defend him."

Always thin, Oppenheimer now looked emaciated. Fatigue had worn away his cheeks, and his crystal blue eyes recessed deep in their sockets, an image of implosion. His voice, dry and scratchy, seemed to cry out for rest, but instead his body was in constant motion, pacing edgily. He vibrated with tension, his cigarette hand moving to his mouth in tiny jerks. Groves feared he might come apart at the last minute. Oppenheimer scarcely breathed and held on to a post to steady himself. "Lord, these affairs are hard on the heart," he whispered.[66]

Twenty miles northwest of Zero, Teller stood atop Compañia Hill where he had hiked with a heavy, uneven step because of his artificial foot to view the long-awaited test. Other scientists who also had been bused in to view the test stood with him in the dark atop the sandy desert ridge. They talked in groups like guests at a tailgate party. Most had been there all night and were stiff with cold and waiting. The wind had died down to a still hush before dawn. Now the crowd members grew quiet, stamping their feet to keep warm.

Although all had been instructed to lie down on the sand and turn their faces away from the blast and bury their heads in their arms, Teller had no intention of doing so. Suspecting the flash might be even bigger than expected, in the pitch black of this early morning, he hurriedly smeared suntan lotion on his face and hands. He put on dark glasses and pulled on a pair of heavy gloves. With both hands, he pressed a piece of dark welder's glass to his face so that the light would not damage his eyes. "A hundred-to-one it's not needed, but what do we know?" he said nervously to those around him.[67] Teller then looked straight toward the distant tower.

Bethe moved into position with Teller on Compañia Hill. Bethe had addressed "T" Division personnel the night before in Los Alamos' biggest community hall, concluding: "Human calculation indicates that the experiment must succeed. But will nature act in conformity with our calculations?"[68] Bethe and his audience had then boarded buses camouflaged with paint and set off on the four-hour journey through thunderstorms and hail to Trinity. Like Teller, Bethe now rubbed suntan lotion on his face and hands for protection against damaging ultraviolet rays from an expected flash twenty miles away. The one-minute warning rocket fired.

Lawrence was also on Compañia Hill, having made the three-hour drive down from Albuquerque in the middle of the night. Lawrence had wagered other scientists on the test's success, but his usual assurance was missing. "Our tenseness grew as zero hour approached," he wrote later that day.[69] Lawrence had planned to watch the shot through the windshield of his olive-drab Plymouth, allowing the tinted glass to filter out the ultraviolet rays, but at the last minute, as the final countdown began, he decided to get out and look toward distant Zero with just sunglasses.

Fermi had gazed over the desert the day before "at the world on the eve of its disintegration."[70] Now he stood at base camp, making some final calculations on his slide rule. He tore up scraps of paper and stuffed them into his pockets. A brilliant and methodical physicist with a mordant wit, he had annoyed Groves by offering to take wagers from other scientists on whether or not the bomb would ignite the atmosphere and destroy the world. Whatever the outcome, Fermi said, the test would be a worthwhile scientific experiment. If the bomb failed, they would have proved that an atomic explosion was impossible. Some of Fermi's colleagues interpreted his remark as thoughtless bravado, but to Fermi it was black satire.

Rabi had spent the night playing poker. Now he stood beside Fermi at base camp. The intermittent lightning and thunder made Rabi fear that the "gadget" might be set off accidentally. A warning siren, fired one minute before the explosion, signaled him, Fermi, and others to go into shallow trenches that had been bulldozed below a reservoir at base camp. Rabi lay down, facing away from Zero. "We were lying there, very tense, in the early dawn, and there were just a few streaks of gold in the east; you could see your neighbor very dimly," he recalled of the final moments. "Those ten seconds were the longest ten seconds that I ever experienced."[71]

The nervous announcer brought the countdown to zero with a scream.

PART II

—

PANDORA'S BOX

CHAPTER 7

Three Fires

A T 5:29:45 A.M. Mountain War Time on July 16, 1945, just as the first faint signs of dawn appeared above the eastern horizon, a pinprick of blinding white light materialized atop the tower that spurted upward in a flaming jet. The light, at its core many times brighter than the midday sun, instantly replaced the dawn's subtle pastels with a blazing radiance. It was so intense that it could be seen in Albuquerque, Santa Fe, and even El Paso — 180 miles away. The heat at the center of the blast was so intense that six miles away it felt like standing in front of a roaring fireplace. In milliseconds, charges imploding inward had compressed the plutonium core beyond critical mass, causing it to explode in a furious frenzy of energy-releasing fissions that instantly vaporized the steel tower.

A white-hot fireball spilled across the desert, kicking up a swirl of radioactive debris that boiled and billowed upward in a massive mushroom. Every living thing within a mile's radius was annihilated. The flash left behind shadows of tiny creatures incinerated in the hard-packed sand. The fireball gouged out a twelve hundred foot crater ranging in depth from ten feet at the periphery to twenty-five feet in the center. Sand in the crater melted into a jadelike substance the color of emerald. Fifteen hundred feet away, a stout four-inch iron pipe, sixteen feet high and set in concrete, had completely disappeared. Slowly the fireball lifted from the desert, a furnace of mammoth, violent, roiling flames. Up it went, a convulsive, quivering mushroom a mile in diameter, changing colors from gold to purple to violet to gray to blue, expanding, growing and rising until it touched the clouds, pushed through them, and kept rising higher and higher.

The mushroom stem appeared twisted like a left-hand threaded screw, and below it, the color of the Jornada was an unearthly green. The whole sky glowed with an intense violet hue for half a minute. Then came a shock wave of hot wind closely followed by a strong, sustained, awesome roar of thunder. The sound reverberated for miles across the desert, mounting in resonance as it raced to the very rim of the Jornada's bowl and ricocheted off the peaks. The ground trembled as in an earthquake.

Across the test site everyone felt infinitely small. The moment was uplifting and crushing, exhilarating and devastating, full of great promise and great foreboding. The spectacle was so overwhelming that most observers' first reaction was speechlessness. No one moved or said a word for several moments. All was silence. They were in awe and at a loss for words. Yet all of them had the feeling that they had just witnessed one of the great events of history. "It was," said an eyewitness, "as awesome a thing as I've ever seen."[1]

Oppenheimer's face relaxed into an expression of tremendous relief as he sensed the flash of light. All his pent-up emotions and burdens evaporated in that instant. He waited until the blast had passed, then stepped out of the control bunker. He watched and listened in silence, then simply muttered, "It worked. It worked." He thought of the immediate future. The success of the test seemed to signal an end to the war against Japan and a promise of life for many American soldiers. It was "terrifying" and "not entirely undepressing," he told the *New York Times* science correspondent who was at Trinity to chronicle the event, adding: "Lots of boys not grown up yet will owe their life to it!"[2] But in the next moments he thought of the longer future, which made him feel "extremely solemn." "We knew the world would not be the same," he said of the explosion many years later, then recalled lines from the Bhagavad Gita: Vishnu is trying to persuade the Prince that he should do his duty, and to impress him he takes on his multi-armed form and says, "If the radiance of a thousand suns / Were to burst forth at once in the sky, / That would be like the splendor / of the Mighty One. . . . / I am become Death, the destroyer of worlds." "I suppose we all thought that, one way or another," he remembered.

When Oppenheimer returned to base camp shortly after the explosion, he was strangely quiet. He appeared distant and distracted, not in a frame of mind to discuss anything. Still shaken, Oppenheimer asked to be driven in a jeep into the surrounding hills for an hour or so in order to calm down. He felt deeply relieved that the bomb had worked — that his creation was a success — and yet terribly frightened by what he had done.

The other scientists at Trinity shared Oppenheimer's feelings. The mushroom cloud symbolized a giant question mark to Teller. Bethe felt overwhelmed by exhilaration and accomplishment. Then he began to feel shock and fear. "What have we done?" he whispered to himself. "What have we done?"[3] Lawrence reacted by slapping another scientist on the back and leaping in the air. Then he began to feel solemn. "The grand, indeed almost cataclysmic proportions of the explosion produced a kind of solemnity in everyone's behaviour," he wrote later that day. "There was restrained applause, but more a hushed murmuring bordering on reverence."[4] Deeply moved, Lawrence still could talk of nothing else even two days later. "The awesome spectacle was an experience I shall never forget."[5]

Even the cool and matter-of-fact Fermi felt its emotional impact. At first, Fermi played the scientist, trying to measure the force of the blast by dropping the scraps of paper from his pocket into the air before, during, and after the shock wave hit base camp. He was so absorbed in his bits of paper that he did not hear the tremendous noise.[6] Then he felt jolted and drained. He confessed that he did not feel capable of sitting behind the wheel of his sand-colored Chevrolet, and asked a friend to drive him back to Los Alamos — something he had never done before. When his wife saw him, "he seemed shrunken and aged, made of old parchment, so entirely dried out and browned was he by the desert sun and exhausted by the ordeal."[7]

Rabi felt jubilant at first. He passed around cups of bourbon as a congratulatory offering. Then he began to notice little things: horses whinnying in fright, the slowly spinning paddle of the windmill above the reservoir, the toads that had stopped croaking. Rabi felt gooseflesh break out all over him. He sensed, he later wrote, "a chill, which was not the morning cold; it was a chill that came to one when one thought, as for instance when I thought of my wooden house in Cambridge, and my laboratory in New York, and of the millions of people living around there, and this power of nature which we had first understood it to be — well, there it was."[8]

When the scientists piled into buses to return to Los Alamos, they sprawled exhausted in their seats and grew solemn. "It was quiet," recalled one who made the ride back. "We were busy with our own thoughts. We were still absorbing the impact of it."[9] The full import of Trinity was beginning to register. A physicist at Los Alamos vividly remembered seeing the grim, silent expressions on the faces of the scientists as they stepped from the buses that evening. "I saw that something very grave and strong had happened to their whole outlook on the future."[10] At last they had a chance to pause and think about what they had done, to face the awesome and chilling consequences of their labors. They realized — because they had seen and felt it — just how terrifying was the force they had unleashed. The bomb's power turned out to be far greater than they had imagined. They sensed the world would never be the same again.

Meanwhile, planning for dropping the bomb on Japan ground forward relentlessly. The institutional machinery created to achieve this goal was powerful, and it was moving inexorably toward its end. By July twenty-fourth, plans were set. The bombs would be used when they were ready. Beforehand, Japan would be given a generally phrased warning of total destruction unless it surrendered. This "last chance" warning, included in the Potsdam Declaration of July twenty-sixth, was dismissed by the Japanese. Groves notified Stimson that a uranium bomb would be available soon after August first. The first plutonium bomb, the type tested at Trinity, would be ready for delivery about August sixth, and a second was expected by August seventeenth or eighteenth. Additional ones would be produced at an accelerated rate from possibly three in September to perhaps seven or more in December. A specially trained B-29 unit in the South Pacific, the 509th Composite Air Group, was to deliver the first bomb as soon as weather permitted visual bombing after August third. The list of targets included Hiroshima and Nagasaki.

Hiroshima was chosen as a target for the atomic bomb because its landscape was flat and it was one of the few Japanese cities left by the summer of 1945 that had not yet been firebombed to ashes. These conditions would afford the most dramatic demonstration of the weapon's power and the most accurate measurement of its destructiveness. There was some military rationale, too: the city was the headquarters of the Second Japanese Army, which commanded the defense of southern Japan. From here the Japanese general staff prepared to direct the defense of the island of Kyushu against an impending American invasion. But it was also the home of more than

300,000 noncombatants. In Hiroshima, civilians outnumbered soldiers by more than six to one.

On July twenty-third Oppenheimer informed Navy Captain Deak Parsons, the Los Alamos ordnance specialist who would ride aboard the attacking aircraft, that the bombs were expected to perform well. "As a result of the Trinity shot we are led to expect a very similar performance from the first Little Boy [U-235 bomb] and the first plutonium Fat Man." Oppenheimer predicted that the energy release of each bomb would fall between twelve to twenty thousand tons, and that the blast effect would be equivalent to eight to fifteen thousand tons of TNT. The fireball would be of greater brilliance and longer duration than the Trinity shot, since no dust would be mixed with it when it detonated at altitude. Yet lethal radiation from the bomb would reach the ground.[11]

At 2:45 A.M. on August 6, 1945, three B-29s belonging to the 509th lifted off from the island of Tinian in the Marianas and headed for the Japanese home islands fifteen hundred miles to the north. In the belly of the lead plane, the *Enola Gay*, was Little Boy — chosen because it had been readied first. It contained twenty-five kilograms of U-235 encased within cordite, steel tamper, casing, and firing controls.* By 7:30 A.M. the bomb had been armed. Fifteen minutes later the plane was over the Japanese mainland.

The morning of August sixth was sunny, calm, and warm in Hiroshima — a beautiful summer day. The sky was sharply blue. "Shimmering leaves, reflecting sunlight from a cloudless sky, made a pleasant contrast with shadows in my garden," a resident of the city noted in his diary.[12] People walked, bicycled, and rode streetcars to work. Soldiers exercised on parade grounds while schoolgirls swept city streets. An air-raid siren sounded just before 8:15 A.M., but few scurried for cover — people were more concerned with getting to work than with sheltering themselves from three planes — although many raised their eyes to watch the B-29s high in the sky. No military alert sounded when the *Enola Gay* and two trailing B-29s loaded with

---

* The U-235 for the Hiroshima bomb was transported to Tinian by the cruiser *Indianapolis* as a safety precaution. Whereas the plutonium for the Nagasaki bomb was the output of about two weeks' production at Hanford by the summer of 1945, the uranium bomb was the output of about six months' production at Oak Ridge. Consequently, Washington did not want to risk losing it by transporting it by plane, which might crash or be shot down. Three days after delivering the U-235 to Tinian, the *Indianapolis* was torpedoed by a Japanese submarine en route to the Philippines, sinking in less than half an hour and taking the lives of nearly one thousand American sailors.

instruments to measure and photograph the blast approached Hiroshima; Japanese officials assumed the three planes were on a routine reconnaissance flight. Unchallenged, the *Enola Gay* flew to the heart of the city.[13]

A minute later the bomb was dropped. Ground Zero was the Aioi Bridge, spanning the delta islands of the Ōta River in central Hiroshima. Whistling and spinning, the bomb had small holes around its midpoint where wires came out as it fell; these started the clock switches of its first arming system. More small holes drilled farther back on its steel casing took in samples of air as it fell; when the bomb reached seven thousand feet, a barometric switch turned, priming the second arming system. Sticking out of the bomb's spinning tail fins were numerous thin radio antennae; these collected returning radio signals, and used the time lag each took to return as a way of measuring the height remaining to the ground. At nineteen hundred feet — the height calculated for maximum damage — the bomb detonated. There was a tremendous flash of light and heat. It lasted only a fraction of a second, but its intensity was sufficient to instantly incinerate everything up to five hundred yards from Ground Zero. Total devastation stretched out half a mile from the point of the explosion, leaving the rubble of one building indistinguishable from that of the next. People within half a mile of the fireball were seared to smoking black bundles, their internal organs boiled away. Thousands of these black bundles littered the smashed streets and bridges and sidewalks of Hiroshima. Farther out, the thermal flash instantly blistered and tore loose people's skin, leaving it hanging from the horribly swollen faces and bodies of severely injured survivors who groaned and staggered like sleepwalkers as they called out names of loved ones in their shock and suffering.

The blast wave, rocketing from Ground Zero at two miles per second, threw up a vast cloud of swirling debris, igniting fires similar to the incendiary raids against other Japanese cities, except this time the fires were everywhere at once. The sickly sweet odor of burning human flesh hung over all of Hiroshima, which had changed to a wasteland of scorched earth. Everything as far as the eye could see was ashes and ruins. Smoke thick enough to obscure the sun covered the sky. Rain that was muddy and chilly (and highly radioactive) began to fall. Children cried for their mothers; mothers searched desperately for their children. Pain and suffering were everywhere. "I know of no word or words to describe the view," a survivor later said.[14] Some people thought the world was ending. Others thought it was Hell on earth.

Hiroshima had been destroyed in an instant. Fire stations, police stations, railroad stations, post offices, telephone and telegraph offices, broadcasting stations, and schools were demolished. Streetcars, roads, and electricity, gas, water, and sewer facilities were ruined beyond use. Hospitals and first-aid clinics were destroyed. Ninety percent of all medical personnel in the city were killed or disabled. An entire community had been shattered. And this was only the beginning. Within hours, victims not killed or horribly burned became sick by what was thought to be a mysterious gas, but was actually radiation poisoning. They seemed to improve for a time, but then they worsened, slowly and painfully. It was a strange and agonizing form of illness: nausea, vomiting, loss of appetite, bloody diarrhea, fever, weakness, ulceration and bleeding in the mouth, the eyes, the lungs — a slow but progressive worsening until death. Those who would survive suffered a greatly increased risk of leukemia. There would also be high mortality rates among fetuses exposed to radiation in the womb, and many infants who lived showed retarded growth and abnormally small heads. Nearly 200,000 people were killed outright or would die in Hiroshima in subsequent years from the effects of heat, blast, and fire. There was to be a continuing toll of radiation-induced genetic disorders in children conceived years afterward.

Nagasaki was a densely populated and cosmopolitan city built around a harbor and up into surrounding hills like San Francisco. And like San Francisco, it was a fabled port of spectacular beauty, particularly now, for autumn had come early to the city and many of its trees were brilliant with red and yellow leaves. The Portuguese and the Dutch had arrived in Nagasaki in the late sixteenth century and helped transform it from a fishing village into Japan's chief port for foreign trade. Portuguese Jesuit priests had brought Christianity with them, spreading the word of the God of Love and the Golden Rule. In 1945 Nagasaki remained the most Christianized city in Japan, a harmonious blend of Eastern and Western cultures with its many churches and western-style houses, including the legendary home of Madame Butterfly, immortalized by Puccini, overlooking the harbor. It was also where the Mitsubishi torpedoes used to devastating effect at Pearl Harbor had been made.

Nagasaki was not the intended target on the morning of August 9, 1945. The intended target was Kokura, on the northeast coast of Kyushu, but heavy ground haze and smoke obscured Kokura and the aiming point could not be seen. So the B-29 flew on to Nagasaki, and found that it, too, was obscured by clouds racing in from the East China Sea. Running low on fuel, the pilot had time for one final pass over the city. At the last minute, the clouds broke just long enough to give the bombardier a view of the target. A plutonium bomb fell from the B-29 and exploded 1,650 feet above Nagasaki just after 11:00 in the morning.

There was a blinding bluish-white flash, accompanied by intense glare and heat. The split-second flash was so intense that it caused third-degree burns to exposed human skin up to a distance of a mile. Clothing ignited, telephone poles charred, thatch-roofed houses caught fire. Black or other dark-colored surfaces absorbed the heat and immediately burst into flames. A blast wave followed that roared like an earthquake. People forty miles away felt the concussion. The sky darkened ominously, turning an eerie red and then a ghostly yellow. Huge radioactive raindrops fell from the sky. The scene on the ground was obscured first by a bluish haze and then by a purple-brown cloud of choking dust and smoke. The victims of Nagasaki, like those of Hiroshima, thought they had descended into Hell. They stumbled around, terrified and helpless, in the twilight gloom. Bodies of the dead were so charred that one could not distinguish men from women, backs from chests. As the dust settled and the smoke cleared, the search for victims buried in the rubble began. The flesh of survivors peeled off their bones like gloves from hands as they were pulled screaming and moaning from the debris.

Far from the human suffering below, the crew of the B-29 stared in shocked amazement at a boiling cauldron where a beautiful, vibrant city had been just moments before. Over four square miles in the center of the city had been flattened and blackened. They watched as a gigantic ball of flame rose in a huge column of thick smoke two miles up in the sky. A massive, swelling mushroom billowed at the top. It seethed like a thousand geysers, changing colors kaleidoscopically. Then it broke free from the stem and a smaller mushroom took its place. It was like a decapitated monster growing a new head.

After a while, countless men, women, and children began to gather for a drink of water at the banks of the Urakami River. Their hair and clothing were scorched and their burnt skin hung off in sheets like rags. Begging for help, they died one after another in the water or in heaps on the banks. Then radiation began to take its toll. Seventy thousand people died in Nagasaki that day and another 70,000 more over the next five years — a slightly smaller death toll than in Hiroshima because the surrounding hills had deflected the blast and radiation. But the victims of Nagasaki endured equally unspeakable suffering. An American naval officer who visited Nagasaki a month after the bombing described in a letter home to his wife what he felt when he saw the once beautiful city:

> A smell of death and corruption pervades the place, ranging from the ordinary carrion smell to somewhat subtler stenches with strong overtones of ammonia (decomposing nitrogenous matter, I suppose). The general impression, which transcends those derived from the evidence of our physical senses, is one of deadness, the absolute essence of death in the sense of finality without hope of resurrection. And all this is not localized. It's everywhere, and nothing has escaped its touch. In most ruined cities you can bury the dead, clean up the rubble, rebuild the houses and have a living city again. One feels that is not so here. Like the ancient Sodom and Gomorrah, its site has been sown with salt and *ichabod* ["the glory is departed"] is written over its gates.[15]

Groves telephoned Oppenheimer from Washington on the afternoon of August sixth with the news that Hiroshima had been bombed. Oppenheimer was tense. He had been pacing his office and chain-smoking. Groves told him he was proud of his lab. "It went all right?" Oppenheimer anxiously asked. "Apparently it went with a tremendous bang," the general replied. Remembering the profound impression that the predawn Trinity test had made on him, and hoping that Hiroshima would similarly shock the world, Oppenheimer asked Groves if the bomb had been dropped before sunrise. No, said Groves, the bomb had been dropped in daylight in order to safeguard the plane's crew. "Everybody is feeling reasonably good about it here and I extend my heartiest congratulations," Oppenheimer said to Groves, his voice trailing off. "It's been a long road." "One of the wisest things I ever did was when I selected the director of Los Alamos," the general crowed. "Well, I have my doubts, General Groves," said Oppenheimer, in no mood for self-congratulation at that moment.[16]

Teller learned about Hiroshima on the afternoon of August sixth as he walked from his apartment along the Jemez Mesa to the Tech Area. On the way, he saw another scientist sitting in a jeep parked beneath the Los Alamos water tower. His face was exuberant. He was as exhilarated as a victorious boxer. He called to Teller excitedly: "One down!" Teller did not know what he meant, and walked on toward the Tech Area. There he heard the news. But word of the Hiroshima bombing created no exuberance, no exhilaration, no elation in Teller that afternoon. Instead, he felt worried, concerned, and anxious. A new force was loose in the world. What this new force would do, Teller could not guess.

When Oppenheimer had returned to Los Alamos after Trinity, he had found Teller's latest report on superbomb research waiting on his desk. Calculations suggested that a thermonuclear reaction could indeed be triggered by an atomic bomb. On the afternoon of Hiroshima, Oppenheimer went to Teller's office for a long and private talk. He made it clear to Teller that he, personally, would have nothing further to do with research on a superbomb. If he had his way, Oppenheimer added, Los Alamos would never develop such a weapon.[17] But even in that case, he was solicitous of Teller's well-being. He did not simply inform Teller of his opinion; he did his best to persuade him that abandoning work on a superbomb was the wisest course.

When news of Hiroshima reached Szilard at the University of Chicago's faculty club on the afternoon of August sixth, he reacted with anger, sadness, and horror. His first stop after he heard the news was University President Robert Maynard Hutchins's office. He asked Hutchins if the Met Lab staff might wear black mourning bands on their arms. Hutchins suggested that Szilard find some less dramatic way for them to demonstrate their grief. That evening Szilard poured out his guilt and regret in a letter to his beloved Trude:

> I suppose you have seen today's newspapers. Using atomic bombs against Japan is one of the greatest blunders of history. Both from a practical point of view on a 10-year scale and from the point of view of our moral position. I went out of my way (and very much so) in order to prevent it, but as today's papers show, without success. It is very difficult to see what wise course of action is possible from here on.[18]

"I always thought it was his way of apologizing," Trude said after Leo's death. "It was one of the most important letters he ever wrote to me."[19]

Compton was in his office at the University of Chicago when news of Hiroshima flashed over the radio. He called together the scientists of the Met Lab, and told them what details he knew. It was a tough audience. Compton expressed his regret for the enormous human suffering caused by the bomb, and accepted his share of responsibility for the decision to drop it. To an acquaintance who decried the atomic attacks, Compton responded, "I favored the use of the bomb, substantially as it was used, and believe now that this was wise." Yet he obliquely acknowledged moral qualms, arguing that the atomic bombing was no worse than the firebombing of Tokyo that had erased any distinction between combatants and noncombatants. The atomic bomb's chief difference, he asserted, "was the psychological effect of its surprise use. It was of about the same destructiveness as a raid by a fleet of B-29s using ordinary bombs." "I say that before God our consciences are clear," Compton declared, somewhat plaintively. "We made the best choice for man's future that we knew how to make."[20]

That night, Oppenheimer called a general meeting in the Tech Area auditorium. He entered at the rear — not from the wings, as was his custom — and made his way up the center aisle amid whistling, cheering, and foot stomping. On the stage Oppenheimer pumped his clasped hands above his head in the classic self-congratulation of a prizefighter. When at last he could speak, he read from a message flashed from the B-29 after the drop. There was no hint of regret in his words — no trace of the ambivalence and guilt the private Oppenheimer had expressed to Groves and Teller. The public Oppenheimer played unashamedly to the crowd. A young physicist in the audience that night remembered him strutting in triumph:

> It was too early to determine what the results of the bombing might have been, but he was sure that the Japanese didn't like it. More cheering. He was proud, and he showed it, of what he had accomplished. Even more cheering. And his only regret was that we hadn't developed the bomb in time to have used it against the Germans. This practically raised the roof.[21]

As the days passed, Oppenheimer grew depressed as what had really happened started to sink in. To one observer, he seemed "a nervous wreck."[22] Many scientists had worked on the bomb, and shared in the moral burden of having built such a devastating weapon, but Oppenheimer was one of the very few who had been given a chance to advise "No"; there was no honest way he could deny that the death of so many Japanese civilians was in some measure his personal doing. When news of Nagasaki reached him on August ninth, he released this statement to the press on behalf of his lab:

> We have believed that the use of this weapon in the war against Japan might help to shorten the war and be a benefit to the world for that reason alone; but above all we have thought that this rather spectacular technical development, and the assured prospect of far more terrifying future developments, would force upon the people of this country, and all the war-weary people of the world, a recognition of how imperative it has become to avert wars in the future; how the cooperation and understanding between nations which has seemed desirable for so long has become a desperate necessity. . . .[23]

Dropping the bomb on Hiroshima was a tragic mistake, Szilard thought; dropping the bomb on Nagasaki was an atrocity. He immediately asked the chaplain of the University of Chicago to include a special prayer for the Japanese casualties of the two devastated cities in any memorial service commemorating the end of the war. He offered to transmit the prayer to the Japanese survivors personally. He then sat down and drafted another petition to President Truman, calling the atomic bombings "a flagrant violation of our own moral standards" and asking that they be stopped. The Japanese surrender on August fourteenth mooted the issue and Szilard never sent his petition. When he tried to publish his first petition to President Truman in *Science* magazine later that month, Groves ordered it classified "secret" and explicitly forbade Szilard from publishing the second petition anywhere, threatening to imprison him if he did.

August 6, 1945, had found Bohr in London, awaiting return to his native Denmark. News of Hiroshima had provoked Bohr to speak out and give citizens of the world an understanding of the revolutionary issues involved and some way to deal with them. He wrote a letter to the *London Times* which appeared on August eleventh under a two-column headline: "Science and Civilization." It was Bohr's first public statement about the need for a more open world:

> The formidable power of destruction which has come within reach of man may become a mortal menace unless human society can adjust itself to the exigencies of the situation. Civilization is pre-

sented with a challenge more serious perhaps than ever before. . . . Against the new destructive powers no defense may be possible [and] no control can be effective without international supervision of all undertakings which unless regulated might become a source of disaster.

Such measures will demand the abolition of barriers hitherto considered necessary to safeguard national interests but now standing in the way of the common security against unprecedented danger. Certainly the handling of the precarious situation will demand the good will of all nations, but it must be recognized that we are dealing with what is potentially a deadly challenge to civilization itself.

Hiroshima and Nagasaki hit home for Bethe when photographs of the devastated cities arrived at Los Alamos by special courier several days later. Although Bethe had witnessed the Trinity test and had calculated the effect of an atomic blast over an urban area, he was unprepared emotionally for what he saw when he looked at the grim pictures. "The total destruction, the total leveling of a wide area was really very shocking," Bethe said with considerable emotion many years later. "It really came to mind when I saw the pictures."[24]

Lawrence learned of Hiroshima while listening to the radio in his living room. He sensed this meant the end of Japan's resistance and looked toward the future. "Now we will have no more war and the most backward countries will be able to start catching up," he told his wife, Molly.[25] On the day Nagasaki was bombed, Lawrence received a phone call from an agitated physicist who condemned the targeting of Japanese civilians and feared the bombings' effect on the reputation of science. The physicist wrote Lawrence later that day:

Many people, including some who are prominent and influential, think that science does more harm than good to humanity. Some of these, and some who think oppositely, contend that scientists ought to control the applications of their discoveries, though I for one cannot imagine how they could exercise any control. Some people go so far as to blame scientists for the consequences of their discoveries. I think that it is not far-fetched nor absurd to conjecture that in time to come, people will be saying, "Those wicked physicists of the 'Manhattan Project' deliberately developed a bomb which they knew would be used for killing thousands of innocent people without any warning, and they either wanted this outcome or at least condoned it. Away with physicists!" It will not be accepted as an excuse that they may have disapproved in silence. We do not excuse the German civilians who accepted Buchenwald while possibly disapproving in silence.[26]

Lawrence responded that same day:

In view of the fact that two bombs ended the war, I am inclined to feel that they made the right decision. Surely many more lives were saved by shortening the war than were sacrificed as a result of the bombs. Further, it goes without saying that all of us hope and pray that there will never be an occasion to use another one. The world must realize that there can never be another war.

As regards criticism of science and scientists, I think that is a cross we will have to bear, and I think in the long run the good sense of everyone the world over will realize that in this instance, as in all scientific pursuits, the world is better as a result.[27]

A short time later Lawrence left Berkeley for Los Alamos, partly to escape reporters clamoring for comment and partly to work with Oppenheimer on a report on postwar atomic efforts. Lawrence reacted impatiently to Oppenheimer's developing remorse. He felt little of Oppenheimer's soul-searching guilt. Although Lawrence had initially believed that the bomb would never be used against people and then had been one of the last members of the Scientific Advisory Panel to abandon the idea of a demonstration, he now thought of the bomb as a terrible swift sword that had forced Japan's surrender. Publicly, Lawrence confidently declared that "the harnessing of atomic energy in a weapon of war will come to be regarded in the future not as a mark of the doom of mankind, but rather as a first step in man's conquest of a new realm of the universe for his own betterment and welfare."[28]

Cool and controlled as always, Fermi did not comment publicly. When Japan surrendered on August fourteenth, residents of Los Alamos came out the next day to celebrate the end of the war. Fermi joined in the celebration, but he never once mentioned Hiroshima or Nagasaki in conversations with close friends that day. Fermi remained characteristically silent about his reaction to the bombing, even when his sister Maria, writing from Italy, reported that "All [here] are perplexed and appalled by its dreadful effects, and with time the bewilderment increases rather than diminishes. For my part I recommend you to God, Who alone can judge you morally."[29]

Fermi had, however, discussed the bomb privately with Oppenheimer. The two had concluded before Hiroshima that nothing could be done to control the bomb after the war if the American people did not even know that it existed, much less how much destruction it could inflict. Fermi and Oppenheimer believed that only its use would breach the wall of secrecy, and do the sort of shocking and horrific damage that might end war altogether.

Having witnessed the Trinity test, Rabi had understood the appalling damage the bomb would do to cities. A sensitive and moral man who had expressed misgivings to Oppenheimer early on in the project about making a weapon of mass destruction, Rabi had learned a "frightening thing" in the course of the war: "how easy it is to kill people when you turn your mind to it." "When you turn the resources of modern science to the problem of killing people," Rabi later wrote of his feelings in August 1945, "you realize how vulnerable they really are."[30]

Pollsters reported that the American public backed the use of the atomic bombs against Japan overwhelmingly because it — along with the Soviet Union's entrance into the conflict — brought the Pacific War to a speedy end. To those who cheered at the time (and they were the vast majority) — that was what mattered most. As Winston Churchill later wrote: "To avert a vast, indefinite butchery, to bring the war to an end, to give peace to the world, to lay healing hands upon its tortured peoples by a manifestation of overwhelming power at the cost of a few explosions, seemed, after all our toils and perils, a miracle of deliverance."[31]

Hiroshima and Nagasaki marked the culmination of a willingness on the part of American policy makers in World War II to tolerate the killing of noncombatants in the pursuit of victory. And of course the war against Japan had acquired such terrible momentum by the summer of 1945 that there was very little argument against waging war in any way, including in a new and terrible way: using a weapon of mass destruction on civilians in undefended cities. It was a bloody sort of progress: by inflicting suffering, the atomic bomb ended the suffering caused by firebombings and starvation blockades, and it obviated the ghastly specter of a U.S. invasion of the Japanese home islands.

The dropping of the atomic bomb was so dramatic, the awed shock it provoked throughout the world was so deep, and the sense that it was, in President Truman's words, "the greatest thing in history" seemed so incontestable that there was a general instinct to think that it had brought one phase of human affairs to an end. The events of the summer of 1945, Hans Bethe concurred, "changed everything."[32]

CHAPTER 8

An End, a Beginning

THE TRINITY TEST, closely followed by Hiroshima and Nagasaki, shook the atomic scientists out of their absorption in the technical problems of building the bomb and awakened them to its enormous moral and political implications. The scientific work was finished, and the awful magnitude of what they had done began to sink in. I. I. Rabi voiced their confused reactions in a widely read magazine article that fall. "I would say that we are frankly pleased, terrified, and to an even greater extent embarrassed when we contemplate the results of our wartime efforts," he wrote. "Our terror comes from the realization — which is nowhere more strongly felt than among us — of the tremendous forces of destruction now existing in an all too practical form."[1] Many felt "a feeling of accomplishment *and* a feeling of revulsion about what we had done," as Bethe said.[2]

All of them were haunted by the sarcasm of a Japanese radiologist in Hiroshima. "I did the experiment years ago, but only on a few rats. But you Americans — you are wonderful. You have made the *human* experiment." "No one," wrote a Los Alamos physicist, "could fail to carry the scar of such a cutting remark."[3] Many decided to leave Los Alamos. They left for many reasons, and not all explained why. Those who watched them go saw answers in their eyes or read them in letters written some time afterward. "We all felt," Bethe remembered, "that, like the soldiers, we had done our duty and that we deserved to return to the type of work that we had chosen as our life's career, the pursuit of pure science and teaching. Moreover, it was not obvious that there was any need for a large effort on atomic weapons in peacetime."[4]

Some felt a sense of unease, even those who believed that ending a bloody war had justified using the bomb. Many came to regard themselves, in the phrase of *Time* magazine, as the "world's guilty men."[5] Oppenheimer spoke for himself and many other physicists when he wrote, "In some sort of crude sense which no vulgarity, no humor, no overstatement can quite extinguish, the physicists have known sin; and this is a knowledge which they cannot lose."[6] Oppenheimer's words expressed the anguish of those caught between the commitment to pursue knowledge wherever it might lead and the realization that the knowledge discovered had caused great misery to other human beings.

Oppenheimer's anxiety was intensified by fear that the bomb threatened popular respect for the discipline of science he revered. Although physicists now seemed to wear the "tunic of Superman," in the phrase of *Life* magazine, and to stand in the spotlight of a thousand suns, the physicists themselves knew better.[7] "If we take the stand that our object is merely to see that the next war is bigger and better," Rabi warned, "we will ultimately lose the respect of the public. In popular demagogy we [will] become the unpaid servants of the 'munitions makers' and mere technicians rather than the self-sacrificing public-spirited citizens which we feel ourselves to be."[8] Their achievement seemed an ominous refutation of the Enlightenment belief — an article of faith to them — that greater knowledge would inevitably bring greater happiness and progress. "We have made a thing, a most terrible weapon," admitted Oppenheimer, one "that has altered abruptly and profoundly the nature of the world, a thing that by all the standards of the world we grew up in is an evil thing. And by so doing we have raised again the question of whether science is good for man, or whether it is good to learn about the world, to try to understand it, to try to control it."[9] Slowly, as if feeling their way in a blinding light, they struggled to understand what it all meant.

Oppenheimer was not the only physicist uneasy about a world armed with atomic bombs, but his exhaustion was deeper than most. The day after Nagasaki, Lawrence flew to Los Alamos (he had overcome his fear of airplanes), where he found his Berkeley colleague looking weary and feeling pessimistic, his hair turning gray. Oppenheimer wondered aloud if the dead at Hiroshima and Nagasaki were not luckier than the survivors, whose exposure to radiation would have painful and lasting effects. "I know that he felt guilty in spite of having told Truman the weapon had to be used," recalled Bethe. "He felt guilty for having directed the project."[10]

Compton and Fermi joined Oppenheimer and Lawrence that weekend to draft a report for Washington on postwar atomic policy. The four were emerging from the secret project as public heroes; not just policy makers but also the American people were clamoring for their views. Understanding this, they eschewed merely technical advice and decided to draft a plea for international control. "Other powers," they presciently warned, "can produce these weapons in a few years and all too soon be in a threatening position. We consider it imperative, therefore, to take determined steps toward international arrangements that will make such developments highly improbable, if not impossible."[11]

"We are convinced," they went on, "that weapons quantitatively and qualitatively far more effective than now available will result from further work on these problems." They were referring to the superbomb. The physicists further emphasized their "firm opinion" that "no military countermeasures will be found which will be adequately effective in preventing the delivery of atomic weapons" on the American homeland. This led to their most sobering but farsighted conclusion:

> We are not only unable to outline a program that would assure to this nation for the next decades hegemony in the field of atomic weapons; we are equally unable to insure that such hegemony, if achieved, could protect us from the most terrible destruction.

> The development, in the years to come, of more effective atomic weapons, would appear to be a most natural element in any national policy of maintaining our military forces at great strength; nevertheless we have grave doubts that this further development can contribute essentially or permanently to the prevention of war. We believe that the safety of this nation — as opposed to its ability to inflict damage on an enemy power — cannot lie wholly or even primarily in its scientific or technical prowess. It can be based only on making future wars impossible. It is our unanimous and urgent recommendation to you that, despite the present incomplete exploitation of technical possibilities in this field, all steps be taken, all necessary international arrangements be made, to this one end.[12]

Oppenheimer took their report to Washington in late August. The timing was unfortunate; the report stood in jarring contrast to the triumphant mood of the capital, where policy makers were exulting in victory over Japan, anticipating trouble with Russia, and more interested in building up the U.S. atomic arsenal than in pursuing international control. Oppenheimer described Washington's reaction in a disappointed letter back to Lawrence at Berkeley:

August 30, 1945

Dear Ernest:
After our meetings [at Los Alamos] I had a few days in Washington: it was a bad time, too early for clarity. I took our letter to Bush and to [Stimson's assistant] Harrison — Conant, Stimson, Compton were all away — and had an opportunity with them to explain in more detail than was appropriate in a letter what our common feelings were in this all-important thing. I emphasized of course that all of us would earnestly do whatever was really in the national interest, no matter how desperate and disagreeable; but that we felt reluctant to promise that much real good could come of continuing the atomic bomb work just like poison gases after the last war. . . . I had the fairly clear impression from the talks that things had gone most badly at Potsdam, and that little or no progress had been made in interesting the Russians in collaboration or control.* I don't know how seriously an effort was made: apparently neither Churchill nor Attlee nor Stalin was any help at all, but this is only my conjecture. While I was in Washington two things happened, both rather gloomy: the President issued an absolute Ukase, forbidding any disclosures on the atomic bomb — and the terms were broad — without his personal approval. The other was that Harrison took our letter to Byrnes, who sent back word just as I was leaving that "in the present critical international situation there was no alternative to pushing the [atomic] program full steam ahead." . . . I do not come away from a profound grief, and a profound perplexity about the course we should be following. . . .

Affectionately,
Robert[13]

---

* The Big Three summit conference outside Berlin was attended by Truman, Churchill, Attlee, and Stalin in late July 1945.

Oppenheimer sensed that policy makers did not grasp what scientists had put into their hands. Just weeks after the war, in response to a reporter's question, he said: "If you ask: 'Can we make [atomic bombs] more terrible?' the answer is yes. If you ask: 'Can we make a lot of them?' the answer is yes. If you ask: 'Can we make them terribly more terrible?' the answer is probably."[14] It was already clear to Oppenheimer that the atomic bomb represented only the *beginning* of a revolutionary new level of destructiveness. And he and the other atomic scientists were no longer in control, if they ever had been. This sobering realization led Oppenheimer, Lawrence, Compton, and Fermi to use even stronger language in a second report they prepared for policy makers in late September. This time, the four intended to jolt Washington into confronting the bomb's dangers. "The realization of atomic weapons constitutes a peril of the first magnitude for this nation and for the world," they bluntly wrote. They warned that America's nuclear monopoly would not last — the atomic genie had been let out of the bottle; other powers would one day develop their own weapons of mass destruction. All of this raised the specter of an atomic arms race, which they doubted America could win because the destructiveness of nuclear weapons could be increased almost infinitely and the development of effective countermeasures was unlikely. "There is no foundation for the hope that this nation can be safe against atomic weapons on the basis of technical prowess or technical ingenuity alone," noted these technical wizards, with deliberate irony.

The looming issue for all of them was the superbomb. As Teller's latest report had suggested, there was a good chance it could be developed. They flatly opposed such development on moral grounds. "We feel that this development should <u>not</u> be undertaken," they wrote, "primarily because we should prefer defeat in war to a victory obtained at the expense of the enormous human disaster that would be caused by its determined use." Their dread was rooted in the superbomb's boggling destructiveness: the atomic bombs dropped on Hiroshima and Nagasaki had leveled four square miles; a superbomb would level one hundred square miles.

They cited other reasons for restraint. "If developed here, other great powers must follow suit," they warned. Within a decade the United States could develop enough atomic bombs to destroy "all major industrial and military facilities throughout the world" anyway. The bomb had transformed the nature of war: "all the world faces a future in which sudden destruction is possible at any time." Instead of building bigger bombs, they urged "work[ing] with speed and determination toward establishing a world 'government'" that, to be effective, would require "the United States, along with the other great powers, to place into its hands all atom bomb and other major war-making facilities, and to submit to international inspection and control of work in the field of atomic energy."[15] It was a bold — even revolutionary — conclusion, requiring an unprecedented — and perhaps unrealistic — political transformation. But they saw no other way. "The only solution to the problem," they pointedly concluded, "must lie in politics, and this implies a profound and shattering alteration in the relations among nations."[16]

Although curious as scientists, they nevertheless had concluded that the superbomb was a problem that should not be solved — some science had become too deadly, its implications too dangerous. Breaking with their past, they had decided to put the interests of humanity above the pursuit of knowledge, a courageous and farsighted stance that reflected the revulsion that the mass killings of Hiroshima and Nagasaki had brought over each of them. They could not foresee that some of them would reverse their stance when America's effort at international control failed and the Cold War set in.

Oppenheimer returned to Los Alamos from Washington tired and dispirited. A few days later, he and Kitty drove across the Rio Grande Valley to Perro Caliente for their first real vacation in nearly three years. Oppenheimer took with him a pile of letters from old friends surprised to find his name prominently associated with the weapon that had ended the war, and answered some of the more personal ones by hand. A prompt reply went to Herbert Smith, his old teacher at the Ethical Culture School, with whom he had first experienced New Mexico. "It seemed appropriate, & very sweet," he wrote Smith, "that your good note should reach me on the Pecos — we had come over for a few days after the surrender. Like so many of the beautiful things of which I learned first from you, the love of it grows with the years. Your words were good to have. You will believe that this undertaking has not been without its misgivings; they are heavy on us today, when the future, which has so many elements of high promise, is yet only a stone's throw from despair. Thus the good which this work has perhaps contributed to make in the ending of the war looms very large to us, because it is there for sure." A letter to Haakon Chevalier the next day seemed an effort to persuade himself that this last point was true. "The thing had to be done, Haakon. It had to be brought to an open public fruition at a time when all over the world men craved peace as never before, were committed as never before both to technology as a way of life and thought and to the idea that no man is an island." To his Harvard classmate Frederick Bernheim, he confessed: "We are at the ranch now, in an earnest but not-too-sanguine search for sanity. . . . There would seem to be some great headaches ahead."[17]

Now that the war was over, the urgency was gone. Oppenheimer had lost the sense of purpose with which he had thrown himself into work on the bomb. He had already written to Groves, making it plain that he did not believe Los Alamos should continue as a weapons lab and that "the Director himself would very much like to know when he will be able to escape from these duties for which he is so ill-qualified and which he had accepted only in an effort to serve the country during the war."[18] On a consulting visit to Washington in late September, he told Undersecretary of State Dean Acheson that physicists as a group opposed doing any more weapons work — "not merely a superbomb but any bomb" — because it went "against the dictates of their hearts and spirits."[19] "There was not much left in me at that moment," said Oppenheimer later.[20] He arranged to quit his post shortly after an army awards ceremony for the lab on October sixteenth.

Almost everyone on the mesa turned out for the ceremony, which was held outdoors under a deep blue sky. Groves, standing in front of Fuller Lodge on a low platform decked in patriotic bunting and American flags fluttering in a cool wind amid the sound of shimmering aspen leaves colored gold by the autumn sun, spoke in loud and clear tones of the patriotic work done by the laboratory. Oppenheimer followed Groves, speaking in a low, quiet voice that he often used in public. He was uncharacteristically nervous as he began his speech. His theme was that the old concepts of war were no longer valid and that the only way to prevent a nuclear arms race leading one day to a nuclear holocaust was some form of international control. The atomic bomb, he said, symbolized "not only a great peril but a great hope of beginning to realize those changes which are needed if there is to be any peace." Under threat of mutual destruction nations might come to understand the imperative need for control of atomic weapons. But then he warned:

If atomic bombs are to be added to the arsenals of a warring world, or to the arsenals of nations preparing for war, then the time will come when mankind will curse the names of Los Alamos and Hiroshima.

The peoples of this world must unite, or they will perish. This war, that has ravaged so much of the earth, has written these words. The atomic bomb has spelled them out for all men to understand. Other men have spoken them, in other times, in other wars, of other weapons. They have not prevailed. There are some, misled by a false sense of human history, who hold that they will not prevail today. It is not for us to believe that. By our works we are committed, committed to a world united, before this common peril.[21]

Oppenheimer spoke for the last time at Los Alamos on November second, the night before he returned to Berkeley. Hundreds jammed the largest auditorium on the Hill to hear him speak about the implications of what they, collectively, had wrought. It was a stormy night and thunder rolled over the mesa. This was the first — really the only — time at Los Alamos that he felt truly free to speak what was on his mind and in his heart:

I should like to talk tonight as a fellow scientist, and at least as a fellow worrier about the fix we are in. . . . I would have liked to talk to you at an earlier date — but I couldn't talk to you as Director. . . . I think that it can only help to look a little at what our situation is — at what has happened to us — and that this must give us some honesty, some insight, which will be a source of strength in what may be the not-too-easy days ahead. . . .

What has happened to us forced us to re-consider the relations between science and common sense. . . . They forced us to be prepared for the inadequacy of the ways in which human beings attempted to deal with reality. . . . In some ways I think these virtues, which scientists quite reluctantly were forced to learn by the nature of the world they were studying, may be useful even today in preparing us for somewhat more radical views of what the issues are than would be natural or easy for people who had not been through this experience. . . .

I think that it hardly needs to be said why the impact is so strong. There are three reasons: one is the extraordinary speed with which things which were right on the frontier of science were translated into terms where they affected many living people, and potentially all people. Another is the fact, quite accidental in many ways, and connected with the speed, that scientists themselves played such a large part, not merely in providing the foundation for atomic weapons, but in actually making them. In this we are certainly closer to it than any other group. The third is that the thing we made . . . arrived in the world with such a shattering reality and suddenness that there was no opportunity for the edges to be worn off.

In considering what the situation of science is, it may be helpful to think a little of what people said and felt of their motives in coming into this job. One always has to worry that what people say of their motives is not adequate. Many people said different things, and most of them, I think, had some validity. There was in the first place the great concern that our enemy might develop these weapons before we did, and the feeling — at least, in the early days, the very strong feeling — that without atomic weapons it might be very difficult, it might be an impossible, it might be an incredibly long thing to win the war. These things wore off a little as it became clear that the war would be won in any case. Some people, I think, were motivated by curiosity, and rightly so; and some by a sense of adventure, and rightly so. Others had more political arguments and said, "Well, we know that atomic weapons are in principle possible, and it is not right that the threat of their unrealized possibility should hang over the world. It is right that the world should know what can be done in their field and deal with it." And the people added to that that it was a time when all over the world men would be particularly ripe and open for dealing with this problem because of the immediacy of the evils of war, because of the universal cry from everyone that one could not go through this thing again, even a war without atomic bombs. And there was finally, and I think rightly, the feeling that there was probably no place in the world where the development of atomic weapons would have a better chance of leading to a reasonable solution, and a smaller chance of leading to disaster, than within the United States. I believe all these things that people said are true, and I think I said them all myself at one time or another. . . .

There are [those] who try to escape the immediacy of this situation by saying that, after all, war has always been very terrible; after all, weapons have always gotten worse and worse; that this is just another weapon and it doesn't create a great change; that they are not so bad; bombings have been bad in this war and this is not a change in that — it just adds a little to the effectiveness of bombing; that some sort of protection will be found. I think that these efforts to diffuse and weaken the nature of the crisis make it only more dangerous. I think it is for us to accept it as a very grave crisis, to realize that these atomic weapons which we have started to make are very terrible, that they involve a change, that they are not just a slight modification. . . .

I think the advent of the atomic bomb and the facts which will get around that they are not too hard to make — that they will be universal if people wish to make them universal, that they will not constitute a real drain on the economy of any strong nation, and that their power of destruction will grow and is already incomparably greater than that of any other weapon — these things create a new situation. . . . I think when people talk of the fact that this is not only a great peril, but a great hope, this is what they should mean. . . . There exists a possibility of realizing those changes which are needed if there is to be any peace.

Those are very far-reaching changes. They are changes in the relations between nations, not only in spirit, not only in law, but also in conception and feeling. I don't know which of these is prior; they must all work together, and only the gradual interaction of one on the other can make a reality. . . . Atomic weapons are a peril which affect everyone in the world, and in that sense a completely common problem, as common a problem as it was for the Allies to defeat the Nazis. I think that in order to handle this common problem there must be a complete sense of community responsibility. I do not think that one may expect that people will contribute to the solution of the problem until they are aware of their ability to take part in the solution. . . .

I think it is important to realize that even those who are well informed in this country have been slow to understand, slow to believe that the bombs would work, and then slow to understand that their working would present such profound problems. We have certain interests in playing up the bomb, not only we here locally, but all over the country, because we made them, and our pride is involved. I think that in other lands it may be even more difficult for an appreciation of the magnitude of the thing to take hold. For this reason, I'm not sure that the greatest opportunities for progress do not lie somewhat further in the future than I had for a long time thought. . . .

The thing which must have troubled you, and which troubled me, in the official statements was the insistent note of unilateral responsibility for the handling of atomic weapons. However good the motives of this country are . . . we are 140 million people, and there are two billion people living on earth. We must understand that whatever our commitments to our own views and ideas, and however confident we are that in the course of time they will tend to prevail, our absolute — our completely absolute — commitment to them, in denial of the views and ideas of other people, cannot be the basis of any kind of agreement. . . .

We are not only scientists; we are men, too. We cannot forget our dependence on our fellow men. I mean not only our material dependence, without which no science would be possible, and without which we could not work; I mean also our deep moral dependence, in that the value of science must lie in the world of men, that all our roots lie there. These are the strongest bonds in the world, stronger than those even that bind us to one another, these are the deepest bonds — that bind us to our fellow men.[22]

The next morning, Oppenheimer and his family piled into their car and drove down off the mesa bound for California.

Down beside the Rio Grande River, at the teahouse where Oppenheimer had often sought refuge from his burdens, Edith Warner read a transcript of his remarks in the newspaper a few days later. She had made a point during the war of never questioning Oppenheimer as she quietly served him dinner, but she had sensed all along that he was thinking about more than just science. On November twenty-fifth, she wrote Oppenheimer a letter:

Dear Mr. Opp,

I have thought of you frequently. . . . So it was especially satisfying to read your recent speech. I hope you do not mind my having it.

As I read, it seemed almost as though you were pacing my kitchen, talking half to yourself and half to me. And from it came the conviction of what I've felt a number of times — you have, in lesser degree, that quality which radiates from Mr. Baker [Niels Bohr]. It has seemed to me in these past few months that it is a power as little known as atomic energy, which has greatly increased man's need for it. It also seems that even recognition of it involves responsibility.

There are many things for which I would express my gratitude. . . .

Your hours here mean much to me and I appreciate, perhaps more than most outsiders, what you have given of yourself in these Los Alamos years. Most of all I am grateful for your bringing Mr. Baker. I think of you both, hopefully, as the song of the river comes from the canyon and the need of the world reaches even this quiet spot.

May you have strength and courage and wisdom,

Edith Warner[23]

In Bohr's view, because the problem of atomic weapons and war *had* to be solved, it *would* be solved; the threat to humanity's survival simply left no other choice. Bohr believed that scientists should not portray the atomic bomb to the public solely as a potential destroyer, but as a "forceful reminder of how closely the fate of all mankind is coupled together," and as "a unique opportunity to remove obstacles to peaceful collaboration between nations and to enable them jointly to benefit from the great promises held out by the progress of science." Bohr saw physicists like himself as the unique agents of this opportunity, both as makers of the bomb and as the teachers of its universal lessons.[24]

Bohr looked to Oppenheimer as a key ally in this effort. After settling back in Copenhagen, Bohr wrote to him in November:

I was very sorry that I was not able see you again before my return to Denmark, but, due to difficulties in arranging passage for Margrethe and me, we could not, as we had intended to, return to the U.S.A. before the secret of the project was lifted, and then it was thought advisable that I no longer postponed my return to Denmark.

I need not say how often Aage and I think of all the kindness you and Kitty showed us in these last eventful years, where your understanding and sympathy have meant so much to me, and how closely I feel connected with you in the hope that the great accomplishment may contribute decisively to bringing about harmonious relationships between nations. I trust the whole matter is developing in a favorable way.[25]

Oppenheimer shared Bohr's goal, and sought to achieve it by courting policy makers, whom he believed would listen to him. He was, after all, now an international celebrity and a national hero.

Oppenheimer urged other physicists to keep the horrors of atomic war fresh in the public's mind. "It will not help to avert such a war," he told them, "if we try to rub the edges off this new terror that we have helped to bring to the world. If I return so insistently to the magnitude of the peril," he continued, "it is because I see in that our one great hope. As a vast threat, and a new one, to all the peoples of the earth, by its novelty, its terror, its strangely promethean quality, it has become, in the eyes of many of us, an opportunity unique and challenging."[26]

Other physicists besides Oppenheimer began lobbying policy makers, their efforts made easier because policy makers now looked on them much as primitive tribesmen had looked on their shamans: as high priests in touch with a supernatural world of mysterious forces whose terrible power they alone could control. Fermi wrote Washington Democratic Senator Warren Magnuson in September 1945 to warn against the fallacy of an atomic monopoly. "The safety offered this country by the attempt to withhold from foreign powers what we know is only limited," Fermi stressed. "Any major power could reach our present stage in this development in five years. It would be extremely dangerous to rely on secrecy."[27] Compton told an audience of civic leaders in St. Louis in November that "if the United States should be a party to an atomic war," America's cities would "follow Hiroshima and Nagasaki into oblivion." "If our nation should eventually win," Compton said, "what would we have gained? Perhaps the control of the world. But of what value would this be with our civilization gone and our population decimated?" "We must keep in mind," he added, "that when all are armed with atomic weapons no superiority of one nation can free it from danger of great damage by another."[28]

Rabi agreed with Fermi and Compton — and set out to do something about it. His solution would not be — indeed, could not be — scientific. Try as he might, Rabi could not recapture the single-minded focus on physics he had enjoyed before the war. Now he was an older and wiser man who had experience dealing with the military, politics, and warfare, aware in a way he had not been as a young professor of the complexity of his own equations. Rabi thought that by working from the "inside," with the government in Washington, he might be able to do something about controlling its dangers.

He decided to map out a plan with Oppenheimer. The two friends met in Rabi's faculty apartment on Riverside Drive in late December

1945. It was a bitterly cold day. Factories across the Hudson in New Jersey belched smoke that hung almost suspended in the frigid air. Oppenheimer and Rabi stood at the window, looking out and watching small ice floes drift downstream, turning pink in the sunset. They sat down and began posing questions to each other and shaping answers. When evening came, they had formed a far-reaching idea for international control of the atom. "We were optimistic because we realized what a terrible state the world was going to get into if something like what we were proposing didn't happen," remembered Rabi. "We assumed the predicament was obvious to others and it was to most — even the military."[29]

Oppenheimer conveyed their ideas to Washington, and the following month a committee was set up to draft an international control plan. The committee was headed by Undersecretary of State Dean Acheson, with Oppenheimer serving as a consultant.* For the next six weeks, committee members met in Washington offices, in railroad cars, at Oak Ridge and Los Alamos, even aloft in a military transport plane. They worked and studied and debated late into the night, then resumed again early the next morning. Once again, through the force of his personality and the power of his intellect, Oppenheimer emerged as the dominant figure of the group.

The committee submitted its report to the Truman administration in March 1946. Although labeled the Acheson-Lilienthal Report, it bore the unmistakable imprint of Robert Oppenheimer, who had drafted it. "Only if dangerous aspects of atomic energy are taken out of national hands," the report noted, "is there any reasonable prospect of devising safeguards against the use of atomic energy for bombs." The committee proposed the creation of an international atomic agency. Believing that an unpoliced agreement placed too great a burden on good faith, the report recommended endowing the international agency with strong inspection powers. It stressed that the risk to the United States of relinquishing its atomic monopoly to an international agency was preferable to the risk of a nuclear arms race.[30]

Other physicists rallied behind the report. Teller called it "a bold and dangerous solution; but inaction and an unplanned drift into

---

* Other members of the committee were Vannevar Bush, James Conant, Leslie Groves, and Assistant Secretary of War John McCloy. The committee's consultants — in addition to Oppenheimer — were former Tennessee Valley administrator David Lilienthal, New Jersey Bell president Chester Barnard, General Electric vice president Harry Winne, and Monsanto executive Charles Thomas.

international competition would be still more dangerous." "If the constructive and imaginative spirit of the State Department report is compared with the 'Maginot-line' mentality of 'keeping the secret,'" Teller added, "one can hardly doubt in which direction our eventual hope for safety lies."[31] Compton called the report "a sound and constructive basis for solving a difficult problem." "We'd be in a much stronger position if the United Nations would have the atomic weapons and no individual nations would have them," he said, "than the position in which we would hold atomic weapons and other nations also would develop them. Military defenses cannot make us safe; we've got to rely on international agreement before we can really be safe."[32] Bethe thought the greatest service physicists could perform was to "make it clear that only a truly international control of atomic energy gives any hope of lasting security from atomic weapons."[33] Any country in the world that possessed sufficient scientific talent and material resources — certainly including the Soviet Union — could, sooner or later, duplicate the accomplishment of the Manhattan Project.

All of them conceded that if no international agreement could be reached, then the United States might have to keep its atomic arsenal for purposes of deterrence. But they stressed that the bomb was not a "winning weapon" in the long run because other countries would eventually have it too, and in any atomic war, all sides would lose.

The Acheson-Lilienthal Report was presented to the world with great fanfare by American diplomat Bernard Baruch in the gymnasium of New York's Hunter College, the temporary home of the United Nations, on June 14, 1946. Oppenheimer and Compton sat in the audience that day. "We are here to make a choice between the quick and the dead," Baruch intoned at the beginning of his speech. He then went on to describe the destructive power of the bomb, to propose an international atomic authority, and to insist on the abolition of the national veto in this one area. Baruch differed from Oppenheimer by focusing attention on the negative aspect of punishment for violators rather than, as did the report, on the positive aspect of mutual cooperation.

Sadly, within weeks the plan was gravely ill and in less than six months it was dead. American military forces were rapidly demobilizing from Western Europe while massive Russian military forces remained deployed in Eastern Europe; under such conditions, Truman was unlikely to agree to relinquish what he considered the principal

American deterrent to Soviet adventurism. Additionally, probably no international control plan could have overcome the fear and suspicion with which Stalin viewed any outside intrusion into Russian territory. Quite simply, Stalin wanted his own atomic bomb and probably would not have accepted any limitation on his own fledgling program, and Truman favored preserving America's atomic monopoly until, and unless, he got firm agreement to international control from the Soviets.* The Acheson-Lilienthal Report had addressed the physical facts of atomic energy, but it had ignored American and Soviet geopolitical interests, which were rooted in different values, different dispositions of military forces, and different perceptions of national security. The scientists had thought leaders would want the bomb to go away, but in fact what they wanted was the bomb.

The plan's failure bitterly disappointed and badly discouraged Oppenheimer. David Lilienthal, who talked with Oppenheimer late into the night that summer about the opportunity both thought had been missed, recorded in his diary:

> He really is a tragic figure; with all his great attractiveness [and] brilliance of mind. As I left him he looked so sad: "I am ready to go anywhere and do anything, but I am bankrupt of further ideas. And I find that physics and the teaching of physics, which is my life, now seems irrelevant." It was this last [remark] that really wrung my heart.[34]

Still, Oppenheimer saw no alternative but to continue working for international control. Writing to Bohr, he tried to put the best face on what he considered a bad situation: "It seems important for all our future hopes that the wrong lessons should not have been learned by the failure of the past year, but that on the contrary there may be a renewed courage for a somewhat deeper attack on the problem."[35]

Szilard was similarly dejected. Szilard had been hopeful, but his mood grew increasingly pessimistic as the months passed. "To me it seems futile to hope that 140 million people of this country can be smuggled through the gates of Paradise while most of them are looking the other way," he said bitterly in 1947. "Nothing much can be achieved now or in the very near future until such time as the people

---

* Russian scientists were well along toward a bomb of their own, due in part to the espionage of Western scientists such as Klaus Fuchs, Theodore Hall, and Allan Nunn May (and perhaps others), whose spying simplified and sped their work.

of this country understand what is at stake. Maybe God will work a miracle — if we don't make it too difficult for him."[36] Lawrence, however, took a completely different view: he blamed the failure of international control on Soviet intransigence, which made him conclude that American restraint was unwise and an agreement with Stalin unattainable. As a result, Lawrence abandoned the nuclear restraint that he had advocated along with Oppenheimer, Fermi, and Compton just after the war, and now turned into an enthusiastic proponent of American nuclear superiority.

The failure of international control came as a deep disappointment to most of the other atomic scientists as well, and they also lacked the political sophistication and stamina to swallow defeat and return to fight another day. This was most plainly the case with Edward Teller, who supported the Acheson-Lilienthal Report, but when it failed, lost all interest in political efforts to control the bomb. Losing his optimism and succumbing to an increasing suspicion of the Soviet Union in the late 1940s, Teller abandoned his support for international control and began to champion a conservative agenda that would remain a constant for the rest of his life: development of a superbomb, opposition to all arms-control efforts as naive and dangerous, and advocacy of an unlimited American nuclear buildup.

The failure of international control did nothing to diminish Robert Oppenheimer's stature, however. The bomb's success had made him a celebrity whose views were in great demand by policy makers and ordinary citizens alike. His face replaced Einstein's as the public image of scientific genius. His portrait appeared on the cover of *Time* magazine, and he was in constant demand as a speaker and writer. A new journal, *Physics Today*, carried a photograph on the cover of its first issue that required no explanation: a porkpie hat slung nonchalantly over a cyclotron. Periodicals featured his remarks with flattering portraits of him holding a pipe, looking erudite and persuasive. He was "the smartest of the lot," a magazine quoted an unnamed colleague.[37] The public romance had begun.

Oppenheimer's vast reputation gave him easy and regular access to top officials. His home and office phones rang constantly — usually someone from Washington was calling — and his office safe was stuffed with classified documents. He served on countless advisory committees and acted as a consultant to many others. All of this was a far cry from the Oppenheimer of Berkeley days. He had changed from a brilliant, arrogant, and in many ways immature intellectual into a gifted administrator and savvy politician with a masterly sense of public relations. He typified the new, worldly scientist of the atomic age who spent more time advising the government and less time teaching students. He saw himself — and others did too — as an oracle for policy makers. A combination of ambition, unrest, and guilt had compelled him into the central political arena of postwar America, and Oppenheimer reveled in the attention and the limelight. He now wore his hair cut very short — as if to signal to Washington that he was no longer one of the longhairs. His frequent public speaking resulted in a solidified persona, his voice now crossing a range of tones, from deliberate arrogance to judicious reflectiveness to irresistible warmth. He reveled at making a difference and being "in the swim" — perhaps too much. A former pupil noted, "I think his sudden fame and the new position he now occupied had gone to his head so much that he began to consider himself God Almighty, able to put the whole world to rights."[38] Among those in the staid realm of academia, Oppenheimer's new life in the political swim of Washington inspired no small amount of envy.

In October 1947 Oppenheimer accepted the prestigious post of director of the Institute for Advanced Study in Princeton, New Jersey. (He had changed his mind about Princeton since his visit there in the 1930s, when he wrote his brother, Frank, that the institute was "a madhouse, its solipsistic luminaries shining in separate and helpless desolation.") Oppenheimer gave up his tenured professorships at Berkeley and Caltech not only because of the intellectual appeal of the institute but also because it moved him close to the political action of Washington, where he really wanted to be.

Not surprisingly, the Institute for Advanced Study soon began to reflect Oppenheimer's personality. Although Oppenheimer's career in original research was over, he remained an effective and articulate critic of others' research, and this gave the institute's weekly seminars in theoretical physics enormous vitality. A young postdoctoral fellow at the institute described Oppenheimer's exacting standards in the seminar room in a letter home to his parents:

> I have been observing rather carefully his behavior during seminars. If one is saying, for the benefit of the rest of the audience, things that he knows already, he cannot resist hurrying one on to some-

thing else; then when one says things that he doesn't know or immediately agree with, he breaks in before the point is fully explained
with acute and sometimes devastating criticisms, to which it is
impossible to reply adequately even when he is wrong. If one
watches him one can see that he is moving around nervously all the
time, never stops smoking, and I believe that his impatience is
largely beyond his control. On Tuesday we had our fiercest public
battle so far, when I criticized some unwarrantably pessimistic
remarks he had made about the Schwinger theory. He came down
on me like a ton of bricks, and conclusively won the argument so far
as the public was concerned. However, afterwards he was very
friendly and even apologized to me.[39]

Oppenheimer's greatest contribution to the institute, however, was
more indirect and subtle. He gave its faculty, as he gave scientists at
Los Alamos during the war, a sense of participation in a great adventure. He still had the ability to inspire and motivate others by convey-
ing an extraordinary sense of excitement and purpose. His talent for
attracting bright people and stimulating them to excellence showed
itself once more. There remained shortcomings, however. Oppenheimer continued to wound others with his cutting tongue when they
failed to clarify a point or missed one entirely, belittling them with
unnecessarily cruel and biting remarks. More than one young fellow
fled to his office sobbing after being humiliated by Oppenheimer.
Such conduct deeply hurt people, some of whom would not forget.

Oppenheimer and his family lived at Olden Manor, the director's
residence on the institute grounds. The large white-frame colonial
house provided a spacious setting. Robert had a library, Kitty a green-
house, Peter a darkroom, and Toni a pony. Summers were spent lecturing in California, and for a few years the Oppenheimers made
regular visits to Perro Caliente in New Mexico. Winter holidays were
spent in the U.S. Virgin Islands, where Oppenheimer rediscovered
his youthful love of sailing. St. John became his preferred retreat.

It was an easy and pleasant life in many respects, but not in others.
Oppenheimer was operating now in the hard and unforgiving arena of
politics, where his sensitive nature was bound to get battered and
bruised. So too was his introspective temperament, which increasingly assailed him with guilt about what he had done. When Oppenheimer visited Truman in the Oval Office shortly after the war, the
Los Alamos director blurted out, "Mr. President, I have blood on my

hands." Truman, offended by what he considered Oppenheimer's melodramatic egocentricity, offered his guest his handkerchief and said: "Well, here, would you like to wipe off your hands?" After Oppenheimer left the room, Truman, angrier and more agitated than he was willing to admit, turned to Dean Acheson, who was also present, and snapped: "I don't want to see that son-of-a-bitch in this office ever again. After all, all he did was make the bomb. I'm the guy who fired it off."[40]

When Oppenheimer began serving as a government adviser, he viewed the assignment as an opportunity to educate policy makers about peaceful applications of atomic energy. Instead, he found most of his time devoted to giving counsel on the development of newer bombs. He grew disenchanted and melancholy when he realized that his "principal job was to provide atomic weapons and good atomic weapons and many atomic weapons."[41] He thought the prospect of superbombs — assuming they could be made — would be a dangerous mistake, inviting Armageddon in the event of another world war. If atomic bombs had to be part of the picture, he thought it better, and wiser, to rely on conventional military forces supported by tactical nuclear weapons as powerful as the bombs that had destroyed Hiroshima and Nagasaki.

The postwar years also brought increased scrutiny of Oppenheimer by government security agencies and their supporters in Congress and the media, where "the internal communist threat" was becoming a popular political issue in the deepening Cold War. The surveillance that had dogged him at Los Alamos was intensified. His phones were tapped, his office was bugged, his movements were watched. In September 1946 FBI agents questioned him for the first time. The interview concerned some of his former Berkeley students and meetings he had attended in the Bay Area before and after the war where communists were present. It was a line of questioning that was to become all too familiar in coming years. Cold War anticommunist feeling was rising, and in this political climate Oppenheimer was going to learn the high price of having an independent mind and a vulnerable left-wing past.

In 1947 responsibility for atomic energy passed from the military to the newly created civilian Atomic Energy Commission. All AEC consultants who had received wartime clearances from the army were reinvestigated, including Oppenheimer. After reading all the material in his FBI file, the AEC commissioners reached the same conclusion as John Lansdale, Groves's wartime counterintelligence chief, who "was absolutely certain of the present loyalty of J. Robert Oppenheimer, despite the fact that he doubtless was at one time at least an avid fellow-traveler." The AEC renewed his security clearance on August 11, 1947.

But hints of trouble to come had already surfaced. A month earlier, on July twelfth, the *Washington Times-Herald* had published a front-page story by a reporter with ties to the FBI under the banner headline U.S. ATOM SCIENTIST'S BROTHER EXPOSED AS COMMUNIST WHO WORKED ON A-BOMB. It began:

> Amid official revelation that security of some of the nation's atom secrets has been jeopardized, this newspaper today can reveal that Dr. Frank Oppenheimer, brother of the American scientist who directed development of the atomic bomb at Los Alamos, was a card-carrying member of the Communist Party who worked on the Manhattan Project and was aware of many secrets of the bomb from the start.

Buried on page six of the same story was the following disclaimer: "The *Times-Herald* wishes to emphasize that the official report on Frank Oppenheimer in no way reflects on the loyalty or ability of his brother, Dr. J. Robert Oppenheimer."

Oppenheimer himself was ordered before the House Un-American Activities Committee on June 7, 1949. The hearing room seemed designed to intimidate witnesses: members of the committee and their staff sat on a raised platform that ran in a semicircle around the witness table. Oppenheimer was called to testify in executive session about leftists he had known at Berkeley before the war. Oppenheimer answered the questions put to him and the session ended with California Republican Congressman Richard Nixon saying, "I think we all have been tremendously impressed with him and are mighty happy we have him in the position he has in our program." Within days, Oppenheimer's testimony was leaked to the press.

A week later, his brother, Frank, appeared before the same committee. Frank and his wife, Jackie, admitted to having been members of the Communist Party — a charge they had denied two years earlier, when the *Times-Herald* article had appeared — but explained that they had left the party before Frank joined the Manhattan Project. (He had terminated his Communist Party membership in 1941, but had not revealed his former membership to wartime security officers.) Less than an hour after testifying at this hearing, Frank learned from one of the journalists covering his appearance that he had "resigned" as an assistant professor of physics at the University of Minnesota, a position he had secured with the help of Ernest Lawrence. Angered that Frank had covered up his Communist Party membership, Lawrence banished him from the Rad Lab. Ten years would pass before Frank was invited to teach physics at the college level again. One did not have to be very smart to know that his brother's position was a shaky one. And Robert Oppenheimer was very smart.

Shortly after the war was over, Oppenheimer's successor as Los Alamos, director Norris Bradbury, invited Teller to succeed the departing Bethe as head of the laboratory's Theoretical Division. The position that Teller had coveted throughout the war seemed within his reach at last. Teller told Bradbury that he would gladly accept, if the lab would take up work on his superbomb idea with the same gusto that it had committed to making the atomic bomb. Bradbury was noncommittal, noting that postwar political conditions made a crash program to build a superbomb unlikely.

That evening, Teller attended a party where the soon-to-depart Oppenheimer was also present. Teller told Oppenheimer about his conversation with Bradbury earlier that day. "This has been your laboratory, and its future depends upon you," said Teller. "I will stay if you will help enlist support for work toward a hydrogen bomb or further development of the atomic bomb." Oppenheimer gave a reply that was short and pointed. "I neither can, nor will do so," he said. Knowing there was little hope without Oppenheimer's help, Teller announced that he would accept a post he had been offered by the University of Chicago. Oppenheimer shook Teller's hand, smiled, and said, "You are doing the right thing." The two spoke again at the end of the party. "Now that you have decided to go to Chicago, don't you feel better?" Oppenheimer asked.[42] He told Teller he would have nothing more to do with the superbomb.[43]

Teller, his wife, Mici, and their young son, Paul, packed up and left Los Alamos for Chicago on February 1, 1946. They moved into a duplex in Hyde Park near the university, where Teller resumed an academic life. The next few years proved to be happy and productive ones for Teller. His second child, a girl named Wendy, was born in the summer of 1946, and Teller quickly took to doting on his baby daughter. Freed from the pressures of political turmoil and war for the first time since the early 1930s — and secure in the knowledge of America's sole possession of the atomic bomb — Teller began to relax. He learned to enjoy the quietly satisfying pleasures of domesticity. He became less choleric, more optimistic, and trusting. He threw himself back into pure research and coauthored numerous papers. He got caught up again in the grandeur and deeply satisfying creativity of basic science. He also wrote articles for the liberal *Bulletin of the Atomic Scientists*, started in 1946 by Met Lab activists. In one article he praised Oppenheimer's plan for international control of nuclear weapons as "ingenious, daring and basically sound."[44] "World government," he wrote in the *Bulletin* as late as July 1948, "is our only hope for survival. . . . I believe that we should cease to be infatuated with the menace of this fabulous monster, Russia."[45] There were moments during these early postwar years when Teller almost forgot about fear and danger.

The Cold War, however, remained an underlying strain on his newfound optimism. He was troubled by the Soviet coup in Czechoslovakia, by the Berlin Blockade, and by the Communist victory over Nationalist forces in China. A more personal challenge was his family in Hungary. His parents were too old and frail to emigrate, but his widowed sister and her small son could. Teller sent the necessary papers to Hungary, but nothing happened. Then his father, wearied by hunger and depressed by Soviet domination, died. His mother was deported from Budapest to the countryside as a bourgeois "undesirable." His sister endured secret-police interrogations about his scientific activities. Although his sibling knew nothing, Teller was greatly agitated and angered by her ordeal. These hardships intensified Teller's childhood fears of the Russians and reinforced his fundamental belief that only the military strength of democracies like the United States kept totalitarian nations like the Soviet Union at bay.

While Teller felt fearful of the Russians, Szilard remained guilty about his part in the making of the bomb. After the war, he sometimes wished that he could undo what he had done and withdraw from the world — or at least change it. Szilard shared his thoughts at a conference at the University of Chicago in September 1945. A participant who kept shorthand notes of Szilard's talk wrote:

We are in an armament race.

If Russia starts making atomic bombs in two or three years — perhaps five or six years — then we have an armed peace, and it will be a durable peace.

But we will not have permanent peace at lesser cost than world government. But this cannot come without changed loyalty of people. If we can't have that, all we can have is a durable peace. Only purpose of a durable peace would be to create conditions 20–30 years from now [that] can bring about world peace. That requires shift of loyalties.

If we are *sure* to get a Third World War, the later it comes the worse for us.

Victor of next war will *make* a world government, even if that victor should be the United States, having lost 25 million people dead.

Szilard's fear of a nuclear World War III appalled him so much that he decided to have nothing more to do with physics, which he had once associated with creativity but now associated with destruction. In 1947 he took up the study of biology, which was for him a rejection of death and an affirmation of life. Hotel lobbies and cafés remained the settings where he communicated his ideas to others in wide-ranging discussions. People who came in contact with Szilard remained impressed by his capacity to see far beyond what most others were seeing or thinking, but some also concluded dismissively that he had become a Don Quixote, tilting against a nuclear windmill that had begun to turn faster and faster.

After the war, Hans Bethe returned to Cornell, but continued doing weapons work at Los Alamos during summers because he thought this would give him the credibility to influence government policy along lines he considered constructive. This "inside" strategy reflected Bethe's pragmatic temperament. He thought that refusing to do any weapons work (as did some of his wartime colleagues) would not accomplish anything: atomic bombs would not go away — Pandora's box had been opened irrevocably — and there would always be other competent scientists willing to do anything he refused. He explained his thinking this way:

In order to fulfill this function of contributing to the decision-making process, scientists (at least some of them) must be willing to work on weapons. They must do this also because our present struggle is (fortunately) not carried on in actual warfare which has become an absurdity, but in technical development for a potential war which nobody expects to come. The scientists must preserve the precarious balance of armament which would make it disastrous for either side to start a war. Only then can we argue for and embark on more constructive ventures like disarmament and international cooperation which may eventually lead to a more definite peace.[46]

As relations between the United States and the Soviet Union deteriorated in the late 1940s, Bethe grew skeptical. By the end of the decade, he expected a nuclear war between America and Russia within ten years.[47] Bethe's sense of foreboding and pessimism intensified with the outbreak of the Korean War in June 1950. He continued, however, to urge that America's atomic stockpile be kept to a minimum compatible with national security. He privately worried that Cold War firebrands in Washington were whipping up a dangerous atmosphere in which scientists might be compelled to invent more frightful weapons.

Ernest Lawrence's direction of the Rad Lab after the war was more absolute and also more distant. The Rad Lab had grown so large that he no longer knew all the people who worked for him. Instead of pausing for brief conversations on inspection walks, he now merely checked to see whether everyone on the staff was busy. This sometimes produced comical results. Once, Lawrence happened upon a man who seemed to be loafing. "What are you doing?" he snapped. "I'm just waiting for the phone to ring." "You're fired," said Lawrence. "I work for the telephone company," the man replied.[48]

If the size of the Rad Lab had changed, its spirit had not. Lawrence still wanted to do big things and tended to treat his staff like servants. He drove them hard as always, but more now through subordinates than through personal contact. When he did see them, the tension he created had a new edge to it. No longer shrugging off an idea when it became a blind alley, Lawrence grew irritated and inclined to fix blame. He was driving himself harder than ever. He began to drink in the evenings, and Rad Lab personnel he encountered on nighttime visits to the lab noticed it. "Although he seemed perfectly sober," said one staffer, "it really smelled."[49] The cumulative toll on Lawrence manifested itself in the form of ulcerative colitis, intestinal bleeding that he found increasingly difficult to stanch.

Lawrence's mission had become one of raising ever more money and building ever larger machines. His intense optimism, his connections to rich donors, and his high-powered contacts in Washington still proved an effective combination. A new laboratory rose at his bidding near Livermore, a quiet town an hour's drive east of Berkeley in a dry, rural valley — tucked in the foothills of the Sierra Nevada Mountains — known for good wines, fields of roses, and grazing horses and cattle. (Today it is known as the Lawrence Livermore National Laboratory.) The navy had used a square mile of the Livermore Valley as a training camp during World War II, and Lawrence converted this camp into a satellite of the Rad Lab. In the tense atmosphere of the Cold War, Livermore quickly became a high-tech compound of hundreds of olive-drab buildings and thousands of employees — all surrounded by barbed-wire fences and guardposts obscured from a distance by tall eucalyptus trees. It was a long way from the early days of the Rad Lab.

Every Friday afternoon, Lawrence drove out to Livermore from Berkeley in his baby blue Cadillac convertible to survey his new domain. He had an office reserved especially for him, where he began his weekly visit by interrogating Herbert York, a young Berkeley postdoctorate whom he picked to run the lab for him. "What's going on?" Lawrence would say to York. "What's new?"[50] Lawrence then would walk the grounds, asking everyone he encountered to explain what they were doing.

Although Lawrence still looked to Oppenheimer to interpret the findings made with his machines, the relationship between the two physicists was changing. Before the war, Lawrence had been the leader in the public mind and his laboratory had been famous. He had won the Nobel Prize; Oppenheimer had not. After the war, Oppenheimer was hailed as the father of the atomic bomb, the wizard of the scientific world. His name carried magic. Crowds gathered around him. Lawrence had reacted by urgently seeking to enlist Oppenheimer in his projects, but instead Oppenheimer had left for Princeton. "To Lawrence," said I. I. Rabi, who spoke with both men during this period, "Oppenheimer's leaving Berkeley seemed treason."[51] On a visit to Berkeley in the summer of 1949, Oppenheimer and his wife, Kitty, encountered Lawrence at a faculty party. Kitty, who was tight, loudly scolded him for banishing Frank from the Rad Lab. Oppenheimer looked on, saying nothing. Their fabled friendship was rapidly deteriorating.

When Enrico Fermi returned to Chicago after the war, he bought a large, three-story house on University Avenue a few blocks east of campus and set about creating an expansive new Institute for Nuclear Studies. (Today it is known as the Enrico Fermi Institute.) Ground was broken for the institute on July 8, 1947, in the block between 56th and 57th Streets and Ellis and Ingleside Avenues, across the street from Stagg Field, where Fermi had achieved the world's first chain reaction five years earlier. Once construction was completed, Fermi moved his office and laboratory into the ground floor of the institute's south wing. Discussions with Teller were frequent and productive. Fermi enjoyed Teller's unusual abundance of original ideas, often developing them far beyond the point reached by Teller, though Fermi always gave his friend full credit for his contributions.

Teller was not the only Manhattan Project colleague hanging around the Midway. Veterans of the Met Lab and Los Alamos thronged to Chicago after the war to study physics, attracted by Fermi's reputation. Fermi did not want to limit his teaching to advanced students; he thought that beginners should be brought into contact with science, and taught the elementary physics course to large classes with great enthusiasm and success. It was "standing room only" when Fermi taught, and he would talk with equal brilliance to a crowd as to a single student. It seemed effortless, but this impression was contrived. Fermi spent hours preparing for each course. Once, when he had to be away from Chicago, Fermi asked a graduate student to take over a session of one of his classes. Fermi handed the student a small notebook in which he had written out the entire lecture.

Once a week, Fermi held an informal seminar for graduate students. The group gathered in Fermi's office and one of his students proposed a topic for discussion. Fermi then searched through his carefully indexed papers to find his notes on that topic and shared them. He always kept the discussion focused on the essential aspects of a topic. He taught his students that physics should not be an esoteric specialty but rather a practical and relevant discipline, and he was always eager to learn — and grateful when he found out something new. Throughout, he was rigorously inductive in his reasoning; theoretical generalizations came only *after* empirical observation. Exploring the mysteries of nature was a great adventure for him, a thrilling sport for the intensely competitive and confident man behind the mask of nonchalance and modesty.

As he had before the war, Fermi continued to dislike pretension and stuffiness. Whenever he and Laura planned a party where the guest list included an important person — as many of the atomic scientists were after the war — Fermi would say, "We've got to dilute him with somebody." He was amazingly unassuming, given his fame and accomplishments. After the war, he helped General Electric build nuclear reactors, telling its engineers what to do and boosting its corporate profits enormously. One night at dinner Laura said, "Enrico, I went to the store today and put our name on the list for a dishwasher." "Fine," said Fermi. "Enrico, you know the president of General Electric. If you tell him you want one, you'll get it tomorrow." "No," he said, "we're on the list, we'll wait and get it when it comes."[52]

But some things had changed. Friends noticed that Fermi was becoming more reflective, and were surprised to glimpse his occasional detachment from physics — unheard of before the war. The steady reading he had been doing since coming to America extended and deepened his cultural interests beyond what they had been in his Italian days. He even began to meditate on literature and philosophical questions, once remarking to Laura that "with science one can explain everything except oneself."[53] Fermi was struggling to understand himself and his place in the new world he had helped to create.

As the atomic scientists strived to warn people about the dangers of nuclear weapons, the political climate began to change, and the Cold War set in. By the early 1950s, American public opinion shifted from sympathy for Russia as a wartime ally to fear of the Soviet Union as an expansionist power. This fear found expression in many ways, including pressure to expand America's atomic arsenal. Partly in response to this pressure, and partly the result of bureaucratic momentum and military demand, the size of the nation's atomic stockpile grew from thirteen in 1947 to nearly three hundred in 1950, with a corresponding increase in strategic delivery capability.[54] What Bohr and the other atomic scientists had feared — a growing reliance on nuclear weapons and the beginnings of a nuclear arms race — was coming to pass. The direction of America's atomic program would soon become a major political issue, struggled over vehemently by those with competing visions of the future.

CHAPTER 9

The Superbomb Debate

IGH IN THE CLEAR, cold air off the Kamchatka Peninsula of Siberia in early September 1949, a chemical filter fitted into the nose of an American reconnaissance plane picked up traces of particles containing disintegrating nuclei. Like cancer cells in their earliest stages, the nuclei portended ominous consequences. Scientists who analyzed the particles determined that the invisible grains of matter caught in the plane's filter were highly radioactive and part of a cloud that was drifting east. Further analysis determined that the particles had been produced by a fission explosion. On August twenty-ninth, over the steppes of Kazakhstan, the Soviet Union had tested its first atomic bomb — a virtual copy of the U.S. plutonium bomb based on data stolen by spies — and had shattered America's short-lived nuclear monopoly.

Robert Oppenheimer had just returned to Princeton after spending the summer at Caltech and Perro Caliente when the phone rang in the study of his Olden Manor home. It was a call from Washington reporting the news. Many officials were incredulous, but Oppenheimer sensed immediately that it was true. Still, he was shaken by the news, and in this he was not alone. Most Americans had accepted the comforting (and mistaken) belief that it would be many years — maybe decades — before the Soviets would have the bomb. The idea of a nuclear-armed Stalinist Russia was ominous, suddenly presenting serious dangers of a kind totally different from any that America had faced before.

Fearing a national panic, Oppenheimer urged Washington to pre-empt Moscow's announcement of the test by breaking the news to the U.S. people first. Many Americans, including those in high places, had great difficulty believing that the Soviets could achieve such a technological feat on their own. Truman, dubious, grudgingly accepted the scientists' conclusion and released news of the Soviet bomb on September twenty-third. That same evening, Oppenheimer received a call from Teller, who was back at Los Alamos doing consulting work. "What should we do now?" Teller asked Oppenheimer excitedly. "Just go back and keep working," said Oppenheimer. Then, after a long pause, he added: "Keep your shirt on."[1]

Teller's anxious "What should we do now?" became the question of the day in Washington as well. The Russian bomb fed fears triggered by earlier Soviet actions: the occupation of Eastern Europe and the use of the Red Army to install governments controlled by local communist parties in East Germany, Hungary, Romania, and Poland. While the United States and its Western European allies made their own contributions to Cold War tensions, the Soviet Union under Stalin readily appeared to be a dangerous totalitarian regime. Coming at a time when the Cold War was rapidly worsening — the Soviet coup in Czechoslovakia, the Berlin Blockade, and Mao's victory in China had all happened within the past year — Russia's atomic test seemed the latest and most spectacular setback for the West against what it saw as a monolithic, aggressive communist axis stretching across Eurasia, encompassing half of the world's people and threatening the rest. Combined with the Soviets' development of long-range aircraft capable of reaching the United States, a Soviet atomic bomb promised to end America's historic sense of invulnerability. Contributing to this vulnerability were fresh memories of Pearl Harbor. These anxieties about nuclear vulnerability fed American fears of the Soviet Union.

The answer that came back from many quarters within the American government and the American scientific establishment was to embark on a crash program to develop the superbomb. In the current crisis atmosphere, the superbomb seemed a quick way for the United States to recapture its lost nuclear hegemony.

The destructive power of a superbomb was as revolutionary in respect to the atomic bomb as the latter was to conventional weapons. Unlike an atomic bomb, which used the explosive energy of fission (the splitting of uranium and plutonium isotopes by neutrons), a superbomb would use the explosive energy of *fusion*, in which the nuclei of two light atoms (usually isotopes of hydrogen such as deuterium or tritium)* combined to form one, heavier nucleus. This combining, or thermonuclear fusion, of two atomic nuclei into one occurred only at extraordinarily high temperatures and pressures (for example, those found at the center of the sun) and released enormous — theoretically unlimited — amounts of heat, energy, and radiation, far greater even than fission.

Advocates of a superbomb, led by Teller, argued that it was only a matter of time before Russia developed one; America *must* have its own in order to avoid falling behind or being blackmailed. They further contended that the superbomb was morally no different from the atomic bomb, or any other weapon for that matter; it all depended on what policy makers did with them. Teller had voiced this view as far back as 1945. Terming moral opposition to the superbomb "a fallacy," he had written to Fermi in October of that year:

> If the development is possible, it is out of our powers to prevent it. All that we can do is to retard its completion by some years. I believe, on the other hand, that any form of international control may be put on a more stable basis by the knowledge of the full extent of the problem that must be solved and of the dangers of a ruthless international competition. The terrible consequences of a superbomb will not be avoided by ignoring or postponing the issue but by wise and provident planning.[2]

His thinking had not changed since then, except to become more fervent. Teller and other advocates of the superbomb believed in the principle — bordering on an imperative — that physicists, like other scientists, had an obligation to understand nature and develop new knowledge. They could not avoid the responsibility of knowing the facts, no matter how terrifying. In Teller's mind, once he and other physicists had realized an atomic bomb was feasible, a thermonuclear weapon was scientifically the next logical step.

Few physicists had challenged the development of the atomic bomb during World War II, and almost no one other than Bohr and Szilard had given thought to the time "after the bomb." Questions did not emerge until shortly before Hiroshima; and even then, few opposed

---

* This is why the superbomb also became known as the hydrogen or H-bomb.

the use of the bomb against Japan. The atomic bomb debate occurred only *after* the weapon was made. The superbomb debate, in contrast, occurred *before* the weapon was made. What is more, no one now could plead ignorance of its effects. Physicists knew they were confronting in the superbomb a scientific issue, and a personal choice, fraught with large moral and political implications.

The superbomb debate played out before secret boards and committees of the U.S. government. But reduced to its barest essentials, the debate amounted to a personal duel between two proud and brilliant men: Oppenheimer and Teller. Everything about the duel was compelling: the drama it sparked, the struggles it produced, and above all, the clashing perspectives and values it revealed.

For Teller, this moment had been a long time coming. The idea of a superbomb had originated in conversations between him and Fermi at Columbia University back in the fall of 1941. One afternoon, as they walked back to Pupin Laboratory after lunch, Fermi had casually — almost offhandedly — asked Teller whether he thought an atomic explosion might be used to produce a thermonuclear reaction. In the center of an exploding fission bomb, extraordinarily high temperatures — approaching 40 million degrees Fahrenheit — were produced, and so at least one of the conditions necessary for igniting a thermonuclear reaction seemed to be feasible, perhaps even within reach.

The idea had intrigued Teller. It appealed to his immense curiosity and competitiveness. It also appealed to his intense ambitiousness. A scientist who knew Teller sensed this quality in him from the start:

> When I first met Teller, he appeared youthful, always intense, visibly ambitious, and harboring a smoldering passion for achievement in physics. He was a warm person and clearly desired friendship with other physicists. Possessing a very critical mind, he also showed quickness, sense, and great determination and persistence. However, I think he also showed less feeling for true simplicity in the more fundamental levels of theoretical physics. To exaggerate a bit, I would say his talents were more in the direction of engineering, construction, and the surveying of existing methods. But undoubtedly he also had great ingenuity.[3]

Teller's mind worked with dazzling swiftness and creativity. He liked to discuss ideas with others, using these conversations to strike sparks and generate insights. Teller would slap his forehead as he corrected or discarded an idea — and then dash off another. Fermi, who knew him well, often said of him: "If only he could find one thing to concentrate on!"[4] With the superbomb, Teller had found his one thing.

Teller's superbomb obsession surprised many people because it was so out of character with his flighty personality. "His trouble was *lack* of concentration on any one problem," said a colleague. "Then this thing hit him and he seemingly couldn't let loose of it."[5] His commitment reflected a personal passion and emotional involvement not uncommon among scientists. No doubt his fear of the Russians, his sense of scientific curiosity and patriotic duty, and his belief that peace could be achieved only through powerful weapons were sincere and genuine. But his personal ambition was even stronger. The superbomb became the territory that Teller staked out as his own, where he could compete successfully against Oppenheimer's esteem and Fermi's achievement. More and more, Teller began to identify himself with the superbomb, mentally classifying physicists into those on "his" side and those "against" him. His emotional temperament also came into play, his habit of getting self-blindingly attached to his own ideas leading him on. Teller pressed his idea forcefully and relentlessly, tirelessly ready at each meeting to start again from the beginning. He was impervious to doubt.

Teller had begun his dogged quest for the superbomb at wartime Los Alamos. In a meeting there with James Conant toward the end of the war, he had pressed for postwar development of the weapon and dismissed moral objections to it as irrelevant to the pursuit of scientific knowledge: "There is among my scientific colleagues some hesitancy as to the advisability of this development on the grounds that it might make the international problems even more difficult than they are now. My opinion is that this is a fallacy. If the development is possible, it is out of our powers to prevent it."[6] After he moved to Chicago, he kept abreast of theoretical developments by spending summers at Los Alamos as a consultant. Unable to get his mind off the superbomb, he lobbied for it whenever and with whomever he could. His message was insistent but simple: If a superbomb could be built (and he believed that it could), then it also could be built by the Russians. America therefore must undertake a crash program to build the superbomb in order to prevent Russia from getting it first, and then using it to intimidate or blackmail the United States in a crisis.

In his insecure mind, greater destructive power meant greater military strength, and greater military strength meant greater national security.

Ever since the end of the war, Teller had been trying to find a way to get serious work going on his pet project. The challenge of the Soviet bomb seemed to provide the impetus that was previously lacking, and Teller resolved to use every means and argument he could think of to exploit it. This was his moment, he thought.

Oppenheimer had hoped that Soviet scientists could not soon duplicate what he and his wartime colleagues at Los Alamos had done. Yet even after he learned of the Soviet atomic test, Oppenheimer remained opposed to development of the superbomb. Fission bombs, destructive as they might be, were limited in power. Now, it seemed, scientists such as Teller were seeking to brush even those limits aside and to build bombs whose destructiveness was boundless. Oppenheimer believed that America, as the world's leading nuclear power, must lead by example. And the example he sought to set was one of restraint.

Oppenheimer's concern was not new; two years before the Soviet atomic test, Arthur Compton

> found Oppenheimer reluctant [about the superbomb]. His chief reluctance was, I believe, on moral grounds. No nation should bring into being a power that would (or could) be so destructive of human lives. Even if another nation should do so, our morality should be higher than this. We should accept the military disadvantage in the interest of standing for a proper moral principle.
>
> He had other reasons — the development of fear and antagonism among other nations, the substantial possibility that the effort to create a [thermonuclear] explosion would fail, questions regarding the H-bomb's military value. He hoped that no urgent need for its development would arise.[7]

Oppenheimer found the superbomb a weapon out of all proportion to whatever America might seek to accomplish in either peace or war. He believed that most policy makers and scientists such as Teller gave far too high a value to nuclear weapons; and that just as the atomic bomb had given America a false sense of security, the nation was in danger of falling into the same error with the superbomb: the fallacy of a cheap, easy alternative to finding a way to coexist — like it or not — with Soviet Russia.

Oppenheimer suspected that most advocates of the superbomb were motivated by a reactive fear of the Soviet atomic test. "Having tried to find something tangible to chew on ever since September 23," he confided to a friend, they "[have] at last found [their] answer: We must have a Super, and we must have it fast." Privately admitting that "it would be folly to oppose exploration of this weapon" — a prediction his own career would tragically bear out — and that the basic scientific research "had to be done," Oppenheimer nonetheless refused to accept the enormously destructive superbomb "as the way to save the country and the peace." Instead, he believed the allure of the superbomb was "full of dangers," and represented a doomed effort to "return to a state of affairs approximating monopoly."[8]

Lawrence did not share Oppenheimer's qualms; he was, as Bethe described him, "a terrific nationalist who was completely devoted to making America infinitely strong."[9] Like Oppenheimer, Lawrence had opposed development of the superbomb just after the war, but the Soviet atomic test had changed his mind. Lawrence hoped the superbomb would prove impossible, but if such a weapon could be built, then he believed the United States must have it first. A longtime associate of Lawrence noted another motivation: "He welcomed it as not only a matter of duty, but a personal opportunity" to return to the "kind of high" experienced in the making of the atomic bomb, the sense that "you were really part of a great movement, doing things which were interesting and consequential."[10] Princeton physicist Henry Smyth, who had known Lawrence for many years, characterized him astutely. "Apart from being an expert in his field and a brilliant scientist," Smyth wrote that fall, Lawrence was "also something of a promoter; . . . several times in the past he may have overstepped the line in pushing projects which add to his own 'Empire.'"[11]

Lawrence knew how to build an empire. He was an experienced, effective, and politically savvy promoter of scientific projects. By 1949 Lawrence had spent a decade at the summit of American physics. His Rad Lab had been centrally involved in the Manhattan Project; he had served as a member of the highest scientific advisory councils since the war; and he continued to play a major role in atomic policy through close but unofficial personal contacts in the Pentagon and Congress. Lawrence had made his own laboratory — the only physicist who had — and this put him in a special category. He was used to acting on his own and having his way, though he did not see himself in this light. Rather, he saw himself as simply opposing those — such as Oppenheimer — who, in his mind, were trying to stifle legitimate and patriotic scientific work for their own political, and therefore improper, reasons.

Although Lawrence often piously cautioned other scientists not to "fool around" with politics, he did not follow his own advice.[12] Soon after Truman announced the Soviet test, Lawrence began lobbying vigorously for the superbomb's development. He phoned Teller at Los Alamos and said he would stop off to see him on his way to Washington. The next morning, October seventh, Lawrence landed in the predawn hours at the airstrip that ran off the eastern end of the Los Alamos mesa, and went straight to a meeting with Teller, who explained to him in convincing detail that a superbomb was feasible. When Teller finished, Lawrence said simply, "In the present situation, there is no question but that you must go ahead."[13]

It was late in the day when the two finished their talk. Lawrence needed to leave for Albuquerque because he was going on to Washington the next day. He asked Teller to accompany him, and during their trip down in the small plane that provided service between Los Alamos and Albuquerque, they talked about the importance of enlisting the help of other top physicists. The place to start, Teller thought, was Fermi — after all, he was undeniably brilliant and he had first suggested the idea of a thermonuclear explosion. But Fermi made it clear that he would not help. "You and I and Truman and Stalin would be happy if further great developments were impossible," he told Teller. "So, why don't we make an agreement to refrain from such development? It is, of course, impossible without an ultimate test and when that happens we shall know about it anyway." "Why should the bomb be bigger?" he asked in conclusion.[14] The intensity of Fermi's refusal was surprising; he was a reserved man, and it was unusual for him to show emotion.

Teller was unhappy, upset, and unwilling to take no for an answer. He goaded Fermi by reminding him that he had opposed the Acheson-Lilienthal Report because he distrusted the Russians — yet now he proposed an arrangement with them without guarantees. "Yes," Fermi shot back, "but what else can we do?" "Go ahead and work on it if you have to," he added. "I hope you will not succeed."[15] "I felt clearly," Teller wrote in a letter after their meeting, that "Enrico wants to be rid of the whole problem. (Why talk about it — why think about it?)"[16]

Having failed to enlist Fermi, Teller turned next to Bethe. If he could convince someone of Bethe's stature to work on the superbomb, other physicists could be persuaded to work on it, too. Bethe seldom suffered from hesitation or indecision, but he did when Teller arrived in Ithaca in late September 1949 seeking his help. The two sat up late into the night in the living room of Bethe's home discussing the issue. Autumn had come early to Ithaca that year and the temperature outside was as cool as it was in the room. "I had very great internal conflicts about what I should do," Bethe remembered. On the one hand, the superbomb was a seductive technical challenge. It meant working with other top scientists and having access to powerful new electronic computers reserved for military research. It also meant the likelihood of exciting discoveries. And there was a political consideration: Bethe worried that Stalin might blackmail the world if he alone had it. "On the other hand," as he later said, "it seemed to me that it was a very terrible undertaking to develop a still bigger bomb."[17]

Undecided, Bethe talked things over with his wife, Rose. She reminded him that he had helped make an atomic bomb only because the western democracies were at war with Nazi Germany. Then, motioning toward their two small children, Henry and Monica, asleep in the next room, she asked him if he wanted them to grow up in a world with superbombs. "She felt that the atomic bomb was bad enough, and that increasing its power a thousand times was simply irresponsible," recalled Bethe. "'You don't want to do this.'"[18]

But Bethe was unsure. "It seemed to me that the development of thermonuclear weapons would not solve any of the difficulties that we found ourselves in and yet I was not quite sure whether I should refuse." He decided to call Oppenheimer, whose judgment he respected, for advice. Oppenheimer suggested he and Teller come visit him in Princeton. Two days later, the three of them met in Oppenheimer's office at the Institute for Advanced Study. It was a far cry from Oppenheimer's spartan office at Los Alamos, where the three had met together often during the war. The bright, well-appointed room looked out over broad green meadows fringed with trees aflame with the golden tints of autumn. At Los Alamos, Oppenheimer had resembled the enthusiastic leader of a rugged pioneer settlement. Now he reminded Bethe of a restrained country gentleman receiving his guests at a stately manor.

Oppenheimer and Teller eyed each other warily, while the object of their unstated but unmistakable competition sat silently between them.

Oppenheimer said nothing as Teller presented his case, either out of caution in Teller's presence or because he did not want to say anything to influence Bethe — or both. When Teller finished, he and Oppenheimer mildly debated, but Oppenheimer did not mount much of a counterattack, which was unusual for him. Perhaps Oppenheimer believed he did not need to argue what he thought was obvious, but it was, at least with regard to the other guest, a tactical mistake. "I did not get from him the advice that I was hoping to get," Bethe recalled. "I did not get from him advice to decide me either way."[19] Teller, who was convinced that Oppenheimer had been using his clout to discourage physicists from working on the superbomb, was elated by his silence. Before going to Princeton, he recalled later, "I had expressed to Bethe the worry that we are going to talk to Oppenheimer, and after that you will not come. When we left the office, Bethe turned to me and smiled and he said, 'You see, you can be quite satisfied. I am still coming.'"[20]

From Oppenheimer's institute office, Bethe walked over to the university campus, where a conference was underway. When he reached the conference hall, he ran into Szilard, who greeted him by saying, "Ah, here is Dr. Bethe from Los Alamos."[21] Szilard's remark was carefully calculated. He knew Bethe was sensitive about his weapons work, and he sought to stir Bethe's conscience against the superbomb by embarrassing him in front of his peers, many of whom opposed its development. "I protested that I was not at Los Alamos," recalled Bethe, "and didn't know if I wanted to go back there."

MIT theoretical physicist Victor Weisskopf was also at the conference. A close friend of Bethe since prewar days in Europe, "Vicky" Weisskopf had eschewed weapons work since the war. He and Bethe took a long walk around the Princeton campus the next evening. Weisskopf imagined the horrors of a war fought with superbombs for his friend as they crunched through the autumn leaves. "Vicky vividly described to me what it would mean to destroy a whole city like New York with one bomb," Bethe recalled. "We both had to agree that after such a war even if we were to win it, the world would not be like the world we wanted to preserve. We would lose the things we were fighting for. This was a very long conversation and a very difficult one for both of us." But it clarified things for Bethe. "Your discussion with me last weekend was most wholesome," he wrote Weisskopf. "I felt very much better after talking to you."[22] Bethe's struggle with his conscience was over. He phoned Teller with his decision. "Edward, I've been thinking it over," said Bethe. "I can't come after all."

"I felt relieved," he recalled later.[23] Teller was sad, disappointed, and angry — but not at Bethe or Weisskopf. As he would increasingly do, with or without evidence, he found his enemy in the form of his former boss. "I knew it after the meeting with Oppenheimer," he grumbled.[24]

Bethe explained his decision later. "It seemed to me then and it seems to me now that it was the wrong thing to do, that we should not have escalated. It seems to me now very clear that we should have developed the atomic bomb during the war when we had a desperate situation with the Nazis. But in 1949 vis-à-vis the Russians we still held the cards of greater production [and] greater delivery capability of nuclear weapons. So I think the right direction would have been to say no, we are not going to do it. We may do some further research on it, but let's not make it a crash program. We really didn't need it, but when we embarked on it, I think it was one of the many examples of overkill that we indulged in in those days."[25]

While Teller sought to enlist Fermi's and Bethe's help, Lawrence lobbied for the superbomb in Washington. One of his first stops was Capitol Hill, where he met with the Joint Congressional Committee on Atomic Energy, including its powerful chairman, Connecticut Democratic senator Brien McMahon. Lawrence warned McMahon that Stalin would go all out to develop a superbomb and that the Soviet Union might be ahead in the race. For the first time in his life, he said, he was afraid that America might lose a war — unless Washington undertook a crash program to build a superbomb. Lawrence also lobbied his high-level contacts at the Pentagon. "It would be disastrous," he warned those close to the secretary of defense and the Joint Chiefs of Staff, "if the Soviets produced a hydrogen bomb before the United States."[26]

Lawrence's next stop was New York, where he went to see Rabi at Columbia. Lawrence was accompanied by Rad Lab associate Luis Alvarez, who recounted their meeting with Rabi in his diary that evening. Rabi was "very happy at our plans," Alvarez wrote. "He is worried, too." According to Alvarez, Rabi had told them, "It is certainly good to see the first team back in. You fellows have been playing with your cyclotron and nuclei for four years and it is certainly time you got back to work." Rabi's recollection was more tentative. "I felt that some answer must be made in some form to regain our lead. There were two directions in which one could look: either the realization of the super or an intensification of the effort on fission weapons." But Rabi felt Lawrence and Alvarez had already made up their minds:

> They were extremely optimistic. They are both very optimistic gentlemen. . . . They had been to Los Alamos and talked to Dr. Teller, who gave them a very optimistic estimate about the [super-bomb]. So they were all keyed up to go bang into it. . . . I generally find myself when I talk with these two gentlemen in a very uncomfortable position. I like to be an enthusiast. I love it. But those fellows are so enthusiastic that I have to be conservative. So it always puts me in an odd position [where I have to] say, "Now, now, there, there," and that sort of thing. So I was not in agreement in the sense that I felt they were, as usual, overly optimistic.[27]

When the meeting ended, Lawrence flew back to Washington and urged the Joint Chiefs of Staff to declare their support for development of the superbomb.

Once Lawrence had brought the superbomb to Washington's attention, the idea went to the AEC's General Advisory Committee (GAC) for study and recommendation. Government advisory committees are almost always more show than substance, but the GAC was different. Composed of a panel of nine leading American scientists, the GAC had established itself since its creation in 1947 as the most influential source of advice to the government on atomic weapons.* Its chairman was Oppenheimer, who had been chosen unanimously by his colleagues. The GAC was not Oppenheimer's puppet, however, because its membership also included Fermi and Rabi. Fermi worked hard and conscientiously on the GAC, but without the pleasure that Oppenheimer felt in counseling on policy — he was a scientist, not a politician. Although the atomic bomb had shaken him up, Fermi remained cold and clinical, even a little ruthless, in the way he disdained human emotions and went directly to the facts in deciding any question. Oppenheimer assessed him cogently: "Not a philosopher. Passion for

---

* The GAC in 1949 also included James Conant; Lee DuBridge, leader of the wartime radar lab at MIT and now president of Caltech; Hartley Rowe, an engineer who had worked on materials procurement for the Manhattan Project; Oliver Buckley, president of Bell Telephone Laboratories and an expert on guided missiles; Glenn Seaborg, discoverer of plutonium and coauthor of the 1945 Franck Report; and Cyril Smith of the University of Chicago, who had been in charge of the metallurgy division at Los Alamos during the war.

clarity. He was simply unable to let things be foggy. Since they always are, this kept him pretty active."[28] Fermi believed the superbomb could be built if America set itself to accomplishing the task, but he feared the devastating consequences of its potential use. It was far wiser, Fermi thought, to try to outlaw this weapon that did not yet exist.

The afternoon of Friday, October 28, 1949, was gray and drizzly when the GAC convened in a cavernous conference room on the second floor of AEC headquarters at 19th Street and Constitution Avenue on the Mall near the White House.* The wood-paneled room looked out on the Reflecting Pool in front of the Lincoln Memorial, but no one was in the mood to peer out the windows that day. Oppenheimer began the meeting by stating the matter to be considered: the prospects and implications of developing a superbomb. The GAC spent the rest of the afternoon talking with top experts. George Kennan, director of the State Department's Policy Planning Staff and an influential and experienced specialist in Soviet affairs, told the committee that it might be possible to negotiate an arms control agreement with Russia. Next they heard from Bethe, who stressed that many technical problems relating to the superbomb remained to be solved. He also talked about his fear that a war fought with superbombs would destroy what it was intended to preserve.

Oppenheimer opened the next morning's session by reading aloud Seaborg's letter. He then asked each committee member to express his view about what to do. Not everyone had made up his mind, and Oppenheimer was careful not to lead or to influence them. A member of the GAC recalled:

> Dr. Oppenheimer did not express his point of view until after all the rest of the members of the committee had expressed themselves. It was clear, however, as the individual members did express their opinions as we went around the table, that while there were differing points of view, different reasons, different methods of thinking, different methods of approach to the problem, that each member came essentially to the same conclusion, namely, there were better things the United States could do at that time than to embark upon

* One GAC member, Glenn Seaborg, was abroad on a visit to Sweden. The GAC had his views, however, in the form of a letter. Seaborg reluctantly supported development of the superbomb.

this super program. . . . Each person took five to ten minutes or thereabouts to express his views.[29]

Oppenheimer spoke last. "There was a surprising unanimity — to me very surprising — that the United States ought not to take the initiative at that time in an all-out program," he said. Then: "I am glad you feel this way, for if it had not come out this way, I would have had to resign as chairman."[30] The fact that there *was* a consensus on such a contentious issue underscored the physicists' moral qualms about building a superbomb. (But there was not unanimity, since Seaborg, in his letter, favored going ahead.)

Four of the five AEC commissioners then joined the GAC at this point.* For an hour the two groups discussed the superbomb. It was a soul-searching session. Many GAC members said they could not see how any country could go from one weapon of mass destruction to another a thousand times more destructive and retain any normal perspective with regard to other countries and world peace. They felt as if they were being asked to endorse an undertaking that might prove to bring down the curtain on human civilization.

At 11:00 A.M. the Joint Chiefs arrived. They came with a very different perspective. Without the superbomb, they asserted, there would be nothing the U.S. military could do to deter or prevent Russia from overrunning Western Europe. They considered a war with the Soviet Union "likely" in four to five years. "Further negotiation with the Russians," they sniffed, "is useless." But they had great difficulty articulating the actual military value of a superbomb. When Oppenheimer asked the JCS chairman, army general Omar Bradley, what military advantages he could see in a superbomb over the largest atomic bombs, Bradley answered, "Only psychological." When Lilienthal asked air force general Lauris Norstad why not simply increase the production of atomic bombs instead of building an even more destructive weapon, Norstad had no answer. The group then broke for lunch.

When discussion resumed in the afternoon, GAC member Hartley Rowe expressed strong opposition to the superbomb on moral grounds. "We built one Frankenstein," he muttered. Oppenheimer nodded in agreement. Speaking carefully as his eyes swept the room,

* David Lilienthal, chairman; financier Lewis Strauss; attorney Gordon Dean; and Princeton physicist Henry Smyth. The fifth AEC commissioner, businessman Sumner Pike, did not attend.

Fermi said the superbomb should be explored but not necessarily developed. "One must explore it and do it," said Fermi, but added, "That doesn't foreclose the question: should it be made use of?"[31] Rabi felt a decision to go ahead was probably foreordained, if for no other reason than domestic politics; the only open question would be who was willing to join in it. The sense of momentum, and inevitability, made Conant recall the development of the atomic bomb, and the parallel made him uneasy. A chemist who had begun his service to the state making poison gas during World War I and then had helped direct the Manhattan Project, Conant had had enough — he wanted nothing more to do with weapons of mass destruction. "This whole discussion makes me feel I'm seeing the same film, and a punk one, for the second time," Conant announced.[32] Conant's and the other scientists' qualms boiled down to this: it was one thing to develop the atomic bomb in wartime; it was quite another to develop a weapon so destructive that it had no rational military use and to introduce it into a world at peace.

At the end of their deliberations, the GAC members sat down to write a report. Emotions were running high and the eight men stayed up late that night drafting the document. The body of the report addressed mainly technical issues, but also larger concerns. They agreed that a superbomb would probably be technically feasible, but that it was unnecessary because the Soviet Union had few large cities and the United States could use atomic bombs against them if necessary. As Oppenheimer later explained: "We thought it was something to avoid because we were infinitely more vulnerable [because more of the American population lived in large cities than did the Russian population] and infinitely less likely to initiate the use of these weapons and because the world in which great destruction has been done in all civilized parts of the world is a harder world for America to live with than it is for the Communists to live with." From a strategic standpoint, the superbomb made no sense. Moreover, even if the Soviets developed the superbomb, the United States would still have more than enough atomic bombs for adequate deterrence or, if deterrence failed, punishing retaliation. Moral *and* military logic argued against building anything bigger.

To these scientists, however, the practical and strategic liabilities of the superbomb were subordinate to a more fundamental concern. The majority of the committee's members opposed the superbomb *per se*. They emphasized the single most distinctive characteristic of a fusion, as opposed to a fission, weapon: if it could be built, it would have unlimited destructiveness. This distinguished the superbomb from even such horrific weapons as atomic bombs — the superbomb was "a weapon of genocide":

> It is clear that the use of this weapon would bring about the destruction of innumerable human lives; it is not a weapon which can be used exclusively for the destruction of material installations of military or semi-military purposes. Its use therefore carries much further than the atomic bomb itself the policy of exterminating civilian populations.

This was surprisingly strong language coming from many of those who had put the atomic bomb in the hands of the United States during World War II. "In determining not to proceed to develop the superbomb," they concluded, "we see a unique opportunity of providing by example some limitations on the totality of war and thus of limiting the fear and arousing the hopes of mankind."[33]

They did not say that following their advice would prevent the development of a Soviet superbomb. Rather, they argued that foregoing the superbomb was a necessary precondition for persuading the Russians to do the same; and that America's atomic stockpile was such that doing so would not entail any substantial risk of upsetting the balance of power. All of this was done in the hope that restraint would replace an ever-deadlier arms race.

There were some divisions. Oppenheimer and most other GAC members opposed *any* development of the superbomb. But Fermi and Rabi, suspecting that a GAC recommendation against development would be ignored by the White House, suggested a more practical alternative: coupling American forbearance on the superbomb with a Soviet pledge to do the same. Fermi and Rabi laid out their proposal in a minority annex to the report:

> We believe it important for the President of the United States to tell the American public, and the world, that we think it wrong on fundamental ethical principles to initiate a program of development of such a weapon. At the same time it would be appropriate to invite the nations of the world to join us in a solemn pledge not to proceed in the development or construction of weapons of this category. If such a pledge were accepted even without control machinery, it

appears highly probable that an advanced stage of development leading to a test by another power could be detected by available physical means. Furthermore, we have in our possession, in our stockpile of atomic bombs, the means for adequate "military" retaliation for the production or use of a "super."[34]

Their hope, said Fermi later, was "to outlaw the thing before it was born."[35] Rabi explained what he and Fermi had in mind: "Fermi and I said that we should use this as an excuse to call a world conference for the nations to agree, for the time being, not to do further research on [superbombs]. We felt that if the conference should be a failure and we couldn't get agreement to stop this research and had to go ahead, we could then do so in good conscience."[36]

But despite this, it was not clear whether Fermi's and Rabi's consciences could be untroubled in any circumstances relating to the superbomb. They behaved uncertainly — favoring the superbomb at the outset of the GAC's deliberations, but conditionally opposing it at the end. And while willing to countenance an American superbomb if the Russians would not forgo one of their own, both clearly condemned the weapon's immorality:

Necessarily such a weapon goes far beyond any military objective and enters the range of very great natural catastrophes. By its very nature it cannot be confined to a military objective but becomes a weapon which in practical effect is almost one of genocide.

It is clear that the use of such a weapon cannot be justified on any ethical ground which gives a human being a certain individuality and dignity even if he happens to be a resident of an enemy country. It is evident to us that this would be the view of peoples in other countries. Its use would put the United States in a bad moral position relative to the peoples of the world.

Any postwar situation resulting from such a weapon would leave unresolvable enmities for generations. A desirable peace cannot come from such an inhuman application of force. The postwar problems would dwarf the problems which confront us at present. . . .

The fact that no limits exist to the destructiveness of this weapon makes its very existence and the knowledge of its construction a danger to humanity as a whole. It is necessarily an evil thing considered in any light. For these reasons we believe it important for the President of the United States to tell the American public, and the world, that we think it wrong on fundamental ethical principles to initiate the development of such a weapon.

Fermi and Rabi's minority annex showed not just moral passion but political imagination. It sought to use the Soviet atomic test as a lever for restarting nuclear arms control talks instead of letting it serve as a stimulus for the development of even more destructive superbombs. The United States could simply agree with the Soviets on a "no super-bomb" pledge even without on-site inspection, relying upon atmospheric and seismic detection to monitor compliance. The Soviets in all likelihood could not produce a superbomb without testing, and American detection was very likely to pick up any evidence of cheating.

The effect of Fermi and Rabi's annex, however, was marginal; it was the majority's call for *total* renunciation of the superbomb that got noticed. Some of this was their fault. "We just wrote our report and then went home, and left the field to the others," said Rabi. "That was a mistake. If we hadn't done that, history might have been different."[37]

Not only had the GAC majority report said that the superbomb was the wrong answer — it had also challenged Teller and Lawrence. This challenge had been political, but it was hard not to see some personal elements in it. Oppenheimer had grown estranged from both men by 1949. The latent friction that had marked Oppenheimer and Teller's first encounter in 1937 had surfaced under the wartime strain at Los Alamos and deepened after Teller began promoting the super-bomb in the wake of the Soviet test.

Oppenheimer's relationship with Lawrence was deeper and more complicated. A mixture of personal affection and professional one-upmanship had characterized their association from the beginning. Their relationship, already weakened when Oppenheimer left Berke-ley for Princeton, had been severely strained when Oppenheimer's brother, Frank, had gotten in trouble for his communist past and Lawrence, stung by the exposure of his Rad Lab as a hotbed of Soviet sympathizers, had exiled Frank from the place where he had worked so hard and effectively during the war. Lawrence's treatment of Frank wounded Frank's sensitive and protective older brother, and shredded all but a vestige of Lawrence and Oppenheimer's long-standing friendship. "I think there was probably warmth between us at all times," Oppenheimer said later, "but there was bitterness which be-came very acute in '49 and which was never resolved."[38] Lawrence felt that bitterness, too. Distinguishing now between "working scientists" like himself and "talkers," Lawrence observed acidly that "those who once thought the atomic bomb was a terrible thing now have no such scruples about it but have transferred their sense of horror to the H-bomb."[39]

This mutual bitterness led Oppenheimer to belittle Lawrence and Teller around this time in a private letter as "two experienced promoters"[40] and served to blind him to the merit of Fermi and Rabi's proposal. Oppenheimer had recognized, as he had written privately, that "it would be folly to oppose the exploration of this weapon. We have always known it had to be done; and it does have to be done." Then he added: "But that we become committed to it as the way to save the country and the peace appears to me full of dangers," failing to recognize that Fermi and Rabi's idea might have allowed the exploration he considered inevitable without the commitment he considered dangerous.[41] Thus a potentially promising avenue went unexplored and the contentious issue became even more personalized.

Once Teller learned the GAC had reached a verdict, he was anxious to know what it was. A few days after the decision, he left Los Alamos for Washington, stopping in Chicago along the way to see if Fermi might give him an inkling of the GAC's verdict. Fermi was aware of Teller's concern, but the GAC report was classified and Fermi refused to discuss its contents. He did not have to. The tone of Fermi's voice and his body language told the story. "It was clear from the tenor of his remarks," Teller later wrote, "that certainly Fermi and possibly the entire GAC did not favor an all-out crash program."[42] Fermi even scolded Teller for joining a "fascist like Lawrence" in pushing for the superbomb.[43]

Fermi's words "thoroughly frightened" Teller, as he confided in a letter to another friend a short time later. Although he had known and liked the Italian for years, Fermi's about-face — he had originally proposed the idea of a superbomb to Teller in 1941 — made Teller angry. "Enrico does not know what I think of him," he wrote. "But — unfortunately — he has an inkling." Teller's words revealed how emotionally invested he had become in the superbomb, an emotional investment that eclipsed even long-standing friendships.[44]

Teller's conversation with Fermi reinforced his fear that Oppenheimer's persuasive powers spelled doom for the superbomb project.

When Teller finally saw the GAC report and the minority annex on November second, he became "morose and almost silent (*very* unusual)," recalled John Manley, associate director of Los Alamos and secretary to the GAC, who had shown him the report. Teller thought the superbomb project was all but dead — and with it, America as he knew it. "Edward offered to bet me that unless we went ahead with his Super . . . he, Teller, would be a Russian prisoner of war in the United States within five years," Manley recalled.[45] Teller suspected a conspiracy, complaining that there were "mysterious actions in the GAC and even higher places." "What disturbs me most," he wrote fellow Hungarian John von Neumann, "is that apparently Enrico is at least temporarily convinced that the action of the GAC is reasonable. One thing is quite clear, that the really fine and unanimous enthusiasm which was building up in Los Alamos [for the superbomb] is now checked at least temporarily."[46] Teller believed that anyone — like Oppenheimer — who opposed the superbomb had become suspect.

Teller had always disliked routine and was ill at ease under any imposed discipline. This maverick streak, combined with his overwhelming ambition and intense commitment to the superbomb, led Teller to mount a countercharge to gain support for the proposed weapon. He had learned after the war that it was necessary for him to become very political in order to accomplish his goals, and so he had become very smart at aligning himself with the powers in Washington. He spent much of the next few months after the GAC report lobbying military officers and congressmen. His excited gestures showed his sincerity, and his anticommunism struck the right patriotic note. Teller had no doubt that his campaign to build a superbomb would require a great deal of effort and work on his part and that of many others — but so, he was fond of saying, had the atomic bomb. "I wonder to how many people it happens that they are sent back where they have been before and that they get a second chance," he wrote to a confidante at the end of the year. "But this time I love the job I am going to do — I shall even love to fight if it must be."[47]

Teller was at least temporarily stymied when, on November ninth, the AEC endorsed the GAC recommendation against the superbomb in a split three-to-two decision, with Lilienthal, Pike, and Smyth (who urged delay more than rejection) against development; Strauss and Dean in favor. Lilienthal presented the views of the AEC commissioners, along with a full copy of the GAC report, to Truman the same day. Truman assured Lilienthal that he would not be "blitzed" into any decision on this important issue.[48] The president turned to a special three-man subcommittee of the National Security Council — Lilienthal, Secretary of State Dean Acheson, and Secretary of Defense Louis Johnson — for a final recommendation. Lilienthal strongly supported the GAC's position, and Johnson was just as clearly determined to develop the weapon.

That left Acheson, who had not just the tiebreaking vote but the most influence with Truman. Acheson was a realist who believed additional military power would enhance American diplomacy, and he was already under withering personal attack from conservative Republicans for weakness in "losing" China. There was even some talk inside the Joint Congressional Committee on Atomic Energy of bringing impeachment proceedings against Truman if he failed to give the go-ahead on the superbomb. It was no surprise that Acheson leaned toward the superbomb's development. But he was a good lawyer and understood that knowing all sides of the argument was essential. So before making up his mind, he talked at length with opponents of the weapon, especially Oppenheimer, who had been a friend since their work together in 1946 on an American plan for international control of atomic energy.

The urbane and pragmatic Acheson, whose first impression of Oppenheimer had been that of a smart but naive idealist, listened closely to Oppenheimer's arguments against the superbomb, which echoed what Bohr had said to FDR and Churchill about the atomic bomb in 1944: it would be easier to negotiate a ban on a weapon not yet made. Acheson thought that Oppenheimer was moved less by logic and reason than by "an immense distaste" for what the scientist himself described as "the whole rotten business."[49] "I listened as carefully as I knew how," Acheson wrote loftily in his memoirs, "but I [did not] understand what Oppie was trying to say. How can you persuade a paranoid adversary to disarm 'by example'?"[50] But that was not the only reason he disagreed. Acheson also did not see, as he later told Oppenheimer, "how any president could [politically] survive a policy of not making the H-bomb."[51]

Such fear, logic, and pressure prevailed. Truman's decision had been solidified by a memo the Chiefs had sent to him in mid-January: (1) "Possession of a thermonuclear weapon by the USSR without such possession by the United States would be intolerable" both by its "profoundly demoralizing effect upon the American people" and by the "tremendous psychological boost" it would afford Soviet leaders;

and (2) "a unilateral decision on the part of the United States not to develop a thermonuclear weapon will not prevent the development of such a weapon elsewhere." Truman zeroed in on these points when he met with his senior advisers on the day of decision. "Can the Russians do it?" the president asked them. All heads nodded. "Yes, they can." "In that case," said Truman, "we have no choice. We'll go ahead."[52]

On January 31, 1950, Truman approved development of the super-bomb. Like Acheson, Truman saw no alternative to going ahead, nor did he seek one after being told that the Russians would probably be able to develop their own superbomb — a belief bolstered by the news around this time that German refugee physicist Klaus Fuchs had been arrested in London for espionage on behalf of the Soviet Union. Fuchs had been at Los Alamos from December 1944 to June 1946, working on, among other things, the primitive superbomb program. He was in a position to have complete knowledge of American efforts up to that point.

Truman's decision to move ahead was so popular that it was greeted with cheers on the floor of the House and the Senate. An opinion poll showed overwhelming public support as well: 73 percent for versus 18 percent against.[53] The *New York Times* editorialized, "Regardless of how dreadful the hydrogen weapon might be, Mr. Truman had no other course in view of the failure so far of negotiations for inter-national control of atomic energy and of the 'atomic explosion' some months ago in the Soviet Union."[54] The fear that Moscow might also be working on a superbomb — and what that would mean for Ameri-can security — overwhelmed moral qualms and worries about escalat-ing the nuclear arms race.

The fear proved well founded, even as the qualms and worries remained. Andrei Sakharov, Russia's top nuclear physicist at the time, later stated that Stalin "already understood the potential of the new weapon, and nothing could have dissuaded [him] from going forward with its development. Any U.S. move toward abandoning or suspend-ing work on a thermonuclear weapon would have been perceived either as a cunning, deceitful maneuver or as evidence of stupidity or weakness. In any case, the Soviet reaction would have been the same: to avoid a possible trap, and to exploit the adversary's folly at the earli-est opportunity."[55]*

---

* Sakharov's disclosure made the effort of Oppenheimer and others to prevent an escalation of the nuclear arms race appear "hopeless" in retrospect, concluded Hans Bethe, reasoning that "Stalin would never have accepted an agreement *not* to develop the H-bomb." (Notes, "TV 1995 — Anniversary," Hans Bethe Personal Papers.)

The evening that Truman announced his decision, AEC commissioner Lewis Strauss hosted a party at Washington's posh Shoreham Hotel — it was Strauss's fifty-fourth birthday. Among the politicians, journalists, bureaucrats, and officers in attendance was Robert Oppenheimer, who had accepted the invitation weeks before. One of the journalists spotted Oppenheimer standing alone, morose, on the sidelines of the celebration. The journalist asked Oppenheimer why he appeared so glum. After an unusually long pause, Oppenheimer finally replied: "This is the plague of Thebes."[56]

Oppenheimer did not publicly criticize Truman's decision. Perhaps he felt that as chairman of the GAC he had no right to engage in public debate with the president. Then, too, dissent had its political risks; it was beginning to be equated with disloyalty in a climate of growing fear of communist subversion, and Oppenheimer's left-wing past made him vulnerable.* Nearly a decade later, when looking back on the GAC report, Oppenheimer remembered that his confidential secretary had been surprised by his strong stand against the superbomb in the October 1949 report and correctly predicted that this would get him in a lot of trouble. Furthermore, Truman imposed a gag order barring all public discussion, and Oppenheimer would not violate the president's directive. He did, however, criticize the atmosphere of secrecy in which the issue of the superbomb had been debated and decided. Shortly after Truman's decision, he told a nationwide television audience that nuclear issues "are complex technical things, but they touch on the very basis of our morality." Debate should proceed in the open. "It is a grave danger for us that these decisions are taken on the basis of facts held secret," said Oppenheimer, adding: "Wisdom cannot flourish and even the truth cannot be established, without the give-and-take of debate and criticism. The facts, the relevant facts, are of little use to an enemy, yet they are fundamental to an understanding of the issues of policy."[57] Thereafter Oppenheimer periodically hinted at his frustration but, reluctant to abandon his access to power, publicly held his tongue.

* Former State Department official Alger Hiss was convicted of perjury on January twenty-first for having denied passing secret documents to Soviet agent Whittaker Chambers during the 1930s. On February third, Klaus Fuchs was publicly arraigned in Britain for atomic espionage during the war. Exploiting these sensational developments, Republican senator Joseph McCarthy of Wisconsin began an anticommunist witch-hunt on February ninth with a speech in which he claimed to have a list of 205 communists working in the State Department.

Truman's decision left Szilard unsurprised but nonetheless disappointed. In a burst of black humor, Szilard drafted (but never published) a fictional letter from inmates in a lunatic asylum to dramatize what he considered the insanity of the superbomb. "We *got* to show him [God] that He cannot get away with [domination] any longer; we got to show him who the master is, and let's not stop until we show him that we can blow up what he created. On to the global bomb!" In despair Szilard warned in a nationwide broadcast that the radioactive fallout from a thermonuclear war could destroy all human life on earth. He believed that recognition of the possibility of mass death was essential to changing policy.[58]

Compton's criticism of Truman's superbomb decision was more indirect. "This is not a question for experts, either militarists or scientists," said Compton. "All they can do is to explain what the results will be if we do or do not try to develop such destructive weapons. The American people must themselves say whether they want to defend themselves with such weapons." He urged his fellow citizens to address these fundamental questions: "Should we take moral responsibility for introducing such greater destruction into war, at the risk of fear and suspicion by other nations? If developed, would its greater destructiveness be outweighed by its influence as a deterrent to war? Would its development provide greater safety — or provoke other nations to yet greater war preparations?"[59]

Rabi regretted the president's decision and put the blame squarely on Teller and Lawrence, whom he felt had whipped up political pressures that forced Truman's decision. One of the results, Rabi concluded, was to lay down a challenge to the Soviet Union:

> However it's worded, this will be taken as a statement that we're going ahead and building a hydrogen bomb. The Russians are certainly going to take it that way. Only we're not building a hydrogen bomb, because we don't know how. We're going to try. We don't even know that it can be done. But the Russians will never believe that an American President could be so stupid as to say we're going to build the most powerful weapon in the world when we don't know how. We've got the worst of both worlds. We haven't got a super, but we've spurred the Russians on to an all-out effort to build one.[60]

A February 1950 manifesto signed by twelve prominent physicists — all Manhattan Project veterans — echoed this point. It went on to warn:

A hydrogen bomb, if it can be made, would be capable of developing a power 1000 times greater than the present atomic bomb. New York, or any other of the greatest cities of the world, could be destroyed by a single hydrogen bomb.

We believe that no nation has the right to use such a bomb, no matter how righteous its cause. This bomb is no longer a weapon of war but a means of extermination of whole populations. Its use would be a betrayal of all standards of morality and of Christian civilization itself. . . .

We shall not have a monopoly of this bomb. . . . the Russians will be able to make one too. In the case of the fission bomb the Russians required four years to parallel our development. In the case of the hydrogen bomb they will probably need a shorter time.* Perhaps the development of the hydrogen bomb has already been under way in Russia for some time. But if it was not, our decision to develop it must have started the Russians on the same program. If they had already a going program, they will redouble their efforts.[61]

The organizer of the manifesto, Hans Bethe, authored an essay for *Scientific American* later that spring in which he wrote:

I believe the most important question is the moral one: can we, who have always insisted on morality and human decency between nations as well as inside our own country, introduce this weapon of total annihilation into the world? The usual argument, heard in the frantic week before the President's decision and frequently since, is that we are fighting against a country which denies all the human values we cherish and that any weapon, however terrible, must be used to prevent that country and its creed from dominating the world. It is argued that it would be better for us to lose our lives than our liberty; and this I personally agree with. But I believe that this is not the question; I believe that we would lose far more than our lives in a war fought with hydrogen bombs, that we would in fact lose all our liberties and human values at the same time, and so thoroughly that we would not recover them for an unforeseeably long time.

We believe in peace based on mutual trust. Shall we achieve it by

* They were right. The Soviets tested their first superbomb, a fission-boosted weapon, on August 12, 1953. Their first "true" superbomb, based on thermonuclear fusion, was tested on November 22, 1955.

using hydrogen bombs? Shall we convince the Russians of the value of the individual by killing millions of them? If we fight a war and win it with H-bombs, what history will remember is *not* the ideals we were fighting for but the method we used to accomplish them. These methods will be compared to the warfare of Genghis Khan, who ruthlessly killed every last inhabitant of Persia.[62]

Bethe believed the principal moral distinction between the United States and the Soviet Union lay in the *means* they used, rather than the *ends* they sought. Should the United States employ such an indiscriminately destructive weapon as the superbomb, it would forfeit that moral claim. He then wrote a private letter to Norris Bradbury outlining his personal views in greater detail:

Dear Dr. Bradbury,
You will probably have heard about my feelings concerning the hydrogen bomb from . . . the newspapers. The announcement of the President has not changed my feelings in the matter. I still believe that it is morally wrong and unwise for our national security to develop this weapon. In most respects I agree with the opinions of the General Advisory Committee although I have not seen their report itself. So much has been said about the reasons on both sides that I do not need to go into them here. The main point is that I can not in good conscience work on this weapon.

For this reason, if and when I come to Los Alamos in the future I will completely refrain from any discussions relating to the superbomb.

Bethe concluded his letter with a caveat: "In case of war I would obviously reconsider my position."[63] Four months later the Korean War broke out, and he indeed returned to Los Alamos. Bethe hoped that by doing so, he could prove to himself and others that a superbomb could not be made, and actually did some calculations attempting to prove this.

Such an outcome offered the best — perhaps the only — solution to Bethe's tortured conscience. For even while working on the superbomb, he "still hated the thing."[64] But Bethe stifled his impulse to tell military officers at Los Alamos "what a horrible thing we were working on,"[65] and, paradoxically, ended up playing a major part in the development of the very weapon that he feared and had initially opposed. Deep down he would long wonder whether his anxieties about the Russians might not have been an attempt to rationalize a simple desire to take part in another clever trick of nature.

The doubts never went away. "I am still not reconciled to the hydrogen bomb although I have myself worked on it," Bethe told an audience of physicists at Los Alamos in 1953. "I still think that it is a more evil thing than the atomic bomb."[66] He finally came to the conclusion that the superbomb "was probably inevitable, but one wishes it could have been avoided."[67] He also reflected on his own role in its development. "I am afraid my inner troubles stayed with me and are still with me and I have not resolved this problem," confessed Bethe. "I still have the feeling that I have done the wrong thing, but I have done it."[68]

Others had also changed their minds. This was most evident at a meeting on superbomb design held at Princeton in June 1951. Those attending included not just Teller — but also Oppenheimer, Bethe, and Fermi.* An eyewitness described what took place:

> Pictures were drawn on the board. Calculations were made, Dr. Bethe, Dr. Teller, Dr. Fermi participating the most in this; Oppy very actively as well. . . . I remember leaving that meeting impressed with this fact, that everyone around that table without exception — and this included Dr. Oppenheimer — was enthusiastic now that you had something foreseeable. The bickering was gone. The discussions were pretty well ended, and we were able within a matter of just about one year to have that gadget ready.[69]

Why did those who had opposed the superbomb so strongly on moral grounds eventually assist in its development? Because, in their minds, the superbomb had become inevitable. With its theoretical feasibility proven, and the nearly limitless resources of the federal government behind it, they thought the superbomb was almost certain to be constructed. Refusing to work on it would not prevent it from being made.[70] Equally important, it now seemed likely that the Russians would be able to make it, too, and the scientists — like America's political leaders — felt it would be intolerable for the superbomb to be in the hands of the Soviet Union but not the United

* Bethe and Fermi subsequently consulted at Los Alamos on the superbomb's development, and Bethe helped design the weapon based on an idea conceived by Edward Teller, Stanislaw Ulam, and Richard Garwin.

States. Once "it was clear that it could be done, not only by us, but also by the Russians," said Bethe, "Oppenheimer and I concluded that it *had* to be done."[71]

There was another, crucially important reason. Oppenheimer himself explained it. "When you see something technically sweet you go ahead and do it and you argue about what to do about it only after you have had your technical success. That is the way it was with the atomic bomb. I do not think anybody opposed making it; there were some debates about what to do with it after it was made. I cannot very well imagine if we had known in late 1949 what we got to know by early 1951 that the tone of our report would have been the same."[72] Oppenheimer's remark conveyed none of the moral anguish that he and Fermi had so forcibly expressed in their October 1949 GAC report, or that he had offered in reply to Teller's question "If the president gave the [superbomb] project the go-ahead, would you come back to Los Alamos?" — "Certainly not."[73]

Oppenheimer's candid admission underscored the Faustian bargain that scientists struck through their work on the atomic bomb and now on the superbomb: whatever their moral and political scruples, what was "technically sweet" was, in the end, simply irresistible to them. Oppenheimer, Bethe, and Fermi were not narrow technocrats oblivious to the larger consequences of their work; they were intelligent, intensely curious men whose moral and political compunctions were exceeded only by their compulsion to understand nature's secrets.

Their adversary in the superbomb debate, Teller, was driven by this compulsion more than anyone. He conceded this fact with remarkable candor in later years:

> One of my main reasons for working on the hydrogen bomb was its novelty. I wanted both as a scientist and also for practical reasons to know how it would work. I believe it is not irresponsible to try to work out those technical developments that can be worked out.[74]

In this sense, the scientists' complicity came not from any ill intentions, but from wanting to know more.

An American superbomb was finally ready for testing on November 1, 1952. The test site was Elugelab, in the Pacific Ocean atoll of Eniwetok in the Marshall Islands. Although invited to witness the test, Teller did not go. "I very much wanted to see the explosion of the device that had consumed my energies and that had dragged me into so many arguments," he later said, "but I knew that I really was not needed at Eniwetok."[75] Yet the curiosity that had driven Teller's quest for the superbomb remained intense and unquenchable. Shortly before the predawn test — it was midday on the West Coast of the United States — Teller crossed the Berkeley campus from the Rad Lab to Haviland Hall, home of the geology department, whose basement housed one of the most sensitive seismographs in the world. There Teller hoped to see signs of the shock wave generated by the detonation five thousand miles away.

The small room was lit only by a dim red lamp, which was turned off. Teller's eyes grew accustomed to the darkness. It would take about a quarter of an hour for the shock wave to travel deep under the Pacific basin to the California coast. He sat alone in the darkness, with a loudly ticking clock hovering anxiously above the sensitive seismograph that would indicate the slightest tremor with a tiny beam of light on a photographic plate. He recalled what happened next:

> I waited with little patience, the seismograph making at each minute a clearly visible vibration which served as a time signal.
>
> At last the time signal came that had to be followed by the shock from the explosion and there it seemed to be: the luminous point appeared to dance wildly and irregularly. Was it only that the pencil which I held as a marker trembled in my hand?
>
> I waited for many more minutes to be sure that the record did not miss any of the shocks that might follow the first. Then, finally, the film was taken off and developed. By that time I had almost convinced myself that what I saw was the motion of my own hand rather than the signal from the first hydrogen bomb.
>
> Then the trace appeared on the photographic plate. It was clear and unmistakable. It had been made by the wave of compression that had traveled for thousands of miles and brought positive assurance that Mike [the bomb's nickname] was a success.[76]

Lawrence was the first to offer congratulations.

The superbomb's explosion expanded in an instant to a blinding white fireball more than three miles wide. (The Hiroshima fireball had measured little more than one-tenth of a mile.) The fireball seemed to blot out the whole horizon. It dug out of the sea floor a crater two hundred feet deep and a mile and a half wide. Observers felt a wall of heat as if someone had opened an oven, heat that persisted for an unnervingly long time. "You would swear that the whole world was on fire," one eyewitness wrote home.[77] Swirling with intense radioactivity, the enormous fireball became a burning mushroom cloud with a skirt of boiling water around its base that fell back to sea with a roar. The ominous cloud began to spread out, its top cresting in the stratosphere at twenty-seven miles across, its stem eight miles wide. "It really filled up the sky," said a physicist who had witnessed earlier atomic tests and was not easily impressed. "It was awesome. It just went on and on."[78] The superbomb had exploded with the force of more than 10 million tons of TNT, a thousand times greater than the atomic bomb that destroyed Hiroshima.

Less than two years later, on March 1, 1954, American scientists developed and tested a superbomb with the explosive force of 15 million tons of TNT. Before the decade was over, the Soviets would develop a superbomb with an explosive yield of 60 million tons of TNT. Where would it all end?

As with the atomic bomb in 1945, the superbomb debate forced scientists once again to reflect on the implications of their work. It made them come face-to-face with moral and political issues of enormous moment and scope — for example, weighing the current national interests of their own country against creating a perpetual catastrophic danger for the world. Teller and other proponents argued that it was in the nature of science to pursue knowledge, and no amount of moral scruples or hand-wringing should — or could — stop this quest. "It is the scientist's job to find the ways in which laws [of nature] can serve the human will," Teller wrote at the time of the debate. "It is not the scientist's job to determine whether a hydrogen bomb should be constructed, whether it should be used, or how it should be used." He put the point more sharply toward the end of his life: "As a scientist, it is my responsibility to make things work that will work. How they're used is not my responsibility."[79] For Teller, trying to stop the pursuit of knowledge was not only futile but irrational and even immoral. Knowledge was inherently good.

In the end, even Teller had to occasionally confront the implications of a weapon whose destructiveness boggled the mind and tortured the conscience. When he did, it left him deeply ambivalent — with elemental feelings of awe mixed with dread. On a spring afternoon in 1950, just weeks after Truman gave the go-ahead to the superbomb, the physicist had a very private and candid talk with his old friend Cloyd Marvin, president of George Washington University, whom Teller had known since arriving in the United States in 1935 to teach at GWU. Teller and Marvin sat together in Marvin's office in Foggy Bottom until the shadows lengthened and the room grew dark. Teller was in a curious mood; he seemed to be searching for something. Finally he got around to his question. "Suppose you could develop a force capable of destroying all life on earth," said Teller, pausing for a moment. "Is it right even to take any steps in that direction?" Marvin said it was, assuring Teller that such a force would be safe in the hands of the United States.[80]

That same spring, Teller began composing a bedtime rhyme for his young son, Paul, basing each stanza on a successive letter of the alphabet. He first wrote rhymes for A and B:

A stands for atom; *it is so small*
No one has ever seen it at all.

B stands for bomb; *the bombs are much bigger,*
So, brother, do not be too fast on the trigger.

Later Teller added a rhyme for *H*:

H has become a most ominous letter.
It means something bigger if not something better.[81]

CHAPTER 10

The Oppenheimer Affair

ROBERT OPPENHEIMER HAD an intellect and eloquence that swayed groups and won admirers, but also an arrogance and impatience that wounded sensibilities and made enemies. His moral sensitivity, moreover, stood at odds with his desire to be near power, an enterprise not often guided by considerations of sin. Famous after the war, Oppenheimer became intoxicated with the Washington environment and his influence within it. He became ever sensitive to the way he appeared; Robert Oppenheimer was on his mind at all times. While Oppenheimer's vanity troubled many of his friends, to his enemies it was insufferable.

Oppenheimer's enemies included men practiced in the subterranean stiletto warfare of Washington who envied his brilliance and influence, resented his liberal politics, suspected his patriotism because of his radical past and their own fear of communism, and felt no qualms about ruthlessly exploiting his vulnerabilities. And because Oppenheimer was vulnerable, the temptation to smear his past politics onto his present policy recommendations could hardly be resisted by the little men who were upset by his advice. So his enemies, who felt intimidated and threatened by him and yet could not cope with him, decided to use these skeletons to shame Oppenheimer and to bring him down with a maximum of disgrace so that his influence would be finished. The atmosphere was even more Machiavellian and predatory than usual in Washington life.

On November 7, 1953, one of Oppenheimer's enemies, William Borden, a former staff director of the Joint Congressional Committee on Atomic Energy who had zealously advocated the superbomb and deeply resented Oppenheimer's opposition to it, mailed a three and a half page, single-spaced letter to FBI director J. Edgar Hoover, who was another Oppenheimer foe. "More probably than not," Borden asserted in his accusatory letter, "J. Robert Oppenheimer is an agent of the Soviet Union." Borden listed the factors that led him to this conclusion: Oppenheimer's financial contributions to the Communist Party during the late 1930s and early 1940s; the fact that his wife, his brother, and his onetime fiancée all had been communists; his contradictory information about espionage approaches in 1943; and his "tireless" work "to retard the United States H-bomb program."[1]

Oppenheimer had been in Hoover's crosshairs for years. In 1947 the FBI director had argued in vain against renewing Oppenheimer's wartime security clearance. Since then, on Hoover's instructions, FBI agents had busily collected further evidence and innuendo against the physicist through minute and ceaseless surveillance of his public and private life. Oppenheimer's phone was tapped. His office and home were bugged. His mail was opened. By 1953 the FBI file on Oppenheimer was four and a half feet thick — plenty with which to tarnish his name. After receiving Borden's letter, Hoover eagerly prepared a digest of Oppenheimer's file and sent it, along with a copy of the letter, to various top government officials, including President Eisenhower. That Eisenhower had recently come under attack by Senator Joseph McCarthy for laxness in confronting communism made it politically imperative that he and his administration be seen as tough in handling Borden's accusation.

Unaware of the storm brewing against him — his celebrity and the caliber of his high-level friends gave him an illusion of invulnerability — Oppenheimer spent the last weeks of 1953 giving the distinguished Reith Lectures over BBC Radio from a studio in Bush House, London. In one of these lectures, Oppenheimer expressed his personal view of communism:

It is a cruel and humorless sort of pun that so powerful a present form of modern tyranny should call itself by the very name of a belief in community, by a word "communism" which in other times evoked memories of villages and village inns and of artisans concerting their skills, and of men of learning content with anonymity.

But perhaps only a malignant end can follow the systematic belief that all communities are one community; that all truth is one truth; that all experience is compatible with all other; that total knowledge is possible; that all that is potential can exist as actual.

This is not man's fate; this is not his path; to force him on it makes him resemble not that divine image of the all-knowing and all-powerful but the helpless, iron-bound prisoner of a dying world.

Whatever the young and naive Oppenheimer's view of communism had been in the late 1930s and early 1940s, in these words an older and wiser Oppenheimer clearly condemned an ideology that held no appeal or sway over him. But perhaps that did not matter. It is a hallmark of Greek tragedy that the selection of the victim is never accidental, and the end is always foreordained.

Borden and Hoover triggered the vendetta against Oppenheimer, but it was AEC chairman Lewis Strauss who brought him down. An owlish and dour-looking man with cool, deep, enormous eyes like a night animal, Strauss had a keen mind and a clever political sense. As a young naval officer in World War I, he had caught Herbert Hoover's attention, and had seen high politics firsthand as Hoover's personal assistant. Between the wars, he had made a fortune on Wall Street before rejoining the navy at the beginning of World War II, where he had risen to the rank of rear admiral and head of the navy's Ordnance Division. Strauss possessed considerable charm and urbanity that cloaked profound insecurity about his limited formal education and humble roots, two areas where he felt particularly inadequate in comparison to Oppenheimer. This was apparent in Strauss's description of Oppenheimer when he first met him in the summer of 1945. "I was enormously impressed with him," said Strauss. "He was a man with an extraordinary mind, a compelling, dramatic personality, a charm for me that I suppose rose out of his poetic approach to the problem we faced together. I'm not his peer, of course."[2]

A self-made millionaire with only a high school education, Strauss had struggled to understand physics and was both proud and anxious about his intellectual accomplishments. He made a cult of science, and since he saw Oppenheimer as the apotheosis of the scientist, he considered him a wizard who would not withhold his powers for good unless he proposed to employ them for evil. There was also something in Strauss that gave him a desperate need to be always agreed with, to dominate. With superiors, he was always pliable and flattering. But from equals and subordinates, he brooked no argument. One acquaintance said of him, "If you disagree with Lewis about anything, he assumes you're just a fool at first. But if you go on disagreeing with him, he concludes you must be a traitor."[3] His face, with its rosy hue and the blandness of its spectacles, gave no hint of his resentments or his long and unforgiving memory. His personality combined extraordinary vanity with a stubborn vindictiveness.

Oppenheimer was fated from the first to get on badly with such a man. The scientist was by no means without fault. He had impossibly high intellectual standards, with more than a trace of intellectual snobbery and sometimes cold scorn for those who fell short. All these faults of Oppenheimer's exaggerated and indeed inflamed those of Strauss.

The triggering incident had occurred in June 1949, when Oppenheimer testified before the Joint Congressional Committee on Atomic Energy about the exportation of radioactive isotopes. Strauss, who had testified against such exports because he thought they might assist in production of an atomic bomb, was present in the hearing room. When asked about the possible military application of exported isotopes, Oppenheimer replied with the laserlike sarcasm that had wounded so many others before:

No one can force me to say you cannot use these isotopes for atomic energy. You can use a shovel for atomic energy. In fact you do. You can use a bottle of beer for atomic energy. In fact you do. But to get some perspective, the fact is that during the war and after the war these materials have played no significant part and in my knowledge no part at all.[4]

As snickers spread around the hearing room, it became clear that Oppenheimer was ridiculing someone. AEC deputy general counsel Joseph Volpe, seated next to him at the witness table, had no doubt who that someone was. He turned around and sneaked a look at Strauss. His eyes had narrowed, his jaw had tightened, and his cheeks had colored. His countenance was cold, hard, and furious. A senator then asked: "Is it not true, doctor, that the overall national defense of a country rests on more than secret military development alone?" "Of course it does," replied Oppenheimer, who could not stop there. "My own rating of the importance of isotopes in this broad sense is that they are far less important than electronic devices, but far more important than, let us say, vitamins. Somewhere in between." There were more snickers. At the end of his testimony, Oppenheimer, delighted and amused by his own wit, turned to Volpe and said, "Well, Joe, how did I do?" Volpe, with the memory of Strauss's twisted face vividly in his mind, shook his head and answered, "*Too* well, Robert. Much too well." Years later, another observer in the hearing room that afternoon could still remember Strauss's expression. "There was a look of hatred there that you don't see very often in a man's face."[5] Like most vain and insecure men, Strauss was a close accountant of small insults. All such sins were entered in a ledger, no less permanent for being kept in Strauss's razor-sharp memory rather than on book-keeper's pages. It concealed interior tides of terrible anger.

Oppenheimer's barbs were unwise — it is always dangerous busi-ness to slight powerful people in Washington — but they were under-standable. Oppenheimer knew that Strauss had whispered doubts about his loyalty to others in Washington, that the FBI had leaked these doubts to friends in the press, that his every action was under round-the-clock FBI surveillance, and that he could never be certain what kind of whispering campaign was being mounted against him or when it would eventually come to a head. He was angry about the backstage politics and it showed in his rude demeanor.

In Strauss, Oppenheimer had antagonized a vindictive man who retaliated from the moment Eisenhower named him AEC chairman in June 1953. During his first week in office, Strauss sent a squad of AEC security officers to Princeton to remove the classified docu-ments which Oppenheimer had always been allowed to store in a spe-cially guarded facility in his office, and then hired former army security agents to dig up derogatory information on Oppenheimer, even per-sonally helping to line up interviews for the agents. Strauss was so obsessed with getting Oppenheimer that he turned the AEC's security office into his personal detective agency. When Borden's letter came in, Strauss could have reassured Eisenhower, but he did not. Oppen-heimer's influence among physicists was so pervasive and, in Strauss's view, so pernicious that it could be thwarted only by destroying him. With the fuse lit by Borden, Strauss calculated that he at last had at hand the means of Oppenheimer's destruction.

Strauss phoned Oppenheimer in Princeton shortly after the physi-cist's return from Europe, but did not mention that his security clear-ance had been suspended or even that there were any serious problems. "I was wondering whether you planned to come down here?" Strauss amiably inquired. "I haven't made plans," Oppenheimer replied, "but I can easily do it if you like."[6] A week later, on the afternoon of December 21, 1953, Oppenheimer called on Strauss at his office at AEC headquarters. The two men took their seats at a long table in the large octagonal room where the Combined Chiefs of Staff had met during World War II. Oppenheimer had not been told the reason for the meeting, so it began with a coldly correct exchange of pleasantries. After a while, Strauss dropped the pleasantries and showed Oppenheimer a letter of charges based on Borden's correspondence but refused to give him a copy. Strauss explained that as a result of Borden's letter, Eisenhower had ordered a "blank wall" placed between Oppenheimer and any further access to secret information. The physicist's clearance was being suspended until his "character, associations, and loyalty" had been judged by a Personnel Security Board hearing, which would be conducted in secret and not bound by courtroom rules of evidence. Strauss told Oppenheimer that he could resign rather than face a hearing and thus "avoid an explicit consideration of the charges."

The issue of clearance was crucial because Oppenheimer's influence depended on access to classified information. "You had to be inside the government if you wanted to have an influence, especially on these military matters," Rabi noted. "Since there was all that secrecy, you couldn't know what you were talking about unless you were a part of it."[7] Oppenheimer's top secret "Q Clearance" allowed him to know what he was talking about; withdrawing it would eliminate his influence immediately and effectively.

Oppenheimer was stunned by the charges. Ignoring the cigarette burning down through his fingers, he wordlessly took the letter of charges handed to him and paged through it rapidly. He grew ashen. Stoicism came hard to Oppenheimer, but he held on. Underneath he was shaken and just wanted to get out of the room. Without saying what he intended to do, Oppenheimer ended the painful confrontation. Leaving AEC headquarters, he walked a few blocks north to 1701 K Street, NW, where he took the elevator to the sixth floor and entered the law office of now former AEC general counsel Joe Volpe. Oppenheimer's personal attorney, Herbert Marks, joined them there. Oppenheimer told Volpe and Marks about his conference with Strauss, and they discussed what measures Oppenheimer should take in his own defense.*

---

* The FBI monitored these and subsequent conversations between Oppenheimer and his lawyers, violating the attorney-client privilege and giving Strauss and the AEC the advantage of anticipating Oppenheimer's defense.

Marks's wife, Anne, had been Oppenheimer's personal assistant at Los Alamos and was a close friend. As she drove Oppenheimer to the Marks's Georgetown home that afternoon, the physicist clenched his fists and fumed, "I can't believe this is happening to me!"[8] The three of them paced the floor late into the night. "It was like Pearl Harbor — on a small scale," Oppenheimer said with some bitterness later. "Given the circumstances and the spirit of the times, one knew that something like this was possible and even probable; but still it was a shock when it came." "I lost my pipe that day; put it down some place and couldn't remember where," he also recalled. "Maybe that sums up about as well as anything my state of mind."[9]

Oppenheimer did not know what to do. If he resigned rather than face a hearing, Senator Joseph McCarthy might target him as the next victim of his anticommunist witch-hunt anyway. And resignation might not end the matter because Borden's charges could be leaked to the press, making resignation, in effect, an admission of guilt. A hearing, on the other hand, could be humiliating. Eliminating Oppenheimer's influence was not enough for his enemies — they hated him and wanted to destroy him. They would not be content until they had ousted him from power and publicly shamed him. His past — his communist associations during the 1930s and his lies to security officers during the 1940s — would be dredged up. The past communist affiliations of his wife, brother, and sister-in-law also might be probed and used against him. As he knew, the FBI had tapped his phone and kept him under surveillance, so various indiscretions could emerge. Yet Oppenheimer could not accept the implication that he was a loyalty or security risk. Moreover, he did not want to lose the power, influence, and prestige that came from government service. He had given up the best years of his life to serve the country, surrendering the opportunity to do basic science and thus missing the great scientific discoveries for which he had seemed destined.

The next day Oppenheimer sent Strauss a letter. "I have thought most earnestly of the alternative suggested [resignation]," his letter read in carefully controlled language. "Under the circumstances, this course of action would mean that I accept and concur in the view that I am not fit to serve this Government that I have now served for some 12 years. This I cannot do. If I were thus unworthy, I could hardly have served our country as I have tried, . . . or have spoken, as on more than one occasion I have found myself speaking, in the name of science and our country."[10] Oppenheimer had decided to fight to maintain his clearance.

For the next three months, both sides marshaled their forces. At Strauss's request, the FBI tapping of Oppenheimer's home and office phones continued. The FBI also followed the physicist whenever he left Princeton. Oppenheimer knew that he was under surveillance. "Even the walls have ears," he told visitors to Princeton.[11] Oppenheimer sought to make light of the stressful situation. He told friends that he wished he had a fraction of the money that was being spent keeping him under surveillance — it would make him very rich. Strauss not only concealed his enlistment of the FBI but flatly denied that there was any taping of anyone on his initiative.

Meanwhile, Oppenheimer sought to line up support from other scientists. He encountered Teller at a physics conference in Rochester, New York, early the next year. Teller told Oppenheimer he was sorry to hear about his current difficulties. "I suppose, I hope, that you don't think that anything I did has sinister implications," Oppenheimer replied. "I said I did not think that — after all, the word 'sinister' was pretty harsh," recalled Teller later. "Then he asked if I would speak to his lawyer, and I said I would."[12] Teller went to see Oppenheimer's lawyer, told of his disagreements with the physicist, but professed that he had no doubts about Oppenheimer's patriotism.

Teller also spoke to the FBI, using these secret interviews to tell a very different story. Teller told Hoover's agents that Oppenheimer had fought development of the superbomb since 1945 and that it would have been built sooner if he had not. He attributed Oppenheimer's opposition not to honest disagreement over policy but to fundamental deviousness and dishonesty:

> [Oppenheimer] delayed or hindered the development of the H-bomb from 1945 to 1950 by opposing it on moral grounds. After the President announced the H-bomb was to be made, [Oppenheimer] opposed it on the ground that it was not feasible. . . . After this, [Oppenheimer] changed his approach and opposed the H-bomb on the basis that there were insufficient facilities and scientific personnel to develop it, which according to Teller is incorrect.

He ascribed Oppenheimer's motives "to a combination of reasons including personal vanity in not desiring to see his work on the A-bomb done better on the H-bomb, and also because he does not feel the H-bomb is politically desirable." Asserting that Oppenheimer had never gotten over the shock of Hiroshima and Nagasaki, Teller

> said that he found Oppenheimer to be a very complicated person, even though an outstanding man. He also said that he understands that in his youth Oppenheimer was troubled with some sort of physical or mental attacks which may have permanently affected him. He has also had great ambitions in science and realizes that he is not as great a physicist as he would like to be.

Teller proceeded to affirm Oppenheimer's loyalty while subtly undermining it. He told the FBI "that in all of his dealings with Oppenheimer he has never had the slightest reason or indication to believe that Oppenheimer is in any way disloyal to the United States" — and then followed that declaration by slyly noting "that Oppenheimer's brother, Frank, is an admitted former member of the Communist Party."* He concluded by stating that "he would do most anything to see [Oppenheimer] separated from the General Advisory Committee because of his poor advice and policies regarding national preparedness and because of his delaying of the development of the H-bomb." Teller asked the FBI to keep his attack against Oppenheimer secret because "such information could prove very embarrassing to him personally" with other scientists.[13]

One of them, Rabi, was furious at what he saw happening to his friend. "My own feeling was just indignation, outrage that this was happening," recalled Rabi. "He was a great man, who had done something very great for his country."[14] Rallying to Oppenheimer's defense, Rabi went to see Strauss and urged appointing an independent board to hear the case and sit in judgment of Oppenheimer. Strauss refused. A short time later, Rabi went to see Strauss again, this time with a letter signed by each member of the GAC, stating their willingness to testify on Oppenheimer's behalf. Strauss was unmoved. Given that Oppenheimer's official influence had greatly diminished when the Republicans took office in January 1953 and that the AEC had an easy and graceful "out" (simply to let his consultant contract expire), the

---

* Teller had told FBI investigators in 1950 that Frank Oppenheimer would not have joined the Communist Party without the "tacit approval" of his brother. (See SAC, WFO to FBI Director, "Dr. J. Robert Oppenheimer," January 5, 1954, FBI J. Robert Oppenheimer Serial File [100–17828]/Freedom of Information Act Files.)

zeal with which Strauss pursued Oppenheimer's banishment belied his vindictiveness.

The selection of the three-member Personnel Security Board to hear the case was a case in point. An AEC attorney at the time later recalled: "Strauss was looking for three members who would have a predisposition to find against Oppenheimer. Although pains were taken to maintain a facade of seeking members with a fair and judicious attitude, the major consideration was whether the candidate would shrink from revoking Oppenheimer's clearance."[15] Strauss wanted a "hanging jury." If Oppenheimer won this fight, he would be back on top of the heap: vindicated and as influential as ever among scientists.

Strauss picked three men whom he thought would give him the verdict he wanted: Gordon Gray, a Yale Law School graduate, former secretary of the army, president of the University of North Carolina at Chapel Hill, and Democrat who had supported Eisenhower over his own party's candidate in 1952, Adlai Stevenson, because he considered Stevenson insufficiently anticommunist; Thomas Morgan, a defense contractor who had been president of the Sperry Gyroscope Company before being appointed to a presidential commission on defense preparedness; and Ward Evans, a conservative Loyola University of Chicago chemistry professor who had served on security boards before and had almost always voted to deny clearance.

Strauss continued his machinations. He chose Roger Robb, one of the most aggressive and conservative trial lawyers in Washington, to prosecute the case before the board — the first time the AEC had gone outside for a lawyer to handle a security hearing — and quickly arranged clearance for Robb to read Oppenheimer's AEC file. When Oppenheimer's attorney for the hearing, Lloyd Garrison, a New York lawyer well known for defending civil liberties cases but with little trial experience, sought similar clearance for himself and two associates, the request was refused — only Garrison would be cleared. Oppenheimer and Garrison decided that unless all of them were cleared, then none of them would be; they would instead rely on the AEC to declassify documents. But the AEC declassified only two documents — after it asserted the right to decide which documents were relevant for declassification and what portions of these "relevant" documents it would be "consistent with the national interest" to permit Oppenheimer's legal team to see. Garrison thus changed course and requested clearance for just himself (as had been promised) seventeen days before the hearing began. It had taken only eight days for Robb to obtain his clearance, yet the AEC not only failed to process Garrison's request in time for the opening of the hearing but declared it was "not possible" to clear Garrison before the hearing ended and the Gray Board had submitted its report — eight weeks after Garrison's initial request. Finally, Robb spent hours going through Oppenheimer's FBI file with the three board members in the week before the hearing, and socialized with them.[16] When Garrison asked if he, too, could spend time with the board and see his own client's FBI file, his requests were refused.

During the week that Robb met with the Gray Board to discuss the contents of Oppenheimer's FBI file, the physicist received letters of support from his friends. Bethe, stunned and angry at what was happening to a great man and a good friend and convinced that it was rooted in Oppenheimer's now unpopular advice about the super-bomb, cabled Oppenheimer: "You know that we believe in you and will do all we can to help." Victor Weisskopf, who had learned of Oppenheimer's predicament from Bethe, wrote Oppenheimer a moving letter:

> I would like you to know that I and everybody who feels as I do are fully aware of the fact that you are fighting here our own fight. Somehow Fate has chosen you as the one who has to bear the heaviest load in this struggle. I know that you are suffering from this as any man would under such enormous strain. On the other hand, I would not know of any better man to bear this load. As a matter of fact, if I had to choose whom to select for the person who has to take this on, I could not but choose you. Who else in this country could represent better than you the spirit and the philosophy of our way of life? Please think of us when you are feeling low. Think of all your friends who are going to remain your friends and who rely upon you. . . . I beg you to remain what you always have been, and things will end well.[17]

The AEC's Building T-3 was one of the "temporary" offices put up during World War I on the Mall in Washington and inherited from the navy in the late 1940s. The white planks of its facade, the wooden bridges that connected its sheds, and its ugly, greenish, makeshift roof were strikingly similar to those of the Tech Area building in Los Alamos where Oppenheimer had his office during the war. Room 2022 on the second floor was an ordinary office whose furnishings were official, functional, and drab; there was no carpet on the composition floor. This became the temporary courtroom where, in the spring of 1954, Oppenheimer stood trial in an inquisition masquerading as a fact-finding proceeding.

Along the north wall of the broad, oblong room ran a row of windows that opened out across Constitution Avenue and onto the grassy ellipse just south of the White House. Along the east wall stood a long, baize-covered table, with three chairs for the hearing board members — the "judges" in the case. Perpendicular to it and forming the stem of a T were two tables running parallel to the windows. To the board's right, with his back to the window, sat prosecutor Robb; to the left, facing the windows, defending counsel Garrison. A witness chair sat at the base of the T. Behind the witness chair, against the west wall, was an old leather couch where Oppenheimer would sit, puffing incessantly on a pipe or cigarette when he was not on the stand, unable to study the witnesses' faces as they spoke. Seldom more than a handful of people would ever be present in the room, but at times a disembodied voice would be heard coming from a tape recorder, statements by Oppenheimer which had been recorded — without his knowledge — during his wartime security interrogations ten and a half years earlier.

On Monday, April 12, 1954, shortly before 10:00 A.M., the various parties began to make their way to room 2022. It was springtime in Washington, and the cherry trees lining the Tidal Basin just south of the Mall were in full and glorious bloom. Upon arrival, the hearing board members took their places at the table. Before each of them lay not a blank notepad but a thick binder of material from the FBI files and investigative reports that they had been studying throughout the previous week. Oppenheimer, his wife, Kitty, and Garrison made an inauspicious, but highly symbolic, entrance. Nervous and strained by her husband's ordeal, Kitty had fallen down some stairs, and she had her leg in a cast and was on crutches. The Oppenheimers and their attorney arrived late and the board was irritated with them.

"The hearing will come to order." With these words, chairman Gray opened the proceeding "in the matter of J. Robert Oppenheimer." The atmosphere of the Cold War pervaded the hearing room. A week earlier, Senator McCarthy, who had been on the scent of Oppenheimer, had alleged in a nationally televised speech that communists in government had delayed research on the superbomb by eighteen months, effectively pressing the Gray Board to produce a culprit. This made it all the harder for Oppenheimer's judges to evaluate him fairly. It was almost as if the Gray Board members were peering at those earlier days through the wrong end of a long telescope. Here were three men of a prosperous, communist-hating, fear-ridden America of the Cold-War 1950s sitting in judgment on Oppenheimer's radical associations and activities in the Depression-ridden 1930s, when the U.S. economy was in total collapse, when fascism was spreading across Europe, and when American communists — far from being treated as political lepers, as they were in 1954 — were openly allied with the noncommunist American Left. It was a dark irony that the proceedings the three led resembled nothing so much as a Stalinist show trial.

Gray began the hearing by reading the AEC letter of charges and Oppenheimer's written reply into the record. It was a self-accusing and self-abasing document. He admitted his political naïveté before the war, acknowledged his association with Communist Party causes, but denied — perhaps falsely — that he had ever belonged to the party, and in effect repudiated his left-wing past.* Summing up, Oppenheimer wrote: "What I have hoped was, not that I could wholly avoid error, but that I might learn from it. What I have learned has, I think, made me more fit to serve my country." Gray then ventured some observations on the nature and ground rules of the hearing. First, said Gray, he wanted to "remind everyone concerned that this proceeding is an inquiry, and not in the nature of a trial. We shall approach our duties in that atmosphere and in that spirit," he asserted.[18] Gray added that the hearing would not be subject to the strict rules and procedures that governed courtroom trials. His implication was that the informality of a hearing worked to Oppenheimer's advantage, affording him more flexibility in meeting the charges — yet later in the hearing, Gray announced that Oppenheimer's witnesses would be heard at times suited "to the convenience of this board, and not the

---

* If Oppenheimer did lie about his Communist Party affiliation in the late 1930s and early 1940s, why did he do so? Most likely because he felt vulnerable in the anticommunist political climate of the 1950s and thought it necessary to cover up his now embarrassing past in order to maintain his influence as a government adviser, which had become so important to him after 1945 as a way of assuaging his guilt over Hiroshima and Nagasaki. One who knew Oppenheimer well during his radical days offered a revealing insight: "This fiction that he was putting forward was presumably necessary for his protection in the carrying out of an ideal purpose which I had no doubt he was pursuing." (Chevalier, *Oppenheimer,* p. 84.)

convenience of the witnesses, as would be true in most [judicial] proceedings in the American tradition."[19]

Now came Garrison's turn. Tall and stately in appearance and manner, Garrison had a reputation for integrity and dedication to good causes, but he was not a litigator who was at home in the ringlike atmosphere of the courtroom. In his opening remarks, Garrison spoke softly and carefully — almost gingerly — as if convinced that if he could just avoid any abrasive actions that might offend the hearing board members, he would be able to persuade them to use the rule of reason in judging "the whole Oppenheimer," and thus find in his client's favor.

Garrison put Oppenheimer on the stand that afternoon. He tried to minimize his client's left-wing past as an indiscretion of youth and ignorance, and by stressing his later patriotic service. Oppenheimer spoke easily and confidently, as though he were addressing a friendly gathering, but there was a quality of desperation about him. He felt oppressed by the unfriendly atmosphere of the proceeding and kept his distance even from his own attorney. He told the facts about his life and career; what he left out were the motives and context. Similar ambiguities exist in the lives of all individuals; they are not usually exposed to harsh examination and judgment. Nevertheless, the board felt something was left out, and it was unlikely to fill the gap with a generous, sympathetic picture that Oppenheimer himself failed to draw.

The next morning Mervin Kelly, president of Bell Telephone Laboratories, took the stand as the first pro-Oppenheimer witness. When Garrison finished his questions, those in the hearing room got their first glimpse of Robb. It quickly became clear that he was not a factfinder but a ruthlessly aggressive prosecutor. Robb cross-examined Kelly in a manner deliberately calculated to intimidate Oppenheimer. The prosecutor turned to Gray and said, "Mr. Chairman, I would like to read the witness something from the report which is classified." For the next few minutes, Oppenheimer remained in the hearing room alone, his attorney having been dismissed from the room. The psychological impact — the demonstration of power that Robb had, based on his privileged access to Oppenheimer's security file — must have unnerved the lonely and embattled physicist. "When I saw what they were doing to Oppenheimer," said another witness, "I was ready to throw chairs. How can a lawyer defend his client's interests if he isn't even in the hearing room? There hadn't been a proceeding like this since the Spanish Inquisition."[20]

Oppenheimer resumed the stand later that day. He talked at length about his service to the country at Los Alamos during the war and in Washington since. He also talked about his fondness and protectiveness toward his younger brother, Frank. Frank, it was recalled, had wed Jacquenette Quann in September 1936. A Canadian majoring in economics at Berkeley who was active in the campus Young Communist League, Jackie had done for Frank what Jean Tatlock had done for Robert: she had opened his eyes to the suffering in the world around him and had turned his attention to left-wing politics. Shortly after their marriage, Frank and Jackie had joined the Communist Party. Later, in Pasadena, where Frank was studying physics at Caltech, the younger brother had invited Robert to attend a Communist Party meeting at his house — the only thing "recognizable as a Communist Party meeting" that Robert allegedly ever recalled attending.

Robb began his interrogation of Oppenheimer the next morning. The prosecutor and the physicist were vastly different: Oppenheimer was intellectual and reflective; Robb was aggressive and combative. Robb, convinced of the physicist's guilt, took a quick and strong personal dislike to Oppenheimer: "My feeling was that he was just a brain and as cold as a fish, and he had the iciest pair of blue eyes I ever saw."[21] Vigorous and bludgeoning, the fleshy, shovel-jawed prosecutor was intent on taking full advantage of Oppenheimer's predicament by impelling him to testify from sheer memory about long-past events, while secretly holding in reserve documents containing the facts about these events. Twisting words and exploiting errors in memory, Robb bullied and browbeat Oppenheimer. Cast on the defense, Oppenheimer seemed not arrogant, aloof, or intellectually agile and precise but often vague, confused, even meandering.

Robb quickly turned to the "Chevalier incident." Sometime in late 1942 or early 1943 (before Oppenheimer moved to Los Alamos), Haakon Chevalier, one of his closest friends and a communist professor at Berkeley, had approached the physicist (and perhaps others, including his younger brother, Frank) on behalf of a West Coast British engineer and communist named George Eltenton. Chevalier had told Oppenheimer that Eltenton could pass secret information about the Manhattan Project to the Soviet Union. Chevalier had gone back to Eltenton almost immediately and had told him, as Eltenton later said, "that there was no chance whatsoever of obtaining any data and Dr. Oppenheimer did not approve."[22]

Although Oppenheimer had rebuffed this espionage approach, he had — seeking to protect his friend Chevalier and perhaps his brother, Frank — delayed reporting the approach to Manhattan Project security officer Colonel Boris Pash, identified Chevalier as the intermediary only after being specifically ordered to do so by Groves, and later changed the details of his story. Oppenheimer was unaware, however, that Pash had secretly recorded his 1943 revelation. With access to these 1943 recordings (access denied to Oppenheimer and his attorneys), Robb — instead of stressing the essence of the matter: that Chevalier got nothing from Oppenheimer and that Oppenheimer had taken the initiative to give the warning about Eltenton — hammered away at the story that Oppenheimer had made up in order to tip off security officers to espionage feelers without implicating those close to him:*

ROBB: Did you tell Pash the truth about this thing?
OPPENHEIMER: No.
ROBB: You lied to him?
OPPENHEIMER: Yes.[23]

Oppenheimer's last response was barely audible. Anguished and surprisingly inarticulate, he slumped in the witness chair. He felt like a man sliding helplessly down a slope toward the sheer cliff that would finish him. His heart was pounding. He rubbed his hands between his knees, his head bowed, the color drained from his face:

ROBB: So that we may be clear, did you discuss with or disclose to Pash the identity of Chevalier?
OPPENHEIMER: No.
ROBB: Let us refer then, for the time being, to Chevalier as X.
OPPENHEIMER: All right.
ROBB: Did you tell Pash that X had approached three persons on the project?
OPPENHEIMER: I am not clear whether I said there were three Xs or that X approached three people.
ROBB: Didn't you say that X had approached three people?
OPPENHEIMER: Probably.
ROBB: Why did you do that, Doctor?

---

*Paradoxically, the implications of Oppenheimer's false story were more serious than what actually happened. His story impeded army security officers, hurt his friend Chevalier, and damned himself in the eyes of both his friend and his judges. To protect others, Oppenheimer accepted the guilt of a made-up story that he could not sustain.

"Because," said Oppenheimer, dropping his voice, "I was an idiot."

ROBB: Is that your only explanation, Doctor?

OPPENHEIMER: I was reluctant to mention Chevalier.

ROBB: Yes.

OPPENHEIMER: No doubt somewhat reluctant to mention myself.[24]

Smelling blood, Robb confronted Oppenheimer with section after section of the 1943 recordings. Then he made Oppenheimer go back over the details of what he forced him to admit was a cock-and-bull story.

ROBB: Isn't it a fair statement today, Dr. Oppenheimer, that according to your testimony now you told not one lie to Colonel Pash, but a whole fabrication and tissue of lies?

OPPENHEIMER: Right.[25]

Even after this, Oppenheimer's ordeal was not over. There was one added humiliation to be suffered that day: intimate questions about his relationship with Jean Tatlock — in particular, his overnight stay with her at her apartment on Montgomery Street in San Francisco on June fourteenth and fifteenth, 1943 — three years after he had married Kitty and three months after he had become director of the secret laboratory at Los Alamos. Robb asked Oppenheimer why he had to see Jean. Oppenheimer explained that his former fiancée was being treated for depression at a San Francisco hospital and had sent word to Los Alamos that she wanted to see him.* Robb continued to probe, pitilessly and relentlessly:

ROBB: Did you find out why she had to see you?

OPPENHEIMER: Because she was still in love with me. . . .

ROBB: You spent the night with her, didn't you?

OPPENHEIMER: Yes.

ROBB: That is when you were working on a secret war project?

OPPENHEIMER: Yes.

ROBB: Did you think that consistent with good security?

OPPENHEIMER: It was, as a matter of fact. Not a word — it was not good practice.[26]

Oppenheimer's blurred, stumbling reply showed that Robb had crushed him. Some in the hearing room thought Oppenheimer might have a nervous breakdown or even commit suicide that night. He did

---

* Jean Tatlock committed suicide the following year.

not. In fact, Oppenheimer's friends were astonished at his resilience during the pressure-filled proceedings. Back in Princeton over the weekend breaks, he attended to physics and institute business. Oppenheimer's friends did, however, notice a change in him: his self-confidence gave way to melancholy. He paced his bedroom floor at night. He felt trapped. To this pressure was added the burden of media scrutiny. Journalists hounded him for interviews, followed him and Kitty as they came and went from the hearing, and dug deep into their newspaper files for background information to add to sketches for their daily reporting. One newspaperman found himself on the same train with Oppenheimer and Kitty between Washington and Princeton. Stuck with the reporter over dinner, Oppenheimer gently but steadfastly refused to comment while the hearing was under way. The reporter was surprised to see two security "shadows" following Oppenheimer's every move on the train.

The day after Robb's withering interrogation about the Chevalier incident and the night with Jean Tatlock, Groves, wartime commander of the Manhattan Project and now a businessman in Connecticut, took the stand. He reaffirmed his 1943 decision to choose, grant clearance to, and retain Oppenheimer as head of Los Alamos because his overriding objective had been "to produce an atomic bomb in the shortest possible time." In that capacity, the general said, Oppenheimer had had Groves's complete confidence. Groves added that he would be "amazed" if Oppenheimer would ever commit a disloyal act. He shrugged off Oppenheimer's reluctance to divulge Chevalier's name to him as "the typical American schoolboy attitude that there is something wicked about telling on a friend." Oppenheimer had said no to the espionage approach and had named Eltenton — those were the essential things as far as Groves was concerned.* Robb cleverly asked Groves whether he would clear Oppenheimer now. (Robb already knew the answer to this question because Strauss, by threatening Groves for having withheld information from the FBI during the war, had compelled the general to submit a letter that stated: "If I am asked whether I think the [AEC] would be justified in clearing Dr. Oppenheimer, I will say 'no.' If I am asked if I think he is a security risk, I will say 'yes'" — thereby compromising the defense's most important witness.)[27] Groves dutifully replied that he "would not clear Dr. Oppenheimer today"

* Years later, Groves recalled that the only reason he had ultimately ordered Oppenheimer to reveal Chevalier's name was to fend off any further agitation from his security officers.

under his interpretation of new and tougher security standards. Thus Groves had covered himself, and the helpfulness of his testimony to Oppenheimer had been blunted considerably.

After Groves finished testifying, Oppenheimer returned to the stand, this time to face questioning about his stance on the super-bomb. The weather outside the hearing room had changed — a rain-storm now beat against the windows — and so had Oppenheimer's bearing from the previous day. No longer subdued, uncertain, and slow to respond, he was now confident, combative, and quick to reply. His upper lip was tense and coldly resolved. Misery had turned to indignation. Robb brought up Oppenheimer's reference to Lawrence and Teller as "two experienced promoters" in a letter he wrote shortly before the October 1949 GAC meeting. Oppenheimer's irritation and resentment toward both men — once friends and now enemies who would speak against him — was apparent:

ROBB: Would you agree, Doctor, that your references to Dr. Lawrence and Dr. Teller and their enthusiasm for the super-bomb . . . are a little bit belittling?

OPPENHEIMER: Dr. Lawrence came to Washington. He did not talk to the Commission. He went and talked to Congressmen and to members of the military establishment. I think that deserves some belittling.

ROBB: So you would agree that your references to those men in this letter were belittling?

OPPENHEIMER: No. I pay my great respects to them as promoters. I don't think I did them justice.

ROBB: You used the word "promoters" in an invidious sense, didn't you?

OPPENHEIMER: I promoted lots of things in my time.

ROBB: Doctor, would you answer my question? When you used the word "promoter" you meant it to be in a slightly invidious sense, didn't you?

OPPENHEIMER: I have no idea.

ROBB: When you use the word now with reference to Lawrence and Teller, don't you intend it to be invidious?

OPPENHEIMER: No.

ROBB: You think that their work of promotion was admirable, is that right?

OPPENHEIMER: I think they did an admirable job of promotion.[28]

Robb then suggested, rather darkly, that Oppenheimer had had qualms about the building of the superbomb. By this time Oppenheimer understood in his bones that moral objection was very bad form in the corridors of power that he loved to stroll, and during cross-examination he desperately fought to conceal his qualms. But Robb goaded and pressed until he extracted from Oppenheimer a confession of at least a certain ethical queasiness about the superbomb:

OPPENHEIMER: I could very well have said this is a dreadful weapon. . . . I have always thought it was a dreadful weapon. Even [if] from a technical point of view it was a sweet and lovely and beautiful job, I have still thought it was a dreadful weapon.

ROBB: And have said so?

OPPENHEIMER: I would assume that I have said so, yes.

ROBB: You mean you had a moral revulsion against the production of such a dreadful weapon?

OPPENHEIMER: This is too strong. . . .

ROBB: Which is too strong, the weapon or my expression?

OPPENHEIMER: Your expression. I had a grave concern and anxiety.

ROBB: You had moral qualms about it, is that accurate?

OPPENHEIMER: Let us leave the word "moral" out of it.

ROBB: You had qualms about it.

OPPENHEIMER: How could one not have qualms about it? I know no one who doesn't have qualms about it.[29]

That night Oppenheimer met with his legal advisers to talk about the case. They invited Joe Volpe to join them. Volpe had warned all along about ploys that Robb might use. Now he listened as Oppenheimer and Garrison recounted what had occurred during the first few days of the hearing:

Robert said to me, "Joe, I would like to have these fellows describe to you what's going on in the hearing." I don't think the others liked it very much, but finally they got around to telling me and honestly I was outraged. I was the one who had drawn up the procedures for these hearings when I was General Counsel and they were very definitely not meant to be an adversary procedure, and this one was. What's more, they told me that they were withholding documents, which was utterly ridiculous. . . . This behavior gave me great concern, and so after an hour or so, I finally said, "Robert, tell them to shove it, leave it, don't go on with it because I don't think you can win."[30]

Oppenheimer listened closely to Volpe, weighing his advice carefully, but in the end he rejected it. Said Volpe:

> He had always known that if someone, someday, wanted to bring all that stuff out and really make an issue of it, he could be made a victim. He lived with this sword of Damocles always suspended over his head; he knew he was deliberately taking risks in putting himself and his ideas forward in all these . . . groups and plans that made him powerful enemies. But he went on anyway, knowing the possible consequences and ready to face them if they came.[31]

Brilliant, amusing, and attractive, Oppenheimer had a way of getting into morally uncomfortable positions from which he hoped to extricate himself without anyone noticing. He had also resigned himself to play the game according to the rules. Like many people who resign themselves in this way, Oppenheimer did so too thoroughly. For most of his time in Washington, this did not affect him; but when he found himself in a situation where the rules were broken, he was at a loss, and he surrendered too easily. A less-disciplined person might have made more of a row, upset the applecart, played to the court of public opinion. For Oppenheimer, however, it was psychologically inconceivable: fighting back wasn't good manners. He had made a place for himself — and, to an extent, from himself — in the corridors of power that was precious to him. In the long run, he could not break away. Any behavior that Washington officials would condemn, even if they sympathized with him, he could not manage. Anything they would not do, he would not do either.

One by one, through the rest of April, an A-list of witnesses testified on behalf of Oppenheimer's character and loyalty. His friends came first, including Bethe, Fermi, and Rabi. These supreme rationalists were the most emotional of the witnesses, because they were depressed and angry. They had talked with some of the other witnesses as they left the hearing room and were shown parts of the testimony. They could see how things were going; it was clear to them that Oppenheimer was going to be judged harshly. And yet, when their time came to take the stand, each of them described why he believed in Oppenheimer's loyalty. Bethe talked glowingly of Oppenheimer as the unifying and driving force at wartime Los Alamos, the person who was recognized as "superior in judgment and superior in knowledge to all of us." He told of how when he had to decide whether to join Teller on the superbomb project, it was to Oppenheimer that he had turned for guidance. Robb did not attempt to challenge Bethe's faith in Oppenheimer but instead tried to undermine his credibility by exposing Bethe's own vulnerability:

ROBB: Doctor, how many divisions were there at Los Alamos?

BETHE: It changed somewhat in the course of time. As far as I could count the other day, there were seven, but that may have been eight or nine at some time.

ROBB: What division was Klaus Fuchs in?

BETHE: He was in my division which was the Theoretical Division.

ROBB: Thank you. That is all.[32]

"A long dark room" — so thought Rabi on entering the hearing room on the morning of April twenty-first. "The board were stationed in front, then Robb, then Oppenheimer in the back. It made me rather indignant to see him there," he reflected afterward.[33] Robb's bullying tactics had unsettled and confused many witnesses, but not Rabi. That testifying for Oppenheimer might jeopardize his own advisory role to the government was of no concern to him. Rabi was confident in himself and his conviction that the hearing was a farce and a travesty. In his view, whatever Oppenheimer's politics before the project, however arrogant Oppenheimer appeared to some, it was nonsense to brand him a security risk. Rabi had a clear perception of what was happening and was more than a match for the inquisitor Robb and for the occasion itself.

Rabi made his points forcefully. First, he urged the board to bear in mind the times in which the Chevalier incident had occurred. While an approach concerning Soviet espionage would be "horrifying" in 1954, a similar overture in 1943 — a time of alliance with Russia and years before the emergence of the Cold War — would not, in Rabi's view, have merited anything more than throwing the man out of the room (that is, would not necessarily have required reporting him to authorities). Second, Rabi stressed that Oppenheimer's shortcomings should be judged against his much larger historic contributions to the national interest. Oppenheimer had given the United States the most powerful weapon in the history of the world up to that time, a weapon that had helped it to successfully end the war against Japan. Something took hold of Rabi's throat. His voice choked and turned guttural with anger. "What more do you want," Rabi asked, his voice dripping with outraged sarcasm, "mermaids?" "This is just a tremendous achievement. If the end of that road is this kind of hearing, which can't help but be humiliating," he added, "I think it is a pretty bad show."[34]

Once again, Robb tried to deflate the witness by exploiting, and trumpeting, his privileged access to information. Rabi would have none of this prosecutorial bullying. He parried Robb's jabs with a lively and sharp tongue:

> ROBB: Perhaps the board may be in possession of information which is not now available to you about the [Chevalier] incident.
> RABI: It may be. On the other hand, *I* am in possession of a long experience with this man, going back to 1929, which is twenty-five years, and there is a kind of seat-of-the-pants feeling [upon] which I myself lay great weight.[35]

Robb persisted by trying to confine Rabi's opinion of Oppenheimer to the Chevalier incident. Rabi would have none of it. "You have to take the whole story," he shot back. "That is what novels are about. There is a dramatic moment in the history of the man, what made him act, what he did, and what sort of person he was. That is what you are really doing here. You are writing a man's life."[36]

Compton, abroad on a world lecture tour during the hearing, took the time to publicly support the embattled Oppenheimer. Compton told wire-service reporters in Istanbul, Turkey, that he believed one of Oppenheimer's qualifications for the job was the fact that he was not innocent about communism. "I considered his acquaintance with communism, and his rejection of it as a result of that acquaintance, was a factor in favor of his reliability." Compton noted he had made a careful personal investigation of Oppenheimer before choosing him to head the bomb theory and design program in April 1942. "I satisfied myself completely that Oppenheimer was reliable and no security risk, and have had no reason since to change my views," he said. Compton stressed that Oppenheimer's postwar stance against the superbomb's development was based on moral grounds. "He did not want the United States to make such a vastly destructive weapon because of the death and suffering to many people, nor did he want people to suspect the United States contemplated its use," Compton said. "It's an argument that any person sensitive to human reaction must respect."[37] Compton elaborated on these points in a detailed affidavit to the Gray Board that resoundingly affirmed Oppenheimer's loyalty.[38]

A distinguished group of public officials also testified enthusiastically on Oppenheimer's behalf. David Lilienthal and Gordon Dean, Lilienthal's successor and Strauss's predecessor as AEC chairman, swore their confidence in Oppenheimer's loyalty and reliability. Other such men appeared: George F. Kennan; John J. McCloy; and Sumner Pike, a tough-minded self-made millionaire and former AEC commissioner — one after another praising Oppenheimer and pledging their reputation to his probity.

Then came the leaders of American science to provide strong endorsements of his character. Vannevar Bush, organizer of the nation's scientific mobilization effort during World War II, said of Oppenheimer: "More than any other scientist that I know of he was responsible for our having an atomic bomb on time," and affirmed his faith in Oppenheimer's loyalty. Bush minced no words in saying that he felt "this board has made a mistake and that it is a serious one." He spoke eloquently. The AEC charges, said Bush, are "quite capable of being interpreted as placing a man on trial because he held opinions . . . and had the temerity to express them." "When a man is pilloried for doing that, this country is in a severe state."[39] James Conant said that Oppenheimer was one of the three or four scientists whose combination of professional knowledge, hard work, and loyal devotion made possible the development of the bomb. Lee DuBridge said, "I feel that there is no one who has exhibited his loyalty to this country more spectacularly than Dr. Oppenheimer. He was a natural and respected and at all times a loved leader."[40]

Other eminent scientists who had played leading roles in America's nuclear weapons program spoke to the same effect. Perhaps the most eloquent was John von Neumann, the brilliant Hungarian émigré mathematician, father of the electronic computer, and friend of both Oppenheimer and Teller. Von Neumann entreated the three-member board to put Oppenheimer's wartime indiscretions in their proper context. The war years were a time, von Neumann observed, when the atomic scientists — none of whom had been educated or conditioned to exist in such a situation — discovered the threat of espionage and the need for security, came to understand that friends might be traitors and that science could no longer be open, and slowly developed the necessary maturity and established the necessary code of ethics.

At the end of April, prosecutor Robb began calling "government" witnesses. The first was Berkeley chemistry professor Wendell Latimer, an ally of Ernest Lawrence who harbored an intense dislike of Oppenheimer. Speaking in a low and barely audible voice, Latimer stoked the board's suspicions by depicting Oppenheimer as a mesmerist who bewitched scores of intelligent and individualistic young scientists:

> It is just astounding the influence he has upon a group. . . . He is a man of tremendous sincerity and his ability to convince people depends so much upon this sincerity. . . . Things started happening immediately after he left Los Alamos. Many of our boys came back from it pacifists. I judged that was due very largely to his influence, this tremendous influence he had over those young men.[41]

Military officers and scientists who worked for the military were the most eager prosecution witnesses. Fervent cold warriors and zealous anticommunists, they had — through their fear, suspicion, and hatred of Oppenheimer as an individual and a political symbol — triggered the case and provided much of the zeal behind the government's savage prosecution of him. The air force in particular considered Oppenheimer's removal from influence "an urgent and immediate necessity" and secretly encouraged their contacts on the Hill and in the executive branch — including Borden and Strauss — to go after him.[42] "They had it out for Oppie," recalled Harold Agnew, a veteran of the Manhattan Project and later the director of Los Alamos National Laboratory in the 1970s, who personally knew many of these officers and scientists in the 1950s.[43]

The military men leveled their fiercest attack on Oppenheimer for opposing the superbomb. In their eyes, Oppenheimer had argued against a weapon that would increase America's military power, and this was by definition a form of treason. Air force major general Roscoe Wilson thought Oppenheimer "might as well go fishing for the rest of his life." David Griggs, former chief scientist for the air force who had felt the sting of Oppenheimer's acerbic tongue, was even less inhibited. An intense and zealous man, Griggs recalled "pretty violent" policy controversies in which he and his air force colleagues found themselves arrayed against Oppenheimer. He challenged the physicist's loyalty and alleged the existence of a scientists' conspiracy, headed by Oppenheimer, committed to the air force's destruction. Griggs recalled an occasion when he told Oppenheimer face-to-face that he could not be sure whether or not the physicist was pro-Russian. Oppenheimer "then asked if I had impugned his loyalty to high officials of the Defense Department, and I responded yes. He said I was a paranoid."[44]

The next witness to appear seated himself in the witness chair with his back to Oppenheimer. He was a figure of considerable importance in political-scientific circles, for he had carried the battle for the superbomb over the head of Oppenheimer's powerful GAC and had cleared the way for its successful creation. Whatever he said was bound to have a major impact. The heavyset, beetle-browed man was sworn in at 4:00 in the afternoon on April twenty-eighth, a day that he would never forget — but would later come to regret.

Edward Teller was nervous and afraid about testifying — he knew it would cause a lot of trouble. He had thought about this moment long and hard. An AEC official who had spoken with him a week earlier found him "interested only in discussing the Oppenheimer case." This official summarized his conversation with Teller in a memo to Strauss, a memo that revealed Teller's intense animosity toward Oppenheimer:

> Since the case is being heard on a security basis, Teller wonders if some way can be found to "deepen the charges" to include a documentation of the "consistently bad advice" that Oppenheimer has given, going all the way back to the end of the war in 1945. . . .
>
> Teller said that "only about one percent or less" of the scientists know of the real situation and that Oppie is so powerful "politically" in scientific circles that it will be hard to "unfrock him in his own church." (This last phrase is mine [wrote the AEC official] and he agrees it is apt. . . .)
>
> Teller feels deeply that this "unfrocking" must be done or else — regardless of the outcome of the current hearing — scientists may lose their enthusiasm for the [superbomb] program.[45]

Teller's personal fears and friendships shaped his politics, and by now he deeply believed that having Oppenheimer in a high advisory role was dangerous for the United States. "Every time you go to Washington and you open a door to go into some high official's office," he told another physicist, "you open the door and there's Oppenheimer, blocking the way. Us good guys who have the correct view of what should be done can't even get in because Oppenheimer's there first."[46] For many years Teller had taken the backseat, but now he had reached a point in his own career where he could challenge Oppenheimer. It was a powerful vendetta. "He was absolutely determined to get Oppenheimer," recalled a close associate, "and he would say whatever he had to" to accomplish this.[47] Teller's mind was set on revenge, and he awaited his opportunity.

The night before his appearance at the hearing, Teller had been the object of a desperate last-minute search by Szilard. Szilard disliked what he considered Oppenheimer's infatuation with power, but he did not think him disloyal or a security risk. Szilard had seen a threat to all scientists when the AEC revoked Oppenheimer's clearance, and he had tried to influence the Gray Board in several ways. He had published a letter whose final sentence read: "Classing Oppenheimer as a Security Risk and subjecting him to a formal hearing is regarded by scientists in this country as an indignity and an affront to all; it is regarded by our friends abroad as a sign of insanity — which it probably is."[48] He had written to scientists who might be called to testify, urging them to support Oppenheimer. He also had helped draft an editorial for the *Bulletin of the Atomic Scientists* that dismissed the charges as "contrary to both decency and common sense." This put Szilard in the position of opposing someone he liked but disagreed with (Teller), while supporting someone he agreed with but personally disliked (Oppenheimer).

Szilard took a plane from New York to Washington on the eve of Teller's scheduled testimony and set out from his hotel to find his friend. According to his wife, Trude, Szilard wanted to save Teller from his own "worst instincts." He feared that Teller would injure his own reputation by testifying and unfairly destroying Oppenheimer. Szilard rode taxis to restaurants and clubs, walked to other hotels, but after hours of searching, finally returned dispirited. "If Teller attacks Oppenheimer," Szilard grumbled to Trude that night, "I will have to defend Oppenheimer for the rest of my life."[49]

Szilard did not find Teller, but Bethe did, at the American Physical Society conference at the Wardman Park Hotel. Bethe, serving as the society's president that year, discovered Teller in one of the hotel's hallways and beseeched him at length to testify in favor of Oppenheimer — or, at least, not to testify against him. "It was a desperate discussion," recalled Bethe, "but he was absolutely set in his opinion that Oppenheimer must be eliminated from an advisory role in the government. Teller was immovable."[50] Teller's determination to testify against Oppenheimer frightened Bethe, who understood only too well the damage that Teller's passion and obsessive tenacity — qualities that seemed so ardently patriotic in 1954 — would do to Oppenheimer. A physicist who saw Bethe later that night asked him, "Are [Oppenheimer's] hearings going badly?" "Yes," sighed Bethe, "but that is not the worst. I have just now had the most unpleasant conversation of my whole life. With Edward Teller."[51]

Teller harbored conflicting emotions about Oppenheimer: memories of the early friendship, the later festering grievances, the respect he felt nonetheless for Oppenheimer's intellect. But if Teller felt any remorse that his rival was crippled and fighting for his life, it vanished when Robb showed him a dossier containing items unfavorable to Oppenheimer just hours before he was to testify. The dossier consisted of material from Oppenheimer's security file and damning excerpts of the Gray Board hearing transcript relating to the Chevalier incident that Teller had never seen before. He read the material with rising agitation and emotion. (Teller later recalled that at this meeting Robb painted Oppenheimer as a devil.) Teller had, of course, known of Oppenheimer's left-wing background in a general and undocumented way, but to be suddenly confronted with a mass of detailed information inflamed him. His resentment rose to the surface. The material put Teller "in shock," as he later said, just as Robb and Strauss had hoped it would.[52]

It was in this troubled frame of mind that Teller entered the AEC hearing room the next afternoon. The atmosphere was expectant. There was a palpable tension in the room as he faced Robb for the first questions. Time seemed almost to be standing still. Jealousy and anger were boiling up inside Teller, but he affected a calm demeanor on the stand. He couldn't wait to begin. His energies were surging, his heart was pounding with extra adrenaline. This was the moment, and he was the man. Victory was his at last in the great rivalry with Oppenheimer. Today he would dispatch this self-important nuclear pundit. All of Oppenheimer's special friends — they no longer mattered. The inspiration of liberal and left-wing physicists brought down. Could one ask for a greater victory?

Teller proceeded to play the reluctant witness, earnest and troubled, anxious not to do an injustice to Oppenheimer:

ROBB: Dr. Teller, ... are you appearing as a witness here today because you want to be here?

TELLER: I appear because I have been asked to and because I consider it my duty upon request to say what I think in the matter. I would have preferred not to appear.

ROBB: You stated to me some time ago that anything you had to say, you wished to say in the presence of Dr. Oppenheimer?

TELLER: That is correct.

Robb then went straight to the heart of the matter:

ROBB: To simplify the issues here, let me ask you this question: Is it your intention to suggest that Dr. Oppenheimer is disloyal to the United States?

TELLER: I do not want to suggest anything of the kind. I know Oppenheimer as an intellectually most alert and a very complicated person, and I think it would be presumptuous and wrong on my part if I would try in any way to analyze his motives. But I have always assumed, and I now assume that he is loyal to the United States. I believe this, and I shall believe it until I see very conclusive proof to the opposite.

ROBB: Do you or do you not believe that Dr. Oppenheimer is a security risk?

TELLER: In a great number of cases I have seen Dr. Oppenheimer act — I understood that Dr. Oppenheimer acted — in a way which for me was exceedingly hard to understand. I thoroughly disagreed with him in numerous issues and his actions frankly appear to me confused and complicated. To this extent I feel that I would like to see the vital interests of this country in hands which I understand better, and therefore trust more. In this very limited sense I would like to express a feeling that I would feel personally more secure if public matters would rest in other hands.[53]

Gordon Gray, dissatisfied with Teller's artful phrase "personally more secure," put the question directly: "Do you feel that it would endanger the common defense and security to grant clearance to Dr. Oppenheimer?" Teller replied:

I believe ... that Dr. Oppenheimer's character is such that he would not knowingly and willingly do anything that is designed to endanger the safety of this country. To the extent, therefore,

that your question is directed toward intent, I would say I do not
see any reason to deny clearance.

If it is a question of wisdom and judgment, as demonstrated by
actions since 1945, then I would say one would be wiser not to
grant clearance.[54]

Oppenheimer sat listening as Teller spoke, his face an expressionless
mask, scrawling notes on a yellow legal pad:

> Teller — aggressive
> had conscience
> hysterical
> two sides on H-bomb[55]

At the close of his testimony, Teller rose from the witness chair,
walked over to the leather davenport where Oppenheimer was sitting,
and offered his hand. Oppenheimer looked at Teller for a long
moment, saying nothing, then shook his hand. "I'm sorry," Teller said,
meeting Oppenheimer's eyes. Oppenheimer looked at him oddly.
"After what you've just said," replied Oppenheimer in a polite but
unbelieving tone, "I don't know what you mean."[56] Teller turned
away, his shoulders heavy, and limped slowly from the room. His
innuendoes and doubts had done their intended damage.

Ernest Lawrence's relationship with Oppenheimer had changed after
the war. Lawrence thought Oppenheimer took too much personal
credit for the collective success of Los Alamos and had become self-
important, while Oppenheimer thought Lawrence simply resented
his new stature. The growing tension between them became apparent
in the press. In response to Oppenheimer's famous remark "The
physicists have known sin; and this is a knowledge which they cannot
lose," Lawrence defiantly replied, "I am a physicist and I have no
knowledge to lose in which physics has caused me to know sin."[57]

A proponent of American nuclear superiority, Lawrence believed
Oppenheimer's persuasive, almost hypnotic, influence made his counsel of restraint dangerous. When Robb visited Berkeley shortly before
the hearing, Lawrence complained how others had been "taken in" by
Oppenheimer, but — "giving him the benefit of the doubt" — still
believed that "everything he did can be attributed to bad judgment."

Lawrence also stressed to Robb that Oppenheimer "should never again have anything to do with the forming of policy."[58] How much better, Lawrence thought, if only Oppenheimer would recognize that accomplishment in science did not confer political competence. Lawrence also resented what he considered his former friend's arrogance toward security rules and regulations. "Lawrence was the sort of person," recalled an associate, "who could say, 'Well, if you haven't done anything wrong, there's nothing to worry about.'"[59] He remembered that in Greek mythology the gods always repaid pride with a fall. It was painful to see a man's life picked apart and exposed, but Lawrence thought Oppenheimer had asked for it. He was convinced that Oppenheimer's clearance should be revoked.

Lawrence hoped Oppenheimer would quietly accept revocation of his clearance, but when Oppenheimer protested and requested a hearing, Strauss insisted that Lawrence testify against his former friend. Lawrence was terrified. A few days before his scheduled testimony in late April, he attended a meeting of national laboratory directors at Oak Ridge. The prime topic of conversation, aside from scientific matters, was the Oppenheimer hearing. Oppenheimer was a close friend of many of those present, and feelings ran high. Angrily confronted at the meeting by Rabi, Lawrence insisted that he was playing no part in any personal vendetta, that he was only concerned about the country's welfare. Yet he was worried that his pending testimony would be leaked to the press and would therefore harm himself as well as Oppenheimer. The stress that Lawrence felt was so great that he suffered an acute attack of ulcerative colitis. He canceled his scheduled appearance before the Gray Board and returned home to Berkeley.

Strauss thought Lawrence was using an illness to avoid an unpleasant duty. He pressed Lawrence for a written statement. Lawrence ultimately did as he was told, delivering a short but damning statement to the Gray Board just two days before the hearings ended. In his statement, Lawrence cast doubt on Oppenheimer's loyalty by recalling an incident that had occurred in the fall of 1949:

> I remember driving up to San Francisco from Palo Alto with Luis W. Alvarez and Dr. Vannevar Bush when we discussed Oppenheimer's activities in the nuclear weapons program. At that time we could not understand or make any sense out of the arguments Oppenheimer was using in opposition to the thermonuclear program and indeed we felt he was much too lukewarm in pushing the

overall AEC program. I recall Dr. Bush being concerned about the matter and in the course of the conversation he mentioned that [air force chief of staff] General Hoyt Vandenberg had insisted that Dr. Bush serve as Chairman of a committee to evaluate the evidence for the first Russian atomic explosion, as General Vandenberg did not trust Dr. Oppenheimer. I believe it was on the basis of the findings of this committee that the President made the announcement that the Soviets had set off their first atomic bomb.

Ernest O. Lawrence[60]

The hearing finally came to an end on May 6, 1954. The board members went home for ten days to consider and to judge. The first thing Gray did was to dictate a memorandum for the record, in which he protested that the proceedings had been as fair as circumstances permitted. When the board reconvened, it voted two to one (Ward Evans dissenting) that Robert Oppenheimer was a security risk and that his clearance should not be renewed.

Garrison broke the news of the board's decision to Oppenheimer on May twenty-eighth. Oppenheimer had expected it all along. Even before the hearing began, he had confided to Bethe: "It is impossible for the AEC to find me innocent. After what has happened, they just have to convict me. But nevertheless I have to go through with it."[61] "Once a thing like that has been started," he added after it was over, "they couldn't *not* go through with it to the end; and they couldn't let me win."[62] Although numbed by his recent ordeal and frazzled by the wait for a verdict, Oppenheimer followed Garrison's advice and agreed to appeal the verdict to the AEC commissioners. But when Garrison asked to argue the case before the AEC, the commission's general manager, a Strauss appointee, rejected his request. Oppenheimer was dazed by now. He was like a man running on a treadmill, anxious to get off but not knowing how. He faced persistent requests for comment by newsmen after the board's verdict broke on June second, which he refused. Yet he did accept a phone call from a reporter in Australia, who quoted him as saying: "Maybe this is the end of the road for me. I have no sympathy for Communism, but I have moral principles from which I will never depart."[63] Underneath his stoic facade, however, Oppenheimer was steaming. To family and friends he privately described the hearing and the verdict — the "whole thing" — as an "outrage." "This is an abuse of the power of the state," he said, "and is a problem [for] everybody, not just [me]."[64]

A majority of AEC commissioners, led by Lewis Strauss, affirmed the Gray Board's verdict on June twenty-ninth by a four-to-one vote, physicist Henry Smyth being the lone dissenter. Strauss himself undertook the composition of the AEC majority opinion. It found that "Dr. Oppenheimer is not entitled to the continued confidence of the Government and of this Commission because of the proof of fundamental defects in his 'character'" and emphasized his questionable "associations."[65]

Strauss released the commissioners' verdict to reporters, but not to Oppenheimer himself; he learned of the verdict from a journalist who had gotten advance word of it. There was no shock this time; he was reconciled to the inevitable. Three days after the AEC's verdict was made public, Oppenheimer granted an interview to the Associated Press. He chain-smoked and fidgeted but volunteered little. Did Oppenheimer think he had received a fair hearing? The scientist would only say he hoped "people will study the record of the case and reach their own conclusions." "I think there is something to be learned from it."[66]

Since Oppenheimer's AEC consulting contract was due to expire on June thirtieth, Strauss had vindictively rushed the decision through to get the humiliating denial of clearance on the record. Strauss also released the unflattering transcript of the board hearing to the public, despite Gray's promise to each witness that the AEC would "not take the initiative" in publishing it. Later that summer, in a final, stunning act of personal vindictiveness, Strauss called a meeting of the Board of Trustees of the Institute for Advanced Study at Princeton and vainly tried to force Oppenheimer's resignation as director. Not satisfied with destroying Oppenheimer's reputation, Strauss also tried to destroy his livelihood.

The verdict against Oppenheimer dismayed, angered, and disgusted American physicists. They reacted to the verdict personally — it struck uncomfortably close to home. Szilard considered it a chilling comment on the times. "Unfortunately for all of us, [the Gray Board members] are as good men as they come," noted Szilard with characteristic dryness, "and if they are affected by the general insanity which is more and more creeping up on us, who can be counted on to be immune?"[67] Szilard disagreed with Teller's testimony, but he gave Teller the benefit of the doubt: Teller had said what he believed was true. The friendship between the two Hungarians endured.

The McCarthyite paranoia that Bethe saw in the verdict angered and frightened him. "I was afraid that they might go after all of us" was the way he put it.[68] Bethe's friendship with Teller went back almost as many years as Szilard's, but he could not bring himself to forgive Teller. "I did not see Teller for a long time after this, and our relationship was strained from then on," Bethe said later. "We still encountered each other from time to time, and we were not unfriendly outwardly, but we never discussed this event. There was no question where I stood, however."[69] Bethe hoped, as he wrote in a letter to Teller in November 1954, "that some day we shall again be in a state where we can again talk about the things we used to talk about — meaning the things we talked about before 1942."[70]

Lawrence thought Teller had been rightly disturbed by Oppenheimer's falsehoods about the Chevalier incident. "I can stand a lot," Lawrence told a colleague that spring, "but when a man lies to security agents, that's it." Although Lawrence had helped to bring Oppenheimer down, he took no pleasure in the outcome. He turned down an invitation to attend a dinner in honor of Strauss shortly after the hearing ended, and his ulcerative colitis worsened. Still, there was a bitterness in Lawrence about Oppenheimer that associates could not miss. "I got Oppenheimer that job in the first place," Lawrence complained with some emotion the summer after the hearing. "Of course, we've got a better man around here now." "Who's that?" the associate asked. "Teller," came Lawrence's reply.[71]

Fermi was saddened by the whole affair. He detested the passions aroused in the dispute — which he believed had impeded a fair judgment of the issues — and the negative effect of these passions on American science. He also was very sick. At first it took the form of increasing indigestion. Fermi took antacid pills, but he began to lose energy and grow very thin. Doctors told him his sickness was psychological, so he began to read medical textbooks in an attempt to diagnose his own illness. Then doctors examined his esophagus by putting a tube down his throat; the visible tissue looked normal. He continued to grow thinner. Finally doctors performed exploratory surgery. They found stomach cancer that had metastasized so widely that nothing could be done. He was in the very prime of life.

Knowing he had very little time to live, Fermi resolved to set straight a friend whose behavior he thought had been reprehensible. A visitor to Fermi's hospital room described his mood:

When I came into his room we talked for a moment about his condition, he apparently knowing very well that these were his last days. We then discussed the characters of some of the people with whom we had been associated together. The thing, however, that he was most interested in was a visit Teller was to pay him the next day. . . . Fermi's principal interest was in talking to Teller in a way that would lead him to mend his ways and restore his own position among his scientific associates. I thought he was far more interested in saving Teller than he was in his own desperate condition.[72]

"What nobler thing for a dying man to do — " Fermi smiled ironically to another friend — "than to try to save a soul?"[73]

Lying in Billings Hospital in Chicago and feeling terribly sick and tired, his condition so grave that he was allowed only a few visitors for brief periods of time, Fermi asked his wife, Laura, to summon Teller. Teller came to his old friend at once. He found Fermi, a man of habit and order whose mind never rested, being fed by a tube that ran directly into his stomach, measuring the flow of the intravenous drip by counting the drops with a stopwatch. Laura, grief stricken, was standing by his bedside.

Although shockingly thin and weak, Fermi seemed only a little tired and sad. He told Teller very calmly about his condition and wondered objectively how much time he had. He was stoically good-humored as always. He said that he had been blessed by a Catholic priest, a Protestant pastor, and a Jewish rabbi. At different times the three had entered his room and politely asked permission to bless him; he had given it. "It pleased them and it did not harm me," he said.[74] Then he quipped: "The doctors have played a dirty trick on me."

Teller, choking up, tried to be witty in return. "It's a dirty trick on your friends," he responded halfheartedly.[75] Teller was crestfallen. As natives of another continent transplanted to the United States, he and Fermi had shared a common culture and many common understandings. They had spent innumerable happy hours in conversations together. Losing Fermi now — at a time when he was so greatly in need of friendly counsel — was particularly hard.

Fermi got right to the point. He asked his friend how he was doing; even as he lay facing death, he was concerned about others' problems. Then Fermi told Teller that, in his judgment, Oppenheimer had rendered outstanding service during the war, and that after the war his advice had been given after thorough study and in good faith. If the advice had not been taken, or if it was thought to be wrong — these offered no grounds for impugning Oppenheimer's loyalty. Fermi told Teller that he considered the AEC hearing — and its verdict — a national disgrace and a disaster for American science. Quietly but urgently, he begged Teller to repair the damage. The emotion of the moment moved Teller to remorse. He spoke more openly than he had ever dared to before. "One usually reads," Teller said in recalling the occasion, "that dying men confess their sins to the living. It has always seemed to me that it would be much more logical the other way about. So I confessed my sins to Fermi. None but he, apart from the Deity, if there is one, knows what I then told him."[76] A month later, on November 29, 1954, Enrico Fermi died at the age of only fifty-three.

Rabi felt sore at the Gray Board — and Oppenheimer, too. Rabi understood his old friend on many levels and was directly honest about him. "I'm a bit angry that Robert let it happen," Rabi later said. "He should've said, 'I have a record, and I'm not going to be badgered by you' . . . and just denounce them. Instead, he let it get dragged over all sorts of things. He shouldn't have stood up there and spilled his guts to those people."[77] As another physicist who knew both men has said, "Rabi appreciated Robert and when you appreciate the man you tell him, at least when you are courageous which Rabi always was, you tell him what's wrong with him."[78] Reflecting on the hearing years later, Rabi felt a sense of both guilt and anger:

> I was one of the few living who could sit down and say [to Oppenheimer], "Now don't be a fool." . . . If I'd been in on it [the defense team] . . . , I would simply have advised him to stand up and say, "This is what I accomplished for the United States. There is a record. I see no reason for a retrial. If you find it in your hearts to do this, there it is. I hope you have a long life and live to regret it. I will have no part of it." Period. And walk out.[79]

Yet even if Oppenheimer had taken the hearing more seriously, or if he had followed Rabi's advice and stormed out, the outcome probably would have been the same. A part of him knew this, and that is why his normally quick and intuitive mind seemed paralyzed by the morbid circumstances. He felt doomed from the start. Months before the Gray Board convened, he confided to Bethe that "no matter what happens during the hearings, the Atomic Energy Commission cannot do anything but find me guilty."[80] In the existing political atmosphere, he sensed that there could be no other outcome. Few people amid the McCarthyism of 1954 could have withstood the pounding of Robb and the pain of having a compromising past examined.

The loss of his security clearance ended Oppenheimer's Washington career. All of his government connections were severed, and his long service to national security came to an abrupt and ignoble end. After having contributed so much during the war as director of Los Alamos and so much after the war in many different capacities, his contribution was now over. If Oppenheimer had suffered previously because of the weight of his power, he now suffered grievously because of the effect of its absence.

"He had spent the years after the war being an adviser, being in high places, knowing what was going on," said a close friend. "To be in on things gave him a sense of importance. That became his whole life. He could run the institute with his left hand. And now he really didn't have anything to do."[81] Bethe felt that Oppenheimer "was not the same person afterward."[82] Rabi said this about his friend's destruction:

> I was indignant. Here was a man who had done so greatly for his country. A wonderful representative. He was forgiven the atomic bomb. Crowds followed him. He was a man of peace. And they destroyed this man. A small, mean group. There were scientists among them. One reason for doing it might be envy. Another might be personal dislike. A third, a genuine fear of communism. He was an aesthete. I don't think he was a security risk. I do think he walked along the edge of a precipice. He didn't pay enough attention to the outward symbols.[83]

Oppenheimer was deeply wounded and hurt. His feelings were raw, his pain so fierce as to be almost physical. The effects of the ordeal began to show. Oppenheimer had always been lithe and vibrant; now he began to age visibly and his body took on a look of frailty. He seemed like a biblical martyr with his sad voice and gaunt, haunted appearance. He even took to quoting biblical scripture: "I cannot sit with anger." When a friend compared his ordeal to a dry crucifixion, Oppenheimer smiled unhappily and said, "You know, it wasn't so very dry. I can still feel the warm blood on my hands."[84] There was now pain and hurt in his eyes. The old intellectual impatience, the flashes of arrogance, were gone.

Oppenheimer disappeared from public view and seemed almost to disappear from the life of his friends. Nearly all of them were scientists engaged in one way or another in government work ruled by security regulations. Their lives revolved around their research, as Oppenheimer's had, but he and they could not talk to each other about work. They could not talk about the case, or even about the old days, because all that was too painful to discuss. So they were left with nothing to talk about. Oppenheimer was kept under surveillance even after the hearing was finished. A friend ran into him at the airport months later, and while they were chatting Oppenheimer motioned toward three bystanders and explained calmly but wearily, "They, or others like them, are with me all the time." They had presumably trailed Oppenheimer out to the airport to make sure he did not skip the country and defect to the Soviet Union.

Oppenheimer always kept his composure, at least outwardly. It was his family that suffered the most. The ordeal abode like a permanent ghost at Olden Manor, the Oppenheimers' Princeton home. Kitty simmered with indignation and remained on a slow, corrosive burn for years to come. She deeply resented the injustice, and blamed herself for part of the mess that her husband had gotten into. Her health deteriorated as she began to drink even more. It was hard for the children, who could not understand what it was all about except that everything seemed unfair. The hearings meant that they were separated from their parents for much of the spring of 1954. Thirteen-year-old-son Peter knew his father was going through some kind of ordeal. He came home from school one afternoon in tears and said a classmate had taunted him: "Your father is a communist!" Peter and Toni both came to resent any intrusion on their father's life, any reminder of his banishment from government. They tried to spend as much time as they could with their father, but Oppenheimer made this difficult by being an absentee parent who found it hard to relate to his children. Still, they remained devoted to him. Peter chalked this on the blackboard in his room:

The Amican Govermerant is unfair to Acuse Certain People that I know, of being unfair to them. Since this true, I think that Certain

People, and may I say, only Certain People in the U.S. govermeant, should go to HELL.

Yours truly
Certain People[85]

Oppenheimer was not the only scientist to suffer as a result of the hearing. Paradoxically, Teller also suffered, for his testimony against Oppenheimer brought down on him a harvest of resentment mingled with cold, angry contempt. Although Teller was aware that he had offended many of his fellow scientists, he had no real idea of what was in store for him. A few weeks after the AEC's verdict had been announced and the hearing transcript had been published, Teller went to Los Alamos, where Oppenheimer was a living legend, for a conference of physicists from across the country. Gatherings like this one were usually jovial affairs, reunions of old friends as well as serious scientific sessions. A few physicists were glad to see Teller, but others went out of their way to avoid him. The first large gathering was a dinner in the main hall of Fuller Lodge. Just as Teller was about to sit down, he spotted Rabi and Robert Christy, a Caltech physicist who had been a graduate student of Oppenheimer and a close wartime colleague of Teller, at a nearby table. With great bonhomie and nonchalance, Teller walked over to Rabi and Christy's table and greeted them with a hearty laugh and outstretched hand. As everyone in the crowded dining room looked on, both Christy and Rabi looked icily at Teller and refused to shake his hand. Rabi then acidly congratulated Teller on the "brilliance" of his testimony before the Gray Board and "the *extremely* clever way" he had phrased his reply concerning Oppenheimer as a security risk. "'I would personally feel more secure' without Oppenheimer in the government," said Rabi caustically and loudly — "a brilliant way of saying, 'don't restore his clearance!'" Teller was stunned and speechless, as if Christy and Rabi had punched him. He staggered back to his table, his face flushed and twisted with emotion. He tried as hard as he could to maintain his composure, but the shock and humiliation were too great. In a choked voice he excused himself, abruptly left the hall, and returned to his room, where he broke down and wept.[86] Teller was to endure this kind of rejection again in the years to come because, in the minds of many scientists, he had destroyed Oppenheimer. But no incident was branded on Teller's soul as deeply as this first, stinging rebuke.

The physicists who shunned Teller were the very people whose respect and friendship he craved most. Twice before he had been forced to relinquish the familiar: first his homeland of Hungary, then the continent of his birth and culture. In America everything had been initially unfamiliar except for the community of physicists, who had afforded him comfort since the day he arrived. Now he lost those closest to him. Teller, who had always cherished his friendships, found the loss very painful and hard to bear. He was more miserable than he had ever been in his entire life. "I am just bewildered and also personally very greatly hurt," he wrote after returning from Los Alamos, "when I hear a great number of hateful words coming from people who used to be close to me."[87]

Teller's ostracism provoked intense hostility — even hatred — in him toward his enemies, particularly Rabi. These feelings of childlike hurt and resentment came pouring out in a letter he wrote to a friend:

> I came back from Los Alamos a few days ago. . . . I felt like Daniel in the lions' den. After some time you learn to distinguish the lions by their growls. . . .
>
> I got so that I can guess what a man is going to say. And I begin to believe that I can guess what he thinks. It is not a nice experience.
>
> The worst of them is Rabi. He was never my friend but now he is terrible. . . .
>
> Last night I dreamed that there was a Raven and I did not dare to go to sleep because he may pick out my eyes. Please translate Raven into German [rabe]. I found this amusing because the Raven started to smile and I slept quite well.[88]

Teller was once again in exile, treated like a leper, or — even worse — a modern-day Judas. As long as he remained in the confines of his home at Berkeley, where he had moved from Chicago in 1952, or his office at Livermore, life went along much as usual. But he could never be sure of the reception he would receive whenever he made one of his frequent trips to scientific conferences or public meetings. Lifelong acquaintances began to ignore him and even to pillory him. Many at Los Alamos made it clear that Teller would no longer be welcome there. Teller perceived this all too well, and he did not return there for nearly ten years.

The animosity against Teller, however, went deeper than just defense of Oppenheimer. Teller was regarded not only as having betrayed one of his peers but as having collaborated with — some thought sold out to — the military-industrial complex. As he raced from his lectures at Berkeley to his bomb laboratory at Livermore or to conferences at the Pentagon, Teller grew to be a vivid symbol and an unpleasant reminder to his peers of the captivity of physics. For someone of Teller's sensitivity and temperament — whose feelings always lay just beneath the surface, who enjoyed human relationships so much, and who wanted so much to be liked — such treatment was traumatic. The more criticism he encountered, the more relentlessly he drove himself to overcome it — and the more impatient and irritable he became. He grew physically and emotionally depleted. Like Lawrence, he developed a painful and dangerous form of ulcerative colitis, an ailment closely associated with emotional tension. His gaiety, spontaneity, and teasing nature disappeared. He became bitter, combative, distrustful, and reclusive. Even his children noticed the difference in his personality. He had always been prone to moods of silence, but they now became more frequent. There were times when Mici would warn Paul and Wendy not to disturb their father. At these times Wendy would say, "Don't bother Daddy, he has black bugs in his head."[89]

Teller's painful ostracism led him to have second thoughts about his testimony against Oppenheimer. "What else could I do at the hearing?" he began pleading to friends. "What else could I say?"[90] He drafted a public statement saying that his testimony had been misunderstood, that he had not meant to imply that opinions should be punished. Teller sent the desperate statement to Strauss, explaining that he now felt his testimony had been a mistake and revealing his alarm at his own conduct:

> I continue to feel that I made a grave mistake when I clearly implied that opinion of a man can make him a security risk. I did not say this, but, rereading my own testimony, I see that I came extremely close to saying it. I therefore would feel very much happier if I could make a statement to the press in which I remedy as much of this damage as I possibly can. After a lot of headache and a waste of much paper, I arrived at this brief statement which I am attaching.
>
> It seems particularly important for me to say something of this kind since my friends among the physicists attach very great importance to this point. If I should lose their respect it would be an extremely hard blow to me.[91]

Strauss would have none of this. The last thing he wanted now was a public recantation by his star witness against Oppenheimer. He bucked up Teller by urging him to consult with Roger Robb. To make sure that Teller did so, Strauss sent Teller's draft statement to Robb. Robb immediately advised Teller to stand by his testimony, which had required "courage and character" and had performed "a public service of great value." Teller remained silent.[92]

Years would pass before Teller would again be tolerated by his peers, but even then he was never really forgiven. And while many conservatives admired Teller for conceiving the superbomb and protecting the state against Oppenheimer, he would remain a pariah to liberals for the rest of his long life. Being a perceptive man with a sensitive ego, Teller saw his fate all too clearly. Questioned about the long-term effects of the Oppenheimer affair nearly twenty years later, Teller replied without hesitation: "I think it made Oppenheimer. I think it destroyed Teller."[93] When he published his memoirs in 2001 — nearly half a century after the affair — Teller was moved to write: "Why did I testify? In retrospect, the answer is simple and obvious: because I was demonstrating my fulsome quantity of that general human property, stupidity. . . . In retrospect, I should have said at the beginning of my testimony that the hearing was a dirty business, and that I wouldn't talk to anyone about it."[94]

Such expressions of personal regret and suffering were rare. But at unguarded moments, Teller would let the bitterness pour forth. "If a person leaves his country, leaves his continent, leaves his relatives, leaves his friends, the only people he knows are his professional colleagues. If more than ninety percent of these then come around to consider him an enemy, an outcast, it is bound to have an effect. The truth is it had a profound effect."[95] The affair crippled both men: Oppenheimer because he lost, Teller because he won. The poignancy of Teller's self-awareness about the pariah status to which he relegated himself spoke volumes about the horrible irony of the larger story.

After Strauss retired as AEC chairman in 1958, a review of the Oppenheimer hearing was made by the commission's general counsel, who found that there was "a messy record from a legal standpoint; that the charges kept shifting at each level of the proceedings; that the evidence was stale and consisted of information that was 12 years old and was known when a security clearance was granted during World

War II, and that it was a punitive, personal abuse of the judicial system."[96] But by then it was too late.

Not long after his hearing was over and his security clearance had
been revoked, Oppenheimer gave a speech at Amherst College where
students asked him why he had not helped his case by showing more
repentance for his past left-wing associations. Oppenheimer replied,
"It may not be the obligation of a man in a position of responsibility to
conform his actions to what the public desires; but if he wishes to play
an effective part in politics, it is clear that he must either conform
himself to what the public desires, or persuade the public to accept
what he is."[97] Oppenheimer refused to do the former and failed to do
the latter.

Freed from the burden of playing the Washington game, Oppenheimer devoted himself to investigating issues raised by modern science and commenting on man's fate in the nuclear age. Those who
encountered him now noticed traces of defeat in his manner. At the
same time, they noticed tranquility in his face. He was calmer than
he had been since going to Los Alamos. "We did the devil's work," he
told a visitor in 1956, summing up his experiences during and after
the war. "But we are now going back to our real jobs. Rabi for instance
was telling me only the other day that he intended to devote himself
exclusively to research in the future."[98] Oppenheimer felt unburdened
at last. The hearing made him a martyr among liberals. The Gray
Board's verdict ended their concern that Oppenheimer had surrendered his independence to establish his political influence. The AEC's
action ironically served as a means of his redemption.

Everywhere people wondered, "How could this happen?" Some
blamed the unpopularity of Oppenheimer's views on the superbomb.
Others blamed Oppenheimer's unscrupulous enemies. Still others
blamed Oppenheimer's own arrogance and past evasions. All of them
were factors, but all of them would not have been enough had the
country not been in the grip of the insecurity and paranoia that
expressed itself in anticommunist witch-hunts. In the spring of 1954,
when McCarthyism was at its peak, the reigning dogma identified
security with superiority in the arms race: the superbomb served as a
powerful buttress against expanding communism and kept the peace
by means of deterrence, the capacity to wreak sufficient destruction
on the enemy so as to discourage any attack. In this climate, it was all
too easy to see a physicist with a radical past who disagreed with this

view as being a security threat. It was a mood fed by hysterical fear; its chief symptom was the belief that anyone who did not share it was dangerously unreliable.

Of course, because of his association with the bomb, because of the fascinating complexities of his personality, and because of his marvelous eloquence, Oppenheimer had come to represent all physicists in the public mind. To liberals frightened by the arms race and obsessed with avoiding a nuclear war, he was a superb scientist and a selfless public servant who had been sacrificed for his unpopular beliefs. To conservatives frightened by communism and obsessed with national security, he was the man who had cavorted with the Cold War enemy. Robert Oppenheimer touched people — then and now — because he was the most sensitive and reflective individual among all those involved in the creation of the terrible new weapons.

Yet the Oppenheimer affair was not just the story of one man; it was also the story of all of the atomic scientists. His personal tragedy was also his profession's. It dramatized physicists' sudden transformation from naive academics into major players in the realm of American national security. The bomb had given once-obscure physicists a new standing akin to the mathematician-astronomer-priests of the ancient Maya, who were both revered and feared as the keepers of the mystery of the seasons and the helpers of the sun and stars. Oppenheimer, the father of the atomic bomb, became the unofficial high priest. Not just Oppenheimer's life had been dissected in the hearing room but the lives — with all their subtle pressures and unsolved problems — of the scientists who had ushered in the atomic age. The hearings revealed the new and influential part these men now played in national security politics, their uneasiness in a nuclear world they had helped to create, and above all their anxiety about losing sight of the deeply rooted set of ethical beliefs out of which science — their passion — had grown. How had it happened that men who had tried to find a more comprehensive truth were in the end obliged to spend the best years of their lives in the search for ever more destructive weapons — and then the best among them punished for it? Science had ceased to be seen as something remote and now was looked upon as something terrible. To an extent, then, Oppenheimer and the other atomic scientists whom he symbolized had fallen victim to the very weapon they had created.

CHAPTER 11

Twilight Years

NIELS BOHR HAD returned to Denmark in August 1945, and two months later had turned sixty. The anxieties of the war and the Manhattan Project had strained and saddened him. His thinning gray hair, the jowls that draped over his massive jaw, the heavy eyebrows that shadowed his intelligent and kindly eyes — all had made him a doleful figure. He had spent more and more time during the ensuing years at his summerhouse in Tisvilde, on the northern shore of Sjælland, a two-hour drive from Copenhagen. The thatched, one-story country house stood in a grove of pine trees on heather-covered hills that met the lavender waters of the Baltic in an unbroken harmony. In a ramshackle barn in this beautiful and tranquil setting that he loved so much, Bohr had found time to think and reflect. For relaxation he had bicycled in the woods, walked on the beach, and read fairy tales and played games with his many grandchildren. Evenings were spent in the family circle, chatting about issues large or small. These had been happy days for Bohr, yet there had been long thoughts, too, of how the world had been changed by the bomb.

During the war, Bohr had foreseen that the atomic bomb would cause trouble with Russia, unless the Russians were made partners rather than rivals. Now the Iron Curtain had come down, and Bohr had watched the growing quarrel between East and West with grave misgivings. He did not surrender in his struggle. Time he could have devoted to science was now devoted to writing innumerable appeals and statements. Although these had often gone unanswered by the officials to whom they were addressed, Bohr saw them as a means of educating the public at large. What could be done to break the stalemate and make security possible? The answer to which he had come with increasing emphasis was the international control of atomic weapons before other countries acquired the bomb. Otherwise, the next big war could be the world's last.

In the spring of 1948, while in residence at the Institute for Advanced Study, Bohr had met privately with Secretary of State George Marshall in Washington. During their talk, Bohr had reiterated his plea for openness and cooperation between the United States and the USSR on atomic weapons. This was essential, he had stressed in a follow-up letter, "in order not to lose the opportunity to forestall a fateful competition in atomic armaments." He had then pointed, prophetically, to an even more frightening future. "The new and ominous menace to world security presented by employing the results of the latest development of bacteriological and biochemical science as terrible life-destructive means cannot be eliminated by any practicable control and will, therefore, remain a latent danger until such cooperation in openness has been achieved." Bohr had believed America should take the initiative because it led in the field of atomic energy. "Your country," he had told Marshall, "possesses the strength required to take the lead in accepting the challenge with which civilization is confronted."[1] Marshall gave no promise.

By 1950 Bohr had recognized that his efforts had come to naught, so he had written an "Open Letter" to the United Nations in June of that year in which he gave an account of his efforts in broad outline and pleaded with the world's great powers to begin a dialogue with one another about the bomb. In the letter, he had predicted that the lack of such cooperation would trigger an escalating nuclear arms race and increased tensions between East and West.[2] The Korean War, which broke out three weeks later, had put Bohr's appeal in the shade, but his predictions turned out to be tragically correct.

Almost everyone who encountered Arthur Compton in his later years noticed his eyes. They had always been deep set, but now they were knowing and penetrating, like an old seer's. When he was invited to become chancellor of Washington University at the end of the war, he had candidly told its board of trustees that he did not know what students' and alumni's attitude toward him would be when they learned of his involvement in the top secret Manhattan Project: either they

would think of him as one of the scientists who had saved civilization —
or had imperiled mankind. As he wrote a year after Hiroshima, "It is
too early to say whether the moral historian, if there be one a thousand years hence, will record the use of the atomic bomb as the work
of the world's guardian angel or as that of the devil bent on man's
destruction."[3] No one could go through what Compton did and come
out quite the same.

Compton's ambivalence had led him to refuse to have anything
more to do with weapons making. Shortly after the Soviet atomic test
in August 1949, Ernest Lawrence came to visit him in St. Louis.
Depressed by the news, Lawrence had tried to estimate how long it
would be until the Russians could attack the United States. He had
said he was going to turn the efforts of his lab toward developing new
weapons that he hoped would be helpful in the approaching struggle.
Compton had told Lawrence that his task was no longer to develop
nuclear weapons but to develop young people to bring about peace by
building a strong society.

Not surprisingly, the superbomb filled Compton with anxiety. If
such weapons were used upon centers of population, he doubted
whether enough survivors would remain to rebuild civilized human
existence. "The world is crying that the weapon itself and those
responsible for its development and use be brought under control of
those whose lives it endangers and at the same time protects," said
Compton. "And this means everyone."[4] He opposed targeting civilian
populations in war, urged limiting the size and number of superbombs, and advocated no-first-use of nuclear weapons by the United
States — all ideas which became central goals of arms control advocates in later years. Above all, Compton urged the avoidance of nuclear
war. "No nation," he said again and again, to political leaders and ordinary people alike, "would expect such a war to end without itself suffering more damage than its possible gains would be worth."[5]

Compton's style as chancellor of Washington University had been
quiet and unpretentious. He told the faculty to call him Mr. Compton, not Dr. Compton, and asked that they do the same among themselves. He slipped easily into conversation with students, who sensed
his disciplined enthusiasm, inner tranquility, and natural friendliness.
In 1954 he retired as chancellor and accepted appointment as professor of natural philosophy at the university. The aging Compton
devoted himself to speaking and writing about the impact of science
on society and the morality of science. When asked to reflect on sci-

entists' role in the creation of the bomb, he would cite the biblical story of Eden — it had highly personal meaning for him. When man and woman wished to return to the garden of innocence, he pointed out, an angel with a fiery sword blocked their way. They had eaten the fruit of the tree of knowledge, and as the serpent had promised, became as gods, knowing good from evil. This was a heavy burden. They longed to be free of the knowledge of good and evil, but they could not. Their only peace lay in working to make the world as they felt it should be. Free will made people responsible for their destiny.

After the war, Berkeley had become the mecca of experimental physics and Ernest Lawrence its aging prophet. Tall and heavyset, with thinning hair set above rimless bifocals, Lawrence ruled the Rad Lab like an impresario, parking his car in a no-parking zone just outside the main door. To anyone who acted without consulting him first, he glared fiercely and with his jowls quivering said, "You had better learn which side your bread is buttered on if you want to remain in this laboratory."[6] At other times he would go out of his way to help a subordinate by counseling on technique, by assisting in the building of equipment, or by suggesting some fruitful line of research. The Rad Lab grew rapidly during these years, aided by almost unlimited government funding. What had begun in the 1930s as Lawrence's personal laboratory in a wooden shed had grown by the 1950s into a vast complex employing more than 2,800 people, including nearly 300 graduate students.[7]

As he had always been, Lawrence was constantly on the move, the rapid character of his life heightened by increased responsibilities. But there were some changes. His legendary energy diminished and he abandoned his lifelong quest for ever larger contraptions, becoming the master tinkerer again. "Why, fellas, you don't want a big machine," he told a group of young experimental physicists at the University of Illinois who were redesigning the cyclotron there. "There's too much emphasis these days on sheer size for its own sake. Build something small and precisely suited to the research information you want from it."[8] It was a sign of a subtle shift, recognition of a connection between invention and application and that things had already moved "so far beyond human scale."[9]

Lawrence had not initially questioned the nuclear buildup (indeed, he had been in favor of it), but the escalating atomic arms race and his growing sense of mortality made him begin to worry whether he had been right. He grew more modest, philosophical, and tentative, and acknowledged uncertainties and vulnerabilities for the first time in his life. "The Nobel Prize in physics, or indeed in any other subject, surely is not to be taken as evidence of special wisdom in philosophy or of unusual insight into metaphysical problems," he wrote a Berkeley neighbor in February 1955.[10] He even began to advocate scientific exchanges as a way of breaking down the Iron Curtain and took to giving visiting Soviet physicists personal tours of the Rad Lab as a way of building the mutual understanding that he now saw as necessary to prevent a nuclear holocaust between Cold War rivals.

Biology had offered Leo Szilard an intellectual challenge and an escape from his guilt over Hiroshima and Nagasaki, allowing him to repudiate death and embrace life. "The mysteries of biology are no less deep than the mysteries of physics were one or two generations ago," he said, "and the tools are available to solve them provided only that we believe they can be solved."[11] Yet he did not abandon arms control. "Theoretically I am supposed to divide my time between finding what life is and trying to preserve it by saving the world," he wrote to Bohr in 1950. "At present the world seems to be beyond saving, and that leaves me more free time for biology."[12] He also found time to write satires on science and politics. In one story, superhuman minds on a distant planet worried that earthlings were smart enough to separate U-235, yet stupid enough to use this knowledge to make atomic bombs.[13]

To strangers Szilard seemed shy, witty, and eccentric. To his peers he seemed gruff, demanding, even arrogant. A friend entertained him at a dinner party one evening at which she served asparagus. When the platter was offered to him, he cut off all the tips and put them on his plate. In astonishment, before she could stop herself, she asked him why he did that, and he replied that he liked the tips the best. Another friend said, "I highly esteem Leo, and I would do anything for him — except work with him." Shy and lonely behind his bombastic quips and wisecracks, he amused, annoyed, and bewildered the people around him. One minute he could be silly and winsome, the next, sullen and withdrawn. Szilard acknowledged his impulsive, erratic manner and moods with pride. At a meeting he had thrown into confusion, he rose and impishly announced, "I think I can best contribute to the progress of this conference by leaving."[14] During such conferences he habitually sat like a drowsy hound, with his round face and potbelly, giving the impression he was asleep while his mind played and wandered. Yet from time to time, he would suddenly wake up, his eyes shining with intelligence and wit, to ask sharp, incisive, unexpected questions that he would impatiently repeat if the answer did not immediately come straight and clear.

Often what was complex and baffling to others was perfectly clear to Szilard. At these moments, he would look at his listener, shake his head impatiently, and say, "You'll never understand." His friends devised the "Szilard Index" based on the number of sentences a speaker could finish before Szilard got bored and — often rather rudely — walked out. Part of this was his mighty ego. But behind his arrogance and apparent contempt was a great compassion for humanity that found expression in his tender solicitude toward children and his commitment to the moral use of knowledge. "A scientist must have certain qualities to be creative," he said, "and the moral qualities are very important. Intelligence is not enough. There must be a religious attitude. By that I mean an inner conviction that life has a meaning. Einstein said and I agree, 'Religion without science is blind, science without religion is lame.'"[15]

In late 1957 Lawrence informed Sproul that he might step down as director of the Rad Lab, after creating and running it with iron-fisted control for more than a quarter of a century. To the elderly former physics department chairman who had hired him nearly three decades before, he talked wistfully about returning to LeConte Hall, where he had arrived as a young physicist from Yale in 1929, and simply puttering around a small laboratory in his office.

It seemed unthinkable that Lawrence would ever scale back to such an extent, but he had his reasons. By shedding the burdens he was carrying, Lawrence hoped to relieve the painful ulcers that were aggravated by the pressures under which he had worked for so long. But it was not to be. In 1958 Eisenhower asked Lawrence to serve as one of three U.S. scientists at a technical conference in Geneva to study whether detection measures were feasible for a suspension of nuclear tests. Lawrence, who favored limiting nuclear tests, answered the president's call despite feeling worse than usual. On the way to Washington for briefings, he stopped in St. Louis to visit Compton, who was himself in the hospital recovering from a heart attack. Among other things, the old experimenter told a sympathetic Compton that limits must be put on nuclear experiments in order to control the arms race.

At Geneva, Lawrence was exhausted and uncomfortable. His intestinal bleeding increased rapidly and he grew more silent each day. Violently ill, he ran a high fever and had to be flown back home, where he was immediately admitted to a hospital. The attending physicians did what they could, but his condition worsened. (The Radiation Laboratory founder adamantly refused to submit to X rays.) Lying in his hospital bed, Lawrence apologized to his wife, Molly, "You know, I wish I'd taken more time off. I would have liked to, you know, but my conscience wouldn't let me."[16] The doctors decided they had to perform a colostomy, a difficult operation that removes the lower section of the digestive tract. Very discouraged, Lawrence was convinced that he would not survive the surgery. Five hours into the ordeal, as his circulatory system failed, he turned to Molly at his side in the operating room and whispered, "I'm ready to give up now."[17] He died at Stanford University Hospital on August 27, 1958, shortly after his fifty-seventh birthday.

Only fifty years old when his security hearing ended in 1954, Robert Oppenheimer was at the height of his abilities and chafed at his forced exile from power. He missed being at the center of scientific action, and the telephone calls from secretaries of state and four-star generals. "He still carried on," said Hans Bethe, but "he was a broken man."[18] His brother, Frank, sensed that he felt defeated by his enemies. "The fact that he was kicked out in this way really got him down," Frank said.[19]

Washington and weapons no longer part of his life, Oppenheimer settled into dignified exile as director of the Institute for Advanced Study. Sitting in his office, he often found himself full of both outrage and regret. Here he was, in one of the most splendid of honorific jobs, but his powers were rusting. He could not help thinking things in Washington would be in better shape if he had not been denied clearance. The creative and organizational energies he once devoted to physics and politics were still running strong and sought an outlet.

Oppenheimer was gradually able to get back to reading, thinking, and talking about physics — his first love — but he would never again be the politically naive professor he had been in the 1930s, when he was so indifferent to the world around him that he did not read newspapers. "I should think," he said now, "that you wouldn't step twice in the same river." His ego and his evangelism would not permit him to withdraw from the public stage, so he became a much-traveled and much-interviewed celebrity who had a talent for self-dramatization and an ability to project a larger-than-life image to his audience. None of this, however, could make up for the sadness and the sense of loss in his life.

Oppenheimer received many visitors during these years. The white, unadorned walls of his office contained a blackboard at one end and a large window looking out on a rich green lawn at the other, with books piled neatly on a metal desk and conference table in between. But if the room was serene, the man occupying it was not. Oppenheimer chain-smoked or puffed on a pipe, pausing nervously to fill it, light it, and relight it from a big box of wooden matches. He fidgeted constantly. He talked cautiously and nervously, usually only in response to questions. There was much he wanted to say but did not because he didn't want to appear to be seeking sympathy. When asked about his feelings — Was he bitter? Did he feel mistreated by the government he had worked for so hard? Was he hurt? — Oppenheimer declined to answer, refusing, as he said, to "bare his soul."[20] All he said about himself was this: "I have tried to prove that a security risk can survive. . . . I had two alternatives. One was to seek ways to appeal the decision. I didn't think we'd buy ourselves anything by that. The other was to prove that, in spite of some incredible words the commission wrote about me, these words would not necessarily be believed by all people. In other words, I had to establish by other means that what was put out as a final judgment about me wasn't the final judgment. And the only way to do this was by surviving."[21] He believed in a religion of endurance.

In 1957 the Atoms for Peace Award had been established in the United States to honor the individual who had contributed most to the peaceful uses of atomic energy "without regard to the recipient's political inclinations or nationality." On October twenty-fourth that year, President Eisenhower had presented the award to Bohr at the National Academy of Sciences in Washington. The citation read: "Niels Bohr personifies the modern advances in science and the concern of the man of science for the broad human implications of scientific knowledge." Applause rolled through the room as the aging, moonfaced Bohr had shuffled to his feet to accept the award. As the applause mounted, shouts could be heard above the uproar, for Bohr not only was esteemed and loved by the audience but stood for all that they wanted physicists to be — and believed they could be, given enough courage and insight. Bohr lived out the final years of his life in quiet retirement in his native Denmark. He died of heart failure at the age of seventy-seven on November 18, 1962. His remains were cremated and his ashes interred in the family cemetery in Copenhagen.

Always one to place himself at the center of things, Szilard continued to argue that the same qualities that produced the atomic bomb would be needed to solve the political and social problems that the bomb created: originality, imagination, resourcefulness, and hard work. His method of attacking the problem was, as in all things, energetic and eccentric. He moved about by train and plane, dictating letters and articles in paper-strewn hotel rooms, crisscrossing the country and the world proselytizing against the nuclear arms race and the Cold War. Sometimes he seemed to take impish delight in creating around himself an air of mystery. A freewheeling genius who preferred working behind the scenes, he generated ideas for people in power and spouted advice to anyone who would listen. He also sought contact with Soviet scientists. His idea was simple yet revolutionary: get scientists themselves to address and solve the problem they had created. This notion materialized in a series of "Pugwash Conferences on Science and World Affairs" that began in the summer of 1957 at the Nova Scotia village of Pugwash, where industrialist Cyrus Eaton offered the scientists use of his estate. The Pugwash Conferences soon became the leading forum for international discussion of the nuclear arms race. At these meetings, Szilard offered proposals to avoid a nuclear cataclysm, many of which would eventually be adopted: creating a Washington-Moscow hotline; reducing stockpiles and limiting proliferation; renouncing first use; devising inspection systems; improving command and control to prevent accidents and hair-trigger launches. He also proposed what would later be called "minimal deterrence" by urging the United States and the Soviet Union to stop their nuclear tests, yet retain just enough weapons to deter each other.[22] Szilard resisted the scholasticism that characterized many academic arms control debates. He did not believe nuclear weapons could, or should, be eliminated; but they should be minimized and their use negated by political accord. He favored multilateral disarmament, carried out step-by-step with proper guarantees.

But while Szilard's proposals were farsighted, he lacked both the subtlety necessary to influence the Washington establishment that would have to carry them out and the patience for the bureaucratic scramble that preceded and followed decisions. He habitually moved outside established channels to try to get things done. His satire did not go over well in a serious and self-important city like Washington and his actions invited suspicion in Cold War America. FBI agents kept him under surveillance long after the Manhattan Project. Still his influence reached official channels, at least indirectly. One route ran through the President's Science Advisory Committee (PSAC), where colleagues sympathetic to Szilard's ideas had access to the White House. "Szilard kept us interested in the subject of arms control," recalled Bethe, who was a PSAC member, "and later on that committee, in turn, sponsored the Arms Control and Disarmament Agency, a part of the government."[23]

Szilard clashed often with Teller during these years; he was one of very few people to whom Teller would seriously listen when there was a disagreement. The two debated on national TV in the fall of 1960. They agreed that the danger of nuclear war was great, noted Szilard, "but Teller meant this danger is great if the U.S. government should listen to me, and I meant the danger was great if the U.S. government should listen to him." As their argument deepened, Szilard suggested, "I think, Teller, we should shake hands because maybe later on we don't." The studio audience laughed and applauded, but this did not keep the two from sparring more aggressively. During one heated exchange, when Teller accused Szilard of "irresponsible trustfulness" toward the Russians, Szilard in turn blamed Teller for his "irresponsible distrust."[24]

Around this time Szilard was diagnosed with bladder cancer, considered terminal by most doctors. But true to character, Szilard did the unexpected: he did not die. He took control of his medical treatment, demanding that a detailed course of radiation worked out by him and his wife, Trude, be administered. The doctors followed his orders, and he was thoroughly cured, although his recovery took the better part of a year. During that time, his hospital room became his office and the hospital solarium his receiving room. Not surprisingly, when Szilard was discharged, the hospital was even more relieved to be rid of Szilard than Szilard was to be rid of the hospital.

When Compton learned of Szilard's bladder cancer in early 1960, he wrote his onetime Met Lab colleague — who had caused him so much trouble with Groves and others in Washington — a nostalgic and moving letter, so open in its emotions that it touched its usually gruff recipient:

Dear Leo:

First let me tell of my deep and sincere sorrow at the news of your serious illness.

Let me further say that with the passing years I have become more clearly aware of the sincerity and earnestness and effectiveness of your efforts to turn the development of nuclear energy to the preservation of freedom and the meeting of man's human needs throughout the world.

It is true that we have not always seen eye to eye as to how these humane ends could best be achieved. But of the sincerity of your intent I have never had a doubt. Also your clear understanding of human reactions is impressive to me, and has led you to foresee with unusual clarity, some trends of history.

May I venture the prediction, which neither of us will probably be able to test, that history will see you not only as one of the important initiators of the "atomic" age but also as one who labored bravely to make of that age a condition of life under which men could enjoy an increasing degree of safety and mutual confidence, in spite of the threats of war.

With sincere friendship,
Arthur C [25]

Two years later, while on a speaking visit to Berkeley, Compton died of a cerebral hemorrhage on March 15, 1962. He was sixty-nine.

As for Szilard, he continued to fight for the issues he cherished, and to struggle with the nuclear fears that haunted him. One night in October 1962 friends saw how deeply he suffered. The Cuban Missile Crisis was at its height. Russian ships were plowing through the Caribbean toward Cuba, American naval vessels waiting to confront them. Szilard sat in his hotel room on Dupont Circle in Washington in the depths of despair. In a moody and rambling talk he confessed that he had failed to control the weapon he had helped create. He viewed himself as the inventor of a monster which soon might destroy the world. "What can be done?" a visitor asked. "Nothing," Szilard answered, his face pale with fear. "It is hopeless." He had failed — he had created a Frankenstein. The next day he packed his bags and flew to Switzerland to ride out the coming disaster.

Oppenheimer's exile had eased gradually with the passage of years. When John F. Kennedy became president in 1961, Oppenheimer's friends, such as McGeorge Bundy and Arthur Schlesinger Jr., moved into high posts in the administration and began seeking ways to restore the physicist's reputation. In 1962 Oppenheimer was invited to a White House dinner for Nobel laureates. Although he was not a laureate himself, Oppenheimer stood out among the honorees who shared the evening with him. During the event, AEC chairman Glenn Seaborg approached Oppenheimer and asked if he would like to have another security hearing to restore his clearance. "Not on your life," replied Oppenheimer with utter certainty.

Since Oppenheimer could not regain his clearance without a new hearing, the best alternative was the Fermi Award, the highest honor the U.S. government could bestow for service in the field of nuclear energy. On April 5, 1963, the White House announced that the Fermi Award would go to Oppenheimer. Oppenheimer immediately issued a statement. "Most of us look to the good opinion of our colleagues, and to the goodwill and the confidence of our government. I am no exception." There was some residual opposition among Oppenheimer's old enemies, but most reaction was positive. "In Victor Hugo's tale," wrote one admirer, "they first decorated the hero, and then shot him. Happily in your case, the order is reversed." Rabi wrote him:

> Dear Robert,
> You must feel like a voyager on a ship when after a long journey the sailor on the crow's nest cries, Land, Land!
>
> I wish the reaction to the award could have been a simple Congratulations but there is too much history for simple rejoicing. The dismal years when injustice, paranoia and hypocrisy seemed to prevail remain all too vivid in the memory.
>
> Now in addition to our gratification perhaps we can hope for better things to come.
>
> Love to you and Kitty,
> Rabi[26]

A handwritten note also arrived from Edward Teller:

> Dear Oppie,
> I just heard on the radio that you are getting the Fermi Award of 1963. This makes me happy for many reasons.
>
> One is the memory of our work together in Berkeley in 1942. The other is your proposal which had become known as the Baruch Plan and

which is the only honest and effective suggestion in this field that was ever made.

I had been often tempted to say something to you. This is the one time I can do so with full conviction and knowing that I am doing the right thing.

I enjoyed getting the Fermi prize last year. If you had gotten it first it might have been perhaps better. But I am glad that the announcement was made early, so you have more time for the pleasure.

With sincere wishes for good luck — which we all need,

Edward

Oppenheimer responded to Teller with a short, conciliatory note of his own:

Dear Edward:
Thank you for writing to me. I am very glad that you did.
With good wishes,

Robert Oppenheimer[27]

On the morning of November 22, 1963, the White House announced President Kennedy's intention to present the award personally to Oppenheimer on December second. Less than twelve hours later, Kennedy was dead in Dallas. On the appointed day — twenty years after Oppenheimer had left Berkeley for Los Alamos and ten years after a "blank wall" had been placed between him and government secrets — President Johnson awarded him the Fermi Medal in the cabinet room of the White House. Once remarkably youthful for his years, Oppenheimer was now, at fifty-nine, painfully thin, gray, and wearied. Overcome with emotion, he grasped Kitty's hand as the president spoke. Oppenheimer silently reflected on the situation and the medal for a few moments and then, turning to Johnson, he said, "I think it is just possible, Mr. President, that it has taken some charity and some courage for you to make this award today. That would seem to me a good augury for all our futures." His eyes shone with unshed tears as he spoke.

After the ceremony, Oppenheimer and Teller posed in a handshake of reconciliation. Both behaved with scrupulous politeness. The former adversaries tried to put the past behind them, to close the wound between them. Teller told the press, "I respect Robert Oppenheimer. There are many things that I admire in him." Oppenheimer, who always found it hard to keep a feud going and was prone to forgive anyone who showed him affection — whatever he really thought of them and their politics — said, "For a long time I thought of Edward Teller as a friend. I do not think of him as an enemy."[28] Kitty would have none of it. The cold look on her face as she watched her husband shake Teller's hand told an entirely different story.

The world still in one piece, in early 1964 Szilard and his wife moved to La Jolla, California, a picturesque seaside village north of San Diego, where he accepted a fellowship at the new Salk Institute for Biological Studies. His bout with bladder cancer had left him thinner and his shock of brown hair had turned gray. He had decided to settle down for the first time in his hectic life because, as he said, La Jolla's sunny climate and ocean surf offered a "foretaste of paradise." He bought a small cottage on Torrey Pines Road, a winding, two-lane coastal road with stunning views of the blue sea below. Most afternoons he sat in a deck chair on the open veranda of the Salk Institute, staring at the sunlight dancing across the Pacific, thinking and churning. He had a rich inner world that engaged him, but his worries about the bomb kept him restless. He died in his sleep on the night of May 30, 1964, at the age of sixty-six, taken by a massive heart attack.*

"Leo Szilard was a very complex personality," Bethe said in summing up his colleague's extraordinary life. "His mind worked quickly and profoundly, and he was able to come to ideas that most of us appreciated only after many hours of talk. He was always ahead of his time."[29] Indeed, Szilard propounded ideas which initially were scoffed at as ridiculous, but had an odd way of looking like hard-headed realism within a few years. He had, of course, been the first scientist to imagine a chain reaction and realize that an atomic bomb was thus possible. During the war, while others toiled at making the bomb a reality, his mind was already exploring what the world would be like after the bomb had been made. This ability to see things honestly and perceptively made him a sage observer of human affairs. His vision of the future applied to politics as much as it did to science, as he once made clear:

---

* Shortly before Szilard died, he said that he wanted his ashes tied to a helium balloon and sent skyward. People, he said, should look up rather than down. But — as had been the case with so many of Szilard's ideas — without him there to fight, pester, and promote, nothing happened. His ashes, kept in a California crematory after his death, would finally be buried during the centenary of his birth in 1998.

Politics has been defined as the art of the possible. Science might be defined as the art of the impossible. The crisis which is upon us may not find its ultimate solution until the statesmen catch up with the scientists and politics, too, becomes the art of the impossible.

This, I believe, might be achieved when statesmen will be more afraid of the atomic bomb than they are afraid of using their imagination, because imagination is the tool which has to be used if the impossible is to be accomplished.[30]

The Fermi Award symbolized Oppenheimer's redemption in official circles. His return to Los Alamos the following spring marked a different kind of redemption, a sentimental homecoming among old friends. In May 1964 Oppenheimer returned to the Hill for his first public appearance there since the war. Much had changed in nineteen years. The Los Alamos he knew no longer existed. Few of the old buildings remained. Most of the original Tech Area had been demolished and the laboratory had been shifted across Los Alamos Canyon. A bridge now separated the vast laboratory from the town, which by 1964 had become a good-sized city, a key component of America's sprawling Cold War military-industrial complex. Oppenheimer was also different, now a skeleton of skin and bones. Yet in other — more important — respects, he had not changed: his voice still resonated and his mind was as sharp as it had ever been.

Oppenheimer had come to Los Alamos to give a memorial address in honor of Niels Bohr and to reconnect with an important place from his past. It was an emotional occasion for the man who had founded the desert laboratory and had learned so much from Bohr. The cavernous auditorium of Los Alamos High School — which had not even existed when he left in 1945 — was jammed when Norris Bradbury introduced Oppenheimer and noted that he had built Los Alamos by the sheer force of his personality and character. Bradbury's next sentence was drowned out by applause that rippled from the front row and gathered to a prolonged, standing ovation.

Oppenheimer was deeply moved by the outpouring of respect and affection. A sensitive man who hated to show emotion, he fought back his tears. He ruminated on the passage of time and all that had happened to him. His mind went back to his walks around Ashley Pond with Bohr, where the two had first discussed how the atomic bomb they were making would change the world. A tiny figure at the podium of the auditorium, Oppenheimer told his audience that the nuclear arms race that Bohr had feared, and struggled to avert, had reached mindless proportions. America and Russia each possessed not tens or hundreds but thousands of nuclear bombs, an arsenal of unimaginable destruction made infinitely more dangerous by each country's suspicion and distrust of the other. New means of delivery and use made command and control of these weapons a nightmare fully known only to those responsible; they had added accident to anger as another potential cause of catastrophe. What Bohr and Oppenheimer had learned first, and some in government had learned since, all people should know and every government should understand: if another major war occurred in which nuclear weapons were used, no country could count on having enough living to bury their dead.

Yet Oppenheimer remained optimistic despite these dangers, he said, because of Bohr. "Bohr often spoke with deep appreciation of mortality," said Oppenheimer, whose words — consciously or not — could be used to describe himself: "mortality that screens out the mistakes, the failures, and the follies that would otherwise encumber our future, and that makes it possible that what we have learned, and what has proved itself is transmitted for the next generations."[31] When he finished, the audience rose in loud and sustained applause.

Oppenheimer never returned to Los Alamos again.

A bout of pneumonia the following year weakened Oppenheimer badly, and he had to give up the directorship of the Institute, accepting Einstein's old post as senior professor of theoretical physics instead. Then he was diagnosed with throat cancer. He began radiation therapy, gave up smoking, and took to sucking lozenges to ease his sore and swollen throat. He was in considerable pain, but he went to his office each day. His spirit grew stronger as his bodily powers declined. He was simple, straightforward, and indomitably courageous.

By now, Oppenheimer had become less nervous than he had been in the past, and he met the misfortune that befell him with determination. Criticism did not bother him as much as it once had. He still reacted passionately to events and was no less self-absorbed, but he had learned to control himself. Tempered by the fire, he seemed to have acquired a new, steely resolve. Those around him saw the arrogance of his earlier years dissolve, replaced by a healthy irony about himself, a humility, a compassion, a gentleness. He once again recalled his legendary partnership with Lawrence in the 1930s with affection. He began to examine himself searchingly, as he did at a public forum in the summer of 1966:

> Up to now and even more in the days of my almost infinitely prolonged adolescence, I hardly took any action, hardly did anything, or failed to do anything, whether it was a paper on physics, or a lecture, or how I read a book, how I talked to a friend, how I loved, that did not arouse in me a very great sense of revulsion and of wrong.
>
> It turned out to be impossible . . . for me to live with anybody else, without understanding that what I saw was only one part of the truth . . . and in an attempt to break out and be a reasonable man, I had to realize that my own worries about what I did were valid and were important, but that they were not the whole story, that there must be a complementary way of looking at them, because other people did not see them as I did. And I needed what they saw, needed them.

To a historian who came to interview him in Princeton for a documentary film about Fermi, Oppenheimer whispered, when the taping was over, "Well, when do we get down to the real business, the real interviews, the real historical personal material?"[32] He was prepared at last to look at himself, and to speak of himself, searchingly and honestly.

A few months before his death, Oppenheimer sat for one final, on-the-record interview. Fighting with stoic grace the painful throat cancer that would soon kill him, he amiably greeted the reporter. He wore a brown tweed jacket, dark slacks, and scuffed shoes. His large blue eyes shone brightly over reading glasses. He was very frail, with deep lines in his face and his hair a white mist. There was all of the quickness of his mind and none of the abrasiveness. The once elegant and rich voice was now only a scraping hush.

Oppenheimer took off his glasses and let his hands fall to his lap. He hunched up his shoulders and brought forth a crooked smile, in which all the ironies in his life danced and played. Speaking in a gritty voice, he reaffirmed that scientists *were* responsible for the consequences of their work. "The central question is this," he said: "how to subject the development of [nuclear] weapons to a notion of what is right." He recalled what Bohr had said during their wartime talks: that the atomic bomb was both a peril *and* a hope for mankind. "Very great evil is inherent in weaponry," Oppenheimer said, "and where there is great evil is the opportunity for great good. We have forgotten now, but right after the war, this is what people were saying: that the discovery of atomic power was good, that, among other things, it created an opportunity for great human grandeur because one was dealing with such great dimensions of evil. Atomic power is *not* the same old problem of evil with which man has always been confronted, but you lose an essential dimension when you view it without considering good and evil." He regretted that the world had grown to include many other atomic powers and believed the United States bore much responsibility for this. "As long as we say, 'It is all right for us, but don't you do it,'" Oppenheimer sadly predicted, "efforts to prevent proliferation aren't going to be very effective." About the future, he said: "I'm not very sanguine, but at least the ideas I expressed are no longer radical."[33]

Oppenheimer remained preoccupied with the morality of nuclear weapons and his role in their creation for the rest of his days. It was not long before his death that, speaking of the role he played in building the atomic bomb, he said he was not entirely free of guilt.[34] Two weeks before the end came, he told Rudolf Peierls, the head of the British wartime team at Los Alamos who had come to see him a final time at Princeton, that he should have resigned from the GAC as soon as Truman overruled his recommendation against the superbomb. "You know," Oppenheimer told Peierls, "there is the attitude that says, 'As long as I keep riding on this train, it won't go to the wrong destination.'"[35] His tone was one of regret rather than bitterness.

Even as Oppenheimer suffered the final ravages of his illness, he remembered his friends. Unable to attend Bethe's sixtieth birthday celebration in Ithaca in October 1966, he sent Bethe a warm congratulatory telegram instead. Bethe replied with a handwritten note that illustrated the deep bond that had grown between them over the years:

Dear Robert,
Thanks for your especially warm telegram. It was very good to see you two weeks ago. Your words express, better than I can, what I feel for you —admiration, affection, enduring gratitude and friendship.

As ever,
Hans[36]

That same month Oppenheimer wrote friends, "My cancer is spreading rapidly; thus I am being radiated further." In November, "I am much less able to speak and eat now." And in the following February, he wrote, "I am in some pain. . . . my hearing and my speech are very poor." But he was content. "I have to die some year, and mine has been a pretty good life," he remarked to a friend.[37] His friends saw what those at Los Alamos had seen: a man carrying a crushing burden with such style and good humor that all around him felt uplifted by his example. On the night of Saturday, February 18, 1967, Robert Oppenheimer died at his home in Princeton at the age of 62. Kitty had his body cremated and his ashes scattered in the quiet seas of the Caribbean, where in his later years he found the peace that had always eluded him.

Reaction to Oppenheimer's death was swift and moving. "It was as if an older brother had died," lamented Bethe, who added wistfully, "Where he was, there was always life and excitement."[38] "We were friends," said Rabi. "Oppenheimer meant a great deal to me. I miss him."[39] Even in Japan, where atomic bombs created largely out of Oppenheimer's genius had incinerated two cities, there were tributes. Nobel Prize–winning physicist Hideki Yukawa called Oppenheimer "a symbol of the tragedy of the modern nuclear scientists." Perhaps Oppenheimer's Princeton colleague and fellow physicist Abraham Pais put it best: "In the years to come, the physicist will speak of him. So will the historian and the psychologist, the playwright and the poet."[40] There were so many facets to him. "Oppenheimer was a man who was put together of many bright shining splinters" in the perceptive words of Rabi.[41]

It was intensely cold on February 25, 1967, the day that friends, associates, and admirers gathered in Princeton University's Alexander Hall to pay their final respects to J. Robert Oppenheimer. In the front row sat Kitty, Peter, Toni, and Oppenheimer's brother, Frank. Behind them sat many notables of American science and government — among them Rabi and Groves, now white haired, who had flown in on a specially chartered plane to attend the service.

Those who delivered eulogies spoke with visible emotion. Bethe talked movingly of Oppenheimer's time of glory:

> Los Alamos might have succeeded without him, but certainly only with much greater strain, less enthusiasm, and less speed. As it was, it was an unforgettable experience for all the members of the labo-

ratory. There were other wartime laboratories of high achievement, but I never observed in any one of these other groups quite the spirit of belonging together, quite the urge to reminisce about the days of the laboratory, quite the feeling that this was really the great times of their lives.

George Kennan, who had become Oppenheimer's colleague at the Institute for Advanced Study, recalled a poignant story. "In the dark days of the early 1950s," said Kennan, "when troubles crowded in upon him from many sides and when he found himself harassed by his position at the center of the controversy, I drew his attention to the fact that he would be welcome in a hundred academic centers abroad and asked him whether he had not thought of taking residence outside this country. With tears in his eyes, he replied, 'Damn it, I happen to love this country.'" "On no one," concluded Kennan, "did there ever rest with greater cruelty the dilemmas evoked by the recent conquest by human beings of a power over nature out of all proportion to their moral strength." Nor was there anyone "who more passionately desired to be useful in averting the catastrophes to which the development of the weapons of mass destruction threatened to lead."[42]

At the end of the service the Juilliard String Quartet performed the adagio and allegro movements of Beethoven's Quartet in C-sharp Minor. Back in the 1930s, the C-sharp minor had been the emblem that Oppenheimer and the aspiring theoretical physicists at his feet in Berkeley had held up to proclaim their own refinement and purity. They had been too innocent to discover that Beethoven had instructed his publisher that "it must be dedicated to Lieutenant General Field Marshal von Stutterheim." The ghost of war had hovered in the background of the seminar rooms where they had dreamed, presaging a future that would haunt each and every one of them. Oppenheimer came to understand this irony and commented on it in the last years of his life. "The atom bomb and nuclear weapons will not go away," he said. "These weapons are as present as the desire to have them and to use them. We can only hope that they will increasingly appear irrelevant and thus in the end preposterous, that some day we will look back ashamed of how stupid we were [to want them]."[43]

"Our experience in World War II had a profound effect on the scientific community," I. I. Rabi had said after the war. "We saw how our command of scientific knowledge and method, aided by vast sums of money and support, have made it absurdly easy to kill human beings. This fateful truth has brought home to many scientists the fact that they cannot escape the social responsibility of their actions. No longer can science be just 'fun and games.' "[44] This realization had changed the direction of Rabi's life. He gave up experimental physics and began advising the government. Trips to Washington came with increasing frequency. Demanding positions on the GAC and the PSAC did not impede his bursts of laughter in moments of amusement, nor did they impede his concern for the state of science and society. A quiet and self-confident man who projected toughness with a smile, Rabi played the inside game, operating behind the scenes to help chart America's course in the new world that the atomic age had created. "I thought that by working from within, we might be able to do something about getting rid of the atomic bomb," he said later.[45] Rabi confined his opinion to the inner councils of government, but in those councils he never had the slightest fear of speaking his mind to anyone.

Throughout these years Rabi had worked closely with Oppenheimer. They had served together on the powerful GAC: Oppenheimer as its first chairman, Rabi succeeding him in 1952. Some physicists questioned the propriety of Rabi succeeding Oppenheimer after his close friend had been hounded from government service. The pragmatic Rabi had offered a quick reply. "If I had quit in a huff, I would have gotten two lines in the *New York Times*, and nobody would ever listen to me again on these questions. If I want to have any influence on what's going on, I have to stay on the inside."[46] His style as an adviser differed from Oppenheimer's. Rabi stayed out of the limelight. He was quiet and wise, where Oppenheimer had been vocal and brilliant. Rabi deliberately played second fiddle because he wanted to be effective. "During the war," he said, "I had learned that you either get the credit or you get it done."[47] Rabi wanted to get it done.

When he was not advising the government, he was teaching. Every morning until he retired as professor of physics at Columbia University, the short, bantamlike Rabi put on his horn-rimmed glasses, left his faculty apartment on Riverside Drive overlooking the Hudson River, and strolled up a gentle slope to Pupin Hall, a red-brick pile with limestone trim, where he rode an elevator to his eighth-floor office. Colleagues always knew when he got off the elevator because he hummed as he walked down the corridor. Inside his large, plain office was a huge blackboard that ran the length of an entire wall to large double windows, beneath which sat a green couch stacked with learned journals. He always kept his door open, did his own filing, and answered his own telephone. He maintained close, warm relations with people ranging from Nobel Prize–winning physicists to freshman students.

Rabi's old sparring partner, Edward Teller, became the bête noire of liberals, who caricatured him as an amoral and unbalanced scientist. Teller's volatile temperament and forbidding appearance contributed to this impression. Always headstrong, he was quick to denounce any and all who opposed him. To a physicist who challenged him on arms control, he said: "You're either stupid or you're treasonous, and I know you're not stupid."[48] His heavy eyebrows grew even bushier as he aged, giving him the shadowy, almost fierce countenance of the diabolical scientist. He talked with a deep voice in a strong, well-enunciated cadence with an accent that was part European university professor, part Cold War inquisitor, and part Bela Lugosi.

Teller's efforts to make amends for his testimony against Oppenheimer got him nowhere. Ostracized within the physics community after 1954, Teller had made new friends, this time among the military, financiers, industrialists, and conservative politicians. He became an ally and a symbol of the American Right — the only one of the nine physicists to do so. It was not long before he was writing and speechifying like the best of them. The higher he flew with the hawks, the more it seemed to compensate for his ostracism by his peers — and the more he was impelled to justify and rationalize his actions. It was a hard and wearying journey.

Lewis Strauss once said that there were three kinds of physicists: theoretical, applied, and political. Teller was the most political of them all. He became extraordinarily well connected, often gaining access to the highest councils of government denied to scientists of lesser note. *Time* featured him on the cover of its November 18, 1957, issue, presenting Teller in a four-page story as the shining example of U.S. science at its best because he, more than any of his peers, had recognized the accelerating pace of Russian scientific achievement before sputnik. Like many Americans of the time, he was staunchly anticommunist. There was no weapon big enough to make him sleep well in a world where the Soviet Union existed. He was given to doom-laden pronouncements about communists taking over the earth and believed it a dangerous illusion that the West could be protected by proclaiming high moral principles from a position of military weakness.

As a result, Teller became a leading critic of all arms control initiatives, beginning with his fight against a nuclear test moratorium in the late 1950s. Eisenhower, at first favorably disposed toward a moratorium, was partly dissuaded when Teller came to the White House and told him that with continued testing the United States could develop "clean" (fallout free) weapons and that the Soviets could negate any moratorium by undetectable clandestine tests. If America was behind, Teller reasoned, it had to test to catch up; and if it was ahead, it had to test to stay there. As usual, Teller committed himself in an all-or-nothing way. To rally public support, he wrote, lectured, and engaged in radio and television debates with pro–test-ban spokesmen; to rally scientific backing, he helped devise experiments to show how the Russians could cheat on a test-ban agreement if they wanted to; to keep the Livermore lab on its toes in weapons development and ready for testing, he took direct charge of operations there.

The accumulated strains of overwork, added to the animosities that he felt increasingly surrounded him, began to take their toll, both physically and emotionally. His health deteriorated. His ulcerative colitis required daily doses of medicine and a doctor-ordered diet, frustrating for a man who had always devoured food with gusto. To a friend he wrote: "On my last medical checkup it was found that I have the same trouble as Ernest. It is a good thing to imitate him, but it seems I am carrying it too far. I have resigned from many of the things I am now doing and will have to lead a more quiet life."[49] His frustration was compounded by continuous concern for the fate of family members he had left behind in Hungary. Their experiences under communist rule were bitter, and they helped to harden the mistrust and hostility he felt toward the Soviets well into his later years. His former zest now gave way to somberness and black moods of near despair. The more opposition that he encountered, the more relentlessly he drove himself to overcome it — and the more impatient and irritable he became. As his isolation grew, so did his stubbornness, irascibility, and sense of self-importance.

The debate over the Limited Test Ban Treaty — which sought to end hazardous radiation fallout from nuclear explosions in the atmosphere — roused Teller's temper to a fever pitch. The treaty, which had the backing of the Joint Chiefs of Staff, was submitted to the Senate for ratification on August 9, 1963. Eleven days later, on August twentieth, Teller appeared before the Senate Foreign Relations Committee. Members of the Armed Services Committee and the Joint Congressional Committee on Atomic Energy also attended. Teller's testimony was presented without any prepared text or notes and was delivered with his usual great force and conviction. Largely for this reason he received far more attention from press and television than any other witness. He told the senators that the treaty would not make it more difficult for Russia to catch up, as some of its proponents had claimed, because "it is by no means certain that the United States is ahead of the Soviet Union in the field of nuclear explosives."* He added that the treaty should not be passed because the Russians would secretly cheat — they might even do tests behind the moon. He ended by warning the senators that if they ratified the treaty, "You will have given away the future safety of our country and increased the dangers of war."[50] When asked his reaction to Teller's testimony, President Kennedy replied, "It would be very difficult to satisfy Dr. Teller in this field."[51] The Senate agreed with Kennedy, ratifying the Limited Test Ban Treaty on September 23, 1963, by an overwhelming vote of eighty to nineteen. No country has detonated a nuclear weapon in the atmosphere since.

During his last years at Columbia, Rabi taught a course called Philosophical and Social Implications of Twentieth-Century Physics. In it, Rabi tried to show the importance of science to modern life. To Rabi, physics was not mysterious — it was an inspiring quest, a great game — and the playing field was the universe itself. "You're playing with a champ," he told students. "You're trying to find out how God made the world, just like Jacob wrestling with the angel."[52] Rabi wanted people to understand scientists: their hopes and fears, their motivations and insecurities, how they thought and worked, in order to see them as flesh-and-blood human beings. To Rabi, scientists were not remote; they had "a vital role — sometimes one thinks of it as a fatal role" to play in the affairs of the world, he would say.[53] But Rabi increasingly worried that those around him were specialists — technicians, really — who ignored the larger significance of their work. The increasing abstractions of modern physics were leading to less, not more, engagement with the world.

---

* Teller was later proved quite wrong. In 1963 the United States led the Soviet Union by a large margin in both nuclear technology and stockpiled nuclear weapons.

Rabi taught his last class in the spring of 1967, ending a forty-year career at Columbia. He had not enjoyed a reputation as a great lecturer and was feared by students as a tough taskmaster, but he was admired — as he had always been — for his moral integrity and an impeccable taste that set a style for the study of physics. He told his final class that American nuclear power was so vast that it was distorting human relationships. "Just because we got there first," he said, "doesn't mean that we should have the power of life and death over the whole world. When you get that powerful you begin to lose pity for the human condition." He closed on the theme of power and responsibility. "I have spent most of my time in directions that would help us diminish our responsibility — relieve us of this burden" of power over life and death of nations, he said. "Although I have worked very hard," he added, "I have not been very successful."

Retirement held no professional terrors for Rabi, who retained his close connection with Columbia's physics department. But he knew his time on the frontier of physics had passed. "I keep somewhat in touch with it," he observed, "but not in a creative way. I'm always afraid of being a stuffed shirt — making do with pretense rather than actuality."[54] In retirement, Rabi watched as the superpowers continued to build up their nuclear stockpiles to absurd levels. He became discouraged, then dejected, and finally angry. He felt America's blind reliance on military strength threatened the ethical principles on which that strength rested. "Americans are a moral people. They have respect for human life even where there are differences of opinion," he stressed.[55] Rabi declared that every military and political leader in the world with responsibility for nuclear weapons ought to observe in person, as he had, at least one detonation of a nuclear weapon, believing the effect would be so overpowering, so frightening and terrifying, that a sane person could draw only one conclusion: that these weapons must never be used and the only way to ensure that was to abolish them.

Teller's image as a hawk in the 1960s and 1970s was balanced by his repeated calls for scientific openness. He made these requests with deep feeling in the face of bitter criticism from those who assailed him as the mastermind of a ruinous arms race and a mad scientist fixated on mass destruction, some of whom disrupted his talks with raucous shouts of "War Criminal!" (In 1970, radical students burned him in effigy a half block from his Berkeley home.) Teller passionately advocated the abolition of secrecy surrounding scientific research, including classified nuclear work. He argued that open scientific work was necessary "so we can clearly understand what we are talking about" in the growing debate over the impact of science and technology on society — a debate that had aroused in many people a sentiment against technology.[56] "In a time of rapid development," he proclaimed on another occasion, "the greatest danger is ignorance."[57]

By the time he turned seventy in 1978, Teller had experienced so much conflict that it seemed there could hardly be room for any more. But his indomitable will and technological exuberance fed his restless ambition, and he continued to promote big new ideas. Not all of his ideas seemed sensible to others. For example, he conceived that super-bombs could be used to dig a sea-level waterway across Central America as an alternative to the Panama Canal. He also assumed a leading role in pushing the Strategic Defense Initiative (SDI or "Star Wars") during the 1980s, the conservative years of Reagan, whose fierce anti-communism matched Teller's own. Teller lobbied congressmen and administration officials indefatigably on behalf of the SDI. He looked on the SDI — an X-ray laser–based antimissile shield — as a silver bullet of sorts. If the United States could defend itself against nuclear missile attack, Teller reasoned, then it would not need to negotiate with the Soviet Union and it could move from a strategy of mutual assured destruction (popularly known as MAD) to a strategy of assured survival. He also was driven by guilt, confessing to an interviewer that "a good part, an important part, of my own psychology" was trying to negate, with antimissile arms, the horror of nuclear annihilation he had helped to give the world.[58] A theory that might or might not become a reality after years of research, SDI had many problems, not the least of which was Teller's tendency to minimize technical problems, to make extravagant claims, and to describe hypothetical outcomes as if they were virtual accomplishments. Critics began calling Teller "the original E.T." and accused him of wanting to create a "pin-ball outer-space war."[59]

Teller remained active — and controversial — into his nineties. Although bent with age and able to walk only with the aid of a five-foot-high walking staff that he carved himself from a tree limb, he behaved in interviews at his office at the conservative Hoover Institution of Stanford University like a ring-wise veteran boxer instinctively responding to the bell, intent on persuading guests of the rightness of his views. Inevitably, he looked tired and worn in his rumpled suit, wash-and-wear shirt, and striped tie. Teller closed his eyes, grown clouded by ulceration, and put his hand to his temple as his guests asked their questions. The short pause they expected before his reply grew into a long and anxious silence. Then the famously thick brows beetled, the melancholy gray eyes bored in, and the apocalyptic words came out slowly — each of them intense, uncompromising, and opinionated. Many of the lines in the script were familiar, but their effect had only grown through recitation. He spoke emphatically, his Hungarian-accented voice rising to punctuate crucial ideas and falling dramatically to almost a whisper at the end of key arguments — all accompanied by thumps of his staff on the floor. He was by turns gentle and charming, dark and brooding, rude and combative, his moods punctuated by outbursts of wry humor and ill temper. To combat his own weariness and occasional boredom, he would sometimes doze. When something came to mind, however, he would come alive and start talking in great detail. (Once finished, he would start dozing again.) At home he played dreamy Mozart sonatas on his battered Steinway for hours at a stretch in search of emotional solace. He was a strangely restless man, still full of the ambition, the fear, and the sadness that had marked his long and busy life.

"I don't mind dying," Rabi said in a widely watched 1983 public television interview. "My ancestors did that. What I do mind is the destruction of civilization. Take all my work — it is in libraries. Well, all that goes up in smoke. I mean the whole civilization. This is the holy thing which they are violating by pushing in the direction of an annihilating war."[60]

Rabi's use of the word "holy" hinted at something deeper. Religious themes increasingly colored his thinking in his final years, as he explained to a biographer near the end of his life:

Nothing in the world can *move* me as deeply as some of these Orthodox Jewish practices. People go to Israel, to Williamsburg in Brooklyn, or to those places where Orthodox Jews go . . . and they pray and shake back and forth. Some people are appalled by it, but to me it is great. These are my people. I could join them, shake back and forth, and feel all right about it. The thing that saves me from *any* of those feelings is that I'm a scientist which I firmly believe transcends, doesn't oppose, but transcends these particular things. I am of this and there is no question, but I'm not *in* it, couldn't be in it. I love it and I respect it, but as a scientist I am at a more universal level . . . and this comes back to God.[61]

In 1983 Rabi attended a reunion at Los Alamos marking the fortieth anniversary of its founding. He returned to where it all began, back to the sunbaked mesa and a sprawl of buildings more numerous and permanent than those that he had last seen during the war. So much had changed since then — not the least Rabi himself. "I'm seeing an abomination," he said as his car approached Los Alamos. "We should have put it to rest years ago." Later he addressed a large gathering of physicists at the lab. It was an emotionally charged moment, and the fervor of the occasion moved Rabi, whose eyesight was failing but whose conscience was not. "We meant well," the white-haired, bespectacled Rabi declared as his mind went back to wartime Los Alamos.

But the way things developed — and this is the folly — it became a thing in itself. The question now is not so much how to protect civilization, but how to destroy other human beings. We have lost sight of the basic tenets of all religions — that a human being is a wonderful thing. We talk as if humans were matter. . . . There is no way for scientists to escape the responsibilities of their knowledge. . . . We now have nations lined up like those prisoners at Auschwitz, going into the ovens and waiting for the ovens to be perfected, made more efficient. I submit that this fatalistic attitude is very un-American. It is not American to stand around waiting for something to happen, hoping it won't, when you see it on the horizon. It would be much more true to our spirit to understand and prevent it. The United States was founded on a very revolutionary principle[:] . . . the greatness of the human spirit. Somehow, rather than this calculus of destruction, we must get back to our true nature as a nation and as part of western civilization. . . . How do we recover it? We cannot put this evil spirit back into the bottle. We have to learn to live with it.[62]

Rabi's words were received at first with a sound of indrawn breaths, followed by a gigantic, collective sigh — then wave after wave of loud applause. Five years later, on January 11, 1988, I. I. Rabi died at his home in New York City after a long illness. He was eighty-nine.

At a time when most people were happy to slow down, Teller continued to look ahead, championing weapons research and military preparedness after the collapse of the Soviet Union with the same intensity that he had during the height of the Cold War. The specter of bolshevism that had frightened him since his boyhood in Budapest disappeared into the dustbin of history, but the world remained a chaotic, hostile place in his mind and his adopted country remained perpetually at risk. At century's end, when the United States reigned as the world's sole superpower, Teller darkly warned that "America is as vulnerable as Poland was in 1939."[63] The pain, insecurity, and paranoia of his refugee past never left him.

Nor did the emotional sting of his ostracism in the wake of the Oppenheimer affair, despite his public damn-the-world attitude. The wound was extraordinarily deep and long lasting. More than thirty years on, Teller was asked how he had handled his loss. "As best I could," he said in a voice that was so soft it could barely be heard. "Does it hurt?" he was asked. Teller exploded, "None of your business!" He then paused and added in a child's high-low singsong, "Perhaps it does, perhaps it doesn't." There was another long pause. "Of course that hurts! It was meant to hurt, and it did! I acquired a new set of friends at an age when most people make no more friends. In the meantime, I had lots of additional problems." With that, he abruptly ended the line of questioning.[64] After he suffered a stroke in 1996, a nurse quizzed him to probe his lucidity. "Are you the famous Edward Teller?" she asked. "No," he snapped, "I'm the infamous Edward Teller."[65]

Toward the end of his long life, in 2001, Teller finally published his memoirs. They were like the man himself: by turns witty, insightful, defensive, and evasive. In them, Teller summarized his philosophy of nuclear-weapons work: "To my mind, in a democracy, using nuclear weapons is an issue entirely different from that of working on their development. Research on nuclear weapons has provided the United States with the ability to deter the use of nuclear weapons throughout the past half century."[66] The ninety-three-year-old author showed occasional flashes of vulnerability and regret that he had never shown before. Perhaps most revealing was his comment that one of H. G. Wells's lesser-known tales, *The Man Who Could Work Miracles*, gave him "particular pleasure."[67] In Wells's story, a skeptic discovers that he can work miracles. In the process of exploring his new talent, he commands the earth to stand still. That produces a catastrophe, because he forgets to command the atmosphere to stand still, too, and as a result everything is blown away. The man wishes he had never been given his power, and the story ends with the skeptic back in the setting where the tale began, where he undoes his recent past and loses forever the talent to perform miracles. Read as an autobiographical metaphor, Teller's admiration for Wells's tale was highly revealing.

It had been a long life. Presidents had come and gone, but Teller had remained on center stage for decades, building bombs, advising leaders, fashioning himself into a force to be reckoned with. He had become the science hero of the Republican right and the patron saint of the military-industrial complex. He had built up an enormous inventory of incredibly deadly weapons that outlived the Soviet Union that he hated and feared, and he had personally hindered or blocked almost every effort to control the atomic arms race. Teller's obsession with thermonuclear fusion may be recalled as a monumental contribution to a world without major war. But if the world ever plunges into a nuclear Armageddon, its few survivors may regard Teller as the real incarnation of the fictional Dr. Strangelove. Eugene Wigner, the Nobel Prize–winning physicist, said of Teller: "He is the most imaginative person I ever met, and this means a great deal when you consider that I knew Einstein." Rabi saw him quite differently: "He is a danger to all that is important," he said. "I do really feel it would have been a better world without Teller. I think he is an enemy of humanity."[68]

When Hans Bethe had witnessed the first atomic explosion at Trinity and then saw the photographs of the devastation of Hiroshima and Nagasaki, he had been shocked by what he saw — and had helped to create. "Everything starts with Los Alamos — with the atomic bomb," said Bethe. "All the tragedies and all the mistakes that haunt us now begin there."[69] His unease at the destructive power of the bomb had forced him to contemplate disquieting questions and to do what he had not done before: struggle deeply with the moral dilemmas and political implications of his work. After 1945 and for more than half a century, he wrote articles and pamphlets, signed petitions, held press conferences, lectured and debated throughout the world, and occasionally buttonholed important government officials — all in an effort to limit and control the terrible weapon that he and others had brought into the world. Beginning in the 1950s and for several decades thereafter, he chaired the CIA's secret, highly influential panel charged with taking all source information about nuclear activities throughout the world and figuring out what was going on. Bethe worked within the system, wishing that by doing so he could help solve the problems presented by the bomb he and others had created.

Bethe had always been and remained a strapping figure with a deceptively distracted look. His graying hair seemed permanently electrified, his tie studiously arranged to miss his collar button, but he was rigorously logical and he had a strong sense of his own abilities. His self-confidence and the force of his personality made it possible for him to act decisively as a moral agent. In contrast to Oppenheimer, Bethe was the same whether he was dealing with a student, a colleague, the president of Cornell, or a senator in Washington. In a world of intellectual egotists and academic prima donnas, Bethe — who won the Nobel Prize in 1967 — was a modest man who liked to say, "The great day is when the student knows more than the teacher." Approachable, he always left his office door open. "When I arrived at Cornell and introduced myself to the great man," said one of his postwar graduate students, "two things about him immediately impressed me. First, there was a lot of mud on his shoes. Second, the other students called him Hans."[70]

Bethe's activities in the postwar years brought him into repeated conflict with Teller. He opposed Teller on development of the superbomb in the 1950s, the Limited Test Ban Treaty in the 1960s, the atomic arms race in the 1970s, the nuclear freeze and SDI in the 1980s, and the Comprehensive Test Ban Treaty in the 1990s. Unlike Teller, who believed scientists should build ever bigger bombs to make it disastrous for either side to start a war, Bethe doubted such bombs would lead to peace. "No technology race can make us secure," he told a congressional committee in May 1985. "Only negotiation and agreements with the other side and a change in the atmosphere of international relations can do that." Having helped lead the world into the dangerous age of nuclear weapons, Bethe wanted to help lead the world out of it.[71]

Bethe and Teller were two lions contesting the legacy of their momentous creation. Their lifelines had run a parallel course since long ago in prewar Europe, their fates intertwined and even mirror images of each other. Even their temperaments and abilities complemented each other, Teller with his high spirits and free-ranging imagination, Bethe with his seriousness and powerful common sense. "I am tired of arguing with Hans," Teller would grumble with a mixture of irritation and admiration.[72] Bethe showed similar feelings toward

Teller. Throughout their letters to one another over the years ran a warm private relationship threaded with harsh differences on policy, frequent reassurances of personal and professional respect, and an occasional expression of hurtful surprise. Their friendship endured many strains, but each labored to preserve it.

At the height of the SDI debate in the 1980s, Bethe wrote Teller a letter outlining his objections to the program. Teller usually reacted to such criticism with aggressive rebuttals, but he dwelled on more personal matters with Bethe:

> *Dear Hans,*
>
> *It is good to have your objections in writing.*
>
> *I would have liked to respond in a prompt manner, but this was impossible for three reasons. The first is that your objections deserve a thorough answer.*
>
> *The second is that my schedule has been even more crowded than usual, and I could not acquire the necessary time. I confess that one unavoidable commitment was to celebrate my fiftieth wedding anniversary with Mici and all our children and grandchildren in Hawaii.*
>
> *The third and most important reason is that I have gotten into really serious trouble with my heart.*
>
> *Yesterday I had an exhaustive and exhausting catheterization of my heart. Tomorrow or Thursday, when I have recovered enough from that procedure, I will have a four or five bypass heart surgery. If and when I recover I will write to you independently.*
>
> *Edward*[73]

Within months Teller had recovered enough to invite Bethe to visit him at Livermore. Bethe accepted, and made the visit in March 1985. He applauded the efforts of scientists while at Livermore, but repeated his doubts about SDI in articles and interviews thereafter. This prompted a pained response from Teller. "From a personal point of view, all this is very sad and I suspect that our feelings may be similar," he wrote. "At the same time, I must pay more attention to my responsibilities as I see them rather than to my feelings. Indeed, the hope and effort for a useful defense in the strict and narrow sense of the word is the one remaining motivation for which I continue to work."[74]

Bethe replied by forcefully summarizing their differing views on nuclear weapons:

Dear Edward,

I am happy that you wrote. Let me go right to fundamentals. We both want security for the United States and for the world, we both want to prevent a big nuclear war. But we differ fundamentally on how to achieve this goal. You think peace will be preserved by inventing ever new weapons, and by having a technology race. In my opinion, the arms race has made us less and less secure. . . . We are not going to convince each other, and we are both firmly committed to our convictions.

Bethe then reached out across the decades of their differences and dis-agreements:

I remember very fondly the years of our friendship, back in the 1930s and 1940s. I am very sad indeed that politics has separated us so far. But can't we be personally friendly?

Yours sincerely,
Hans[75]

"Thank you for your kind letter," Teller replied several weeks later, then testily asked: "Is peace better assured by negotiation with the Sovi-ets or by working on defense?" "At this time, I do not urge work on weapons of mass destruction, but rather an effective defense against these weapons," he summed up. "The conflict between the Soviets and us strikes me like the religious conflicts and wars lasting from 1517 to at least 1648," Bethe replied, referring to the Protestant Reformation and the ensuing power struggles throughout western Europe. "But must we have the analogy of the Thirty Years War? With nuclear weapons, this would mean the end of civilization in the countries involved, and the ideological differences would become irrelevant."[76]

That summer, Bethe and Teller both found themselves at Los Alamos. A party was held to which each was invited. Bethe arrived first and sat down at a table on the patio, where a group of people sur-rounded him. Then Teller arrived, stomping in in good humor. The hostess said, "Edward, there is someone here I want you to meet," and she took him over to Bethe. They shook hands, sat down, and talked together to the exclusion of everyone else for the rest of the party. They were like two old high-school chums who hadn't seen each other in forty years and had just found one another.[77] Thereafter until ill health and old age slowed them both, Bethe, who visited Caltech each winter, would somehow find a way to see Teller, who was up the California coast at Stanford.[78]

By then, Bethe was in his eighties and the grand old man of American physics. His friendly blue eyes, thin white hair, and broad smile gave him the look of a favorite grandfather. He was deeply troubled by the irrationality and excesses of the nuclear arms race, but he remained what he had always been: thoughtful and meticulous. He still received visitors in his small office lined with bookcases on the third floor of the Newman Laboratory of Nuclear Studies at Cornell. He and his guests sat in straight-backed chairs around a simple metal desk covered with papers as Bethe listened attentively, barely shifting position. His eyes focused hawklike on his visitors as they asked their questions. He paused after each one, considering his response before answering. Then he spoke precisely in his deep, German-accented voice with a strength and orderliness that brooked no interruption but radiated honesty and curiosity. Asked if he sensed himself as a historical figure, he laughed. "Yes," he said, and added: "As my son said after a talk, 'Well, they got it from the horse's mouth. And there aren't so many horses left."[79] His work ethic remained strong, but he preferred to work now on the theory of binary stars — a peaceful theory, he liked to note, one that required experience and wisdom.

As Bethe aged, his interests broadened beyond the natural world to the world of man. He took to reading history — lots of it. A visitor to his home was more likely to see Tacitus's *Germania* than *The Physical Review* on the table by his reading chair. He increasingly put his faith not in technology but in human beings — a remarkable stance for a man who had dedicated his life to science. Only humane reasoning and political understanding, he felt, would prevent nuclear war. "If a man does not constantly ask himself what is the right thing to do," he said, "I do not know what will become of him."[80] Where before he was willing to play the insider in the hope of influencing policy, he now assumed the role of blunt sage and critic. On the fortieth anniversary of the Trinity test in July 1985, Bethe had journeyed to Washington and spoke to Congress like a latter-day Jeremiah:

> The Bible tells us that the children of Israel wandered forty years through the desert. Our desert has been the fear of nuclear war. But I don't see any sign of the Promised Land.
>
> U.S. policy has tried to rely on superior technology. Whenever

there was a chance to make nuclear weapons more devastating, we took it. We introduced the H-bomb and the transcontinental bomber, we escalated the number of nuclear weapons and later that of nuclear missiles, and (worst of all) we introduced MIRV [multiple-warhead missiles]. In every case, the Soviets followed suit, three to five years later, and we were less secure than before. . . .

Nuclear explosives have shattered the meaning of the age-old words "weapon," "war," and "defense." A weapon is intended to achieve some definite military or political objective, but any use of nuclear explosives carries the risk of virtually unlimited destruction. Hence plans that assume that nuclear devices can be used to wage war are irrational. Nuclear "weapons" have only one purpose — that of deterring war. . . .

The first forty years of the nuclear age should have taught us that we have only two choices: mutual security or mutual insecurity. During the past forty years we have blundered, and in effect chose mutual insecurity. In the next forty years we must strive for mutual security. If we do we will steadily decrease the risk of nuclear war, and restore confidence that we are masters of our fate.[81]

Ten years later, on the fiftieth anniversary of Hiroshima in August 1995, Bethe returned to Los Alamos and implored scientists there to withhold their talents from creating new weapons of mass destruction. "Enough is enough," he said in a weak but insistent voice, speaking from notes written in a careful but shaky hand. "We shouldn't design any more."[82] He issued this statement:

As director of the Theoretical Division of Los Alamos, I participated at the most senior level in the World War II Manhattan Project that produced the first atomic weapons.

Now, at the age of 88, I am one of the few remaining such senior persons alive. Looking back at the half-century since that time, I feel the most intense relief that these weapons have not been used since World War II, mixed with the horror that tens of thousands of such weapons have been built since that time — one hundred times more than any of us at Los Alamos could ever have imagined.

Today we are rightly in an era of disarmament and dismantlement of nuclear weapons. But in some countries nuclear development still continues. Whether and when the various nations of the world can agree to stop this is uncertain. But individual scientists can still influence this process by withholding their skills.

Accordingly, I call on all scientists in all countries to cease and desist from work creating, developing, improving and manufacturing further nuclear weapons — and for that matter, other weapons of potential mass destruction such as chemical and biological weapons.

Hans Bethe[83]

These confessions were part of a gradual but powerful disaffection with the profession of nuclear weaponeering he had done so much to create. In his final years, Bethe grew acutely sensitive to the moral implications of the bomb. "I still believe that we contributed to the security of the United States" in first developing the atomic bomb, he said. "However, while working on weapons I wonder whether our security was really served by their perfection." He paused. "It seemed quite logical," he said in defense of the choices he had made, then added almost wistfully: "But sometimes I wish I were more consistent an idealist."[84] His poignant remark captured the dilemma that each of the atomic scientists confronted, and resolved, with varying degrees of success and guilt. Bethe took to quoting the famous dictum: "Sin must needs come into the world, but woe to him who brings it about." "Perhaps that applies to us," he confessed.[85]

The Atomic Scientists
and Today

TODAY THE GREAT blue sky of New Mexico meets the parched white sand of its high desert just as it did early on the morning of July 16, 1945, but now flowers and scrub grow, camera crews shoot footage, and tourists inspect the parched ground of Trinity Site. All that is left of the giant steel tower where the first atomic bomb exploded 100 feet above ground are the melted tentacles of one of its legs. Nearby is a squat obelisk of black lava rock commemorating the event and a patch of sand scorched so intensely that July morning in 1945 that it was fused into green glass called trinitite. Despite the faded warning on the fence around the site, radiation has long since dropped to tolerable levels. The area is closed to the public, but twice a year — on the first Saturday of April and October — the U.S. government opens the site, part of the normally restricted White Sands Missile Range, so that people can make a pilgrimage to the spot where the nuclear age began. The number of visitors, a trickle at first, has grown steadily over the years.

B Reactor, which opened in 1944, rises above the desolate semidesert plain at Hanford, in southeastern Washington, a windowless, dilapidated, and ominous landmark of the nuclear age. The brass-knobbed control room containing the reactor's looming panel of antique nozzles and tubes looks as if Enrico Fermi had just gotten up from his chair. Here, where the plutonium for the Nagasaki bomb was bred in gigantic piles, underground tanks containing the country's greatest concentration of radioactive wastes have been leaking for decades. Because of the contamination, the byproduct of fifty years of nuclear weapons production, the government allows only occasional visitors, and nobody younger than eighteen. Yet this hazardous structure, a crucible of the Manhattan Project, may become a national landmark, too. The U.S. Department of Energy, at the behest of Congress, is studying the feasibility of decontaminating and preserving B Reactor, and perhaps one day opening it to the public. They are also considering the Ice House on Ashley Pond in Los Alamos, where components for the first atomic bomb were stored, and a fragment of the sprawling, forty-four-acre K-25 building in Oak Ridge where U-235 was separated for the Hiroshima bomb. Nations traditionally make monuments of their most important places — even those that evoke unpleasant and painful memories — and the birthplaces of the atomic bomb are no exception. "When you're standing in front of the reactor," said a visitor to Hanford in the spring of 2001, "you realize this is what humans can do if pushed to the limit. It's a great place to contemplate war."[1]

When Otto Hahn stumbled upon fission in December 1938, he had no idea that his discovery would mark the first step on the road to an atomic bomb. When news of Hiroshima and Nagasaki reached Hahn in August 1945, he was so shocked and aggrieved at how his discovery had been used that his friends were afraid he would kill himself. Hahn's discovery reminds us that science, like all human endeavors, is unpredictable — full of unanticipated and unwanted consequences. It is a cautionary tale of what comes from unleashing forces that one neither fully understands nor controls. Individuals, no matter how intelligent and well meaning, can rarely see far enough ahead to know the effect of their actions.

So it was with the atomic scientists. The bomb changed them, and the world, in ways they could not have foreseen or even imagined. Before the war physicists almost never occupied themselves with problems and questions that could in any way be called practical. During the war they gave up pure science and built a terrible weapon of mass destruction. In some ways, it is not hard to understand their decision. Nazism had to be fought, and since the Nazis might be making atomic bombs, then the Manhattan Project physicists had to make them, too; they had no choice. They felt a patriotic desire to serve their cause and country in an hour of danger, and in this endeavor they did not want to lose a single moment.

They were also quite unaccustomed, by nature and by nurture, to pondering any nonscientific implications of their work. No ethical framework or sensibility existed for them because of the abstract nature of prewar physics. It was an aesthetic pursuit wholly unrelated to questions of politics and morality. They were discoverers, not inventors. The physical universe they worked in had its own set of rules and was so absolutely pure that it isolated them — or so they thought — from the world of man. Compelled by the exigencies of war and their received outlook on science, they did not stop to consider the long-term effects of what they were doing until after the bomb had been made.

Of course, the atomic bomb was an untried weapon; they did not make the decision to use it; they did not pilot the plane that dropped it. Their sense of personal responsibility was diluted by distance, by evasion, by denial, and by the way in which creation of the weapon was shared by so many people. All of these things diminished their moral sensitivity and made them feel removed from responsibility. The few among them who did confront these unsettling issues either argued against using the bomb on Japan or felt that war itself forced a stark choice among lesser evils and that using the bomb to end it was the moral price that had to be paid. It brought death to innocent civilians, but it also brought surrender and peace.

Once this first, albeit uneasy, moral compromise had been made, the atomic scientists found it less difficult and disquieting to make subsequent compromises. The mysteries of fission and then fusion had a seductive appeal to those who had devoted their lives to physics and whose curiosity was insatiable. To understand and exploit nature at its most fundamental and powerful level was an intoxicating exercise of human intelligence and imagination that compelled curious minds to make ever more destructive weapons.

The feeling of power was difficult to resist. Nuclear weapons became all important to the state, and so therefore did the exceptional minds that created them. This link powerfully reinforced and magnified the egos and ambitions of physicists who saw the development of atomic and then thermonuclear weapons as the grandest arenas for the exercise of their vast talents. The secrecy and funding that surrounded these exercises made professional rivalries more intense and lent a false glamour to the new technology. Physicists understood, even if they did not often acknowledge, that a fundamental change had occurred. The prewar functions of a physicist — teaching and basic research — had given way to an entirely different postwar function — huge and costly weaponeering driven by an almost mindless momentum.

The atomic scientists rationalized all of this by reasoning that the bomb's destructive power was so vast that it would become obvious to political leaders throughout the world that war would no longer be a rational means for achieving political goals, no matter what those goals were. They desperately wanted to believe that the death and destruction of World War II — culminating in Hiroshima and Nagasaki — would never be repeated, and that the bomb they had created would be the ironic but irrefutable instrument for not repeating them. They had mastered the atom *and* they had made all-out war obsolete.

In the ensuing years, as the atomic scientists became wiser, more mature, and more sophisticated, they gradually turned away from such simple notions. They came to realize that claims similar to theirs had been made before. Each time a weapon of great destructiveness was introduced, its inventors soothed their consciences with the thought that this finally made war impossible. When the machine gun was invented, its creators felt they had made war so horrible as to be obsolete. This claim also accompanied the introduction of dynamite, poison gas, and many other innovations in military technology.

In fact, the atomic bomb most likely *did* deter major war between the great powers after 1945 — an unusually long period in historical terms — but security against aggression now rested on the fear of retaliation against civilian populations, and during that time the great powers found only one way to maintain this state of affairs: to indulge in an ever-escalating nuclear arms race. The atomic bomb prevented large-scale war, but it did so by raising the price of failure — through accident, misperception, aggression, or whatever — to annihilation and the possible end of all civilization, if not of all mankind. And we are arguably moving closer to the edge now that smaller states webbed into bitter argument have nuclear capabilities and a host of others seem intent on acquiring them.

All of this made the atomic scientists intensely self-conscious about what they had done and poignantly challenged their optimistic faith in reason and the benevolence of science. The bomb's fundamental message directly undermined their cherished belief — bordering on faith — that science was good. The shattering of this faith was particularly traumatic in American scientific circles, where it had taken especially deep root. Until the atomic bomb, science had remained almost unchallenged as a source of enlightenment, understanding, and hope for a better, healthier, safer world. It enjoyed worldwide respect almost akin to reverence. After Hiroshima and Nagasaki, a significant change took place: a pursuit once held in high esteem was now equated in the minds of many people with the destruction of life and a threat to civilization. Physics — especially nuclear physics — became associated in the popular imagination with mass destruction and the threat of ultimate annihilation. An entire part of physical reality — nuclear energy — was now regarded with distrust and profound fear of its dangers.

Nuclear symbols became symbols of the horrors of modern war. The popular image of the scientist shifted from that of Prometheus, who had helped mankind by giving him fire, to that of Faust, who had imperiled mankind by arrogantly divorcing knowledge from moral responsibility. Some thought physicists were like children playing with matches. I. I. Rabi felt this sentiment during a taxi ride after the war. Driving from the airport, the cabbie asked Rabi what he did. Rabi replied that he was a professor of physics. The atmosphere suddenly became cool. "You're going to blow us all up, ain't you?" the cabbie said.[2] Robert Oppenheimer put it well when he wrote that atomic bombs "touched very deeply man's sentiments about the evil of having too much power."[3] This threat was made even more acute by the fact that it would never go away. What the atomic scientists created cannot be uninvented. If enough bombs were made by enough different states, some of them would eventually blow up — through accident, or folly, or madness. How many, or when, did not really matter. What did matter, given the sobering combination of human imperfection and enough time, was the *eventuality*.

What a shattering realization this was for sensitive, thoughtful men who had believed that knowledge was an absolute good, who had assumed that science — and particularly physics — always led to progress, and who had meant to do well. While they felt their work on the bomb was vital to ending World War II, many — indeed most — of them later came to see what they had done as a great tragedy. They never dreamed in 1945 that there would be so many bombs in the arsenals of so many countries more than half a century later. There was the pride of accomplishment — and the shame of being associated with it. They saw themselves as smart — and foolish. They saw the bomb as a great achievement — but not as a good achievement. These central, painful contradictions remained with all of them to the end of their lives.

Disassociating action from feeling and failing to consider the broader consequences of what they were doing, the atomic scientists made a terrible weapon. But in time they came to terms with their creation. They learned from their experience to ask the fundamental questions. And in doing so, questions of usage ultimately became more important to them than questions of research. Their tragedy was also their triumph.

A dozen years after the end of the Cold War, America still possesses 6,000 nuclear weapons. The price for this arsenal is nearly $6 trillion, about one-tenth of all federal government expenditures from 1940 to 1996. Washington plans to reduce the number of operational nuclear warheads in its arsenal to 3,800 by 2007, and to between 1,700 to 2,000 warheads by 2012. It is a step in the right direction, accomplishing in one bold stroke what years of arms control negotiations had failed to deliver. But Washington has no plans to destroy warheads removed from strategic systems or to eliminate the capacity of these platforms to be rapidly refitted with these reserve warheads. America's nuclear stockpile would still have an explosive force equivalent to *forty thousand* Hiroshima bombs. Russia has a similar force. It is very hard to imagine any plausible contingency that requires this kind of capability. After destroying all conceivable military targets, the remaining weapons of just these two countries could obliterate thousands of cities with populations of more than 100,000 people; there are fewer than five hundred such cities in both countries. Even taking into account other potential nuclear-armed adversaries over the next decade, it is difficult to see how these possible adversaries, projected by U.S. Intelligence to have a total of fewer than 200 nuclear weapons over the next decade, justify U.S. retention of 1,700 to 2,000 operationally deployed warheads and the much larger force being held in reserve.

On the other hand, the strategy of deterrence — the idea that because nuclear war would be so horrible, it is inconceivable — has worked since World War II in the sense that there have been no wars among the major powers. The threat of mutual assured destruction has deterred this catastrophic result, and to that extent, the "balance of terror" has turned out to be stable. This record reinforces the assumption that strategic issues and war in the nuclear age lend themselves to careful calculation and control. The long history of deterrence in politics and war going back to ancient Greece reinforces its credibility. But the consequences of deterrence's failure in earlier wars were always limited. Nuclear war entails no such limits, and this radically distinguishes nuclear deterrence from that earlier tradition.

Who, moreover, believes deterrence can work *everywhere* and *forever*, no matter how effective it has been and currently may be? Who, looking at the long record of human folly and accident — to say nothing of human wickedness — that led to international catastrophes of the past, believes that rational decision will prevail always in the future? It should be noted that even rational political leaders in the past have made wishful, mistaken, and foolish estimates of consequences that have led to catastrophic wars. And there is no telling what might happen if fanatics, driven by a zealotry that knows no ethical constraints, gain possession of nuclear weapons. There are at least eight nuclear powers in the world today, and many more nations — such as Iran and Iraq, and transnational movements such as Al Qaeda — seem intent on joining them. Third World countries are racing to acquire warheads and the ballistic missiles to deliver them. The spread of nuclear weapons is now not only a global fact but also a project and intention for some of the Third World's most belligerent and angry regimes. All of this threatens the stability of deterrence. The consequences of deterrence's failure are simply awful: the use of only a *fraction* of the world's nuclear stockpiles would shred the delicate fabric of human civilization and leave the survivors so miserable that they might envy the dead.

Many things are known. It is true that fears, ambitions, and political differences — not weapons — trigger most conflicts. It is true that military strength *can* be a critical element in a political confrontation. It is true that perceptions of a military advantage, or even of a trend in relative military capability that reflects a likely future balance, can affect the thinking and behavior of potential adversaries and third parties in contemplating what actions to take in a crisis. It is true that arms control negotiations cannot substitute for the settlement of political differences. And it is true that the probability of nuclear war depends more on political factors than on the numbers and technical characteristics of weapons. Yet it is also true that the possession of even a few nuclear weapons will not guarantee a country its fundamental national security.

All of this seems a rather grim picture. Yet there is hope. Fear need not lead to passive despair; it can also get people moving. In this race we are riding a wild horse, and we must learn to tame it, for we have no choice but to ride — what the atomic scientists did assured that. We must recognize, and accept, that the clock that determines our destiny moves in one direction only — forward — and that is the direction on which we must fix our gaze, teaching future generations to do the same.

We sometimes overlook the fact that every future age of man will be an atomic age, and if man is to have a future, it will be one overshadowed with the permanent possibility of thermonuclear holocaust. About that sobering fact there is no doubt; our freedom consists only in facing the danger and minimizing it by minimizing our reliance on nuclear weapons. The means for doing so are primarily moral and political, not military or technological. Morally, we must rouse people to ponder the truly terrible destructiveness of nuclear weapons, awakening an abhorrence that pushes governments and their military establishments to minimize reliance on instruments of mass destruction that in the long run endanger everyone. Politically, we must negotiate verifiable international agreements that reduce national nuclear arsenals as much as possible.

Niels Bohr once defined a pessimist as a man who is always right, but who gets no pleasure out of it. There has never been a time in human history when one was not able to make a good case for pessimism. Goals are of little use if they are not set so high that we always fall short of their fulfillment. The pessimist will be able to make a good case against this goal, too, but it will be a cheap and hollow victory. Hopes and goals are the mortar with which we must build, and any "realism" which doesn't admit that isn't serious.

An all-too-common human weakness is a refusal to face and deal with unpleasant facts. And we face a fact of truly gigantic unpleasantness: namely the existence of atomic and thermonuclear weapons capable of inflicting death and destruction on an unlimited scale. The reaction of most people to this fact is apathy, which covers over profound feelings of vulnerability and helplessness. Inattention and irony, silence and suspicion, are just some of the materials out of which we build our defensive walls of denial. Perhaps we can break through such walls and honestly face the human implications of nuclear weapons.

One has to find a place for that truth within the self, morally and psychologically, in order to live and act from it. The atomic scientists did this over the course of their own lives, even though they started out having less knowledge — and came to bear more personal responsibility — than do we. Facing the realities of nuclear weapons and coming to terms with them may be a tall order, but to fail to try is certainly a dereliction. For the first time in history it is not humankind's limited abilities that prevent us from destroying ourselves, but only our good sense. Not the atom, not physics, not science and technology, but man's fears and hopes — these are the determinative forces, now as always. The atomic scientists — very intelligent men — came to understand that.

ACKNOWLEDGMENTS

This book owes a primary debt to Geoff Shandler, Executive Editor of Little, Brown and Company. He brilliantly edited the manuscript, seeing how it should be structured and precisely where it should be cut. I am deeply indebted to him for enriching the book and bringing it to publication. Emily Loose of Crown Publishers was another splendid editor: demanding in her expectations and incisive in her criticisms. In clarifying many problems of writing and interpretation, she made this a better book than it would otherwise have been, and for that I am grateful.

Few readers are aware of the endless, essential details of transforming a long manuscript into a printed book. Elizabeth Nagle of Little, Brown has been superb at this, working with problems of text and photographs and many other things. There were others at Little, Brown whom I must also thank for helping to create this book: Steve Lamont and especially Karen Landry for their careful copyediting; and Debbie Lindblom for thoroughly preparing the index.

My literary agent, Anne Sibbald of Janklow and Nesbit Associates, did something special: she kept the faith — giving me unwavering support and encouragement over the many years it took to research and write this book. Anne never doubted the project, even when I had occasion to doubt it myself. Thank you, Anne.

Robert Dallek, a steadfast mentor since my graduate school days at the University of California, Los Angeles, nearly twenty years ago, offered incisive comments on an early version of the manuscript and wise counsel from beginning to end. I feel very fortunate to call him not just my teacher but my friend. The same holds true of Robert McNamara, whom I had the privilege of assisting on his Vietnam memoirs. Although a busy man, he always found time to share keen insights into the people and policies addressed in this book during conversations over the years.

I am thankful to the many archives and libraries — and the dedicated people who work in them — where I have been privileged to conduct research: the Niels Bohr Library at the American Institute of Physics in College Park, Maryland; the Bancroft Library at the University of California, Berkeley; the Geisel Library at the University of California, San Diego; the Regenstein Library at the University of Chicago; the Carl A. Kroch Library at Cornell University in Ithaca, New York; the Lamont and Pusey Libraries at Harvard University in Cambridge, Massachusetts; the Hagley Museum and Library in Wilmington, Delaware; the Manuscript Division at the Library of Congress in Washington, D.C.; the Archives of the Los Alamos National Laboratory in Los Alamos, New Mexico; the National Archives in Washington, D.C.; the Bodleian Library at the University of Oxford in Oxford, England; the Hoover Institution Archives at Stanford University in Palo Alto, California; the Nimitz Library at the U.S. Naval Academy in Annapolis, Maryland; and the University Archives at Washington University in St. Louis, Missouri.

I also profited from discussions during my stints as Freeman Professor of History at the Johns Hopkins University Nanjing University Center for Chinese and American Studies from 1999 to 2000 and as a Visiting Fellow at St. Catherine's College and the Rothermere American Institute at the University of Oxford in 2002. I had the privilege of lecturing on this book at both universities. In Nanjing, I benefited from discussions with economics professor emeritus Clark Reynolds of Stanford University; and in Oxford, with Daniel Walker Howe, recently retired Rhodes Professor of American History.

Toby Godfrey, who transcribed the tape recordings of my interviews (and spotted unseen errors in them), proved as before — when we worked together with Richard Holbrooke on Clark Clifford's memoirs — that she is a secretary without equal.

Among many others who helped in various ways, I wish to acknowledge the administration of the U.S. Naval Academy, which supported a sabbatical that allowed me to finish the book; the Naval Academy Research Council, for summer research stipends; my colleagues in the history department at Annapolis — especially Ernest

Tucker — all of whom offered valuable friendship and useful suggestions; and — not least — my lively and intelligent students at Annapolis, past and present, whose commitment to service inspired me to do
my best.

My wife, Dian, and our son, Grey, have given me their love, their
support, and above all their patience for many — too many — years.
All the while, they never questioned that "the book" would someday
be finished. How can I adequately express my admiration and gratitude for all they have done?

NOTES

Preface

1. I am thinking here especially of Richard Rhodes's two magisterial works, *The Making of the Atomic Bomb* and *Dark Sun*.
2. I have used primary sources wherever feasible, but I have also relied on a large body of work by other writers for historical and biographical information, general guidance, and many insights and references. In addition to the two books by Richard Rhodes, the following works were indispensable throughout:

   On Bethe: Bernstein, *Hans Bethe, Prophet of Energy*, and Schweber, *In the Shadow of the Bomb*.

   On Bohr: Moore, *Niels Bohr*, and Pais, *Niels Bohr's Times in Physics, Philosophy, and Polity*.

   On Compton: Blackwood, *The House on College Avenue*, and Johnston, *The Cosmos of Arthur Holly Compton*.

   On Fermi: Fermi, *Atoms in the Family*, and Segrè, *Enrico Fermi, Physicist*.

   On Lawrence: Childs, *An American Genius*; Davis, *Lawrence and Oppenheimer*; and Heilbron and Seidel, *Lawrence and His Laboratory*.

   On Oppenheimer: Goodchild, *J. Robert Oppenheimer*; Kunetka, *Oppenheimer*; and Michelmore, *The Swift Years*.

   On Rabi: Bernstein, "Profiles: Physicist," and Rigden, *Rabi*.

   On Szilard: Grandy, *Leo Szilard*, and Lanouette with Silard, *Genius in the Shadows*.

   On Teller: Blumberg and Owens, *Energy and Conflict*, and Blumberg and Panos, *Edward Teller*.

   Four general works — one of scientific history and three of political history — were particularly germane: Kevles, *The Physicists*; Bundy, *Danger and Survival*; Herken, *Brotherhood of the Bomb*; and Sherwin, *A World Destroyed*.

Prologue: Nine Physicists and the Discovery of Fission

1. Quoted in Kevles, *The Physicists*, p. 324.
2. Ernest O. Lawrence to Enrico Fermi, February 7, 1939, Ernest O. Lawrence Papers, Bancroft Library, University of California, Berkeley (hereafter cited as EOLP, BL, UCB).
3. Quoted in Smith and Weiner, *Robert Oppenheimer*, pp. 208–209.

Chapter 1: Exodus

1. Weisskopf, *The Joy of Insight*, p. vii.
2. Quoted in Bernstein, "Profiles: Physicist — I," p. 70.
3. Paul Ewald interview with Charles Weiner, May 17–24, 1968, Oral History Collection, Niels Bohr Library, American Institute of Physics (hereafter cited as OHC, NBL, AIP), College Park, Md.
4. Quotes are in William L. Shirer, *The Rise and Fall of the Third Reich: A History of Nazi Germany* (Simon and Schuster, 1960; reprint, Fawcett Crest Books), pp. 345–346.
5. John von Neumann to Oswald Veblen, June 19, 1933, Oswald Veblen Papers (hereafter cited as OVP), Manuscript Division, Library of Congress (hereafter cited as MDLOC), Washington, D.C. Hitler quote is in Edward Y. Hartshorne, Jr., *The German Universities and National Socialism* (Allen and Unwin, 1937), p. 112.
6. Quoted in Weart and Szilard, *Leo Szilard*, p. 5.
7. Ibid., p. 4.
8. "Outline," Leo Szilard Papers, Mandeville Special Collections Department, Geisel Library, University of California, San Diego (hereafter cited as LSP, MSCD, GL, UCSD).
9. Leo Szilard to I. I. Rabi, July 1, 1932, I. I. Rabi Papers (hereafter cited as IIRP), Box 7, MDLOC.
10. Quoted in Weart and Szilard, *Leo Szilard*, p. 17.
11. Leo Szilard to Hugo Hirst, March 17, 1934, quoted in ibid., p. 38.
12. "Atom Energy Hope Is Spiked by Einstein," *Pittsburgh Post-Gazette*, December 29, 1934.
13. Quoted in the *New York Times* (hereafter cited as *NYT*), April 13, 1935.
14. Lord Rutherford, *The Newer Alchemy* (Cambridge University Press, 1937), p. 65.
15. Maurice Goldhaber interview with Gloria Lubkin and Charles Weiner, January 10, 1966, OHC, NBL, AIP.
16. Leo Szilard to Gertrud Weiss, March 26, 1936, quoted in Weart and Szilard, *Leo Szilard*, p. 38.
17. Author's interview with Rose Bethe and Jane Wilson, Ithaca, N.Y., June 8, 1997.
18. Quoted in Segrè, *Enrico Fermi, Physicist*, p. 98.
19. Quoted in Lanouette with Silard, *Genius in the Shadows*, p. 167.
20. Quoted in *NYT*, January 12, 1988, p. A1.
21. Quoted in Howe, *World of Our Fathers*, p. 256.
22. Quoted in Rigden, *Rabi*, p. 23.

23. Quoted in ibid., p. 21; and Bernstein, "Profiles: Physicist — I," p. 50.
24. Quoted in Bernstein, "Profiles: Physicist — I," p. 53.
25. Quoted in *NYT,* January 12, 1988, p. A24.
26. Quoted in Rigden, *Rabi,* p. 117.
27. "Reminiscences of Norman F. Ramsey (1962)," Oral History Research Office, Columbia University (hereafter cited as OHRO, CU).
28. Fermi, *Atoms in the Family,* p. 154.
29. Addendum D.9, Rudolf Peierls Papers, Bodleian Library, University of Oxford (hereafter cited as RPP, BL, UO).
30. Quoted in Weisskopf, *Joy of Insight,* p. 63.
31. See John Wheeler interview with Finn Aaserud, May 23, 1988, OHC, NBL, AIP.
32. Leo Szilard, Book Manuscript "Book — Apology (in lieu of a foreword)," LSP, Box 40, Folder 4, MSCD, GL, UCSD.
33. Quoted in Laurence, *Men and Atoms,* p. 9.
34. Quoted in Weart and Szilard, *Leo Szilard,* p. 54.
35. Ibid.
36. Remarks at *Nation* banquet, December 3, 1945, reprinted in ibid., p. 55.

Chapter 2: The Gathering Storm

1. Teller with Brown, *The Legacy of Hiroshima,* p. 10.
2. Teller with Shoolery, *Memoirs,* p. 139.
3. Quoted in Sebastian Cody, "Edward Teller," December 1985, RPP, BL, UO.
4. Author's interview with Herbert York, La Jolla, Calif., March 12, 2001.
5. Quoted in Teller with Shoolery, *Memoirs,* p. 15.
6. Quoted in Coughlan, "The Tangled Drama," p. 89.
7. Ibid., p. 49.
8. Quoted in Cody, "Edward Teller."
9. Quoted in Teller with Shoolery, *Memoirs,* p. 143.
10. Ibid.
11. Quoted in Moore, *Niels Bohr,* p. 267.
12. George Pegram to Admiral S. C. Hooper, March 16, 1939, Enrico Fermi Papers (hereafter cited as EFP), Box 9, Department of Special Collections, Joseph Regenstein Library, University of Chicago (hereafter cited as DSC, JRL, UC).
13. Quoted in Szilard, "Reminiscences," p. 114.
14. Quoted in Szilard, "Book — Apology."
15. Szilard notes for interview, April 18, 1955, Weart and Szilard, *Leo Szilard,* p. 83.
16. Transcript, *A Is for Atom, B Is for Bomb* (WGBH-TV, 1980), p. 2.
17. Albert Einstein to President Roosevelt, August 2, 1939, Roosevelt-PSF, Confidential File, Alexander Sachs Folder, Franklin D. Roosevelt Library, Hyde Park, New York (hereafter cited as FDRL).
18. Ulam, *Adventures of a Mathematician,* p. 116.
19. Leo Szilard to Albert Einstein, October 3, 1939, reprinted in Weart and Szilard, *Leo Szilard,* p. 101.
20. See Alexander Sachs's testimony before the U.S. Senate Special Committee on Atomic Energy, 79th Congress, 1st Session, November 27, 1945, pp. 2–29.

21. Quoted in Blumberg and Owens, *Energy and Conflict*, p. 98; and Edward Teller, *Energy from Heaven and Earth* (W. H. Freeman, 1979), p. 144.
22. Weart and Szilard, *Leo Szilard*, p. 85.
23. Quoted in Hewlett and Anderson, *The New World*, p. 20.
24. Wigner, "Are We Making the Transition Wisely?" p. 28.
25. Albert Einstein to Alexander Sachs, March 7, 1940, LSP, Box 17, Folder 4, MSCD, GL, UCSD.
26. Vannevar Bush to James B. Conant, February 24, 1942, Bush-Conant File Relating to the Development of the Atomic Bomb, 1940–1945, Records of the Office of Scientific Research and Development, Record Group 227, Manhattan Engineering District Records, National Archives, Washington, D.C. (hereafter cited as BCF, ROSRD, MEDR, NA).
27. Lieutenant Colonel S. V. Constant, Acting Chief of Staff, G-2, War Department, August 13, 1940, U.S. Intelligence and Security Command, Freedom of Information/Privacy Office, Fort George G. Meade, Md.

Chapter 3: The Manhattan Project

1. Quoted in Jungk, *Brighter than a Thousand Suns*, p. 114.
2. Quoted in Rudolf Peierls interview with Charles Weiner, August 11–13, 1969, OHC, NBL, AIP.
3. Rudolf Peierls to Mr. Murphy, May 2, 1993, Addendum D. 110, RPP, BL, UO.
4. "On the Construction of a 'Super-bomb; Based on a Nuclear Chain Reaction in Uranium,'" reprinted in Gowing, *Britain and Atomic Energy*, pp. 389–393.
5. Frisch, *What Little I Remember*, p. 126.
6. MAUD Committee Report, reprinted in Gowing, *Britain and Atomic Energy*, pp. 394–436.
7. Quoted in Weart and Szilard, *Leo Szilard*, p. 146.
8. Author's interview with Philip Abelson, Washington, D.C., March 23, 1999.
9. Robert Wilson interview with Spencer Weart, May 19, 1977, OHC, NBL, AIP.
10. Cited in Herken, *Brotherhood of the Bomb*, p. 7.
11. Author's interview with Herbert York, La Jolla, Calif., March 12, 2001.
12. Edwin McMillan interview with Charles Weiner, June 1, 1972, OHC, NBL, AIP.
13. Quoted in Childs, *An American Genius*, p. 251; and Davis, *Lawrence and Oppenheimer*, p. 48.
14. Quoted in Childs, *American Genius*, p. 281.
15. Quoted in Davis, *Lawrence and Oppenheimer*, p. 87.
16. Ernest O. Lawrence to Carl and Gunda Lawrence, August 29, 1939, EOLP, BL, UCB.
17. Quoted in Groueff, *The Manhattan Project*, p. 40.
18. Martin Kamen to Edwin McMillan, EOLP, BL, UCB.
19. See Vannevar Bush to James B. Conant, October 9, 1941, BCF, ROSRD, MEDR, NA.
20. Quoted in Davis, *Lawrence and Oppenheimer*, p. 131.
21. Quoted in Johnston, *The Cosmos of Arthur Holly Compton*, p. 11.
22. Quoted in Compton, *Atomic Quest*, p. 6.
23. Ibid., p. 8.

24. National Academy of Sciences Committee on Uranium Report to the President, November 6, 1941, BCF, Folder 18, ROSRD, MEDR, NA.
25. Quoted in Compton, *Atomic Quest*, p. 62.
26. See December 6, 1941, entry, Diary, Harold Urey Papers (hereafter cited as HUP), Box 145, Folder 19, MSCD, GL, UCSD.
27. Vannevar Bush to Frank Jewett, November 4, 1941, BCF, ROSRD, MEDR, NA.
28. Vannevar Bush to James B. Conant, February 24, 1942, in ibid.
29. Quoted in Frank Oppenheimer interview with Charles Weiner, February 9, 1973, OHC, NBL, AIP.
30. Quoted in Childs, *An American Genius*, pp. 343–344.

Chapter 4: The Met Lab

1. Quoted in Arthur H. Compton, "Operation of the Metallurgical Project by the University of Chicago," July 28, 1944, BCF, ROSRD, MEDR, NA.
2. Quoted in Hewlett and Anderson, *The New World*, pp. 54–55.
3. Leo Szilard, "Memorandum on My Visit to Chicago, January 23–24," January 26, 1942, LSP, Box 41, Folder 6, MSCD, GL, UCSD.
4. Leo Szilard to Enrico Fermi, December 31, 1941, LSP, Box 8, Folder 6, in ibid.
5. See Leo Szilard to Arthur Compton, January 27, 1942, LSP, Box 6, Folder 30, in ibid.
6. Author's interview with Philip Morrison, Cambridge, Mass., May 18, 1998.
7. Quoted in Hewlett and Anderson, *The New World*, pp. 54–55.
8. Author's interview with Philip Morrison, Cambridge, Mass., May 18, 1998.
9. Arthur Compton to Members of the Metallurgical Project, February 11, 1942, Courtesy of Harold Agnew.
10. Quoted in Davis, *Lawrence and Oppenheimer*, p. 125.
11. Author's interview with Philip Morrison, Cambridge, Mass., May 18, 1998.
12. Diary entries, January 3, 1943, and February 3, 1943, Crawford Greenewalt Manhattan Project Diary, Crawford Greenewalt Papers, Hagley Museum Library (hereafter cited as CGMPD, CGP, HML), Wilmington, Del.
13. Quoted in Groueff, *The Manhattan Project*, p. 29.
14. Kenneth Nichols, quoted in Goodchild, *J. Robert Oppenheimer*, p. 56.
15. Groves, *Now It Can Be Told*.
16. Vannevar Bush to Harvey Bundy, September 17, 1942, Folder 7, Harrison-Bundy Files Relating to the Development of the Atomic Bomb, 1942–1946, Record Group 77, Manhattan Engineer District Records, National Archives, Washington, D.C. (hereafter cited as HBF, MEDR, NA).
17. Minutes of Coordination Meeting, April 16, 1943, Box 19, Lawrence Berkeley National Laboratory Archives, Berkeley, California.
18. "What Is Wrong with Us?" September 21, 1942, reprinted in Weart and Szilard, *Leo Szilard*, pp. 153–160.
19. Transcript, Lansing Lamont Oral History Interview, Harry S Truman Library, Independence, Missouri, p. 258.
20. Quoted in Jungk, *Brighter than a Thousand Suns*, p. 120.
21. L. R. Groves to the Attorney General, October 28, 1942, 201 File (Leo Szilard), MEDR, NA.
22. Ibid.

23. Quoted in Davis, *Lawrence and Oppenheimer*, pp. 243–244.

24. Brigadiar General Groves to Major Calvert, June 12, 1943, MEDR, NA.

25. Arthur Compton to Vannevar Bush, June 1, 1942; and Arthur Compton to Leslie R. Groves, November 13, 1942, BCF, ROSRD, MEDR, NA.

26. Quoted in Smith and Weiner, *Robert Oppenheimer*, pp. 71–72; and *NYT*, February 19, 1967, p. 66.

27. Quoted in Goodchild, *J. Robert Oppenheimer*, p. 15.

28. See Herbert Smith interview with Charles Weiner, August 1, 1974, OHC, NBL, AIP.

29. Quoted in Goodchild, *J. Robert Oppenheimer*, p. 77.

30. Quoted in *NYT*, February 19, 1967, p. 66.

31. Quoted in Smith and Weiner, *Robert Oppenheimer*, p. 195.

32. Robert Oppenheimer to Frank Oppenheimer, Box 294, J. Robert Oppenheimer Papers (hereafter cited as JROP), MDLOC.

33. Quoted in Smith and Weiner, *Robert Oppenheimer*, p. 143.

34. Ibid., p. 135.

35. Author's interview with Robert Christy, Pasadena, Calif., July 29, 1998.

36. Quoted in Davis, *Lawrence and Oppenheimer*, p. 103.

37. Quoted in Smith and Weiner, *Robert Oppenheimer*, p. 135.

38. Emilio Segrè interview with Charles Weiner and Barry Richman, February 13, 1967, OHC, NBL, AIP.

39. Author's interview with Herbert York, La Jolla, Calif., March 12, 2001.

40. Author's interview with Robert Christy, Pasadena, Calif., July 29, 1998.

41. Frank Oppenheimer interview with Charles Weiner, February 9, 1973, OHC, NBL, AIP.

42. Quoted in Goodchild, *J. Robert Oppenheimer*, p. 25.

43. U.S. Atomic Energy Commission, *In the Matter of J. Robert Oppenheimer*, p. 8.

44. Ibid., p. 10.

45. Quoted in Goodchild, *J. Robert Oppenheimer*, p. 36.

46. Author's interview with Rose Bethe and Jane Wilson, Ithaca, N.Y., June 8, 1997.

47. Quoted in Schweber, *In the Shadow of the Bomb*, p. 108.

48. Quoted in Davis, *Lawrence and Oppenheimer*, p. 80.

49. Robert Oppenheimer to Ernest Lawrence, October 2, 1931, in Smith and Weiner, *Robert Oppenheimer*, p. 144.

50. Ernest O. Lawrence to Arthur Compton, October 17, 1941, EOLP, BL, UCB.

51. Carl Anderson interview with Harriett Lyle, 1981, California Institute of Technology Oral History Project.

52. U.S. Atomic Energy Commission, *In the Matter of J. Robert Oppenheimer*, p. 11.

53. Quoted in Jungk, *Brighter than a Thousand Suns*, p. 127.

54. Hans Bethe interview with Charles Weiner, November 17, 1967, OHC, NBL, AIP.

55. See Powers, *Heisenberg's War*, p. 37.

56. Author's interview with Hans Bethe, Ithaca, N.Y., June 6, 1997.

57. Hans Bethe interview with Charles Weiner, November 17, 1967, OHC, NBL, AIP.

58. "A Conversation with Hans Bethe and Victor Weisskopf," Cornell University, 1993, videotape copy in Audiovisual Archives (hereafter cited as AA), AIP.

59. Hans Bethe to Arnold Sommerfeld, May 20, 1947, Sommerfeld Papers, Deutsches Museum, Munich, Germany, cited in Schweber, *In the Shadow of the Bomb.*
60. Quoted in Blumberg and Owens, *Energy and Conflict,* p. 72.
61. "A Conversation with Hans Bethe and Robert Wilson," Cornell University, 1993, videotape copy in AA, AIP.
62. Quoted in Bernstein, *Hans Bethe,* p. 73.
63. Robert Oppenheimer to John Manley, July 1, 1942, Accession #A-92–024/2–25, Los Alamos National Laboratory Archives (hereafter cited as LANLA), Los Alamos, N.Mex.
64. Edward Teller to Enrico Fermi, July 17, 1942, Accession #A-84–019/73–17, in ibid.
65. Author's interview with Harold Agnew, Solana Beach, Calif., March 13, 2001.
66. Quoted in Groueff, *The Manhattan Project,* p. 77.
67. Ibid.
68. Quoted in Ackland, "Dawn of the Atomic Age," p. 12.
69. Compton, *Atomic Quest,* p. 137.
70. Ibid., p. 138.
71. Fermi, *Collected Papers,* p. 270.
72. Quoted in Lanouette, *Genius in the Shadows,* p. 243.
73. Author's interview with Robert Christy, Pasadena, Calif., July 29, 1998.
74. Quoted in Groueff, *The Manhattan Project,* p. 96.
75. Ibid.
76. Herbert Anderson, quoted in Wilson, *All in Our Time,* p. 95.
77. Diary entry, December 2, 1942, CGMPD, CGP, HML.
78. Compton, *Atomic Quest,* p. 144.
79. Anderson, "Fermi, Szilard and Trinity," p. 45.
80. Eugene Wigner, *Symmetries and Reflections,* pp. 240–241.
81. Weart and Szilard, *Leo Szilard,* p. 146.
82. Author's interview with Kathleen Manley, Los Alamos, N.Mex., July 21, 1997.

Chapter 5: Los Alamos

1. Jon Else, *The Day After Trinity* (KTEH-TV, 1980); and I. I. Rabi, "How Well We Meant," Speech at Los Alamos National Laboratory, 1983, LANLA.
2. Groves, *Now It Can Be Told,* p. 63.
3. Quoted in Joseph J. Ermenc, ed., *Atomic Bomb Scientists: Memoirs, 1939–1945* (Meckler, 1989), p. 257.
4. Enclosure to Frederick T. Hobbs to H. T. Wensel, June 10, 1942, BCF, ROSRD, MEDR, NA.
5. Leslie Groves to the District Engineer, United States Engineer Office, Manhattan District, Station F, July 20, 1943, in ibid.
6. Quoted in Herbert Smith interview with Charles Weiner, August 1, 1974, OHC, NBL, AIP.
7. Rabi, "How Well We Meant."
8. See Robert Oppenheimer to John Manley, November 10, 1942, Accession #A-84–019/63–1, LANLA.

9. Quoted in Edwin M. McMillan, "Early Days at Los Alamos," in Badash et al., *Reminiscences of Los Alamos*, p. 15.

10. Quoted in Davis, *Lawrence and Oppenheimer*, p. 161.

11. Quoted in "Julius Robert Oppenheimer" in Charles Montz, ed., *Current Biography Yearbook, 1964* (H. W. Wilson, 1964), p. 331.

12. "Reminiscences of Norman F. Ramsey," OHRO, CU.

13. Franklin D. Roosevelt to J. Robert Oppenheimer, June 29, 1943, Box 62, JROP, MDLOC.

14. J. R. Oppenheimer to the President, July 9, 1943, Box 36, in ibid.

15. Author's interview with Donald Hornig, Cambridge, Mass., May 14, 1998.

16. Quoted in Jungk, *Brighter than a Thousand Suns*, p. 118.

17. Quoted in Compton, *Atomic Quest*, p. 113.

18. See Graph 1 in Hawkins, *Toward Trinity*, p. 483.

19. Robert Wilson to Henry Smyth, November 27, 1943, Accession #A-84–019/7–7, LANLA.

20. Major N. E. Davis to Occupants of Dormitory T-187, March 8, 1945, Accession #A-84–019, in ibid.

21. Elsie McMillan, "Outside the Inner Fence," in Badash et al., *Reminiscences of Los Alamos*, p. 43.

22. Robert Wilson to Henry Smyth, November 27, 1943, Accession #A-84–019/7–7, LANLA.

23. Author's interview with Donald Hornig, Cambridge, Mass., May 14, 1998.

24. U.S. Atomic Energy Commission, *In the Matter of J. Robert Oppenheimer*, pp. 12 ff.

25. Author's interview with Louis Rosen, Los Alamos, N.Mex., July 16, 1997.

26. Ibid.

27. Smith and Weiner, *Robert Oppenheimer*, p. 226.

28. Quoted in Powers, *Heisenberg's War*, p. 216.

29. Ibid.

30. "Reminiscences of Norman F. Ramsey," OHRO, CU.

31. Author's interview with Beverly Agnew, Solana Beach, Calif., March 13, 2001.

32. Norris Bradbury with Arthur Lawrence Norberg, February 11, 1976, History of Science and Technology Program, BL, UCB.

33. Author's interview with Kathleen Manley, Los Alamos, N.Mex., July 21, 1997.

34. Quoted in Davis, *Lawrence and Oppenheimer*, p. 178.

35. Quotes are in Blumberg and Owens, *Energy and Conflict*, p. 124.

36. Author's interview with Robert Christy, Pasadena, Calif., July 29, 1998.

37. J. R. Oppenheimer to General L. R. Groves, October 6, 1944, Box 36, JROP, MDLOC.

38. See I. I. Rabi to Robert Oppenheimer, "Suggestions for Interim Organization and Procedure," February 10, 1943, Box 59, in ibid.

39. Quoted in Blumberg and Owens, *Energy and Conflict*, p. 129.

40. Teller with Shoolery, *Memoirs*, p. 177.

41. Ibid., pp. 177–178.

42. Quoted in Smith and Weiner, *Robert Oppenheimer*, p. 273.

43. Author's interview with Philip Morrison, Cambridge, Mass., May 18, 1998.

44. Hans Bethe Personal Papers (hereafter cited as BPP), Ithaca, N.Y.

45. Author's interview with Kathleen Manley, Los Alamos, N.Mex., July 21, 1997.

46. Author's interview with Hans Bethe, Ithaca, N.Y., June 6, 1997.

47. Author's interview with Kay Mark, Los Alamos, N.Mex., July 19, 1997.

48. Author's interview with Rose Bethe and Jane Wilson, Ithaca, N.Y., June 8, 1997.

49. Quoted in Bernstein, "Profiles: Physicist — II," p. 53.

50. Quoted in Rigden, *Rabi*, p. 217.

51. Quoted by Hans Bethe in ibid., p. 149.

52. Quoted in Peierls, *Bird of Passage*, p. 192.

53. Quoted in J. Robert Oppenheimer to I. I. Rabi, February 26, 1943, JROP, MDLOC. Rabi had apparently suggested this to Oppenheimer in a prior letter or conversation.

54. Author's interview with Hans Bethe, Ithaca, N.Y., June 6, 1997.

55. The physicist was John Wheeler, then at Hanford, Washington. His brother Joe, an army private with a Ph.D. in history, was killed on October 25, 1944. Wheeler with Ford, *Geons, Black Holes, and Quantum Foam*, pp. 18–19.

56. Darol Froman interview with Arthur Lawrence Norberg, HSTP, BL, UCB.

57. Blue Corn, quoted in Mason, *Children of Los Alamos*, p. 147.

58. Quoted in Peggy Pond Church, *The House at Otowi Bridge* (University of New Mexico Press, 1960), pp. 65–66.

59. Bohr handwritten notes, Document 10, Niels Bohr Archives Document Release, February 6, 2002, *www.nba.nbi.dk/NBA/papers/docs/d10tra.htm*.

60. Quoted in James Glanz, "New Light on Physicist's Role in Nazi Bomb," *NYT*, February 7, 2002, pp. A1 and A8.

61. Quoted in Rudolf Peierls to Mr. Masters, February 20, 1988, Addendum D.9, RPP, BL, UO.

62. Quoted in Moore, *Niels Bohr*, p. 324.

63. Quoted in Teller with Shoolery, *Memoirs*, p. 186.

64. Niels Bohr to President Roosevelt, July 3, 1944, JROP, Box 34, MDLOC.

65. Quoted in Powers, *Heisenberg's War*, p. 255.

66. Author's interview with Robert Christy, Pasadena, Calif., July 29, 1998.

67. Richard Feynman interview with Charles Weiner, June 28, 1966, OHC, NBL, AIP.

68. Felix Frankfurter to Lord Halifax, April 18, 1945, JROP, Box 34, MDLOC.

69. Quoted in Moore, *Niels Bohr*, p. 343.

70. See R. V. Jones, "Winston Leonard Spencer Churchill," *Biographical Memoirs of Fellows of the Royal Society*, 1966, p. 88; and Gowing, *Britain and Atomic Energy*, p. 355.

71. See Aage Bohr, "The War Years and the Prospects Raised by the Atomic Weapons," in Rozental, *Niels Bohr*, pp. 206–207.

72. Hyde Park Aide-Memoire, September 18, 1944, President's Map Room Papers, Naval Aide's File, Box 172, FDRL.

Chapter 6: The Decision to Use the Bomb

1. Leo Szilard to Vannevar Bush, January 14, 1944, LSP, Box 5, Folder 21, MSCD, GL, UCSD.

2. Compton himself addressed the political implications of atomic bombs for the first time in a memorandum to James Conant in August 1944. See Arthur H. Compton to James B. Conant, August 15, 1944, BCF, ROSRD, MEDR, NA.

3. See Arthur H. Compton to Alice K. Smith, September 30, 1958, Series 3, Box 27, Arthur H. Compton Papers (hereafter cited as AHCP), Washington University Archives (hereafter cited as WUA), St. Louis, Mo.

4. Bohr Memorandum, May 8, 1945, summarizing his communications with Roosevelt, JROP, Box 34, MDLOC.

5. Leo Szilard, "Atomic Bombs and the Postwar Position of the United States in the World," March 12, 1945, reprinted in Weart and Szilard, *Leo Szilard*, pp. 196–204.

6. See Leo Szilard to Ernest Lawrence, April 3, 1945; and Ernest Lawrence to Leo Szilard, April 9, 1945, EOLP, BL, UCB.

7. Quoted in Wyden, *Day One*, p. 141; and Weart and Szilard, *Leo Szilard*, p. 182.

8. Quoted in Allan R. Millett and Peter Maslowski, *For the Common Defense: A Military History of the United States of America* (revised, Free Press, 1994), p. 482.

9. Quoted in John W. Dower, *War Without Mercy: Race and Power in the Pacific War* (Pantheon Books, 1986), pp. 39–40.

10. Quoted in Steve Birdsall, *Saga of the Superfortress* (Doubleday, 1980), p. 195.

11. Henry L. Stimson Diary, December 31, 1944, Sterling Library, Yale University.

12. Harry S Truman, *Memoirs, Vol. I: Year of Decisions* (Doubleday, 1955), p. 10.

13. Henry L. Stimson, "Memo Discussed with the President," April 25, 1945, Box 151, Folder 60, HBF, MEDR, NA.

14. J. Robert Oppenheimer, "The Atomic Bomb as a Great Force for Peace," *New York Times Magazine*, June 9, 1946, p. 60.

15. Leo Szilard to J. Robert Oppenheimer, May 16, 1945, LSP, Box 14, Folder 27, MSCD, GL, UCSD.

16. Author's interview with Louis Rosen, Los Alamos, N.Mex., July 16, 1997.

17. Ibid.

18. U.S. Atomic Energy Commission, *In the Matter of J. Robert Oppenheimer*, pp. 32–33.

19. James Byrnes to President Roosevelt, March 3, 1945, Box 147, HBF, MEDR, NA.

20. See Szilard, "Reminiscences," pp. 122–128; Smith, *A Peril and a Hope*, pp. 28–30; and James F. Byrnes, *All in One Lifetime* (Harper and Brothers, 1958), pp. 284–285.

21. Szilard, "Reminiscences," p. 129.

22. Arthur H. Compton, Statement to Interim Committee, May 28, 1945, BCF, ROSRD, MEDR, NA.

23. Compton, *Atomic Quest*, p. 238.

24. Stimson Diary, May 31, 1945, SL, YU.

25. Handwritten Notes "To the Four [Scientists]," May 31, 1945, HBF, MEDR, NA.

26. Diary entry for May 31, 1945, Series 4, Box 1, AHCP, WUA.

27. Quoted in Moore, *Niels Bohr*, p. 369.

28. Quoted in Davis, *Lawrence and Oppenheimer*, p. 142.

29. Compton, *Atomic Quest*, pp. 238–239.

30. Quoted in Davis, *Lawrence and Oppenheimer*, p. 247.

31. Arthur H. Compton to Colonel Kenneth D. Nichols, June 4, 1945, MUC-AC-1306/7, MEDR, NA. See also Diary entry for June 3, 1945, Series 4, Box 1, AHCP, WUA.

32. Franck Report, June 11, 1945, reprinted as Appendix B in Smith, *A Peril and a Hope*, pp. 560–572.

33. See James Franck, "Washington Trip Memo," April 21, 1945, James Franck Papers, Box 18, DSC, JRL, UC.

34. Compton, *Atomic Quest*, p. 236.

35. Ibid., p. 247.

36. Ibid., pp. 239–240.

37. See Leo Szilard to Arthur H. Compton, July 19, 1945, LSP, Box 6, Folder 29, MSCD, GL, UCSD; and Wyden, *Day One*, p. 171.

38. Compton, *Atomic Quest*, pp. 240–241.

39. Recommendations on the Immediate Use of Nuclear Weapons, June 16, 1945, HBF, MEDR, NA.

40. Oppenheimer, "Niels Bohr and His Times," Part 3, p. 15, JROP, Box 247, MDLOC.

41. Quoted in Moore, *Niels Bohr*, p. 370.

42. HBF, MEDR, NA.

43. Leo Szilard, "The Story of a Petition," July 28, 1946, LSP, Box 40, Folder 15, MSCD, GL, UCSD.

44. HBF, MEDR, NA.

45. "A Petition to the President of the United States," July 17, 1945, JROP, Box 70, MDLOC.

46. Quoted in Weart and Szilard, *Leo Szilard*, p. 167; and Compton, *Atomic Quest*, p. 262.

47. Leo Szilard to Frank Oppenheimer, July 10, 1945, JROP, Box 70, MDLOC.

48. Quoted in Teller with Shoolery, *Memoirs*, p. 206; and author's interview with Edward Teller, Stanford, Calif., July 27, 1998.

49. Edward Teller to Leo Szilard, July 2, 1945, LSP, Box 18, Folder 36, MSCD, GL, UCSD.

50. Edward Teller to Gregg Herken, February 26, 1999, cited in Herken, *Brotherhood of the Bomb*, p. 365.

51. Teller with Brown, *The Legacy of Hiroshima*, p. 14.

52. Teller, *Better a Shield than a Sword*, p. 60.

53. Teller with Brown, *The Legacy of Hiroshima*, p. 19.

54. Author's interview with Edward Teller, Stanford, Calif., July 27, 1998.

55. Quotes are in Wyden, *Day One*, p. 150.

56. Quoted in Jungk, *Brighter than a Thousand Suns*, p. 171.

57. See Farrington Daniels and Arthur H. Compton, "A Poll of Scientists at Chicago," *Bulletin of the Atomic Scientists* (hereafter cited as *BAS*), February 1948, p. 44.

58. Arthur Compton to Kenneth Nichols, July 24, 1945, MUC-AC-1306/7, MEDR, NA.

59. Quoted in Knebel and Bailey, "The Fight over the A-Bomb," p. 20.

60. Jette, *Inside Box 1663*, p. 99.

61. Quoted in Groueff, *The Manhattan Project*, p. 44.

62. Quoted in *Los Alamos: Beginning of an Era, 1943–1945* (Los Alamos National Laboratory Public Relations Office), p. 44.

63. Leslie R. Groves Diary, Boxes 1–4, Papers of Leslie R. Groves, Entry 7530G, Record Group 200, NA.

64. Quoted in *Los Alamos: Beginning of an Era*, p. 46.

65. Author's interview with Donald Hornig, Cambridge, Mass., May 14, 1998.
66. Quoted in Bush, *Pieces of the Action*, p. 148; and Lamont, *Day of Trinity*, p. 226.
67. Quoted in Glenn T. Seaborg, *Journals: Volumes 1–4, April 19, 1942–May 19, 1946* (Lawrence Berkeley National Laboratory, 1992), vol. 4, p. 4.
68. Quoted in Jungk, *Brighter than a Thousand Suns*, p. 199.
69. "E. O. Lawrence's Thoughts," July 16, 1945, Correspondence ("Top Secret") of the Manhattan Engineer District, 1942–1946 (hereafter cited as CTS, MED), Record Group 77, NA.
70. Quoted in Sid Moody, "Proving Ground," *Albuquerque Journal* Special Reprint, July 1995, p. 3.
71. Rabi, *Science*, p. 138.

Chapter 7: Three Fires

1. Author's interview with Donald Hornig, Cambridge, Mass., May 14, 1998.
2. Quoted in Laurence, *The Story of the Atomic Bomb*, p. 17.
3. Hans Bethe to Anne Longley, June 7, 1995, BPP; and Else, *The Day After Trinity* (KTEH-TV, 1980).
4. "E. O. Lawrence's Thoughts," July 16, 1945, CTS, MED, Record Group 77, NA.
5. Ernest O. Lawrence to George L. Harrison, July 18, 1945, EOLP, BL, UCB.
6. Enrico Fermi, "My Observations During the Explosion at Trinity on July 16, 1945," A-84–019, LANLA.
7. Laura Fermi, "Bombs or Reactors," *BAS*, June 1970, p. 27.
8. Rabi, *Science*, p. 138; and Bernstein, "Physicist: Profile — II," p. 58.
9. Author's interview with Raemer Schreiber, Los Alamos, N.Mex., July 17, 1997.
10. Quoted in *Albuquerque Journal*, July 12, 1970.
11. Robert Oppenheimer to Thomas Farrell and William Parsons, July 23, 1945, CTS, MED, NA.
12. Michihiko Hachiya, M.D., *Hiroshima Diary: The Journal of a Japanese Physician, August 6–September 30, 1945* (University of North Carolina Press, 1955), p. 1.
13. The following account of Hiroshima and Nagasaki is based on the U.S. Strategic Bombing Survey, *Effects of Atomic Bombs on Hiroshima and Nagasaki, Summary Report (Pacific War)* (U.S. Government Printing Office, 1946), and Rhodes, *The Making of the Atomic Bomb*.
14. Hachiya, *Hiroshima Diary*, p. 31.
15. Captain William C. Bryson, U.S. Navy, September 14, 1945, reprinted in *BAS*, December 1982, p. 35.
16. August 6, 1945, Transcript, L. R. Groves Telephone Conversations, MEDR, NA.
17. See Teller with Brown, *The Legacy of Hiroshima*, p. 41.
18. Leo Szilard to Gertrud Weiss, August 6, 1945, quoted in Rhodes, *The Making of the Atomic Bomb*, p. 735.
19. Quoted in Leigh Fenly, "The Agony of the Bomb, and Ecstasy of Life with Leo Szilard," *San Diego Union*, November 19, 1978, pp. D1, D8.
20. Arthur Compton to A. J. McCartney, March 18, 1946, Series 3, Box 5, AHCP, WUA; and Arthur Compton in *St. Louis Post-Dispatch*, October 7, 1945, p. 4D.

21. Sam Cohen, *The Truth About the Neutron Bomb* (Morrow, 1983), pp. 21–22.
22. Cited in Field Report, April 18, 1952, Robert Oppenheimer File, FBI, Washington, D.C.
23. J. R. Oppenheimer to All Division Leaders, August 9, 1945, LANLA.
24. Author's interview with Hans Bethe, Ithaca, N.Y., June 6, 1997.
25. Quoted in Herken, *Brotherhood of the Bomb*, p. 139.
26. Karl K. Darrow to Ernest O. Lawrence, August 9, 1945, EOLP, BL, UCB.
27. Ernest O. Lawrence to Karl K. Darrow, August 17, 1945, in ibid.
28. Ernest O. Lawrence to Citizens of Berkeley, August 22, 1945, in ibid.
29. Quoted in Fermi, *Atoms in the Family*, p. 245.
30. Rabi, *Science*, p. 70.
31. Winston Churchill, *Triumph and Tragedy* (Houghton Mifflin, 1953), p. 639.
32. Quoted in Alice Kimball Smith, "Los Alamos: Focus of an Age," in Lewis, Wilson, and Rabinowitch, *Alamogordo Plus Twenty-Five Years*, p. 40.

Chapter 8: An End, a Beginning

1. I. I. Rabi, "The Physicist Returns from the War," p. 107.
2. Talk to FAS Members, Los Alamos, N.Mex., July 9, 1953, #14/22/976, Hans A. Bethe Papers (hereafter cited as HABP), Carl A. Kroch Library, Cornell University (hereafter cited as CAKL, CU).
3. Philip Morrison, "The Laboratory Demobilizes," *BAS*, November 1946, pp. 5–6.
4. Quoted in Rhodes, *The Making of the Atomic Bomb*, p. 754.
5. *Time*, November 5, 1945, p. 27.
6. Robert Oppenheimer, "Physics in the Contemporary World," *BAS* 4, no. 3 (March 1948): 66.
7. Francis Sill Wickware, "Manhattan Project," *Life*, August 20, 1945, p. 100.
8. I. I. Rabi to the Research Board for National Security, April 3, 1945, OVP, Box 33, MDLOC.
9. J. Robert Oppenheimer, "Atomic Weapons," *Proceedings of the American Philosophical Society*, January 1946, pp. 7–10.
10. Author's interview with Hans Bethe, Ithaca, N.Y., June 6, 1997.
11. Telegram, Ernest Lawrence to J. R. Oppenheimer, August 16, 1945, Box 45, JROP, MDLOC.
12. J. R. Oppenheimer, "For the [Scientific Advisory] Panel," to Secretary of War Henry Stimson, August 17, 1945, Box 291, in ibid.
13. Oppenheimer to Lawrence, August 30, 1945, EOLP, BL, UCB.
14. Quoted in *Time*, October 29, 1945, p. 30.
15. Arthur Compton to Henry A. Wallace, September 27, 1945, Box 73, JROP, MDLOC.
16. Scientific Advisory Panel, "Proposal for Research and Development in the Field of Atomic Energy," September 28, 1945, Accession #A-92–024, 1–18, LANLA.
17. Robert Oppenheimer to Herbert W. Smith, August 26, 1945, Box 294, JROP, MDLOC; to Haakon Chevalier, August 27, 1945, Supplemental Files, Jon Else, *The Day After Trinity: J. Robert Oppenheimer and the Atomic Bomb* (Voyager CD-ROM, 1999); and to Frederick Bernheim, August 27, 1945, reprinted in Smith and Weiner, *Robert Oppenheimer*, pp. 297–298.

18. Robert Oppenheimer to General Leslie Groves, May 7, 1945, MEDR, NA.
19. George Harrison, Memorandum for the Files, September 25, 1945, HBF, MEDR, NA.
20. Quoted in Davis, *Lawrence and Oppenheimer*, p. 251.
21. Quoted in Hawkins, *Toward Trinity*.
22. Speech to the Association of Los Alamos Scientists, November 2, 1945, reprinted in Smith and Weiner, *Robert Oppenheimer*, pp. 315–325.
23. Edith Warner to J. Robert Oppenheimer, November 25, 1945, reprinted in ibid., pp. 325–326.
24. Niels Bohr, "A Challenge to Civilization," *Science*, October 12, 1945, pp. 363–364.
25. Niels Bohr to Robert Oppenheimer, November 9, 1945, JROP, MDLOC.
26. Robert Oppenheimer to W. A. Higinbotham, March 1946, quoted in Smith, *A Peril and a Hope*, p. 350; and Oppenheimer, "Atomic Weapons," p. 9.
27. Enrico Fermi and Samuel K. Allison to Senator Warren G. Magnusson, September 13, 1945, EFP, DSC, JRL, UC.
28. Arthur Compton to Leslie Groves, November 28, 1945, Series 2, Box 6, AHCP, WUA.
29. Quoted in Goodchild, *J. Robert Oppenheimer*, pp. 180–181.
30. *Report on the International Control of Atomic Energy*, Department of State Publication No. 2498 (U.S. Government Printing Office, March 16, 1946), p. viii.
31. Edward Teller and James Franck, Proposed Statement of the Atomic Scientists of Chicago on the Acheson Report, April 10, 1946, Box 9, James Franck Papers, DSC, JRL, UC.
32. Arthur Compton, Statement with Regard to State Department's Proposal for Development and Control of Atomic Energy, April 3, 1946; and Richard Baumhoff to Arthur Compton, April 2, 1946, Series 3, Box 4, AHCP, WUA.
33. Hans A. Bethe to J. M. Burgers, May 16, 1946, Federation of American Scientists Papers (hereafter cited as FASP), Box 12, DSC, JRL, UC.
34. David Lilienthal, *The Journals of David E. Lilienthal*, pp. 69–70.
35. Robert Oppenheimer to W. A. Higinbotham, May 20, 1947, FASP, DSC, JRL, UC; and Robert Oppenheimer to Niels Bohr, September 3, 1947, JROP, Box 21, MDLOC.
36. Leo Szilard, "The Physicist Invades Politics," pp. 33–34.
37. Quoted in *Time*, October 29, 1945, p. 30.
38. Quoted in Jungk, *Brighter than a Thousand Suns*, p. 241.
39. Dyson, *Disturbing the Universe*, p. 73.
40. Quotes are in Merle Miller, *Plain Speaking: An Oral Biography of Harry S Truman* (G. P. Putnam's Sons, 1974), p. 248; and Goodchild, *J. Robert Oppenheimer*, p. 180.
41. Quoted in Bernstein, "Four Physicists and the Bomb," p. 251.
42. U.S. Atomic Energy Commission, *In the Matter of J. Robert Oppenheimer*, p. 23.
43. See Libby, *The Uranium People*, p. 247.
44. Teller, "The State Department Report," p. 13.
45. Teller, "Comments on the 'Draft of a World Constitution,'" p. 204.
46. Hans Bethe, *BAS*, December 1958, p. 428.
47. Author's interview with Hans Bethe, Ithaca, N.Y., June 6, 1997.
48. Author's interview with Herbert York, La Jolla, Calif., March 12, 2001.
49. Ibid.

50. Ibid.
51. Quoted in Davis, *Lawrence and Oppenheimer*, p. 254.
52. Author's interview with Harold Agnew, Solana Beach, Calif., March 13, 2001.
53. Quoted in Segrè, *Enrico Fermi*, p. 176.
54. Quote is in Herken, *The Winning Weapon*, p. 214. Stockpile figures are in David Alan Rosenberg, "U.S. Nuclear Stockpile, 1945–1950," *BAS*, May 1982, pp. 25–30.

Chapter 9: The Superbomb Debate

1. Teller with Brown, *Legacy of Hiroshima*, p. 33.
2. Edward Teller to Enrico Fermi, October 31, 1945, LANLA.
3. Quoted in Ulam, *Adventures of a Mathematician*, p. 151.
4. Quoted in Moss, *Men Who Play God*, p. 68.
5. Quoted in Coughlan, "Dr. Edward Teller's Magnificent Obsession," p. 61.
6. See George Harrison and Harvey Bundy Files, Folder 76, MEDR, NA.
7. Arthur Compton to Gordon Gray, April 21, 1954, AHCP, Series 3, Box 18, WUA.
8. Robert Oppenheimer to James Conant, October 21, 1949, reprinted in U.S. Atomic Energy Commission, *In the Matter of J. Robert Oppenheimer*, pp. 242–243; and transcript of interview with Warner Schilling, JROP, MDLOC.
9. Author's interview with Hans Bethe, June 6, 1997, Ithaca, N.Y.
10. Herbert York, quoted in Lifton and Markusen, *The Genocidal Mentality*, p. 116.
11. Quoted in Herken, *Brotherhood of the Bomb*, pp. 204–205.
12. Author's interview with Herbert York, La Jolla, Calif., March 12, 2001.
13. Quoted in Teller with Shoolery, *Memoirs*, p. 281.
14. See "National Defense and the Scientists: An Open Letter to Hans Bethe from Edward Teller," HABP, Box 33, CAKL, CU; and Palevsky, *Atomic Fragments*, p. 53.
15. Author's interview with Edward Teller, Stanford, Calif., July 27, 1998.
16. Edward Teller to Maria Mayer (undated), Maria Mayer Papers (hereafter cited as MMP), MSCD, GL, UCSD.
17. U.S. Atomic Energy Commission, *In the Matter of J. Robert Oppenheimer*, p. 328.
18. Quoted in Bernstein, *Hans Bethe*, pp. 92–93.
19. U.S. Atomic energy Commission, *In the Matter of J. Robert Oppenheimer*, p. 328.
20. Ibid., p. 715.
21. Hans Bethe interview with Charles Weiner, May 8, 1972, OHC, NBL, AIP.
22. Hans Bethe to Victor Weisskopf, October 31, 1949, HABP, Box 9, CAKL, CU.
23. Quotes are in Bernstein, *Hans Bethe*, pp. 93–94; U.S. Atomic Energy Commission, *In the Matter of J. Robert Oppenheimer*, p. 328; and Jungk, *Brighter than a Thousand Suns*, p. 281.
24. Quoted in Hans Bethe interview with Charles Weiner, May 8, 1972, OHC, NBL, AIP.
25. Quoted in Blumberg and Owens, *Energy and Conflict*, p. 209.

26. Quoted in Shepley and Blair, *The Hydrogen Bomb*, p. 64.

27. U.S. Atomic Energy Commission, *In the Matter of J. Robert Oppenheimer*, pp. 460–461.

28. Quoted in Davis, *Lawrence and Oppenheimer*, p. 266.

29. Lee DuBridge, U.S. Atomic Energy Commission, *In the Matter of J. Robert Oppenheimer*, pp. 518–519.

30. Quoted in Goodchild, *J. Robert Oppenheimer*, p. 200.

31. Manuscript Journal, David E. Lilienthal Papers, Seeley G. Mudd Library, Princeton University.

32. Quoted in Lilienthal, *The Atomic Energy Years*, p. 581.

33. GAC Report, October 30, 1949, reprinted in York, *The Advisors*, pp. 152–160.

34. Enrico Fermi and I. I. Rabi, "An Opinion on the Development of the 'Super,'" October 30, 1949, reprinted in York, *The Advisors*, pp. 161–162.

35. U.S. Atomic Energy Commission, *In the Matter of J. Robert Oppenheimer*, p. 395.

36. Quoted in Bernstein, "Profiles: Physicist," p. 77.

37. Quoted in Rigden, *Rabi*, p. 208.

38. Herbert Childs interview with Robert Oppenheimer, EOLP, BL, UCB.

39. Quoted in *Foreign Relations of the United States: 1950*, vol. 1, pp. 200–201.

40. See note 8.

41. Ibid.

42. Teller with Brown, *Legacy of Hiroshima*, p. 44.

43. Quoted in Bernstein, "Four Physicists and the Bomb," p. 260.

44. Edward Teller to Maria Mayer (undated), Box 3, MMP, MSCD, GL, UCSD.

45. John H. Manley, "Recollections and Memories," unpublished manuscript, LANLA.

46. Edward Teller to John von Neumann, November 9, 1949, John von Neumann Papers, Box 7, MDLOC.

47. Edward Teller to Maria Mayer (undated), Box 3, MMP, MSCD, GL, UCSD.

48. J. H. Manley Diary, November 15, 1949, p. 14, Accession #A-92-024, 1-1, LANLA.

49. Dean Acheson, *Present at the Creation: My Years in the State Department* (W.W. Norton, 1969), p. 346.

50. Quoted in R. Gordon Arneson, "The H-Bomb Decision," *Foreign Service Journal*, May 1969, p. 29; and Acheson, *Present at the Creation*, p. 346.

51. Transcript of Warner Schilling interview, Box 65, JROP, MDLOC.

52. Quoted in ibid., p. 27.

53. See *The Gallup Poll: Public Opinion, 1935–1971*, vol. 2, p. 888.

54. Quoted in *NYT*, February 1, 1950, p. 3.

55. Andrei Sakharov, *Memoirs* (Alfred A. Knopf, 1990), pp. 94, 98–101.

56. Quoted in Davis, *Lawrence and Oppenheimer*, pp. 330–331.

57. Transcript, "Mrs. Franklin D. Roosevelt's Simulcast on Sunday, February 12, 1950, NBC Network," JROP, MDLOC.

58. "We Got to Go On," unpublished letter, March 6, 1950, LSP, MSCD, GL, UCSD; and Leo Szilard at University of Chicago Roundtable Discussion, February 26, 1950, reprinted in "The Facts About the Hydrogen Bomb," *BAS*, April 1950, pp. 107–109.

59. Arthur Compton to George Gallup, January 21, 1950, AHCP, Series 3, Box 12, WUA.

60. Quoted in Moss, *Men Who Play God*, p. 40.

61. Statement by S. K. Allison et al., Samuel Allison Papers, Box 2, DSC, JRL, UC.

62. Hans Bethe, "The Hydrogen Bomb," *Scientific American*, April 1950, pp. 102–103.

63. Hans Bethe to Norris Bradbury, February 14, 1950, LANLA.

64. Quoted in Lifton and Markusen, *The Genocidal Mentality*, p. 117.

65. Ibid., p. 139.

66. "Talk to FAS Members and Others at Los Alamos, July 9, 1953," HABP, CAKL, CU.

67. Notes on "The Social Responsibilities of Scientists and Engineers," November 6, 1963, HABP, Box 4, CAKL, CU.

68. Quoted in Jungk, *Brighter than a Thousand Suns*, p. 291.

69. AEC chairman Gordon Dean, quoted in ibid., p. 295.

70. See Hans Bethe to John Strauss, February 28, 1950, HABP, CAKL, CU.

71. Notes, "TV 1995 — Anniversary," BPP.

72. Quoted in Jungk, *Brighter than a Thousand Suns*, p. 296.

73. Quoted in Teller with Shoolery, *Memoirs*, p. 289.

74. Quoted in Blumberg and Owens, *Energy and Conflict*, p. 251.

75. Quoted in Blumberg and Panos, *Edward Teller*, p. 141.

76. Teller, "The Work of Many People," *Science*, February 25, 1955, p. 274.

77. Quoted in Chuck Hansen, *The Swords of Armageddon: U.S. Nuclear Weapons Development Since 1945*. CD-ROM. (Chukelea Publications, 1995).

78. Raemer Schreiber, quoted in Rhodes, *Dark Sun*, p. 509.

79. Author's interview with Edward Teller, Stanford, Calif., July 27, 1998.

80. Quoted in Relman Morin, "Dr. Cloyd Marvin Discusses Teller's 'Fear in His Heart,'" *Washington Post*, June 23, 1954.

81. Quoted in Coughlan, "Dr. Edward Teller's Magnificent Obsession," p. 74.

Chapter 10: The Oppenheimer Affair

1. U.S. Atomic Energy Commission, *In the Matter of J. Robert Oppenheimer*, pp. 837–838.

2. Quoted in Davis, *Lawrence and Oppenheimer*, p. 278.

3. Quoted in Alsop, *We Accuse!*, p. 19.

4. Joint Congressional Committee on Atomic Energy, *Investigation into the United States Atomic Energy Project* (U.S Government Printing Office, 1949), pp. 277–315; and *NYT*, June 16, 1949, p. 20.

5. Quoted in Stern with Green, *The Oppenheimer Case*, p. 131; and Lilienthal, *The Atomic Energy Years*, p. 522.

6. "Record of Telephone Conversation (Robert Oppenheimer and Lewis Strauss)," December 14, 1953, AEC Records, Historian's Office, Department of Energy, Germantown, Md.

7. Quoted in Bernstein, "Profiles: Physicist — II."

8. Quoted in Stern with Green, *The Oppenheimer Case*, p. 235.

9. Quoted in Coughlan, "The Tangled Drama," p. 88.

10. J. Robert Oppenheimer to Lewis Strauss, December 22, 1953, reprinted in *NYT*, April 13, 1954, p. 16.

11. Author's interview with Ralph Lapp, Alexandria, Va., March 12, 1999.
12. Quoted in Blumberg and Owens, *Energy and Conflict*, p. 360.
13. Edward Teller, paraphrased in McCabe to FBI Director, May 14, 1952; and SAC, Albuquerque, to Director, FBI, "Dr. J. Robert Oppenheimer," May 27, 1952, J. Robert Oppenheimer FBI/Freedom of Information Act File.
14. Jon Else interview with I. I. Rabi, quoted in Bernstein, "In the Matter of J. Robert Oppenheimer," p. 222.
15. Harold Green, "The Oppenheimer Case: A Study in the Abuse of the Law," *BAS*, September 1977, pp. 59–60.
16. See Transcript of Gordon Gray Oral History, p. 187, Dwight D. Eisenhower Library, Abilene, Kansas.
17. Hans Bethe and Victor Weisskopf to J. Robert Oppenheimer, Box 202, JROP, MDLOC.
18. U.S. Atomic Energy Commission, *In the Matter of J. Robert Oppenheimer*, p. 20.
19. Ibid., p. 56.
20. David Lilienthal, quoted in Stern with Green, *The Oppenheimer Case*, pp. 309–310.
21. Quoted in Goodchild, *J. Robert Oppenheimer*, p. 248.
22. Eltenton FBI interview, June 26, 1946, cited in Herken, *Brotherhood of the Bomb*, p. 92.
23. U.S. Atomic Energy Commission, *In the Matter of J. Robert Oppenheimer*, p. 137.
24. Ibid.
25. Ibid., p. 149.
26. Ibid., p. 154.
27. Leslie Groves to Lewis Strauss, February 1, 1954, Groves Papers, Modern Military Records, NA.
28. U.S. Atomic Energy Commission, *In the Matter of J. Robert Oppenheimer*, p. 243.
29. Ibid., p. 229.
30. Quoted in Goodchild, *J. Robert Oppenheimer*, p. 244.
31. Quoted in Coughlan, "Tangled Drama," p. 101.
32. U.S. Atomic Energy Commission, *In the Matter of J. Robert Oppenheimer*, p. 331.
33. Quoted in Davis, *Lawrence and Oppenheimer*, p. 346.
34. U.S. Atomic Energy Commission, *In the Matter of J. Robert Oppenheimer*, p. 468.
35. Ibid., p. 469.
36. Ibid., p. 470.
37. "Familiarity, Rejection of Reds Favor Oppenheimer — Compton," *Washington Post*, April 19, 1954, p. 10.
38. See Arthur H. Compton to Gordon Gray, April 21, 1954, AHCP, Series 3, Box 18, WUA.
39. U.S. Atomic Energy Commission, *In the Matter of J. Robert Oppenheimer*, pp. 565, 567.
40. Ibid., p. 517.
41. Ibid., p. 660.
42. See Herken, *Brotherhood of the Bomb*, pp. 248, 258.
43. Author's interview with Harold Agnew, Solana Beach, Calif., March 13, 2001.

44. U.S. Atomic Energy Commission, *In the Matter of J. Robert Oppenheimer*, p. 754.
45. Charter Heslep to Lewis Strauss, "Conversation with Edward Teller at Livermore on April 22, 1954," May 3, 1954, Lewis Strauss Papers, Herbert Hoover Library, West Branch, Iowa.
46. Author's interview with Herbert York, La Jolla, Calif., March 12, 2001.
47. Ibid.
48. Draft of a Statement, 1954, in Helen Hawkins, G. Allen Greb, and Gertrud Weiss Szilard, eds., *Toward a Livable World* (MIT Press, 1987), p. 129.
49. See ibid., p. xliii.
50. Hans Bethe interview with Charles Weiner, May 9, 1972, OHC, NBL, AIP; and Bernstein, *Hans Bethe*, p. 99.
51. Quoted in Dyson, *Disturbing the Universe*, p. 90.
52. Quoted in Jonathan Weisman, "Teller Recants Oppenheimer Denunciation," *Tri-Valley Herald*, December 16, 1992.
53. U.S. Atomic Energy Commission, *In the Matter of J. Robert Oppenheimer*, pp. 709–710.
54. Ibid., p. 726.
55. Handwritten Notes, Box 205, JROP, MDLOC.
56. Quoted in Stern with Green, *The Oppenheimer Case*, p. 345.
57. Quoted in York, *The Advisors*, p. 64.
58. Quoted in Herken, *Brotherhood of the Bomb*, p. 283.
59. Author's interview with Herbert York, La Jolla, Calif., March 12, 2001.
60. Ernest O. Lawrence for C. A. Rolander, AEC, picked up by courier on May 4, 1954, LWA-1234, EOLP, BL, UCB.
61. Quoted in Hans Bethe interview with Charles Weiner, May 9, 1972, OHC, NBL, AIP.
62. Quoted in Coughlan, "Tangled Drama," p. 98.
63. Quoted in *NYT*, June 4, 1954, p. 19.
64. Notes of Phone Conversation with Joseph Alsop, June 8, 1954, Box 200, JROP, MDLOC.
65. Decision and Opinions of the United States Atomic Energy Commission in the Matter of Dr. J. Robert Oppenheimer, reprinted in U.S. Atomic Energy Commission, *In the Matter of J. Robert Oppenheimer* (MIT Press edition), pp. 1047–1066.
66. Quoted in *NYT*, July 4, 1954, p. 15.
67. Quoted in Alsop, *We Accuse!*, p. 21.
68. Quoted in Lifton and Markusen, *The Genocidal Mentality*, p. 136.
69. Quoted in Bernstein, *Hans Bethe*, p. 101.
70. Hans Bethe to Edward Teller, November 30, 1954, Edward Teller Papers, Hoover Institution on War, Revolution and Peace, Stanford University.
71. Quoted in Herken, *Brotherhood of the Bomb*, p. 299.
72. Crawford Greenewalt to Herbert Anderson, August 22, 1960, Personal Papers of Crawford Greenewalt, Accession 2016, HML.
73. Quoted in Segrè, *Enrico Fermi*, p. 182.
74. Quoted in Segrè, *A Mind Always in Motion*, p. 252.
75. Quoted in Blumberg and Owens, *Energy and Conflict*, p. 374.
76. Quoted in Jungk, *Brighter than a Thousand Suns*, p. 331.
77. Jon Else interview with I. I. Rabi, quoted in Bernstein, "In the Matter of J. Robert Oppenheimer," p. 222.

78. Felix Bloch, quoted in Rigden, *Rabi*, pp. 218–219.

79. Quoted in ibid., pp. 230–231.

80. Quoted in Bernstein, *Hans Bethe*, p. 99.

81. Robert Serber quoted in Rhodes, *Dark Sun*, p. 558.

82. Quoted in Else, *The Day After Trinity* (KTEH-TV, 1980).

83. Quoted in Moyers, "Meet I. I. Rabi."

84. Quoted in John Mason Brown, *Through These Men* (Harper and Brothers, 1956), p. 288.

85. Quoted in Coughlan, "Tangled Drama," p. 104; and Brown, *Through These Men*, pp. 228–229.

86. Quoted in Coughlan, "Tangled Drama," p. 104.

87. Edward Teller to William L. Borden, July 9, 1954, excerpted in Teller with Shoolery, *Memoirs*, p. 390.

88. Edward Teller to Maria Mayer (undated), MMP, MSCD, GL, UCSD.

89. Quoted in Blumberg and Owens, *Energy and Conflict*, p. 378.

90. Quoted in Moss, *Men Who Play God*, p. 78.

91. Excerpted in Blumberg and Owens, *Energy and Conflict*, p. 368.

92. Teller-Strauss Correspondence File, Lewis Strauss Papers, Herbert Hoover Library.

93. Quoted in Blumberg and Owens, *Energy and Conflict*, p. 364.

94. Teller with Shoolery, *Memoirs*, pp. 371, 383.

95. Quoted in Blumberg and Owens, *Energy and Conflict*, p. 365.

96. See *NYT*, April 5, 1963, p. 1.

97. Quoted in Michelmore, *The Swift Years*, p. 232.

98. Quoted in Jungk, *Brighter than a Thousand Suns*, p. 333.

Chapter 11: Twilight Years

1. Niels Bohr to George C. Marshall, June 10, 1948, JROP, MDLOC.

2. Niels Bohr, "Open Letter to the United Nations," June 9, 1950, reprinted in Rozental, *Niels Bohr*, pp. 340–352.

3. Arthur Compton, "The Moral Meaning of the Atomic Bomb" (1946), quoted in Johnston, *The Cosmos of Arthur Holly Compton*, pp. 304–305.

4. Arthur Compton, "How Peace with the Hydrogen Bomb?" (1954), reprinted in ibid., p. 325.

5. Arthur Compton to Senator Stuart Symington, May 8, 1958, AHCP, Series 3, Box 28, WUA.

6. Quoted in York, *Making Weapons, Talking Peace*, p. 39.

7. See Ernest O. Lawrence to Mrs. Martin Johnson, January 31, 1955, EOLP, BL, UCB.

8. Quoted in Davis, *Lawrence and Oppenheimer*, p. 351.

9. Quoted in Herken, *Brotherhood of the Bomb*, p. 320.

10. Ernest O. Lawrence to Mrs. Edwin S. Spencer, February 17, 1955, EOLP, BL, UCB.

11. Quoted in Coffin, "Leo Szilard."

12. Leo Szilard to Niels Bohr, November 7, 1950, LSP, Box 4, Folder 34, MSCD, GL, UCSD.

13. See Szilard, *The Voice of the Dolphins*.

14. Quoted in Coffin, "Leo Szilard."
15. Ibid.
16. Quoted in Childs, *An American Genius*, p. 531.
17. Quoted in Herken, *Brotherhood of the Bomb*, p. 328.
18. Author's interview with Hans Bethe, Ithaca, N.Y., June 6, 1997.
19. Frank Oppenheimer interview with Charles Weiner, May 21, 1973, OHC, NBL, AIP.
20. "Dr. Oppenheimer Discusses Future," *NYT*, July 4, 1954.
21. Victor Cohn, "Can a Security Risk Survive?" *Minneapolis Tribune*, June 16, 1957.
22. See Leo Szilard, "Memorandum Based on a Meeting Held on the Initiative of Bertrand Russell at Pugwash, Nova Scotia, in July 1957," July 29, 1957; and "Has the Time Come to Abrogate War?" May 25, 1960, Eugene Rabinowitch Papers, Box 9, DSC, JRL, UC.
23. Quoted in Lanouette, *Genius in the Shadows*, p. 371.
24. Szilard-Teller Debate, reprinted in Hawkins, Greb, and Szilard, *Toward a Livable World*, pp. 238–250.
25. Arthur Compton to Leo Szilard, March 3, 1960, LSP, MSCD, GL, UCSD.
26. I. I. Rabi to Robert Oppenheimer, April 5, 1963, IIRP, MDLOC.
27. Edward Teller to Robert Oppenheimer (undated); and Robert Oppenheimer to Edward Teller, April 23, 1963, Box 71, JROP, MDLOC.
28. Quoted in Coughlan, "Tangled Drama," p. 110.
29. Quoted in Lanouette, *Genius in the Shadows*, p. xix.
30. "Address by Dr. Leo Szilard," reprinted in *The Nation*, December 3, 1945.
31. J. Robert Oppenheimer, "Niels Bohr and Atomic Weapons," May 18, 1964, LANLA.
32. Quoted in Herbert Smith interview with Charles Weiner, August 1, 1974, OHC, NBL, AIP.
33. Thomas B. Morgan, "With Oppenheimer, on an Autumn Day," *Look*, December 27, 1966, pp. 63, 67.
34. Robert Reid to the Editor, *The [London] Times*, August 26, 1975.
35. Quoted in Peierls, *Bird of Passage*, p. 315.
36. Hans Bethe to Robert Oppenheimer, JROP, MDLOC.
37. Quoted in Michelmore, *The Swift Years*, p. 254.
38. Quoted in *Science*, March 3, 1967, p. 1080.
39. Quoted in Rigden, *Rabi*, p. 211.
40. Quoted in Royal, *The Story of J. Robert Oppenheimer*, p. 180.
41. Quoted in Rigden, *Rabi*, p. 231.
42. Quoted in Stern with Green, *The Oppenheimer Case*, p. 514.
43. Robert Oppenheimer, "The Power to Act: The Scientific Revolution and Its Effects on Democratic Institutions" (1963), in Metropolis, Rota, and Sharp, *Uncommon Sense*, p.144.
44. Quoted in Rigden, *Rabi*, p. 178.
45. Quoted in Bernstein, "Profiles: Physicist — II," p. 66.
46. Author's interview with Herbert York, La Jolla, Calif., March 12, 2001.
47. Quoted in Rigden, *Rabi*, p. 220.
48. The physicist was Richard Garwin. Cited in author's interview with Herbert York, La Jolla, Calif., March 12, 2001.
49. Edward Teller to Lewis Strauss, 1957, quoted in Blumberg and Owens, *Energy and Conflict*, p. 420.

50. Quoted in *NYT,* August 14, 1963, p. 6.
51. Quoted in ibid., August 24, 1963, p. 18.
52. Quoted in ibid., January 12, 1988, p. A24.
53. I. I. Rabi Lecture, Columbia University, May 13, 1966, Manuscript Biographies, AIP.
54. Quoted in Bernstein, "Profiles: Physicist — II," p. 94.
55. Quoted in *NYT,* January 12, 1988, p. A24.
56. See John Noble Wilford, "Teller Deplores Secret Research," in ibid., December 28, 1970, pp. 1, 25.
57. Quoted in "Edward Teller and His Critics," Part 1, *Bridges: A Liberal/Conservative Dialogue with Larry Josephson,* National Public Radio, November 1995.
58. Transcript, *Firing Line,* Southern Educational Communications Association, June 15, 1982, p. 7.
59. Quoted in Douglas C. Waller, *Congress and the Nuclear Freeze* (University of Massachusetts Press, 1987), p. 191.
60. Quoted in "Our Times with Bill Moyers," CBS TV, June 27, 1983.
61. Quoted in Rigden, *Rabi,* p. 229.
62. Quoted in Charles Claffey, "A Father of the A-Bomb Looks Back in Torment," *Boston Globe,* April 15, 1983, p. 1; and I. I. Rabi, "How Well We Meant."
63. Author's interview with Edward Teller, Stanford, Calif., July 27, 1998.
64. Quoted in Broad, *Teller's War,* pp. 270–271.
65. Quoted in Gary Stix, "Profile: Infamy and Honor at the Atomic Café," *Scientific American,* October 1999, p. 44.
66. Teller with Shoolery, *Memoirs,* p. 396.
67. Ibid., p. 22 n.
68. Quoted in Blumberg and Panos, *Edward Teller,* p. 2.
69. Quoted in Lee Edson, "Scientific Man For All Seasons," *New York Times Magazine,* March 10, 1968, p. 124.
70. Dyson, *Disturbing the Universe,* p. 47.
71. See Testimony before House Subcommittee on Arms Control, International Security, and Science, May 13, 1985; and Notes of Remarks at Los Alamos National Laboratory, April 13, 1983, BPP.
72. Quoted in Blumberg and Panos, *Edward Teller,* p. 198.
73. Edward Teller to Hans Bethe, February 28, 1984, in ibid., p. 264.
74. Edward Teller to Hans Bethe, May 23, 1985, in ibid., pp. 265–266.
75. Hans Bethe to Edward Teller, June 20, 1985, BPP.
76. Edward Teller to Hans Bethe, July 8, 1985; and Hans Bethe to Edward Teller, August 5, 1985, in ibid.
77. Author's interview with Louis Rosen, Los Alamos, N.Mex., July 16, 1997.
78. Author's interview with Herbert York, La Jolla, Calif., March 12, 2001.
79. Quoted in Palevsky, *Atomic Fragments,* p. 158.
80. Handwritten Notes, "28 Nov 72," HABP, CAKL, CU.
81. "Talk to Members of Congress," July 16, 1985, BPP.
82. Quoted in *Chronicle of Higher Education,* January 31, 1997, p. A14.
83. Hans Bethe, *FAS Public Interest Report,* September–October 1995.
84. Quotes are in John W. Finney, "Bethe Receives Atom Award," *NYT,* December 2, 1961; and Edson, "Scientific Man for All Seasons," p. 125.
85. Quoted in Judith Horstman, "Hans Bethe: A Reluctant Warrior," *Ithaca Journal,* December 18, 1981, p. 5.

NOTES

Epilogue: The Atomic Scientists and Today

1. Patricia Leigh Brown, "Preserving the Birthplaces of the Atom Bomb," *NYT,* April 7, 2001, p. A10.
2. Rabi, *My Life and Times as a Physicist,* p. 3.
3. J. Robert Oppenheimer, "Atomic Physics in Civilization," *Bulletin of the Atomic Scientists* Papers, Box 29, JRL, UC.

BIBLIOGRAPHY

Manuscript Collections

Samuel Allison Papers. Department of Special Collections. Joseph Regenstein Library, University of Chicago.

Hans A. Bethe Papers. Division of Rare and Manuscript Collections. Carl A. Kroch Library, Cornell University.

Hans Bethe Personal Papers. Newman Laboratory of Nuclear Studies, Cornell University.

Niels Bohr Manuscripts, 1904–1962 [Microfilm]. Archive for the History of Quantum Physics. Lamont Library, Harvard University.

Bulletin of the Atomic Scientists Papers. Department of Special Collections. Joseph Regenstein Library.

Vannevar Bush Papers. Manuscript Division. Library of Congress, Washington, D.C.

Bush-Conant File Relating to the Development of the Atomic Bomb, 1940–1945. Records of the Office of Scientific Research and Development. Manhattan Engineer District Records. National Archives, Washington, D.C.

Arthur Holly Compton Papers. University Archives, Washington University.

Correspondence ("Top Secret") of the Manhattan Engineer District, 1942–1946. National Archives, Washington, D.C.

Federation of American Scientists Papers. Department of Special Collections. Joseph Regenstein Library, University of Chicago.

Enrico Fermi Papers. Department of Special Collections. Joseph Regenstein Library, University of Chicago.

Richard Feynman Papers. Archives. Niels Bohr Library. American Institute of Physics, College Park, Md.

James Franck Papers. Department of Special Collections. Joseph Regenstein Library, University of Chicago.

George Gamow Papers. Manuscript Division. Library of Congress, Washington, D.C.

BIBLIOGRAPHY

Samuel Goudsmit Papers. Archives. Niels Bohr Library. American Institute of Physics, College Park, Md.

Crawford H. Greenewalt Manhattan Project Diary, 1942–1945. Hagley Museum and Library, Wilmington, Del.

Crawford H. Greenewalt Personal Papers, 1948–1992. Hagley Museum and Library, Wilmington, Del.

Harrison-Bundy Files Relating to the Development of the Atomic Bomb, 1942–1946. Manhattan Engineer District Records. National Archives, Washington, D.C.

George B. Kistiakowsky Papers. Harvard University Archives. Pusey Library, Harvard University.

Ernest O. Lawrence Papers. Bancroft Library. University of California, Berkeley.

Los Alamos National Laboratory Archives. Los Alamos National Laboratory, Los Alamos, N.Mex.

Maria Goeppert Mayer Papers. Mandeville Special Collections Department. Geisel Library, University of California, San Diego.

Elsie Blumer McMillan. "The Atom and Eve" [Manuscript]. Archives. Niels Bohr Library. American Institute of Physics, College Park, Md.

John von Neumann Papers. Manuscript Division. Library of Congress, Washington, D.C.

J. Robert Oppenheimer FBI Security File. Federal Bureau of Investigation. Department of Justice, Washington, D.C.

J. Robert Oppenheimer Papers. Manuscript Division. Library of Congress, Washington, D.C.

Rudolf Peierls Papers. Modern Papers Room. Bodleian Library, University of Oxford.

George Placzek Papers. Archives. Niels Bohr Library. American Institute of Physics, College Park, Md.

I. I. Rabi Papers. Manuscript Division. Library of Congress, Washington, D.C.

Eugene I. Rabinowitch Papers. Department of Special Collections. Joseph Regenstein Library, University of Chicago.

Glenn T. Seaborg Diary. Manuscript Division. Library of Congress, Washington, D.C.

Leo Szilard Papers. Mandeville Special Collections Department. Geisel Library, University of California, San Diego.

Edward Teller Papers. Hoover Institution Library and Archives. Hoover Institution on War, Revolution and Peace, Stanford University.

Harold Clayton Urey Papers. Mandeville Special Collections Department. Geisel Library, University of California, San Diego.

Oswald Veblen Papers. Manuscript Division. Library of Congress, Washington, D.C.

Interviews

Philip Abelson. Washington, D.C. March 23, 1999.
Harold and Beverly Agnew. Solana Beach, Calif. March 13, 2001.
Robert Bacher. Santa Barbara, Calif. July 29, 1998.

BIBLIOGRAPHY

Hans Bethe. Ithaca, N.Y. June 6, 1997.
Rose Bethe. Ithaca, N.Y. June 8, 1997.
Robert Christy. Pasadena, Calif. July 29, 1998.
Jean Critchfield. Los Alamos, N.Mex. July 1997.
Arthur and Peggy Hemmendinger. Santa Fe, N.Mex. July 22, 1997.
Donald and Lily Hornig. Cambridge, Mass. May 14, 1998.
Jerome and Isabella Karle. Washington, D.C. December 10, 1998.
Ralph Lapp. Alexandria, Va. March 12, 1999.
Kathleen Manley. Los Alamos, N.Mex. July 21, 1997.
Kay Mark. Los Alamos, N.Mex. July 19, 1997.
Philip Morrison. Cambridge, Mass. May 18, 1998.
Louis Rosen. Los Alamos, N.Mex. July 16, 1997.
Raemer Schreiber. Los Alamos, N.Mex. July 17, 1997.
Edward Teller. Stanford, Calif. July 27, 1998.
Françoise Ulam. Santa Fe, N.Mex. July 1997.
Victor Weisskopf. Newton, Mass. May 17, 1998.
Jane Wilson. Ithaca, N.Y. June 8, 1997.
Herbert York. La Jolla, Calif. March 12, 2001.

Oral Histories

Luis Alvarez. American Institute of Physics, College Park, Md.
Carl Anderson. California Institute of Technology, Pasadena, Calif.
Hans Bethe. American Institute of Physics, College Park, Md.
Rose Bethe. Carl A. Kroch Library, Cornell University.
Norris Bradbury. Bancroft Library, University of California, Berkeley.
Gregory Breit. American Institute of Physics, College Park, Md.
Betty Compton. American Institute of Physics, College Park, Md.
Paul Ewald. American Institute of Physics, College Park, Md.
Richard Feynman. American Institute of Physics, College Park, Md.
Darol Froman. Bancroft Library, University of California, Berkeley.
Maurice Goldhaber. American Institute of Phyics, College Park, Md.
Carson Mark. Bancroft Library, University of California, Berkeley.
Edwin McMillan. American Institute of Physics, College Park, Md.
Philip Morrison. American Institute of Physics, College Park, Md.
Lothar Nordheim. American Institute of Physics, College Park, Md.
Frank Oppenheimer. American Institute of Physics, College Park, Md.
Robert Oppenheimer. American Institute of Physics, College Park, Md.
Abraham Pais. American Institute of Physics, College Park, Md.
Wolfgang Panofsky. American Institute of Physics, College Park, Md.
Rudolf Peierls. American Institute of Physics, College Park, Md.
Norman Ramsey. Columbia University, New York, N.Y.
Leon Rosenfeld. American Institute of Physics, College Park, Md.
Emilio Segrè. American Institute of Physics, College Park, Md.
Robert Serber. American Institute of Physics, College Park, Md.
Herbert Smith. American Institute of Physics, College Park, Md.
John Wheeler. American Institute of Physics, College Park, Md.

Robert Wilson. American Institute of Physics, College Park, Md.
Herbert York. Bancroft Library, University of California, Berkeley.

Published Primary Sources

Allison, Samuel K. "Arthur Holly Compton." *Biographical Memoirs of the National Academy of Sciences* 38 (1965): 81–94.

Alvarez, Luis W. *Alvarez*. Basic Books, 1987.

———. "Ernest Orlando Lawrence." *Biographical Memoirs of the National Academy of Sciences* 41 (1970): 251–284.

Anderson, Herbert L. "Fermi, Szilard and Trinity." *Bulletin of the Atomic Scientists*, October 1974, 40–47.

———. "The Legacy of Fermi and Szilard," *Bulletin of the Atomic Scientists*, September 1974, 56–62.

Bacher, Robert F. "Robert Oppenheimer." *Proceedings of the American Philosophical Society* 116, no. 4 (August 15, 1972): 279–293.

Badash, Lawrence, et al. *Reminiscences of Los Alamos*. D. Reidel, 1980.

Bainbridge, Kenneth T. "A Foul and Awesome Display." *Bulletin of the Atomic Scientists* 31, no. 5 (May 1975): 40–46.

———. *Trinity*. Los Alamos Scientific Laboratory, 1945.

Barnard, Chester I., et al. *A Report on the International Control of Atomic Energy*. U.S. Department of State, 1946.

Bethe, Hans A. "Comments on the History of the H-Bomb." *Los Alamos Science*, Fall 1982.

———. "J. Robert Oppenheimer." In *Biographical Memoirs of Fellows of the Royal Society*. The Royal Society, 1968.

———. *The Road from Los Alamos*. AIP Press, 1985.

Bohr, Niels. *Atomic Physics and Human Knowledge*. John Wiley, 1958.

———. *Collected Works*. North-Holland, 1972–1981.

———. *Essays 1958–1963 on Atomic Physics and Human Knowledge*. Interscience, 1963.

Brode, Bernice. "Tales of Los Alamos." *LASL Community News*, June 2 and September 22, 1960.

Bush, Vannevar. *Pieces of the Action*. William Morrow, 1970.

Chevalier, Haakon. *Oppenheimer: The Story of a Friendship*. George Braziller, 1965.

Compton, Arthur Holly. *Atomic Quest: A Personal Narrative*. Oxford University Press, 1956.

———. *The Freedom of Man*. Yale University Press, 1935.

———. *The Human Meaning of Science*. University of North Carolina Press, 1940.

———. "The Religion of a Scientist." Jewish Theological Seminary of America, 1938.

Conant, James Bryant. *My Several Lives*. Harper and Row, 1970.

Feld, Bernard. "Leo Szilard, Scientist for All Seasons." *Social Research* 51, no. 3 (Fall 1984).

Fermi, Enrico. *Collected Papers*. University of Chicago Press, 1962.

———. "Development of the First Chain-Reacting Pile." *Proceedings of the American Philosophical Society*, 1946, 20–24.

———. *Nuclear Physics*. University of Chicago Press, 1949.

BIBLIOGRAPHY

Fermi, Laura. *Atoms in the Family: My Life with Enrico Fermi.* University of Chicago Press, 1954.

Feynman, Richard. *Surely You're Joking, Mr. Feynman!* W.W. Norton, 1985.

Frisch, Otto. "The Life of Niels Bohr." *Scientific American,* June 1967.

———. "Scientists and the Hydrogen Bomb." *Listener,* April 1, 1954.

———. *What Little I Remember.* Cambridge University Press, 1979.

Groves, Leslie R. "The Atom General Answers His Critics." *Saturday Evening Post,* May 19, 1948.

———. *Now It Can Be Told: The Story of the Manhattan Project.* Harper and Brothers, 1962.

Hawkins, David. *Toward Trinity,* Part I of *Project Y: The Los Alamos Story.* Los Alamos National Laboratory, 1947. Reprint, Tomash Publishers, 1983.

Jette, Eleanor. *Inside Box 1663.* Los Alamos Historical Society, 1977.

Johnston, Marjorie, ed. *The Cosmos of Arthur Holly Compton.* Alfred A. Knopf, 1967.

Kamen, Martin D. *Radiant Science, Dark Politics: A Memoir of the Nuclear Age.* University of California Press, 1985.

Kathren, Ronald L., Jerry B. Gough, and Gary T. Benefiel, eds. *The Plutonium Story: The Journals of Professor Glenn T. Seaborg, 1939–1946.* Battelle Memorial Institute, 1994.

Kistiakowsky, George B. "Trinity — A Reminiscence." *Bulletin of the Atomic Scientists* 36, no. 6 (June 1980): 19–22.

Laurence, William L. *Dawn over Zero.* Alfred A. Knopf, 1946.

———. *The Story of the Atomic Bomb.* U.S. War Department, 1945.

Lewis, Richard S., and Jane Wilson, with Eugene Rabinowitch, eds. *Alamogordo Plus Twenty-Five Years.* Viking Press, 1971.

Libby, Leona Marshall. *The Uranium People.* Crane Russak, 1979.

Lilienthal, David E. *Change, Hope, and the Bomb.* Princeton University Press, 1963.

———. *The Journals of David E. Lilienthal.* Volume 2: *The Atomic Energy Years, 1945–1950.* Harper and Row, 1964.

Los Alamos Historical Society. *Behind Tall Fences: Stories and Experiences About Los Alamos at Its Beginning.* Los Alamos Historical Society, 1996.

Mason, Katrina R. *Children of Los Alamos: An Oral History of the Town Where the Atomic Age Began.* Twayne, 1995.

McKibben, Dorothy S. "Los Alamos Project: The Santa Fe Office." Manuscript, November 23, 1959.

Metropolis, N., Gian-Carlo Rota, and David Sharp, eds. *Uncommon Sense: J. Robert Oppenheimer.* Birkhäuser, 1984.

Moyers, Bill. "Meet I. I. Rabi." In *A Walk Through the Twentieth Century.* WNET, 1984.

Nichols, K. D. *The Road to Trinity.* William Morrow, 1987.

Nielson, J. Rud. "Memories of Niels Bohr." *Physics Today,* October 1963.

O'Keefe, Bernard J. *Nuclear Hostages.* Houghton Mifflin, 1983.

Oliphant, Mark L. "The Two Ernests." *Physics Today,* September and October 1966.

Oppenheimer, J. Robert. "The Atom Bomb and College Education." In *General Magazine and Historical Chronicle.* University of Pennsylvania General Alumni Society, 1946.

————. *The Open Mind*. Simon and Schuster, 1955.

————. *Science and the Common Understanding*. Simon and Schuster, 1954.

————. "Secretary Stimson and the Atomic Bomb." *Andover Bulletin*, Spring 1961.

————. "Talk to Undergraduates." In *Engineering and Science Monthly*. California Institute of Technology, 1957.

Peierls, Rudolf. *Atomic Histories*. AIP Press, 1997.

————. *Bird of Passage*. Princeton University Press, 1985.

Rabi, I. I. *My Life and Times as a Physicist*. Claremont College, 1960.

————. "The Physicist Returns from the War." *Atlantic*, October 1945.

————. *Science: The Center of Culture*. World, 1970.

Rabi, I. I., Robert Serber, Victor F. Weisskopf, Abraham Pais, and Glenn T. Seaborg. *Oppenheimer*. Charles Scribner's Sons, 1969.

Rabinowitch, Eugene. "Leo Szilard." *Bulletin of the Atomic Scientists*, October 1964, 16–20.

Rozental, Stefan, ed. *Niels Bohr: His Life and Work as Seen by His Friends and Colleagues*. John Wiley and Sons, 1967.

Seaborg, Glenn T. *Journal of Glenn T. Seaborg, 1946–1958*. Lawrence Berkeley Laboratory, 1990.

————. *Kennedy, Khrushchev, and the Test Ban*. University of California Press, 1981.

Seaborg, Glenn T., with Eric Seaborg. *Adventures in the Atomic Age: From Watts to Washington*. Farrar, Straus and Giroux, 2001.

Segrè, Emilio. *Enrico Fermi, Physicist*. University of Chicago Press, 1970.

————. "Fifty Years Up and Down a Strenuous and Scenic Trail." *Annual Review of Nuclear Particle Science* 31 (1981).

————. *A Mind Always in Motion: The Autobiography of Emilio Segrè*. University of California Press, 1993.

Serber, Robert. *The Los Alamos Primer*. University of California Press, 1992.

Serber, Robert, with Robert P. Crease. *Peace & War: Reminiscences of a Life on the Frontiers of Science*. Columbia University Press, 1998.

Shils, Edward. "Leo Szilard: A Memoir." *Encounter*, December 1964.

————. ed. *Remembering the University of Chicago: Teachers, Scientists and Scholars*. University of Chicago Press, 1991.

Smith, Alice Kimball, and Charles Weiner, eds. *Robert Oppenheimer: Letters and Recollections*. Harvard University Press, 1980. Reprint, Stanford University Press, 1995.

Sudoplatov, Pavel, and Anatoli Sudoplatov, with Jerrold L. Schecter and Leona P. Schecter. *Special Tasks: The Memoirs of an Unwanted Witness — A Soviet Spymaster*. Little, Brown, 1994.

Szanton, Andrew. *The Recollections of Eugene P. Wigner*. Plenum Press, 1992.

Szilard, Leo. "Reminiscences." In *The Intellectual Migration: Europe and America, 1930–1960*, edited by Donald Fleming and Bernard Bailyn. Harvard University Press, 1969.

————. *The Voice of the Dolphins and Other Stories*. Simon and Schuster, 1961.

————. "We Turned the Switch." *Nation*, December 22, 1945.

Teller, Edward. "Atomic Scientists Have Two Responsibilities." *Bulletin of the Atomic Scientists*, March 1947.

————. *Better a Shield than a Sword*. Free Press, 1987.

————. "Comments on the 'Draft of a World Constitution.'" *Bulletin of the Atomic Scientists*, July 1948.

————. "How Dangerous Are Atomic Weapons?" *Bulletin of the Atomic Scientists*, February 1947.

————. "Scientists in War and Peace." *Bulletin of the Atomic Scientists*, March 1946.

————. "Seven Hours of Reminiscences." *Los Alamos Science*, Winter/Spring 1983.

————. "The State Department Report — 'A Ray of Hope.'" *Bulletin of the Atomic Scientists*, April 1946.

Teller, Edward, et al. *Report of Conference on the Super*. Los Alamos Scientific Laboratory, 1950.

Teller, Edward, with Allen Brown. *The Legacy of Hiroshima*. Doubleday, 1962.

Teller, Edward, with Judith L. Shoolery. *Memoirs: A Twentieth-Century Journey in Science and Politics*. Perseus Publishing, 2001.

Truslow, Edith C., and Ralph Carlisle Smith. *The Los Alamos Project*. Los Alamos Scientific Laboratory, 1946–1947.

Ulam, Stanislaw. *Adventures of a Mathematician*. Scribner's, 1976.

U.S. Atomic Energy Commission. *In the Matter of J. Robert Oppenheimer: Transcript of Hearing before Personnel Security Board, Washington, D.C., April 12, 1954, through May 6, 1954*. U.S. Government Printing Office, 1954.

U.S. Special Committee on Atomic Energy. *Hearings Pursuant to Senate Resolution 179*. U.S. Government Printing Office, 1945.

Weart, Spencer R., and Gertrud Weiss Szilard, eds. *Leo Szilard: His Version of the Facts*. MIT Press, 1978.

Weisskopf, Victor. *The Joy of Insight: Passions of a Physicist*. Basic Books, 1991.

Wells, H. G. *The World Set Free*. E.P. Dutton, 1914.

Wheeler, John Archibald, with Kenneth Ford. *Geons, Black Holes, and Quantum Foam: A Life in Physics*. W.W. Norton, 1999.

Wigner, Eugene P. "An Appreciation on the 60th Birthday of Edward Teller." In *Properties of Matter Under Unusual Conditions*, edited by Hans Mark and Sidney Fernbach. Interscience, 1969.

————. "Are We Making the Transition Wisely?" *Saturday Review of Literature*, November 17, 1945.

————. "Leo Szilard, 1898–1964." *Biographical Memoirs of the National Academy of Sciences* 40 (1964).

————. *Symmetries and Reflections*. Indiana University Press, 1967.

Wilson, Jane, ed. "All in Our Time: The Reminiscences of Twelve Nuclear Pioneers." *Bulletin of the Atomic Scientists*, 1975.

Wilson, Robert R. "Niels Bohr and the Young Scientists." *Bulletin of the Atomic Scientists*, August 1985.

————. "A Recruit for Los Alamos." *Bulletin of the Atomic Scientists*, March 1975.

York, Herbert F. *Arms and the Physicist*. AIP Press, 1995.

————. *Making Weapons, Talking Peace: A Physicist's Odyssey from Hiroshima to Geneva*. Basic Books, 1987.

Secondary Sources

Ackland, Len. "Dawn of the Atomic Age." *Chicago Tribune Magazine*, November 28, 1982, 10 ff.

Allardice, Corbin, and Edward R. Trapnell. *The First Pile*. U.S. Atomic Energy Commission, 1955.

Alsop, Joseph, and Stewart Alsop. *We Accuse!: The Story of the Miscarriage of American Justice in the Case of Robert Oppenheimer*. Simon and Schuster, 1954.

Bernstein, Barton A. "Four Physicists and the Bomb: The Early Years, 1945–1950." *Historical Studies in the Physical and Biological Sciences* 18, no. 2 (1988).

———. "In the Matter of J. Robert Oppenheimer." *Historical Studies in the Physical and Biological Sciences* 12, no. 2 (1982).

———. "Truman and the H-Bomb." *Bulletin of the Atomic Scientists*, March 1984, 12–18.

Bernstein, Jeremy. *Hans Bethe, Prophet of Energy*. Basic Books, 1980.

———. "Profiles: Physicist." *The New Yorker*, October 13, 1975, 47–110, and October 20, 1975, 47–101.

Beyerchen, Alan D. *Scientists Under Hitler: Politics and the Physics Community in the Third Reich*. Yale University Press, 1977.

Blackwood, James R. *The House on College Avenue: The Comptons at Wooster, 1891–1913*. MIT Press, 1968.

Blaedel, Niels. *Harmony and Unity: The Life of Niels Bohr*. Science Tech, 1988.

Blumberg, Stanley A., and Gwinn Owens. *Energy and Conflict: The Life and Times of Edward Teller*. G.P. Putnam's Sons, 1976.

Blumberg, Stanley A., and Louis G. Panos. *Edward Teller: Giant of the Golden Age of Physics*. Charles Scribner's Sons, 1990.

Bodanis, David. *E=mc²: A Biography of the World's Most Famous Equation*. Walker and Company, 2000.

Broad, William J. *Teller's War: The Top-Secret Story Behind the Star Wars Deception*. Simon and Schuster, 1992.

Bundy, McGeorge. *Danger and Survival: Choices about the Bomb in the First Fifty Years*. Random House, 1988.

Childs, Herbert. *An American Genius: The Life of Ernest Orlando Lawrence*. E.P. Dutton and Co., 1968.

Christman, Al. *Target Hiroshima: Deak Parsons and the Creation of the Atomic Bomb*. Naval Institute Press, 1998.

Clark, Ronald W. *The Greatest Power on Earth: The International Race for Nuclear Supremacy*. Harper and Row, 1980.

Coffin, Tristram. "Leo Szilard, the Conscience of a Scientist." *Holiday*, February 1964.

Coughlan, Robert. "Dr. Edward Teller's Magnificent Obsession." *Life*, September 6, 1954.

———. "The Tangled Drama and Private Hells of Two Famous Scientists." *Life*, December 13, 1963.

Davis, Nuell Pharr. *Lawrence and Oppenheimer*. Simon and Schuster, 1968.

Dawidowicz, Lucy S. *The War Against the Jews, 1933–1945*. Holt, Rinehart, and Winston, 1975.

de Latil, Pierre. *Enrico Fermi: The Man and His Theories*. Paul S. Eriksson, 1966.

Dupré, J. Stefan, and Sanford A. Lakoff. *Science and the Nation: Policy and Politics*. Prentice Hall, 1962.

Dyson, Freeman. *Disturbing the Universe*. Harper and Row, 1979.

———. *Weapons and Hope*. Harper and Row, 1984.

Eiduson, Bernice T. *Scientists: Their Psychological World*. Basic Books, 1962.

Esterer, Arnulf K., and Louise A. Esterer. *Prophet of the Atomic Age: Leo Szilard*. Julian Messner, 1972.

Feld, Bernard. "Leo Szilard: Scientist for All Seasons." *Social Research* 51, no. 3 (Fall 1984): 675–690.

Fermi, Laura. *Illustrious Immigrants*. University of Chicago Press, 1968.

FitzGerald, Francis. *Way Out There in the Blue: Reagan, Star Wars and the End of the Cold War*. Simon and Schuster, 2000.

Frank, Waldo. "An American Tragedy: The Oppenheimer Case." *The Nation*, September 25, 1954, 245–249.

Galison, Peter, and Barton Bernstein. "In Any Light: Scientists and the Decision to Build the Superbomb, 1942–1954." *Historical Studies in the Physical and Biological Sciences* 19, no. 2 (1989): 267–347.

Gilpin, Robert. *American Scientists and Nuclear Weapons Policy*. Princeton University Press, 1962.

Gleick, James. *Genius*. Pantheon, 1992.

Goldberg, Stanley. "Inventing a Climate of Opinion: Vannevar Bush and the Decision to Build the Bomb." *Isis* 83, no. 3 (September 1992): 429–452.

Goodchild, Peter. *J. Robert Oppenheimer: Shatterer of Worlds*. Houghton Mifflin, 1981.

Goodrich, H. B., et al. "The Origins of U.S. Scientists." *Scientific American*, July 1951.

Gowing, Margaret. *Britain and Atomic Energy, 1939–1945*. Macmillan, 1964.

Grandy, David A. *Leo Szilard: Science as a Mode of Being*. University Press of America, 1996.

Grodzins, Morton, and Eugene Rabinowitch. *The Atomic Age*. Basic Books, 1963.

Groueff, Stephane. *The Manhattan Project: The Untold Story of the Making of the Atomic Bomb*. Little, Brown, 1967. Reprint, Bantam Books, 1968.

Gruber, Carol S. "Manhattan Project Maverick: The Case of Leo Szilard." *Prologue*, Summer 1983, 73–87.

Heilbron, J. L., and Robert W. Seidel. *Lawrence and His Laboratory: A History of the Lawrence Berkeley Laboratory*. University of California Press, 1989.

Herken, Gregg. *Brotherhood of the Bomb: The Tangled Lives and Loyalties of Robert Oppenheimer, Ernest Lawrence, and Edward Teller*. Henry Holt and Company, 2002.

———. *The Winning Weapon*. Alfred A. Knopf, 1980.

Hershberg, James. *James B. Conant*. Alfred A. Knopf, 1993.

Hewlett, Richard G., and Francis Duncan. *Atomic Shield, 1947/1962*. Vol. 2 of *A History of the United States Atomic Energy Commission*. Pennsylvania State University Press, 1969.

Hewlett, Richard G., and Jack M. Holl. *Atoms for Peace and War, 1953/1961*. Vol. 3 of *A History of the United States Atomic Energy Commission*. University of California Press, 1989.

Hewlett, Richard G., and Oscar E. Anderson, Jr. *The New World, 1939/1946*. Vol. 1 of *A History of the United States Atomic Energy Commission*. Pennsylvania State University Press, 1962.

Howe, Irving, with the assistance of Kenneth Libo. *World of Our Fathers*. Harcourt, Brace, 1976.

Johnson, Charles W., and Charles O. Jackson. *City Behind a Fence*. University of Tennessee Press, 1981.

Jungk, Robert. *Brighter than a Thousand Suns: A Personal History of the Atomic Scientists*. Harcourt, Brace, 1958.

Kane, Joseph. "Los Alamos: A City upon a Hill." *Time*, December 10, 1979.

Kempton, Murray. "The Ambivalence of J. Robert Oppenheimer." *Esquire*, December 1983, 236–248.

Kevles, Daniel J. *The Physicists: The History of a Scientific Community in Modern America*. Alfred A. Knopf, 1978.

Knebel, Fletcher, and Charles W. Bailey. "The Fight over the A-Bomb." *Look*, August 13, 1963, 19–23.

Kunetka, James W. *City of Fire*. University of New Mexico Press, 1979.

———. *Oppenheimer: The Years of Risk*. Prentice Hall, 1982.

Lamont, Lansing. *Day of Trinity*. Atheneum, 1965.

Lang, Daniel. *Early Tales of the Atomic Age*. Doubleday and Co., 1948.

Lanouette, William. "The Odd Couple and the Bomb." *Scientific American*, November 2000, 104–109.

Lanouette, William, with Bela Silard. *Genius in the Shadows: A Biography of Leo Szilard, the Man Behind the Bomb*. Charles Scribner's Sons, 1992. Reprint, University of Chicago Press, 1994.

Laurence, William L. *Men and Atoms: The Discovery, the Uses and the Future of Atomic Energy*. Simon and Schuster, 1959.

Lifton, Robert Jay, and Eric Markusen. *The Genocidal Mentality: Nazi Holocaust and Nuclear Threat*. Basic Books, 1990.

Michelmore, Peter. *The Swift Years: The Robert Oppenheimer Story*. Dodd, Mead, 1969.

Moore, Ruth. *Niels Bohr: The Man, His Science, and the World They Changed*. Alfred A. Knopf, 1966.

Moss, Norman. *Men Who Play God: The Story of the H-Bomb and How the World Came to Live with It*. Harper and Row, 1968.

Murphy, Charles J. V. "The Hidden Struggle for the H-Bomb." *Fortune*, May 1953, 100–101, 230.

Norris, Robert S. *Racing for the Bomb: General Leslie R. Groves, the Manhattan Project's Indispensable Man*. Steerforth Press, 2002.

Pais, Abraham. *Niels Bohr's Times in Physics, Philosophy, and Polity*. Clarendon Press, 1991.

Palevsky, Mary. *Atomic Fragments: A Daughter's Questions*. University of California Press, 2000.

Peterson, Aage. "The Philosophy of Niels Bohr." *Bulletin of the Atomic Scientists*, September 1963.

Powers, Thomas. *Heisenberg's War: The Secret History of the German Bomb*. Alfred A. Knopf, 1993. Reprint, Back Bay Books, 1994.

Rhodes, Richard. *Dark Sun*. Simon and Schuster, 1995.

———. *The Making of the Atomic Bomb*. Simon and Schuster, 1987.

Rigden, John S. "J. Robert Oppenheimer: Before the War." *Scientific American*, July 1995, 76–81.

———. *Rabi: Scientist and Citizen*. Basic Books, 1987.

Robison, George O. *The Oak Ridge Story*. Southern Publishers, 1950.

Royal, Denise. *The Story of J. Robert Oppenheimer*. St. Martin's Press, 1969.

Sachs, Robert G., ed. *The Nuclear Chain Reaction — Forty Years Later*. University of Chicago Press, 1984.

Schlesinger, Arthur M., Jr. "The Oppenheimer Case." *Atlantic*, September 1954, 29–36.

Schweber, S. S. *In the Shadow of the Bomb: Oppenheimer, Bethe, and the Moral Responsibility of the Scientist*. Princeton University Press, 2000.

Seidel, Robert. *Lawrence and His Laboratory: A History of the Lawrence Berkeley Laboratory*. University of California Press, 1987.

Shepley, James R., and Clay Blair, Jr. *The Hydrogen Bomb: The Men, the Menace, the Mechanism*. David McKay, 1954.

Sherwin, Martin J. "How Well They Meant." *Bulletin of the Atomic Scientists*, August 1985, 9–15.

———. *A World Destroyed: The Atomic Bomb and the Grand Alliance*. Alfred A. Knopf, 1975.

Smith, Alice Kimball. "Behind the Decision to Use the Atomic Bomb: Chicago 1944–45." *Bulletin of the Atomic Scientists*, October 1958.

———. *A Peril and a Hope: The Scientists' Movement in America, 1945–47*. University of Chicago Press, 1965.

———. "The Elusive Dr. Szilard." *Harper's*, July 1960.

Snow, C. P. *The Physicists*. Little, Brown, 1981.

———. *Science and Government*. Harvard University Press, 1961.

———. *Variety of Men*. Scribner's, 1967.

Stern, Philip M., with Harold P. Green. *The Oppenheimer Case: Security on Trial*. Harper and Row, 1969.

Strout, Cushing. "The Oppenheimer Case: Melodrama, Tragedy, and Irony." *Virginia Quarterly Review*, Spring 1964, 268–280.

Szasz, Ferenc Morton. *The Day the Sun Rose Twice: The Story of the Trinity Site Nuclear Explosion, July 16, 1945*. University of New Mexico Press, 1984.

Wang, Jessica. *American Science in an Age of Anxiety: Scientists, Anticommunism, and the Cold War*. University of North Carolina Press, 1999.

Weart, Spencer R. *Nuclear Fear: A History of Images*. Harvard University Press, 1988.

———. *Scientists in Power*. Harvard University Press, 1979.

Weiner, Charles. "A New Site for the Seminar: The Refugees and American Physics in the Thirties." In *The Intellectual Migration: Europe and America, 1930–1960*, edited by Donald Fleming and Bernard Bailyn. Harvard University Press, 1969.

Williams, Robert Chadwell. *Klaus Fuchs: Atom Spy*. Harvard University Press, 1987.

Wyden, Peter. *Day One: Before Hiroshima and After*. Simon and Schuster, 1984.

York, Herbert F. *The Advisors: Oppenheimer, Teller, and the Superbomb*. W.H. Freeman, 1976.

Zachary, G. Pascal. *Endless Frontier: Vannevar Bush, Engineer of the American Century*. Free Press, 1997.

Zuckerman, Solly. "Nuclear Wizards." *New York Review of Books*, March 31, 1988, 26–31.

INDEX

ABOUT THE AUTHOR

Brian VanDeMark teaches history at the U.S. Naval Academy, Annapolis. He has lectured throughout the world, including at Oxford, where he was a Visiting Fellow at St. Catherine's College and the Rothermere American Institute. He coauthored Robert S. McNamara's #1 bestseller, *In Retrospect*, and assisted Clark Clifford with his bestseller, *Counsel to the President*. His *Into the Quagmire*, published by Oxford University Press, is one of the classic works on Lyndon Johnson and Vietnam. He lives with his family in Annapolis, Maryland.